The Land of Prehistory

The Land of Prehistory

A Critical History of American Archaeology

ALICE BECK KEHOE

Routledge
New York and London

Frontispiece: "An Eclosion," by Brian Leister, reproduced from a card ©1991 Smithsonian Institution. Card Design by Chris Noel.

The American archaeologist joins a Renaissance geographer at the pinnacle of the Smithsonian Castle to survey the Land of Prehistory. The Castle is shown atop a Cahokia temple mound; Columbus and Isabella stand at the Castle's door. A Chicano artist paints the Virgin of Guadalupe at lower right, and America's fauna appear and domesticated at left. The naked white ladies near the Castle door represent a nineteenth-century exhibition demonstrating American artists' mastery of European painting style.

Published in 1998 by
Routledge
29 West 35th Street
New York, NY 10001

Published in Great Britain by
Routledge
11 New Fetter Lane
London EC4P 4EE

Library of Congress Cataloging-in-Publication Data

Kehoe, Alice Beck, 1934–
    The land of prehistory : a critical history of American archaeology /
Alice Beck Kehoe.
        p.   cm.
    Includes bibliographical references and index.
    ISBN 0-415-92054-X (hb). —ISBN 0-415-92055-8 (pb)
    1. Archaeology—United States—History.   2. Indians of North America, Historiography.   3. United States—Intellectual life—20th century.   I. Title.
CC101.U6K44   1998
973.1—dc21
                                                                97-49609
                                                                CIP

To Daniel, David, and Cormac,
who so wonderfully enrich the present.

It's the right thing to do. Americans press forward.
We overcome the unexpected. We discover the unknown.
That has been our history. That's America's destiny.

—*Daniel Goldin, NASA's administrator, speaking at the*
September 25, 1997, launch of the space shuttle Atlantis

Contents

Acknowledgments

As a woman entering graduate school at Harvard at the end of the 1950s, a married woman—a married woman with a CHILD yet!—I lived outside the social circle of promising young archaeologists and their mentors. Then and later, my marginalized status brought me into the company of a host of interesting people, women and men, avocational and professional researchers and those who lived what we researched. For the information, support, and stimulation you all have given me, I thank you. And to you bastards who are too important to engage with someone lacking a prestigious position, I thank you, too, for illuminating the social structure of American archaeology. Without you, I couldn't have written this book.

Peter Jones of the Institute for Advanced Study in the Humanities, Edinburgh, provided camaraderie and a 1989 Fellowship that enabled me to research Daniel Wilson and his milieu, and to discuss sociology of science with the Science Studies Unit, Edinburgh University, notably Barry Barnes. Barry's recognition of the broad value of this study has been particularly sustaining. Margaret Mackay and Emily Lyle of the School of Scottish Studies, Edinburgh University, greatly enhanced my understanding of nineteenth-century Edinburgh, and James Secord lent his research into Robert Chambers' work. All of the Edinburgensians—Peter and Jean, Barry, Carole Tansley, David Bloor, Maggie, Emily, Dale Idiens, Callum Calder and the late Sheila Barker of Gardner's Crescent—extended warm personal hospitality that made Edinburgh a paradise.

Among other treasured colleagues who have materially contributed to this work, I especially acknowledge JoAllyn Archambault, Paul Bahn, Karen Bruhns, Christopher Chippindale, Philip Duke, Joan Gero, Guy Gibbon, Robert Hall, Barry Isaac, Stephen Jett, Susan Kent, Kristian Kristiansen, Sarah Nelson, Patricia O'Brien, Thomas Patterson, Valerie Pinsky, Kent

Reilly, Jonathan Reyman, Jeremy Sabloff, Paul Shao, Andrea Stone, David Wilcox, Alison Wylie, and above all, Jane and David Kelley. Through Donald B. Smith, Bennett McCardle supplied me with her thesis on Daniel Wilson. Dena Dincauze and our professors Richard and Nathalie Woodbury stand by me, though I've never quite managed to meet Dick's academic standards. Bruce Trigger has consistently been courteously collegial, in spite of his conviction that I mistake Sir Daniel's significance. At Routledge, editor Bill Germano and production editor Brian Phillips, and their staff, made the metamorphosis of manuscript into book form a really pleasant experience.

Finally—and regretfully it is final—my gratitude to the late Joseph Needham and Lu Gwei-Djen. To have earned their respect, and the privilege of their friendship, is the highest honor I can imagine.

Introduction

American archaeology is a scientific discipline using principles of systematic data collection and analysis to discover the lifeways of prehistoric and historic Americans and generalizations leading to the formulation of laws of human behavoir. Archaeologists work primarily as natural scientists, viewing human societies of the past within their ecosystems. As professional scientists, American archaeologists derive and validate their interpretations from their data, free from political bias. American archaeology produces knowledge that enriches the common good.

So goes the credo of mainstream American archaeology. A critical history of the discipline cannot accept the standard picture of objective research pursued for its intrinsic value by scientists who have abjured ideological bias. The history of American archaeology instead is a remarkable example of post hoc objectification of the doctrine of Manifest Destiny. From its inception, American archaeology has been politically charged, legitimating domination of North America by capitalists imbued with British bourgeois culture. This study expounds that thesis.

The approach here is empirical history of science, contextualizing the deeds, events, and practitioners of American archaeology in their social milieu. The questions posed by journalists—who? what? where? when? why?—are the scaffold of this approach. The book becomes critical because it includes a broader roster of practitioners than appears in the more conventional histories of American archaeology, and this breadth raises the issue of selection: Why are these practitioners deemed significant here but not by other historians of the discipline? Attending to this question, the factor of class stands out; a history of American archaeology that neglects to

discuss practitioners' social position, and the ramifications of social position, is a chronicle, not a history.

American archaeology, as a scientific practice, may be said to have begun
with Carlos de Sigüenza y Góngora trenching Teotihuacán in 1675 (Schávelzon 1983; 1990, 20). Like Thomas Jefferson a century later, Sigüenza y
Góngora displayed wide erudition and a patriotic appreciation of even the
precolumbian monuments of his homeland. It may be said that these
savants appropriated the glories of the preconquest nations, but their commitment to recording their strategies and observations gave their investigations lasting scientific value. Sigüenza y Góngora and Jefferson stand out
for scientifically planned and recorded *excavations* in America, but in the
seventeenth and eighteenth centuries there were congeries of educated men
and women actively contributing to the natural sciences through field and
laboratory studies. Modern science began in the seventeenth century and
was solidly established in the eighteenth, culminating in the genius of
Alexander von Humboldt (1769–1859). In this book, I place early archaeological research in America within its context of what may be termed preindustrial modern science.

What have been the milieux of American archaeology? Invoking Don
Carlos Sigüenza y Góngora and Thomas Jefferson intimates one characteristic only very recently weakened: *Recognized* archaeology has been associated with patrician gentlemen. This book argues that this association masks
the effective foundation of scientific archaeology in nineteenth-century
bourgeois culture, and more specifically, in Scottish bourgeois culture.
While gentlemen of private income published the fruits of their interest in
the monuments of the past, bourgeois investigators doggedly working in
precious free time created the bulk of the eventual data base and, most
importantly, the framework of interpretation for prehistory. Standard histories of archaeology (Daniel 1967; 1976; 1981; Trigger 1989; Willey and
Sabloff 1993) have highlighted the gentlemen of wealth, as if to insinuate
archaeology into the social status of these commanders of labor. The bourgeois professional men who published the results of their own exertions
found support from organizations promoting national identity, using
archaeology to establish a preconquest past crying out for the technological
breakthroughs brought to the continent by the superior race now dominating the hemisphere. American archaeology complemented European prehistoric archaeology, establishing the story of progress read through
technology that demonstrated the superiority of that race. Standard histories of archaeology have failed to penetrate the mystification of class domination created by aristocrats' assumption of leadership. Failing to realize
that prehistoric archaeology is a bourgeois science (White 1987, 86), these
historians of the discipline have missed its fundamental positioning within
nineteenth-century bourgeois political economy, including both the forces

promoting its mainstream development and those hindering deviant interpretations.

The history of the discipline of prehistoric archaeology, to which the entire preconquest American past has been assigned, begins with its formal construction for English speakers in the late 1840s by Daniel Wilson. That the tradesman's son Daniel Wilson is consistently overlooked in favor of the baronet John Lubbock in the standard histories is perhaps the single most telling demonstration of the power of the patron class. Wilson was the first to use the word "prehistory" in English (1851), the first to publish a British prehistory organized into the scientific framework pioneered in Denmark, the first to publish (1862) the model of interpretation through analogy with American ethnography and ethnohistory. This model, suggested by John Locke's famous dictum "In the beginning, all the World was *America,*" served simultaneously to elucidate European antiquity and to present the indigenous history of America as prehistory. Wilson's seminal work is examined in this book.

Intervening between the history and the sociology of American archaeology is the history of science in America. One reason Daniel Wilson's work was both influential and seldom specifically cited is that his approach was solidly grounded in the same Scottish Common-sense Realism that formed the bourgeois worldview and the understanding of science dominant in America. Thus Wilson's books were more than simply accessible to American and bourgeois British readers, they constituted bricks in the edifice of public knowledge built from this worldview. Obscuring Daniel Wilson's contributions obscures the nature of civil society in America.

Recognition of the extent of Scottish bourgeois influence on its American counterpart brings out the persistence of the Scottish Common-sense concept of scientific method—"Baconian science"—in mainstream American archaeology. It is not enough to call it positivism, because it flows from the establishment of modern science in the late seventeenth century, through the spin given by the Scottish Enlightenment, into the mid-twentieth-century formation of an American middle class extending through (and co-opting) the skilled working class. Much of the New Archaeology of the first postwar generation parallels Scientific Creationism in its obsolescent conceptualization of science, and this is no coincidence because both movements were drawn from the worldview taught in conservative American Protestant congregations. Lewis Binford acknowledges his Southern "hills-south, hard-working" origin (Binford 1972, 340), though he hasn't discussed his undergraduate training at Virginia Polytechnic, a school that would soon after his graduation hire Henry Morris, later a founder of the Institute for Creation Research. The hills-south, hard-working society that conditioned the young Binford owes a substantial portion of its heritage to the Scots emigration that also gave America the

Presbyterian Princeton Seminary, fountainhead of Fundamentalism. Contextualizing intellectual history does uncover some unexpected bedfellows.

What will appear from most recent trends in American archaeology is that the true revolution was not, certainly not, the New Archaeology, but the remarkable shift in the 1970s from a profession visibly nearly exclusively white, male, Protestant, and American-born, to one that now reflects a far broader range of social positions. To understand this shift, we must not only comprehend the societal revolution instigated by the mid-century G.I. Bill, but also the contributions of professional women omitted from the standard histories of archaeology. Between the influx of men from working-class and "ethnic" backgrounds into the academy, and the protection given women by the 1964 Civil Rights Act, the old guard lost its power to exclude. American archaeology exhibits a radical change in personnel within a generation. Only now, in the middle 1990s, are consequences emerging within the intellectual content of the discipline. This book is offered as background to the American archaeology aborning, an archaeology that may at last throw off the heavy hand of Manifest Destiny.

Note: In this book, I use "human" as the generic or inclusive term, and "man" only when my references were in fact assuming the male human.

CHAPTER I

The Construction of the Science of Archaeology

Archaeology as a science, the *systematic* study of the human past, was constructed in the mid-nineteenth century by men committed to an interpretation of history untrammeled by the authority of texts. "The testimony of things" (Toulmin and Goodfield 1965, 237) would constitute an incontrovertible history untainted by ideology. For well over a century, this transparent mystification of the process of writing history accorded archaeology a powerful status supporting the imperial aspirations of the Western bourgeoisie. The very innocence of things, their enduring presence underneath the winds and storms of politics, carried their mute witness over the suspect claims of conventional authors. Archaeology proferred the Book of Nature, *Naturwissenschaft,* in place of sectarian dogmas.

Including ancient monuments and other artifacts in natural history presaged the Darwinian worldview placing humans in an embracing natural world. Collingwood—let me introduce him here, the only practicing field archaeologist who was at the same time a first-rate philosopher—locates the formulation of a modern approach to history in the work of Giambattista Vico (1668–1744), specifically in Vico's formulation of history as research into human societies independent of speculation about divine plan. Collingwood emphasizes (1946, 66) that Vico recognized the study of history rests upon human social experience and arises from the effort to deal with living in society; the practical demands of such experience removes it from the realm of abstruse philosophy. From this common

1

experience, Vico was able to rebut Cartesian denial of ordinary reality and to focus on human agency and its detritus, artifacts. Further, Vico saw oral tradition and documents as artifacts to be examined for their reflection of past states of mind rather than as authority. Vico was not an archaeologist, but his formulation of the field of human history laid the philosophical foundation for the discipline of archaeology.

To pinpoint the appearance of the active side of archaeology is like traipsing through sand. One can celebrate Princess Bel-Shalti-Nannar of Babylon, sixth century B.C., for her collection of antiquities, or the Chinese historian Si-ma Qien, second century B.C., who examined ruins and objects as well as texts (Trigger 1989, 29–30). Collingwood (1946, 58) cited William Camden of England for his survey data, published 1586, parallel to his contemporary Francis Bacon's advocacy of the scientific method of observations that would later be termed "Baconian science." My preference is for Edward Lhwyd because he was a *professional* (cf. Hunter 1975, 191, 214), that is, he earned his living by fieldwork, collections curation, and methodical description as assistant and then Keeper of the Ashmolean Museum in Oxford. Lhwyd exemplified the pursuit of field surveys interpreted through comparisons with both Classical texts and contemporary ethnographies. Lhwyd's significance, to me, lies particularly in his milieu, the decades of the formal founding of modern science. The Royal Society of London for Improving Natural Knowledge, incorporated 1662 and chartered 1669, embodied quite literally the privileging of knowledge gained through direct and systematic observation (Shapin and Schaffer 1985). A year later, the same king chartered the Company of Adventurers of England Trading Into Hudson's Bay, similar in signifying royal encouragement of gentlemen actively promoting a daring extension of English power, in one case the power of verified knowledge, in the other the power of economic entrepreneurship.

John Aubrey's *Monumenta Britannica* is said to be "the first English book that can be called 'archaeological' in the modern sense" (Hunter 1975, 159). Aubrey earns this distinction by questioning the convention of deriving identifications of antiquities through Classical references; instead, he gives primacy to accurate plans and attempts to classify them from attributes in the manner of natural history: "to make the Stones give Evidence for themselves" (quoted in Hunter 1975, 180). Inigo Jones's *Stoneheng Restored* (1655) suffers, Aubrey averred, because Jones "framed the monument to his own Hypothesis, which is much differing from the Thing itself" (quoted in Hunter 1975, 180). Attacks upon the hypothetico-deductive method in archaeology are centuries old.

Aubrey was the first to recognize Avebury as a major component in Britain's heritage, although Camden had recorded its ditch. Happening to hunt to hounds with other young gentlemen in January 1649, Aubrey was "wonderfully surprized at the sight of these vast stones, of which I had never heard, as also at the mighty Bank and Grasse about it" (quoted in Tylden-Wright 1991, 70). Later, he described this stupendous site to his antiquarian friend Dr. Walter Charleton, who happened to be King's Physician to Charles II. Chatting with the king in May, 1663, Charleton mentioned Aubrey's claim that the unknown Avebury was to the famous "Stoneheng as a Cathedral [is to] a Parish church" (quoted in Tylden-Wright 1991, 72). The king requested Aubrey to meet him the next morning, and arranged that he should escort a royal party to the site two weeks later, when the court was journeying to Bath. Charles noticed Silbury Hill and chose to walk up it before rejoining his retinue. At Charles' solicitation, Aubrey made a plane-table plan of Avebury, but he refused to interpret the construction on the grounds that he had not sufficient firsthand observation of comparable monuments in Wales to derive any generalization. That Avebury, Stonehenge, and the Welsh monuments were pagan temples, probably Druid, was inferred years later after Edward Lhwyd had conducted the requisite survey in Wales (Hunter 1975, 182; Tylden-Wright 1991, 74).

Lhwyd's salaried position placed him in the ranks of the technicians who carried out much of the work attributed to their aristocratic employers. This hierarchy of knowledge production is as prevalent, and as contestable, in archaeology as in any other science. John Aubrey was born to an independent income but eventually came to depend, like Lhwyd, upon the patronage of wealthy virtuosi. Aubrey's *Monumenta Britannica* was never published in spite of the king's wish that it be—Aubrey lacked money to publish it himself and no patron was sufficiently interested to do so. The fruitful meeting with King Charles came about through Aubrey's gentleman rank and initial family welfare that enabled him to attend Oxford, where he formed lasting friendships with fellow scholars. In 1663, Aubrey was elected to the Royal Society. Dr. Charleton was a member; so were Robert Hooke, Sir William Petty, Christopher Wren, Robert Boyle, Edmund Halley, and others who, like the king himself, found the antiquarian a stimulating companion. Aubrey's position in the gentry enabled him to move in this rank, yet his impecunious condition constrained his explorations (Tylden-Wright 1991, 251) and in attending to patrons' interests (Hunter 1975, 213), gave him the appearance of a dilettante.

"The Battle of the Ancients and the Moderns" waged on into the eighteenth century (J. M. Levine 1987, 1991), pitting the premise of an ancient Golden Age against that of the persistence of human capabilities. The notion that modern men had the same intellectual capacities as those of Classical times gave those modern men the audacity to ignore or dismiss Classical texts that seemed at odds with observation—if some men today have intellectual capacities comparable to those of the great Ancients, it follows that some Ancients likely had inferior, naive, or perfidious intellects. The Royal Society was a beacon for the Moderns, exhibiting noblemen attending to novel feats of disciplined ingenuity, and presenting their learning in English. The modern mind could explore beyond the world of the Ancients, as navigators and traders were exploring domains outside ancient geographies, and in both spheres, applause hailed the courage to counteract received ideas. Exploration of the past through firsthand examination of its remnants fit this modern license to build knowledge.

Walter Scott, Focal Point of Transition

Among the most intrepid explorers of the past was Sir Walter Scott (1771–1832). Daniel Wilson affirmed:

> The zeal for Archaeological investigation which has recently manifested itself in nearly every country of Europe, has been traced, not without reason, to the impulse which proceeded from Abbotsford [Walter Scott's home]. Though such is not exactly the source which we might expect to give birth to the transition from profitless dilettantism to the intelligent spirit of scientific investigation, yet it is unquestionable that Sir Walter Scott was the first of modern writers "to teach all men this truth, which looks like a truism, and yet was as good as unknown to writers of history and others, till so taught—that the bygone ages of the world were actually filled by living men." [footnote, *Carlyle's Miscellanies,* 2nd Ed. Vol. V:301](Wilson 1851, xi)

Growing up in a classically balanced genteel house in Edinburgh (today appropriately between the School of Scottish Studies and the Department of Archaeology on George Square), Scott was drawn to the hills of the lawless Borders inland from the city.[1] He enjoyed long visits to his grandfather's farm, where his grandmother recounted to him the valorous deeds of his lineage and sang ballads that the boy precociously transcribed into books. Briefly attending college in his early teens, Scott managed to learn only little Latin and no Greek, instead acquiring a reading knowledge of the modern Romance languages Italian, Spanish, and French. An illness allowed him recuperation in the country, rides and walks of as much as thirty miles, often to examine places of historical significance. These field excursions were balanced by reading, Scott gaining a familiarity with Anglo-Saxon and with Norse sagas, and as a young man, with contemporary German. His collecting of ballads and stories of Border history, including interviews with local elders, continued enthusiastically and distinguished him in his Edinburgh gentlemen's clubs. By 1802, he published *Minstrelsy of the Scottish Border,* two volumes (a third the next year) of gathered ballads augmented by imitations of his own and friends' composition. In 1805, his epic *Lay of the Last Minstrel* was published and sold so well that Scott felt he could give up the practice of law and earn his living principally by writing.

From the extended ballad form he increasingly found tedious, Walter Scott moved to an innovation, the historical novel. *Waverley* was published anonymously in 1814, first of the trilogy with *Guy Mannering* and *The Antiquary* (both 1815). More Scottish historical novels came out until in 1819 he leaped into *Ivanhoe*'s more exotic medieval realm. Writing was Scott's vocation; his avocation was Abbotsford, an accumulation of farms he transformed into an estate with a baronial mansion displaying his antiquarian interests. As in his literary productions, Scott's Abbotsford drew upon solid firsthand field study of human and artifactual sources, dramatically vivified through his imagination. Contemporaries saw his Scottish novels as romans á clef, arguing over who—out in the Borders, met in Highland excursions, or among themselves in town—were the originals for the telling fictional portraits. (Jonathan Oldbuck, according to Scott himself, was drawn from Scott's father's friend George Constable of Wallace Craigie near Dundee. Oldbuck was also Scott himself, a second son trained to the law but enjoying a landed property Monk-barns/Abbots-ford.) The novelist's lively personifications of historical factors—"Jacobite," "Royalist," "Highland chief"—richly set amongst a host of peasants, artisans, wanderers, shepherds, gentry, aristocrats, fisherfolk, beggars, and hawkers are rendered with a generous sauce of Scots dialect, an early salvo in the battle over whether Scots should be recognized as a language or as only a dialect of English. Through his empathetic Scottish characters, his depictions of the landscape, and his commitment to transcribing Scots speech, Walter Scott made his set of Scottish novels part of his compatriots' resistance to the English dominance threatened through the 1707 Act of Union. Walter Scott winningly displayed the patrimony of the nation, in his ballads and novels for a wide public, and at Abbotsford for a coterie of his own class.

Those admittedly inventive fictions might not have stimulated serious scientific archaeology, were it not for Scott's lifelong antiquarian activities. The largest of these was his successful petition in 1819 to George IV that the big cannon Mons Meg be returned to Edinburgh Castle from the Tower of London. More mundane was his regular attendance at meetings of antiquarian organizations. There was too little systematic method in their inquiries for these to be judged scientific, but Scott's research—weighted by his training for the law—was seen as sufficient to invite him to assume the presidency of the Royal Society of Scotland in 1820, the year he was knighted. Scott's camaraderie lent status and glamor to his fellow antiquarians. His own favorite among his novels, *The Antiquary*, displays the critical intelligence he brought to the study of Scotland's past.

The eponymous hero Jonathan Oldbuck is a complex figure. Scott described him as the descendant of a German printer who early in the Reformation immigrated to Scotland and bought a modest estate from a dissipated aristocrat. Jonathan is contrasted with his neighbor Sir Arthur Wardour, scion of an old Scots landed family, "above him in fortune, and beneath him in intellect." Oldbuck chose as frequent companions only this one of the "country gentlemen," plus the local doctor and the clergyman. Instead of the fishing and fowling that diverted his neighbors, Oldbuck preferred "correspondence with most of the virtuosi of his time, who, like himself, measured decayed entrenchments, made plans of ruined castles, read illegible inscriptions, and wrote essays on medals in the proportion of twelve pages to each letter of the legend" (W. Scott [1815] 1871, 23).

We observe that the Antiquary deeply respects the more renowned of the virtuosi. Disputing with his one companionable neighbor whether the Picts had been Celtic or Goths, Oldbuck corrects his friend:

"I say the *Pikar, Pihar, Piochtar, Piaghter,* or *Peughtar,*" vociferated Old-buck; "they spoke a Gothic dialect"—

"Genuine Celtic," again asserverated the knight.

"Gothic! Gothic! I'll go to death upon it!" counter-asseverated the squire.

"Why, gentlemen," said Lovel, "I conceive that is a dispute which may be easily settled by philologists, if there are any remains of the language."

"There is but one word," said the Baronet, "but, in spite of Mr. Oldbuck's pertinacity, it is decisive of the question."

"Yes, in my favour," said Oldbuck: "Mr. Lovel, you shall be judge—I have the learned Pinkerton on my side."

"I, on mine, the indefatigable and erudite Chalmers."

"Gordon comes into my opinion."

"Sir Robert Sibbald holds mine."

"Innes is with me!" vociferated Oldbuck.

"Riston has no doubt!" shouted the Baronet. (W. Scott [1815] 1871, 61)

Out in the field, the Antiquary encounters another kind of authority, the grizzled local bard who "had the exterior appearance of a mendicant . . . one of that privileged class which are called in Scotland the King's Bedesmen." Standing in a meadow on his property, Oldbuck had been expounding to young Mr. Lovel the

"tumulus, exhibiting the foundation of ruined buildings—the central point —the *prætorian,* doubtless, of the [Roman] camp. From this place, now scarce to be distinguished but by its slight elevation and its greener turf from the rest of the fortification, we may suppose Agricola to have looked forth on the immense army of Caledonians, occupying the declivities of yon opposite hill. . . . . Yes, my dear friend, . . . from this very Prætorium"—

A voice from behind interrupted his ecstatic description—"Prætorian here, Prætorian there, I mind the bigging o't." . . .

"What is that you say, Edie?" said Oldbuck, hoping, perhaps that his ears had betrayed their duty—"what were you speaking about?"

"About this bit bourock, your honour," answered the undaunted Edie; "I mind the bigging o't."

"The devil you do! Why, you old fool, it was here before you were born, and will be after you are hanged, man!"

"Hanged or drowned, here or awa, dead or alive, I mind the bigging o't. . . . What profit have I for telling ye a lie?—I just ken this about it, that about twenty years syne, I, and a wheen hallenshakers like mysell, and the mason-lads that built the lang dike that gaes down the loaning, and twa or three herds maybe, just set to wark, and built this bit thing here that ye ca' the—the—Prætorian, and a' just for a bield at auld Aiken Drum's bridal. . . ."

"This," thought Lovel to himself, "is a famous counterpart to the story of *Keip on this syde*."* [See the *Town and County Magazine* for 1771, p. 595.] (W. Scott [1815] 1871, 41)

Scott appended his Note :

> It may be worth while to mention that the incident of the supposed Prætorium actually happened to an antiquary of great learning and acuteness, Sir John Clerk of Penicuik. . . . Sir John Clerk proceeded to point out . . . to the distinguished English antiquarian Roger Gale, . . . a small hillock near the centre of the enclosure as the *Prætorium*, . . . an aged shepherd . . . like Edie Ochiltree, . . . forgot all reverence, and broke in with nearly the same words—"Prætorium here, Prætorium there, I made the bourock mysell with a flaughter-spade." (421)

Scott juxtaposes two forms of authoritative knowledge, learned texts, and local experience. He emphatically reiterates the importance of the latter, with Lovel's footnote to the magazine story and his own direct note on Sir John Clerk.[2] To this simple contrast between sources of "fact" Scott adds a third dimension, the factor of class,

> [Sir Arthur speaking to his daughter about Oldbuck] "one must allow for the original descent: something of the German boorishness still flows in the blood; something of the whiggish and perverse opposition to established rank and privilege. You may observe that he never has any advantage of me in dispute, unless when he avails himself of a sort of pettifogging intimacy with dates, names, and trifling matters of fact, a tiresome and frivolous accuracy of memory which is entirely owing to his mechanical descent."

"He must find it convenient in historical investigation, I should think, sir?" said the young lady.

"It leads to an uncivil and positive mode of disputing; ... that habit of minute and troublesome accuracy leads to a mercantile manner of doing business, which ought to be beneath a landed proprietor, whose family has stood two or three generations." (W. Scott [1815] 1900, 17)

That "transition from profitless dilettantism to the intelligent spirit of scientific investigation" to which Daniel Wilson gives homage, enfolded a movement from aristocracy to bourgeois. Through the three centuries of modern science, aristocrats' easy assumption of dominance sparred with middle-class tenacity overtly engaged as scrupulous adherence to method and detail. Scott's extraordinary sensibility to social nuance makes *The Antiquary* a rich document.

"In the end all roads lead to Walter Scott," remarked a survey of Scottish social history during Scott's lifetime (Murdoch and Sher 1988, 140). Scott led the transition from the Scottish Enlightenment into nineteenth-century Romanticism. He took courses from Dugald Stewart and knew well Adam Ferguson through friendship with his son (P. H. Scott 1983, 209). He admired Coleridge and hosted, at Abbotsford, Wordsworth, Maria Edgeworth, Washington Irving, and Sir Humphry Davy. Exuberant as his imagination might be in his fiction, in his Edinburgh circle he appeared highly disciplined, hard-working, scrupulous in legal and historical research.

Robert Chambers

A penniless young man ambitious to advance in the bookselling trade insinuated himself into Walter Scott's charmed circle by publishing, first, *Illustrations of the Author of Waverley* (1822) (Scott had not yet admitted his authorship of the popular novels), then *Traditions of Edinburgh* (1823), reputed to "have delighted Scott, who wondered 'where the boy got all the information'" (Watt 1887, 24). The assiduous boy was Robert Chambers, eventually to publish a *Memoir of Sir Walter Scott* (1872) including source material lacking in Lockhart's biography. Chambers is the link between Walter Scott and Daniel Wilson, the unmarked figure "behind the veil, behind the veil" limned by Tennyson *In Memoriam* (1850).

Robert Chambers (1802–1871) was the second son of a manager for cottage cotton weaving in the village of Peebles, a man, as his brother William put it, "aspiring in his tastes." He frequented the local bookstore, characterized by William as "considerably superior to the common booktrader" even though a cow could always be glimpsed at the shop, contentedly creating milk for the bookman's household. William and Robert read at the bookshop as well as at home where lay the set of the fourth *Encyclopædia Britannica* and many other books improvidently purchased by their father. Robert recalled how joyous his eleventh year had been, the year he read through the *Britannica*—the year before the family sold the set to pay off creditors. Machine-woven cloth produced in mills along Border streams dealt a catastrophic death to hand weaving, forcing the Chambers family to move to Edinburgh to find means of living. The father's ill-advised loans to captured French officers quartered in Peebles during the Napoleonic war further ruined the family's economic position. Neither Robert nor his elder brother William could continue formal education beyond the early teens.

William apprenticed to an Edinburgh bookbinder who permitted the youth to take books overnight to his garret lodging. Both brothers studied such works as Adam Smith's *Wealth of Nations* and Locke's *Treatise on Human Understanding* from dawn until time to report for work at 7:30; in the shop until nine each night including Saturdays, and paid too little to buy candles, William used the early morning light to excerpt these volumes into notebooks. When Robert was sixteen, William urged him to take what was left of the family books, plus some cheap Bibles, and set up a bookseller's stall on Leith Walk, the business street connecting Edinburgh with its port at Leith. Robert parlayed his tiny stock into a sustained enterprise, while William bought an old press and began printing. Once he had acquired suitable fonts, William wrote and published a sixpenny pamphlet on Scottish gypsies. Its single illustration "represented a savage gipsy-fight at a place called Lowrie's Den, on the top of Soutra Hill" (W. Chambers 1883, 106). Then as now, gore sold, and William not only earned a profit but heard opportunity knocking. Twenty-one and nineteen years of age, the Chambers brothers launched a literary periodical, Robert the principal writer, William the publisher, printer, binder, and occasional contributor, and little brother James inking the plates.

George IV's visit to Edinburgh in 1822 spurred William to print popular songs and programs for the processions, all selling very well. Robert capitalized on the occasion by writing out speeches in an ornamented penmanship. It was this art that had gained him entry to Sir Walter Scott: The brothers on Leith Walk had been befriended by a former Peebles resident who introduced them to an established bookseller in Leith. He too befriended the zealously working youths; he was impressed by Robert's ornate penmanship displayed on a sheet of extracts from Scott's poems, and he arranged that Robert should show this art to Scott's publisher Archibald Constable. Constable commissioned a handwritten volume of the songs in Scott's *Lady of the Lake,* to be presented to the great author. Building on this opening, Robert composed a set of sketches of country people and places supposed to be the originals of those in the Waverley novels. Constable's kindness did not, in the event, extend to publishing young Robert's original work, and William had to do it. They sold a thousand copies of their 1822 *Illustrations of the Author of Waverley*, and a more professionally produced edition was printed in 1824 by a better-known firm. Robert then prepared a manuscript from interviews he had conducted with elderly Edinburgh people on personages, events, and the Old Town style of tenements housing members of all social classes in the same building, from duchesses on the first floor to whores in the garret five or six flights up. *Traditions of Edinburgh* came out in 1823.

His name now made, if modestly, Robert turned out a long series of books on Scottish history (some published by Constable), landscape, ballads and songs, amusing anecdotes, and biographies. In all these works he utilized field excursions and interviews to extend what could be gleaned from written sources, published and unpublished; in other words, Robert Chambers relied substantially on his own firsthand research. In recognition of this, the Royal Society of Edinburgh elected him to membership in 1840. Eight years before, he and William inaugurated *Chambers's Edinburgh Journal,* to appear every Saturday "when the poorest labourer in the country draws his humble earnings, he shall have it in his power to purchase with an insignificant portion of even that humble sum [threepence], a meal of healthful, useful, and agreeable mental instruction" (W. Chambers 1883, 233).[3] Nearly every line would be written by Robert, supplemented by whatever William could find time to draft. Realizing that recent inventions in industrial-process papermaking and printing presses made mass-market publishing possible for the first time in history, William gambled on feeding a thirst for reading fostered by the Scottish provision of subsidized inexpensive schooling in the parishes. The institution of the Society for the Diffusion of Useful Knowledge in 1825, and Constable's 1827 *Miscellany,* a venture in cheap popularly written volumes, were immediate prods to Chambers' enterprise. With *Chambers's Edinburgh Journal* their flagship, W. & R. Chambers became a major publisher pioneering and profiting in reading matter for the lower bourgeoisie and artisans. Robert himself stated, "It was my design from the first to be the essayist of the middle class—that in which I was born, and to which I continued to belong" (W. Chambers 1883, 240).

[Robert Chambers] was always writing down odds and ends, as if assembling materials for books.... His casual thoughts, things he heard spoken of, anecdotes, stories, fragments of family history—all sooner or later assumed shape in sentences and paragraphs. He never forgot anything. His memory, from a faculty of concentrativeness, was altogether remarkable. He could tell you any date in history; he remembered all the people of any note he had converse with, and how they looked, and what they said, if it was at all worth remembering. Every place he had visited was fresh in his recollection. (W. Chambers 1883, 327)

Particularly between 1840, the year he became a member of the Royal Society of Edinburgh, and 1850, Robert assiduously amassed through correspondence and fieldwork scientific data and theories. He traveled throughout Scotland, Ireland, the Faroes, and Scandinavia tracing ancient shorelines and glacial formations, publishing *Ancient Sea-margins* in 1848 and a series of papers subsequently, "full of excellent observations relating to various geological questions connected with the glacial and other phenomena of the Quaternary period . . . collected with great care and labour" (Joseph Prestwich,[4] president of the Geological Society, 1872, quoted in W. Chambers 1883, 342). Charles Darwin consulted with Chambers in London in 1847, seeking to resolve the controversy over whether the ridges in the Glen Roy valley were ancient sea-margins or the margins of glacial lakes, as Louis Agassiz argued (Desmond and Moore 1991, 323).

"A wide circle of acquaintances" enjoyed the "conversaziones," William reports, in Robert's home where he might be "shewing antiquities of historical interest, and saying something regarding them for the amusement of the guests; or of discussing some curious point in geology" (W. Chambers 1883, 281). Daniel Wilson recalled:

Dr. Robert Chambers [St. Andrews gave him an LL.D. in 1863] presented a curious admixture of antiquarian and conservative instincts, and old nonjuring [to the Church of Scotland] sympathies, with an extreme liberalism in thought on all educational or scientific questions of his own day, which often gave occasion for friendly banter in the lighter moods of social intercourse. . . . With his keen Jacobite sentiment, and his no less ardent sympathy with all modern progress; his archaic veneration, and the bold scientific radicalism . . . there was a rare compass in the genial sympathy of the man. (Wilson 1878, II:150)

His vacations as productive of useful knowledge as his workdays, this genial host consolidated a reputation for solid bourgeois worth.

There was one break in Robert's exemplary career. He was said to have suffered a nervous breakdown in 1842, presumably from overwork. With his family of eight daughters and three sons, he retired to a villa outside St. Andrews, convenient for golfing and a university library. Here he had the pastoral solitude long held to be necessary to the true savant (Yeo 1993, 135–38; Chambers himself [1844, 387] alludes to this premise). Two years later, he had recovered his health and resumed residence in Edinburgh, the happy conversaziones and his labors for *Chambers's Edinburgh Journal* and the publishing enterprise. Outwardly, there would seem no connection between this excellent burgher and a bombshell of a book exploding into print in 1844. *Vestiges of the Natural History of Creation*—like the Waverley novels—came out anonymously. For many years, "Mr. Vestiges" could not be named, no more than the Author of Waverley had been for thirteen years. Why Scott refused to acknowledge authorship has never been quite clear (Sutherland 1995, 172); why "Mr. Vestiges" concealed himself is very clear indeed.

Vestiges of the Natural History of Creation was the scandal of the decade in British literary circles. Gossip guessed its author might be Prince Albert, the queen's young consort, a student of von Humboldt; or Charles Lyell, the geologist who had made his name with his five-volume *Principles* only ten years before; or the prolific magazine contributor William Thackeray, not yet the author of *Vanity Fair*; or a lady—Harriet Martineau? or perhaps Ada, Countess Lovelace, Byron's dashing daughter; or Sir Richard Vyvyan, a powerful politician who three years previous had privately printed an evolutionist cosmology (Secord 1994, xli); or Charles Darwin, that impressive naturalist known for his *Journal of the Voyage of the Beagle,* issued five years before. Any regular reader of *Chambers's Edinburgh Journal* must have suspected Robert Chambers, that fluent essayist whose prose matched the easy style of *Vestiges* and whose *Journal* pieces of the early Forties had considered many of the book's topics.[5] By the same token, any sensible citizen would understand that W. & R. Chambers could not jeopardize their firm's reputation by condoning a heretical work. The anonymous manuscript was transmitted to Churchill, a London publisher, through Chambers' friend Alexander Ireland living in England. Only in 1884 did the vow of silence dissolve on the identity of "Mr. Vestiges," dead thirteen years.

Why was *Vestiges* scandalous? The usual answer is that it initiated the war between science and religion, propounding an inexorable evolution: "The inorganic has one final comprehensive law, GRAVITATION. The organic, the other great department of mundane things, rests in like manner on one law, and that is—DEVELOPMENT" (R. Chambers 1844, 360). But Chambers immediately proposed, "Nor may even these be after all twain, but only branches of one still more comprehensive law, the expression of that unity which man's wit can scarcely separate from Deity itself" (360) "Deity," "God," "Creator," "the Great Ruler of Nature" receives deference on almost every page, one might say obsequiously. *Vestiges'* concluding note aligns its hypotheses with geology, reminding readers that "Geology at first seems inconsistent with the authority of the Mosaic record" but "In time, its truths, being found quite irresistible, are admitted, and mankind continue to regard the Scriptures with the same respect as before" (389). In this sense, *Vestiges* followed the early modern position of acknowledging the Book of Nature separate from the Bible but equally testamentary, a position spelled out by Thomas Sprat in his 1667 insider's explication of the founding of the Royal Society of London. *Vestiges* was crafted to read as an accessible account of current mainstream Natural Philosophy theories including those of Roget, Buffon, Cuvier, Lamarck, Prichard, Agassiz, Lyell, and even Dr. Buckland. Its sticking-point can easily be missed by readers today: *Vestiges* nowhere mentions Jesus Christ as Savior. *Vestiges* is a manifesto of the doctrine of Progress, denying the Fall, outcasting the historic Messiah. Fulsome as are *Vestiges'* praises of the One, it acknowledges only One—one God, one organic world, one human race under the domain of an absolutely nonpartisan Lawgiver.

Vestiges' Deity is a benevolent, merciful constitutional monarch.

> Those who would object to the hypothesis of a creation by the intervention of law, do not perhaps consider how powerful an argument in favour of the existence of God is lost by rejecting this doctrine. When all is seen to be the result of law, the idea of an Almighty Author becomes irresistible, for the creation of a law for an endless series of phenomena—an act of intelligence above all else that we can conceive—could have no other imaginable source, and tells, moreover, as powerfully for a sustaining as for an originating power. (R. Chambers 1844, 157–58)

To clinch the irresistibility of his argument, Chambers ended the passage by quoting the Reverend Dr. Buckland, Oxford geologist and in 1848, Dean of Westminster Abbey, that "such an aboriginal constitution ... could comprehend such an infinity of future uses under future systems" (R. Chambers 1844, 158; he does not reference the quotation). How could law-abiding Britons see heresy here? Buckland and his peers penetrated *Vestiges'* veneer of suprarespectability. The author claimed:

> Amongst the arrangements of Providence is one for the production of original, inventive, and aspiring minds, which, when circumstances are not decidedly unfavourable, strike out new ideas.... nothing can be more clear than that ambitious aggression has led to the civilization of many countries. (R. Chambers 1844, 321–22)

And then he closes by quoting "Dr. Gall," the Swiss anatomist and notorious phrenologist whose theory, if true, would demand a meritocracy should supersede the false institution of inherited privilege. Chambers admits:

> We are ignorant of the laws of variety-production; but we see it going on as a principle in nature, and it is obviously favourable to the supposition that all the great families of men [i.e., races] are of one stock (R. Chambers 1844,

283) [and] the beauty of the higher ranks in England is very remarkable, being, in the main, . . . clearly a result of good external conditions. (281)

The learned gentlemen of the higher ranks in England excoriated "Mr. Vestiges" as an amateur prone to accepting erroneous theories, unacquainted with the latest in science (since he was not in their circle). The bourgeoisie rushed to buy: There were eleven editions in Chambers' lifetime, 22,974 copies sold, plus a twelfth edition in 1884 and Dutch, German, and American editions (Secord 1994, xxvi–xxvii). "Mr. Vestiges" was a dangerous radical.

Robert Chambers was crucial to the construction of a science of prehistory for English speakers, on two counts: As the mentor of Daniel Wilson, and through the foundation he articulated for nineteenth-century anthropology. The two counts are coupled, for I am convinced that Chambers *used* Daniel Wilson—benignly—to advance his own agenda; that the suspicions inevitably, and especially in Edinburgh, associating Robert with *Vestiges* forced him to be extremely circumspect in pushing his bold vision of an archaeology scientifically documenting his Law of Development in human history. Wilson would write, under Chambers' tutelage:

[T]his science [archaeology] is the key to great truths which have yet to be reached . . . its importance will hereafter be recognised in a way little dreamt of by those students of kindred sciences. (Wilson 1851, xvi)

Untainted by the intimation of *Vestiges* radicalism that deprived Robert Chambers of the honor, proposed in 1848, of becoming lord provost of Edinburgh (Watt 1887, 24), Daniel Wilson could matter-of-factly proceed with the reorganization of antiquities that established the science of prehistoric archaeology.

Chambers and Wilson: From the Society of Antiquaries of Scotland to the National Museum

Daniel Wilson[6] (1816–1892) came from the same lower middle class as the Chambers brothers. Wilson's father and uncle supported the family through their liquor store; Daniel's father, like the Chambers' father, was a poor businessman and inclined to imbibe, but his elder brother managed the enterprise and, a bachelor devoted to his nephews and nieces, maintained the family more securely than the Chambers. Daniel and his beloved younger brother George finished Edinburgh High School and took courses in Edinburgh University, but Daniel had to give up his studies in 1835 for lack of funds. He had apprenticed to an engraver in 1830, and moved to London in 1837 hoping for advancement in this trade. The thrilling highlight of this sojourn was a commission to engrave one of J. M. W. Turner's dramatic seascapes, "The Embarkation of Regulus," the artist himself much involved in the project. By 1842, Wilson concluded that London was not the most promising venue, and returned to Edinburgh, opening a shop to sell artists' supplies, prints, and his services as an engraver. Throughout, he wrote what he himself termed pot-boilers for the rapidly growing popular press, including W. & R. Chambers.

Wilson gratefully remembered that Robert Chambers, "amid all the prosperity of maturer years, never forgot his early struggles, or allowed himself to grow callous to early strugglers" (Wilson 1878, II, 150). In 1836, Wilson had gone with two fellow apprentices to see the collections in the Society of Antiquaries of Scotland. Once more in Scotland after 1842, he seriously pursued antiquarian studies, discovering that a small arsenal in Edinburgh Castle was the chapel built by Queen (St.) Margaret in the early twelfth century. On the model of Robert Chambers' *Traditions of Edinburgh*, but much more scholarly and with much finer illustrations from his own drawings, Wilson compiled a lively two-volume *Memorials of Edinburgh in the Olden Time*, published serially 1846–47 and bound in two volumes in 1848. As Chambers gained entrée to Scott's salon with his *Traditions*, so Wilson's antiquarian accomplishments installed him in Chambers' cabal, the company of the bookseller and librarian David Laing and the aristocratic Charles Kirkpatrick Sharpe. Wilson was elected to fellowship in the Society of Antiquaries of Scotland in 1846, to honorary secretary of the society in 1847, and editor of its journal. An honorary secretary could be titular only, but in Wilson's tenure it was a busy post; he corresponded with members and other antiquarians, reorganized the society's collections and prepared an interpretive catalog. In 1848, Wilson sold his shop, relying on his writing and work through the society. He applied, in December 1848, for the position of Keeper of the Library of the Faculty of Advocates of Edinburgh (in effect, Edinburgh University Library). Robert Chambers recommending him wrote:

> Your age, your active habits, your obliging and courteous manners, and your general taste and talents in literature ... you would conduct the business of the establishment vigorously and with great attention to details. You would maintain order, punctuality, and despatch. You would be accessible and serviceable on all occasions. (R. Chambers, 18 XII 1848, printed in *Testimonials in favour of Mr. D. W.*, Edinburgh 1848)

Scott's Sir Arthur Wardour disdained such mercantile qualities, and so, apparently, did the faculty of advocates.

When Robert Chambers, restored to health by getting *Vestiges* out of his system, returned to active membership in the Society of Antiquaries of

Scotland, it was a gentlemen's club. Chambers and Laing deplored its dilettante atmosphere. Chambers invited the young Danish archaeologist Jens Worsaae, protégé of Christian Thomsen of the Danish National Museum, to visit Edinburgh in 1846 and counsel them on reorganizing the society's collections. The Antiquaries had maintained ties with their counterparts across the North Sea since Grímur Thorkelin, an Icelander, was elected a member in 1783. Thomsen's museum innovations were described to the society by a member in 1829, followed by formal alliance with the four-year-old Danish Royal Society of Northern Antiquaries (Ash 1981). Daniel Wilson was not available to meet Worsaae; he had only the copy of Worsaae's *Danmarks Oldtid* (1843), not yet translated, left in Edinburgh by its author, and what Chambers and other older members of the Society could tell him.

> If, however, the impulse to the pursuit of Archaeology as a science be thus traceable to our own country, neither Scotland nor England can lay claim to the merit of having been the first to recognise its true character, or to develop its fruits.... It was not till continental Archaeologists had shewn what legitimate induction is capable of, that those of Britain were content to forsake laborious trifling, and associate themselves with renewed energy of purpose to establish the study on its true footing as an indispensable link in the circle of the sciences. (Wilson 1851, xii)

Wilson's catalog of the collections was ready by 1849, and in 1851 a narrative version was published as *The Archaeology and Prehistoric Annals of Scotland*—"I coined the word *prehistoric* for my own use; and it made its appearance for the first time, unless I deceive myself, in my Prehistoric Annals of Scotland in 1851," Wilson wrote Charles Lyell in 1865. That year, Chambers triumphed, transmitting the gentlemen antiquaries' collections, now scientifically classified, to the new National Museum of Antiquities of Scotland for which he had politicked.

As Chambers had enlisted geology to argue for an incontrovertible, scientific basis for his "Natural History of Creation," Wilson quotes Hugh Miller, considered an

> eminent geologist.... "The antiquities ... piece on in natural sequence to the geology; and it seems but rational to indulge in the same sort of reasonings regarding them. They are the fossils of an extinct order of things newer than the tertiary ... one has to grope one's way along this comparatively modern formation, guided chiefly, as in the more ancient deposits, by the clue of circumstantial evidence."
>
> The archaeologist applies to the accumulated facts of his own science the same process of inductive reasoning which the geologist has already em-

ployed with such success in investigating still earlier states of being ... The detritus records archaeological as well as geological facts. (Wilson 1851, 6–7)

C. J. Thomsen's "*Stone, Bronze,* and *Iron* periods ... simple as it may appear," laid "the foundation of Archaeology as a science" (Wilson 1851, 18). The Danish system found "universal acceptance," Wilson stated, therefore it was "the system on which the following data are arranged, subject only to such modifications as seem naturally to arise from national or local peculiarities" (18). Wilson was aware that Thomsen "enlisted the more important element of public sympathy, and nationality of feeling, in his pursuits," an important factor and one certainly significant to Robert Chambers (Kristiansen 1981, 24–25; 1985).

In 1851, St. Andrews University applauded the thirty-five-year-old Daniel Wilson with an honorary degree. Robert Chambers chaired the Board of the Society of Antiquaries of Scotland as it signed over its now-scientific collections to a public National Museum on the Mound in the center of Edinburgh, between the historic Old Town and the classical elegance of New Town, under Edinburgh Castle on its ancient volcanic crag. Sir Walter Scott's Monument stood close by, near Waverley Railroad Station. Four hundred miles south, the astounding Crystal Palace Exhibition would open that year. National pride filled the air, not least because at last industrial capitalism was beginning to benefit working people. The Law of Development could not be gainsaid.

Prehistoric Man

For Daniel Wilson, 1851 held special poignancy,

> On a bright day in the early summer of [1851] ... I set out, in company with my old friend Dr. Robert Chambers, on an exploratory expedition [to a] ... rude stone cist.... It was such an archaeological prize as one may wait and long for in vain for a lifetime, and it chanced to fit in most aptly with special researches then in hand. I had been busy with the supposed evidences of pre-Celtic races, as shown in certain strange types of head found in bog and barrow; and had experienced the utmost difficulty in obtaining the needful materials for any adequate test of the theory, set forth before the end of that year in one of the sections of the British Association as an "Inquiry into the evidence of the existence of Primitive Races in Scotland prior to the Celtae." It is amusing now to recall the undisguised incredulity with which a theory was then received which has since met with universal acceptance as a mere truism necessarily involved in greatly more comprehensive assumptions.... But primitive British crania were in special request, and here was a disclosure which revealed undreamt-of affinities between those of the Old and the

New World. [Here he describes what sounds like a Beaker grave.] . . . We started homeward with our new-found treasures [skull and pot].

No pleasanter companion could have been selected . . . than Robert Chambers . . . we had a theme now in view which excited his keenest interest. . . . Only the year before there had been added to the English vocabulary the convenient term prehistoric. . . . The . . . skull . . . disclosed a special feature which had not attracted my attention before. The occiput was flattened, precisely as in some of the skulls figured in Morton's *Crania Americana.* What if it were traceable to the same cause?

Here was a theme pregnant with all the charms of a novel discovery; and our evening's talk led us through many a curious speculation on ethnical affinities, evolutionary development, perpetuated peculiarities, backward to the very origin of man. I still recall the startled interest with which I then listened to glimpses of Lamarckian and Darwinian views, now very familiar to all [Wilson published this memoir before Chambers' authorship of *Vestiges* was acknowledged]. (Wilson 1878, 140–47)

Variety-Production, the Law of Development, monogenesis—had Wilson not read *Vestiges?* More likely, he had gone through it, and perhaps von Humboldt's *Kosmos* of the next year, as must-reads for an educated man, without quite giving himself to the thrust of the argument. Trying to make a go of his shop, dedicated to the hard footwork of researching the tenements of Old Town for *Memoirs of the Olden Time,* meeting respected antiquarians, Wilson in the mid-Forties had concrete interests and immediate goals. Once *Archaeology and Prehistoric Annals* was at the printers, and the Antiquaries' collections designated for the National Museum, Wilson, it seems, was ready for new preoccupations. The suburban construction in Juniper Green that chanced to hit a prehistoric grave opened cosmological dimensions to Wilson's archaeology. *Prehistoric Man* was conceived.

Wilson wrote to a fellow antiquary in 1853 that he had "materials in my mind for an Ethnological work, linking geology and Archaeology," but found it hard slugging "amid laborious and irksome literary drudgery" (letter to Albert Way). Feeling desperate, Wilson applied for the professorship of English literature and history at the provincial University College in Toronto, a raw colonial town. The St. Andrews' degree and commendable reviews of his two books, *Memoirs of Edinburgh in the Olden Time* and the *Archaeology and Prehistoric Annals,* looked good; he got the job through the recommendation of the governor-general, fortunately a fellow of the Society of Antiquaries of Scotland (and son of the now-infamous Greek antiquities collector Lord Elgin). University College was literally being built when Wilson arrived in Toronto, the teaching load was heavy, the atmosphere backwoods, but there was potential. (He eventually became first president of the University of Toronto, and somewhat begrudgingly accepted a knighthood from the queen.) Regretfully leaving his beloved Edinburgh, his colleagues and friends, Wilson settled in Canada.

Canada was not without advantages. In 1855, he used his summer break to travel up the Great Lakes to Lake Superior, where he was excited, as he wrote David Laing that year, "to observe thus the manners and habits of a people probably closely resembling those of Scotlands primitive eras, which constitutes one of the favourite themes on which I used to bore you, at our S.A.S. meetings. . . . I shall try and write a paper for the Antiquaries this winter. I intended to have sent you one last winter. But my lectures took all my time" (Wilson 1855). The next year, he toured the Midwest, visiting the great Hopewell constructions and other "Moundbuilder" sites (he would go to see these again in 1874, before the third edition of *Prehistoric Man*).

The broadened perspective nurtured by Robert Chambers incorporated these firsthand experiences unavailable in Europe. Not only did Wilson stand in front of an Ojibwe chipping a stone blade, he absorbed the amazing scale of Hopewell earthworks, beside which Silbury Hill and even Avebury are almost pedestrian.

> When I left Edinburgh, I had sketched out a work partly historical, partly ethnological relating to Scotland on which I fancied I had something new to say. But transported here I found not only that I had no books or other needful facilities for the task; but that I was in an uncongenial atmosphere for such work; and if I would be both useful and happy I must find my work in my new sphere. . . . I have been for some time collecting materials, and meditate some time or other trying to dip behind the historic dawn of America as I have already attempted for Scotland. There were great men before *Columbus* as well as Agamemnon! But leisure is a rarity with me here; and any such extra-academical work progresses very slowly. (Wilson 1860 to J. S. Blackie in Edinburgh; Wilson's italics)

To his boyhood friend Blackie, Wilson bemoaned the impediments to his original goal of a direct successor to *Archaeology and Prehistoric Annals of Scotland*. He did not describe the course he instituted in 1857 that allowed him to correlate researches under the aegis of academic preparation, a third-year honours course entitled "Ethnology." This may well have been the first college course in the subject regularly offered anywhere (McCardle 1980, 22). That Wilson did not merely include material on prehistory and non-Western societies in his history course reveals the breadth of his vision for the emerging field of prehistory.

The manuscript of *Prehistoric Man* was completed by the end of 1860 and mailed to Macmillan in London in January 1861. It was out in October 1862, and nearly sold out by the following March. This success stimulated

Macmillan to request a revised manuscript for a second edition, with which Wilson concurred. A better-organized and somewhat updated *Prehistoric Man* was printed and, after some delay while the publisher filled political campaign commissions (Wilson to Lyell, 1865), for sale late in 1865. A third, substantially emendated edition came out in 1876. The value of *Prehistoric Man* was marked by the Société d'Anthropologie de Paris electing Wilson to fellowship in 1864, and by the Anthropology section of the American Association for the Advancement of Science making him its chairman for 1877. The most telling sign of the impact of *Prehistoric Man* was the invitation by the London publishers Williams and Norgate to Sir John Lubbock to get up a rival, to be titled *Pre-historic Times* (Wilson deplored the ignorant insertion of the hyphen, in a letter to Charles Lyell, December 1865). Lubbock's volume came out in 1865, before Wilson's second edition was for sale although not before its pages had been printed.

The standard histories of archaeology cite Lubbock's *Pre-historic Times* as the inauguration of modern prehistoric archaeology. Bruce Trigger offers the intriguing view that Wilson's liberal humanitarian respect for non-Western societies was not advanced, but obsolete, a last gasp of the Scottish Enlightenment, whereas Sir John Lubbock presented cutting-edge theory in 1865, strongly Darwinian in his premise of human descent from primate stock (Trigger 1992, 69–71). Trigger does not discuss Robert Chambers' relations with Wilson, other than to point out *Traditions of Edinburgh* as the model for Wilson's *Memorials of Edinburgh in the Olden Time*. In the light of Wilson's own memoir on that bright summer day of 1851, Chambers' seminal influence on *Prehistoric Man* seems irrefutable. James Secord (1994, xlv) states that *Vestiges* "defied the structure of authority which was being created for the sciences in the nineteenth century" and concludes that "is why these writings deserve to be read today" (xlv). I believe Secord's evaluation holds also for *Prehistoric Man*. In the next chapter, I explore the differences between Wilson and Lubbock, differences reflecting their strongly contrasting social class positions and those of their mentors in science, Robert Chambers and Charles Darwin.

CHAPTER 2

Science Boldly Predicts

Sir John Lubbock (1834–1913), fourth Bart., was in 1865 "a brash young man" (quoted in Bynum 1984, 178) blessed with not one, but two most beneficent fathers, Sir John Lubbock the third baronet, astronomer and banker at Sir John William Lubbock, Forster & Co., plus the family's neighbor at their three-thousand-acre country estate, Mr. Charles Darwin (Desmond and Moore 1991, 361). Darwin, said to display an "instinctive reverence for rank" (528), taught young John to be his research assistant in entomology, and later depended on John for archaeological data.

John Lubbock, IV, attended Eton but never university, going instead into the family bank as a partner. He followed both natural and avocational father into the Royal Society, where the younger scientists drawn by Darwin into his research formed in 1864 a very select London dining club. Its purpose was to maneuver these Young Turks into power within the Society (Barton 1990). Two members of the X-Club, Thomas Henry Huxley and Herbert Spencer, had been habitués of the *Westminster Review* offices in the early 1850s, clustering around the young publisher John Chapman and his editorial right hand Mary Ann Evans—she whose pseudonym would be George Eliot. John Stuart Mill was the most eminent of Chapman's friends. Robert Chambers stopped in when he was in London, and William Carpenter, who wrote on biology for W. & R. Chambers (Desmond and Moore 1991, 392–93). A decade later, the cachet of science was stronger than that of philosophy. Spencer's high-Victorian prolixness purveyed evolution in ponderous tomes. Huxley and Lubbock enthusiastically embraced evolution, both Spencer's and Darwin's. Lubbock concluded his *Pre-historic Times*, "science boldly predicts [that] Utopia, which we have long looked upon as synonymous with an evident impossibility . . .

turns out, on the contrary, to be the necessary consequence of natural laws" (Lubbock 1865, 491–92).

A century and a half later, the difference between Chambers and Darwin seems much less than the difference between Spencer and Darwin. Given that Chambers was quite openly a popularizer, and drawing upon science of the 1830s rather than 1850s, his *Vestiges* could easily encompass Darwin's theory of natural selection—that could be a codicil to the Law of Variety-Production, the great Law of DEVELOPMENT. Where Spencer invoked an ineffable Vital Force or Energy, Chambers wrote of a law-giving Deity; neither constrained himself as Darwin did to a narrowly scientific argument. Why was *Vestiges* so vehemently attacked, and Spencer befriended? Why was Lubbock's *Pre-historic Times* quickly made the *fons et origo* of prehistoric archaeology, and Wilson's much more carefully crafted work largely ignored by the London intelligentsia? Was it simply a matter of who dined with the X-Club in London?

The crux of the rejection of what may be called the Scottish group, and the fervent embracing of Spencerian utopianism, lies in the political import of the contending cosmologies. Chambers, his Edinburgh associate George Combe, and Daniel Wilson worked to bring about a meritocracy, with "merit" mirroring the values of the bourgeoisie. Lubbock and Darwin were gentry—not aristocrats, gentry—committed to a social order that permitted a degree of social mobility paternally overseen by landed families. Their England was no longer a nation of defined Estates, but a gentler terrain wherein Parliament under duress passed reform bills and mobs retreated back to work. Pound by pound, Englishmen were obtaining suffrage as the property requirement was lessened. The Sir John Lubbocks were businessmen, like Darwin's uncle/father-in-law Josiah Wedgwood. A haute bourgeoisie? Yes, with the emphasis on *haute*. These families' affinity was to the true upper class, the nobility. They shared the basic characteristic of deriving income from landed property. They sent their sons to the best schools, where comrades' families held titles. Though like Jonathan Oldbuck they and their associates acknowledged a self-made ancestor, he was an *ancestor*; they themselves had been born into a comfortable inheritance. This very pleasant scheme of things was worth defending—it had the glow of welcome to truly outstanding men of lower birth, without jeopardizing inherited privilege.

The Chambers and Combe brothers, as I shall describe, were in their hearts radicals. They wanted a system that would identify ability in young children, whatever their family position, and educate these children to become a meritorious ruling class. While neither the Combes nor the Chambers agitated to overthrow the economy that allocated such a disproportionate share of wealth to landed proprietors, the Scottish reformers would negate the political power of wealth. The Chamberses and Combes associated with men such as themselves and the Wilson brothers, Daniel and George, whose abilities had carved out their place with a minimum of patronage.

Prehistoric archaeology's *raison d'être* was to reveal the trends operating on human development, in order that laws and government might be refined to conform synergistically, rather than conflict foolishly. Daniel Wilson asked, "Whence is man? What are his antecedents? What—within the compass with which alone science deals,—are his future destinies?" (Wilson 1876, 7). A contemporary Englishman explained:

> [W]ithout a knowledge of the Past, most of the facts of present life are incomprehensible. Nay, all power of regulating the future comes from a knowledge of the present state of things, gained by a knowledge of the past. . . . [T]he antiquarian is able to arrive at general ideas which explain present matters and which may be used by the philosopher for the regulation of the future. . . . The archaeologist . . . is not, therefore, the useless person that is sometimes thoughtlessly portrayed, but a valuable contributor to the world's progress. (quoted from *The Antiquarian* by Hudson 1981, 100)

Should the petit-bourgeois reformers in Edinburgh and their emigrant scion present the answers? Or should the gentlemen of science (Morrell and Thackray 1981) control the production of knowledge?

Social Reform

Scotland contrasted with England in the degree to which social classes were marked. Until the building of New Town across the Nor' Loch in Edinburgh at the close of the eighteenth century, tall tenements housed all ranks in the same buildings, sharing the common stairs although stratified by floor. Chambers and Wilson, in their Edinburgh histories, describe commoners pushing past titled ladies' voluminous skirts in the tenement staircase. The elegant pale-golden classical facades of the rectangular blocks of the New Town segregated the genteel from the noisy bustle of Old Town's dark grimy wynds. University, courts, St. Giles Cathedral remained in Old Town, doubling segregation by divorcing professional men's work from their ladies' sphere. Particularly in Edinburgh, which as the seat of government employed the largest proportion of professional men, a middle class became visible by the early nineteenth century (Nenadic 1988). An indication of the segregation in effect by 1800 comes from George Combe's note that "the first instance . . . in which I had seen moving and heard speaking, persons whom I considered to be ladies and gentlemen" (in C. Gibbon 1878, I:56) was at a performance of "As You Like It." Combe, son of a brewer living beneath Castle Rock in southwest Edinburgh, was then about eleven.

What is striking about Scotland in the eighteenth and early nineteenth century is that boys such as Combe (1788–1858) and his brothers attended school as a matter of course. The Chambers and Wilson families, though poor, enjoyed books. Combe's parents were functionally literate but showed no inclination for intellectual pursuits (Combe in C. Gibbon 1878, I:3-4). Of their sons, John carried on the brewery, Abram and James became tanners, William, a baker, Walter, a currier—and George became a lawyer and Andrew a medical doctor of international repute (Gibbon 1878, i:83). This social mobility was facilitated by the Scottish provision of cheap schools supported by parishes or burghs. Even in rural areas, at least in the Lowlands and Borders where population density was relatively high (Withrington 1988), schooling was so general that not only the "Ettrick Shepherd" James Hogg but his picturesque mother were literate to the degree that Mrs. Hogg complained to Walter Scott, visiting her cottage in 1802, how previous ballad-collectors "prentit . . . my sangs . . . nouther richt spell'd nor richt setten down" (quoted in Sutherland 1995, 82).

Scotland's dominant Calvinist Protestantism was a strong element in the support for general literacy. The Church of Scotland served as one focus for Scottish nationalist feeling; the Scottish Enlightenment, promoting a distinctive secular philosophy, paralleled the Kirk in this respect. Kirk and literary salon in Scotland were recruited from a system of schools that after the 1707 Act of Union with England increasingly came to be seen as a sine qua non for national identity (Davie 1964; A. Noble 1982; Shapin 1981, 320–22). One consequence of Scottish valuation of common schools, relatively inexpensive secondary schooling, and unrestricted access to a four-year university program was the replication of this structure in the United States, carried by the large number of Scottish emigrants.

Reformers in Scotland looked to schooling to create a better society (L. J. Saunders 1950). State intervention in children's education was established at the end of the seventeenth century, just before the Act of Union. George Combe is remembered for his advocacy of phrenology, whereas for him, phrenology was only the means to discern children's native capacities, so to educate each to his best and give authority to men naturally gifted to govern well. Robert Chambers collaborated with George Combe toward this utopian goal, for some years willing to accept Combe's confidence in phrenology, then losing faith in its potential. Both men shared an optimism born of their own success in rising from impecunious circumstances to comfort and public esteem; in Combe's case, the relative democracy of Edinburgh in 1804, and its connection with general, inexpensive schooling, is well attested by the chance that launched his career. Fifteen-year-old George was to be apprenticed to a shopkeeper selling cloth, when on the High Street he and his father met the latter's brother-in-law, the bailie (alderman) of Canongate. Mr. Comb (the brewer didn't use a final "e") explained his errand, and the bailie told him:

> "I think you are wrong. You have given George a good education: We have a numerous connection in the town, and there is no writer [lawyer] among us. I think he would find some employment among us as a Writer to the Signet." My father replied that he always understood that high, rich, and influential connections were necessary to success in the law, and that in the case of his son all these would be wanting. . . . The case ended by [the bailie] finding a Writer to the Signet . . . who agreed to take me as an apprentice for five years. (Combe, quoted in C. Gibbon, I:62–63)

Walter Scott's father, son of a yeoman farmer, had similarly obtained social advancement as a Writer to the Signet, and his son initially followed that profession.

Combe was like Scott professionally and also in having been a feeble boy whose lively imagination substituted for the rough and tumble pastimes of other boys. Unlike Scott, Combe found no particular charm in the rural folk he met during stays on relatives' farms. Not until 1815 did the cerebral young man encounter his great avocation:

> It chanced that on leaving the Court of Session one day, a friend of mine, a barrister, said, "Would you like to see Dr. Spurzheim dissect the brain?" . . . "Yes, very much." "Then come to my house to-day at one o'clock." I went and saw Dr. Spurzheim . . . display the structure of the brain in a manner inexpressibly superior to that of my late teacher, Dr. Barclay; and I saw with my own eyes that the [*Edinburgh Review*] had shown profound ignorance . . . and gross misrepresentation in regard to the appearances presented by this organ when dissected by a skilful anatomist. . . . All my former interest in the study of mind was now re-awakened . . . at the end of three years' study I became convinced that Phrenology was true . . . and important. . . . In humble gratitude to God and in justice to man, I make the acknowledgment that my own prosperity and happiness increased every day after I had resolved to brave all dangers [of public condemnation] in defence of phrenology. (Combe, 1838 lecture, quoted in C. Gibbon, I:94–96)

Phrenology as initiated by Gall and developed by Spurzheim, two superb neurological anatomists, was a fine example of Baconian science, premising a natural-world cause for a recurrent observable phenomenon, then collecting and comparing data to lead to generalizations. Phrenology, like its contemporary evolutionary cosmology, fell afoul of sectarian Christianity and, in Britain, of the established societal order, evident in the polemnical attack in the *Edinburgh Review*, 1815 (Shapin 1979; Cooter 1984). (Ironically, at that time the *Edinburgh Review* was the organ of young, liberal Whig lawyers, and financed by Scott's publisher Archibald Constable [Murdoch and Sher 1988, 133]. Their supercilious disdain of phrenology reflects their loyalty to the ordained class structure, whatever charges they might bring against sitting politicians.) The Scottish Enlightenment had created a ground for Deism rather than Christianity, but it had not disestablished the legitimacy of inherited privilege.

Herein lay a tension that would cause many a thinker to dance on a tightrope: The Scientific Revolution advanced replicable empirical observations to be the guarantee of truth. An unfortunate consequence of this principle has been the insistence by many more or less reprehensible persons that they have faithfully observed conditions from which an inevitable induction challenges existing social structure. Thomas Jefferson was quite aware of the discomfiting factor when he wrote in the Declaration of Independence, "*We* hold these truths to be self-evident" (Cohen 1995, 121–34; emphasis added). The American rebels posited their political axioms to have the impervious power recognized in scientific axioms such as those presented by Newton. George Combe was more radical, insisting that social behavior flows directly from brain matter as movement flows from muscles; therefore, an enlightened and moral society would no more cripple people's mental growth than deliberately cripple their bodies; and if it is shown, as he believed he was demonstrating by observations of heads, that mental endowment is not correlated with ascribed social rank, then a society that fails to foster the natural growth of all persons endowed with mental organs for socially beneficent action is foolishly hindering its own moral and material progress.

George Combe understood quite well that his observations lacked the force of quantifiable measurable physical actions. "Phrenology is the Physiology of the Brain.... In no department of Physiology can mathematical measurements be applied to determine the *size* of organs, to which, *cæteris paribus*, the amount of their vital power is in proportion: We must *estimate*" (Combe [1847] 1872, 12). This of course was its Achilles' heel. Nineteenth-century Western society, its Biblical faith scourged by the lashes of geology, vastly expanded geography, the success of the American republic, and many other unconformities, eagerly sought certainty. Robert Chambers followed Combe beginning in 1834, but saw, in time, that phrenology could not produce incontrovertible conclusions and cast his argument instead on analogy with Newton's greatly admired "law," gravitation. Combe was, for Chambers, a stalking-horse, as Chambers' *Vestiges* would be for Charles Darwin (Desmond and Moore 1991, 322). Chambers would not, however, reject Combe. In *Vestiges* he quoted "Dr. Gall" immediately after the Scottish Enlightenment leader "Dr. Adam Ferguson," both on the "spontaneous" appearance of the arts of civilization "wherever" (said Ferguson) "men are happily placed" (R. Chambers 1844, 322). The next chapter, "Mental Constitution of Animals," artfully covers the main points of phrenology without citing Combe or Spurzheim, and straightforwardly introducing Gall on "perception . . . [who] has shewn, by induction from a vast number of actual cases, that there is a part of the brain devoted to perception" (341). From that assertion of scientific method, Chambers segues into stating, "The system of mind invented by this philosopher—the only one founded upon nature, or which even pretends to or admits of that necessary basis" (341).

Chambers and Combe's agenda of gradual progress through education to a meritocracy depended less on convincing the public through their books than on promoting actual mass education by means of the high-volume presses installed by William Chambers. Both the Chambers brothers and Combe realized that overt political reform would be mediated by legislative bodies controlled by Britain's alliance of landed proprietors (aristocracy cum gentry) and financially succcessful bourgeoisie. Producing and selling basic knowledge tracts cheaply and abundantly circumvented Establishment control. William Chambers' business acumen in developing this niche through industrial technology, Robert Chambers' voluminous output of clear, fluently written essays in *Chambers's Journal* and the firm's books, and a bequest to George Combe for dissemination of phrenology combined to actualize a significant portion of their reform agenda. Artisans and tradespeople craved the Chamberses' line, purchasing enormous runs of the periodical and books (the *Journal* alone selling eighty thousand weekly! [Secord 1994, xx]).

The Constitution of Man, Combe's most influential book, was published in 1828. It was a revision of "Essay on the Constitution of Man and its Relatons to External Objects" prepared in 1826 for public lectures in Edinburgh. For general publication, Combe removed an introductory section on "lower animals" and environment, lest readers be offput by the implication of continuity between animals and humans, and a final chapter, "On human responsibility," delineating his reformist views. In his autobiography, Combe recounts the miseries he suffered as a child from the polluted surroundings of the family home and from ill-ventilated schoolrooms and lodgings. "External objects" he early learned are powerful determinants of human happiness. Again remembering boyhood tortures, he decried the stupidity of rote memorization and corporal punishment in schools. The focus of *The Constitution* is on recognition that

> If the Creator has bestowed on the body, on the mind, and on external nature, determinate constitutions . . . it is obvious that the very basis of useful knowledge must consist in an acquaintance with these natural

arrangements;—and that education will be valuable in the exact degree in which it communicates such information, and trains the faculties to act upon it ... the natural laws must be obeyed as a preliminary condition to happiness in this world, and if virtue and happiness be inseparably allied, ... the moral and physical welfare of mankind be not at variance with each other (which they cannot be). (Combe [1828] 1860, 355–57)

Phrenology is discussed at great length in this as in Combe's several other books, but the basic call to reform social practices founded in ignorance need not depend on acceptance of phrenological hypotheses. Combe himself, of course, was convinced of their inestimable worth.

It happened that a young man named William Ramsay Henderson, son of an Edinburgh banker but displaying "an aversion to business" (C. Gibbon 1878, I:256), became so engrossed with Combe's phrenology that only a speech impediment prevented him from assisting Combe on the lecture platform. Henderson died in 1832, barely thirty, and his will directed his trustees to convey the residue income from his estate, after paying certain annuities, "for the advancement and diffusion of the science of phrenology, and the practical application thereof in particular" (quoted in C. Gibbon 1878, I:257). First fruit of the bequest was subsidizing the cost of *The Constitution* to students attending Combe's lectures. Three years later, the book was selling so well that volume enabled the price to be reduced, and the trust income was no longer judged necessary (I:256). By the time his executors readied a posthumous edition in 1860, 96,500 copies of the earlier editions had been sold in Britain, plus thousands more in America, and in translation in France, Germany, and Sweden (Cox and Coxe 1860, iii). The Chambers firm did not publish Combe's own major books, but it did produce a simpler textbook on phrenology (Secord 1994, xxii) and several of Combe's essays were printed in *Chambers's Journal* (C. Gibbon 1878, II:112).

George Combe and Robert Chambers remained intimate friends to the end of Combe's life (Gibbon 1878, II:261), sharing a faith in the probability of human improvement—material and moral—and implementing Progress by providing means to satisfy the populace's desire for knowledge. Both were attacked in the most scathing terms as irreligious; both believed the charge unjustified. When Chambers in 1842 decided to devote himself to writing his magnum opus, he could draw heavily on Combe's work, particularly *The Constitution*, without leaning too heavily on phrenology, for Combe was more dedicated to the melioration of humanity, in accordance with his reading of the Book of Nature, than to phrenology per se. Combe's association with Robert Chambers was significant for the practical and personal reinforcement these like-minded, intelligent reformers gave each other, and particularly for the evolutionary schema propounded by Combe as early as 1828.

Neither Combe nor Chambers, sensible Scotsmen that they were, would have accepted the label "millennarian" for their faith in human progress. An argument can nevertheless be made that both envisioned a future so perfect that in the broad sense it should be seen as millennarian. When Stephen McKnight says of the seventeenth-century reformer Campanella that his platform "offered an alternative religion and a redefinition of human nature that identified the present Christian disorder as a cause of ignorance and alienation" (McKnight 1992, 110), he could have been referring to Combe. McKnight continues, "The humanist tradition emphasized human dignity, autonomy, and creativity. . . . [K]nowledge as power . . . profoundly influenced Bacon and other early moderns to see science as the new source of soteriological power in the world" (116; see also Vondung 1992). Witness Combe's ringing conclusion to *The Relation of Science and Religion*:

> the day will come when these Divine rules for the guidance of our conduct, with the basis in science on which they are founded, will be taught in every school, preached from every pulpit, promulgated by the press, enforced by the law, and supported by an overwhelming public opinion; and then the incapable, and the ill-constituted in brain and body, whose actions now form the great afflictions of society, will be protected, restrained, and guided by social power, directed by benevolence, intelligence, and justice, and their crimes and sufferings will be circumscribed. Under the illuminating influence and discipline of the Divine law, Hell will probably appear unnecessary, Heaven will be realised on earth. (Combe [1847] 1872, 286)

Chambers, too, confesses a soteriological

> faith derived from this view of nature sufficient to sustain us under all sense of the imperfect happiness, the calamities, the woes, and pains of this sphere of being . . . we are in the hands of One who is both able and willing to do us the most entire justice. . . . Thinking of all the contingencies of this world as to be in time melted into or lost in the greater system, to which the present is only subsidiary, let us wait the end with patience, and be of good cheer. (R. Chambers 1844, 386)

A decade and a half separated Combe and Chambers in years, and *The Constitution* from *Vestiges*. Combe was molded by the late-Enlightenment impulse to action, proselytizing direct educational reform to realize his millennial vision. Chambers was entirely of the nineteenth century, working in a universe he saw to be so law-governed that direct *political* action (though not practical implementations) would be superfluous. The critical factor differentiating Combe and Chambers was the doctrine of uniformitarianism, which as Arthur Lovejoy showed (1959, 365),[1] was established in the early 1830s principally through Lyell's *Principles of Geology*. Under uniformitarianism, Progress to ever higher (literally and figuratively) forms of being *must* continue. Uniformitarianism gave Chambers, and Lubbock, the power to boldly predict societal change.

Virtually Witnessing Progress

With his health so wonderfully restored after completing *Vestiges*, Chambers sallied from his solitude once again the man of business. He took the time, the next year, to rebut his critics, reiterating his foundational premise "that the natural laws work on the minutest and the grandest scale indifferently" (R. Chambers 1845, 6). His new project apparently was to be the creation of a National Museum of Scotland arranged on scientific principles—another medium for empowering the populace through education. David Laing, Edinburgh's respected bibliophile, would cooperate; who could assist these men of affairs? Daniel Wilson had already, in 1842, penned a popular tract on "Archaeology" for *Chambers's Information for the People* series. The energetic young artist-shopkeeper demonstrated real research talent in his antiquarian studies of Edinburgh buildings, he was personable and from the same petit-bourgeois rank as the Chambers. With Laing's and Chambers' approbation, Wilson was elected a Fellow of the Society of Antiquaries of Scotland early in 1846, then the next year made an "honorary secretary," a position that for him was in effect a professional position as the society's curator. Selling his shop, he worked full time carrying on the society's correspondence and systematically organizing its collections—on uniformitarian principles analogous to geology, implicitly demonstrating the Law of Development.

When Chambers' politicking had succeeded, in 1851, in transforming the society's collections into the National Museum of Scotland, that museum illustrated both uniformitarianism, in cases containing prehistoric and ethnographic objects such as stone axes side by side, and Progress in the series, clockwise around the main room, of Stone, Bronze, and Iron Ages (Stevenson 1981, 147). Three years later, a Scottish Industrial Museum was constructed in Edinburgh to exhibit Technology, an unfamiliar word, first used in 1826 (D. Noble 1992, 263), defined by the museum's director as "Science in its application to the Useful Arts" (Ash 1986, 46). And who was this director? None other than Daniel Wilson's brother George, two years younger and a chemist trained at Edinburgh University. George published a successful textbook on chemistry with the

Chambers firm in 1849, and regularly gave popular lectures. The charter of the Industrial Museum called for such lectures and a library for public use as well as exhibits. "Savage technologists" were represented in the Industrial Museum, through brother Daniel passing on George's request for "Red Indian work" to the Governor of the Hudson's Bay Company, Sir George Simpson. (Thanks to George Wilson's broad vision, the Royal Scottish Museum, descendant of the Industrial Museum, preserves a collection of northern Canadian Indian manufactures of superb quality.) By 1855, Scotland's capital featured two popular museums displaying national history and its contemporary manifestation, national industry, the pair of museums a four-dimensional diorama of the Law of Development.

Close as the two museums' openings were, they fell on either side of the "precipice in Time [a]s in a geological 'fault'" (Thomas Hardy, quoted in Fay 1951, 96) embodied in London's Great Exhibition of 1851. Its truly extraordinary Crystal Palace impressed George Wilson, when he saw it in 1851, as the Celestial Sphere of a man-made universe concomitant with the Deity's older heavenly vault (Ash 1987, 45). Huge panes of clear glass arched within a visible framework of iron girders, glass and girders alike technical breakthroughs breaktakingly freeing mankind from loadbearing walls. The palace's Promethean engineer was Joseph Paxton (1801–1865), "only a gardener's boy," Queen Victoria noted (Fay 1951, 26). In his career to his knighthood in October, 1851, Paxton had become a foreman in the Royal Horticultural Society gardens in London, where the duke of Devonshire hired him to be head gardener at the duke's Chatworth estate. There Paxton had engineered a remarkable Lily House that perhaps deserves to be named the first Biosphere. Paxton had the audacity to draw up a plan for the Great Exhibition that was an enormous greenhouse—it even allowed existing trees on the Hyde Park site to be enclosed in the entry transept. Paxton's plan was submitted late, after the appointed Building Committee had agreed on a massively dull brick edifice, but his plan was urged upon the committee by influential gentlemen (one of the royal commissioners overseeing the project was nephew to the duke of Devonshire) and it had the sterling virtue of being an order of magnitude cheaper[2]—if it would work—than the brick fortress. That it would work was the opinion of the highly successful engineer Robert Stephenson, a member of the Building Committee who happened to have met Paxton on the train to London the day Paxton was taking in his submission, and had examined the plans with him in the railway carriage. Paxton's existing relatively large glass greenhouses further supported the feasibility of his radical design.

The Crystal Palace dramatically opened up vistas of the proliferation of industrial manufactures over the land, much as Louis XIV's gardens at Versailles conveyed the sense that the Sun King's dominion extended to and over the horizon. The Great Exhibition of all manner of products culminated in its Machinery Hall pulsing with steam-powered behemoths. Every day, thousands of the visitors to the palace had experienced the unprecedented rapidity and ease of railway travel; for the first time in history, hordes of working people enjoyed day excursions to the capital, encouraged by employers' nationalistic pride, cheap fares, and fast-food service in the palace. Britain was unified as never before through this common experience of the display of its power, the colonies represented by raw materials in contrast to the gleaming metal of the imperial center. The symbolism of the Crystal Palace Exhibition is as transparent as its glass walls. No one could fail to see the

> principle which has wrought out civilization by assiduous application from small beginnings; from the arrow head, which expresses the thought in the brain of a savage, to the smelting of iron ore, which represents the higher intelligence of the barbarian, and, finally, to the railway train in motion, which may be called the triumph of civilization. (L. H. Morgan [1877] 1985, 553)

Through the Great Exhibition, millions in 1851 "virtually witnessed" Progress and the triumph of British civilization. Shapin and Schaffer (1985, 60) called attention to the practice, so embedded in modern Western culture, of virtual witnessing: the practice of presenting for view evidence asserted to validate a proposition. Oral argument is subsumed, in modern science, to adducing physical demonstration for a claim. That is to say, rhetoric including mathematical proof is not abandoned, but tangible evidence is demanded as well, and in the absence of tangible demonstration, a thesis is "merely theory." The long aisles of the Crystal Palace provided in-your-face, throbbing in your gut proof of the Story of Mankind constructed by eighteenth-century philosophes to legitimate the power of their class (Meek 1976). Dugald Stewart had labeled this, in 1794, conjectural history (quoted in J. Slotkin 1965, 460). Now there seemed no reason to doubt the reality of this scientifically demonstrated history.

Few could be more pleased with the success of the Great Exhibition than George Combe. Shortly after its official closing, Prince Albert wrote, in his own hand:

> My dear Mr. Combe, you have been several times so good as to give me a portrait of the *phrenological* conformation of our children; I take the liberty to-day of sending you Winterhalter's view of their physiognomies. . . . I likewise send you an illustrated catalogue of the Exhibition, knowing that you have taken a lively interest in that child of mine also. We have attempted to give the work as much as possible a scientific character; the shortness of time allowed for the completion has, however, been a great drawback. You

will be pleased to hear that the importance of science to all industries and commercial pursuits is beginning to make itself strongly and generally felt and may be soon publicly recognised by the establishment of institutions for its connection with those pursuits. (quoted in C. Gibbon 1878, II:299)

Combe had, of course, seen the exhibition, making a special trip to London to do so. The previous winter, 1850–51, he had taught phrenology to Albert's secretary, Dr. Ernest Becker, a young German scientist appointed to supervise the Prince of Wales' recreation as well as serve the prince consort. Albert had openly defended Chambers' *Vestiges* in 1844 (Bennett 1977, 236), a valuable testimonial particularly because the prince had received an excellent modern university education at Bonn. His liberal convictions had caused political problems before his leadership of the Great Exhibition team gained him public glory; once his star was in the ascendant, it promised that the second half of the nineteenth century should realize the societal reforms that Combe and Chambers derived from the laws of nature.

Ten years after the fault-line year of 1851, the Edinburgh gynecologist and avocational archaeologist Sir James Simpson reminded the Society of Antiquaries of Scotland that thanks to

the masterly Prehistoric Annals of Scotland by Professor Daniel Wilson . . . Archaeology . . . is [now] a very different pursuit from the Archaeology of our forefathers, and has as little relation to their antiquarianism as modern Chemistry and modern Astronomy have to their former prototypes. (J. Simpson 1861, 16, 5)

[Archaeology has] traced by . . . many and valuable collections . . . the stratifications, as it were, of progress and civilization, by which our primæval ancestors successively passed upwards through the varying eras and stages of advancement from their first struggles in the battle-of-life. (10)

Wilson himself specified:

The alliance of archæology with geology, and the direction of geological research to the evidences of the antiquity of man, [which] have largely contributed to its expansion, until in its comprehensive unity it embraces the entire range of human progress from the infantile stage of primeval arts to the earliest periods of written records. (Wilson 1900 [1878], 333)

Archaeology is, Wilson continued, the "systematic science" for the study of progress; its alliance with geology meant that it could use Lyell's principles and the methodology through which geologists obtained and presented their data. As a sister science to geology—almost a Siamese twin—archaeology must exhibit stratifications, geology's version of the laboratory experiment. Archaeologists must excavate to reveal stratifications, must record the strata and their artifact fossils, and must present reproductions of strata in their publications so that their peers may virtually witness the (natural) experimental condition. The Crystal Palace Exhibition was a man-made visualization of Progress; archaeologists must unveil the hidden evidence that Progress follows natural laws. The Great Exhibition fault-line separates Thomsen's Linnaean methodology aiming at classification, from the newer goal of uncovering in-situ sequences that are visual witness to the successive stages of societal progress.

Progress Naturalized

Robert Chambers had the perspicacity to cater to the pervasive human hubris that sees the cosmos as man's history writ large. He candidly admitted that he "first had his attention attracted to the early history of animated nature, on becoming acquainted with an outline of the Laplacian hypothesis of the solar system" (R. Chambers [1853] 1994, 204), and saw that a universal law of development might be framed to encompass "the great pageant of nature ... in which we ourselves have a place" (205). Enlightenment histories of mankind, like the contemporary Linnaean system for biology, are essentially static, a series of types of societies in which humanity moves as from one room to another. Chambers' narrative moves dynamically as galaxies form, twirling suns "throw off" planets and whirling planets "throw off" moons (R. Chambers 1844, 36, 40). Quickly he leads his readers into the earth's primeval seas "swarming" with invertebrates and soon also with fishes, and so to the "commencement of present species" and a chapter on "animated nature," language that appealed to an audience that could see the triumph of civilization in a railway train in motion.

Jens Worsaae, whom Chambers knew from geological fieldtrips seeking Quaternary shorelines in Scandinavia, was in the 1840s just beginning, tentatively, to develop the methodology of excavation. Worsaae naturalized history by moving, over the course of two decades, from seeking primarily to confirm a static typology, to deriving typology from the exposed sequentiae. In his precocious *Danmarks Oldtid* of 1843, the twenty-two-year-old Worsaae appended recommendations for excavating barrows, emphasizing the value of "the relation between the tomb itself, and the objects deposited within it," in order to "apply the objects discovered to the positive advantage of science" (Worsaae 1843[1849 English translation], quoted in Daniel 1967, 104). Not until the 1850s did he internalize the model of geology whereby the physical superposition of strata is the crux of interpretation. Wilson's 1851 *Archaeology and Prehistoric Annals of*

Scotland similarly failed to grasp the power of in-situ stratigraphy, although he clearly grasped that without systematic comparisons of assemblages, "Collections of antiquities" were no more than "private hoards of 'nick nackets' ... nearly without value" (Wilson 1851, 16). During the 1850s, even these most ambitious younger scientific archaeologists struggled like chicks within eggs to break out of the world that premised the singular object to be the goal of archaeological research.

The singular object versus the "typical" object; the unique treasure— whether it be St. Margaret's Chapel or Priam's hoard from Troy—contrasted with the detritus of everyday life; in a word, the aristocratic versus the bourgeois. Orienting archaeology to the recovery of common patterns of living led to the reception of the geological model elucidating the histories of the mass of organisms. It is not likely to be mere coincidence that the elemental shift appears after 1848, the Year of Revolutions in Europe, when the bourgeois classes consolidated the centrality of their goals and interests. First, in the 1850s, the cutting edge of archaeological methodology turned to systematically demonstrating the common history of the populace, presenting the similarity between artifacts from ancient finds and those from foreign hemispheres. Then, stratigraphic excavations were increasingly presented as the proof of the common ancient heritage of mankind *and* the subsequent unequal evolution leading to the triumph of European civilization in, as the eighteenth-century philosophes had put it, the Age of Commerce.

If the symbolism of the Crystal Palace was transparent, the symbolism archaeology lent to post-revolutionary Europe was earthy. Kristian Kristiansen quotes an 1893 Danish poet:

> We Danes ... have a fatherland in which ancient monuments lie spread out in fields and moors, one after the other, so that at every step we are reminded of our relatives in the far-distant past ... whose bones rest in our soil. But this feeling of having a history and a fatherland, this actually means that we are a nation, a people ... this feeling ... simmers in people's minds, during the wear and tear of the day, like an underground spring, and it is just as clear and pure in the mind of the common man as in that of any other. This spring also fertilises present-day life.... Today's life grows out of respect for the memories of our forefathers. (Skjoldborg, quoted in Kristiansen 1993, 21)

"Today this outlook has taken root," Kristiansen continues, falling into the same metaphor, "the message found fertile soil" (Kristiansen 1993, 23). He quotes a popular author, "Much of what Denmark is actually about and strives for can be *seen and touched* in Lejre" (a reconstructed Iron Age village) (22; my italics). Virtual witnessing: the past is tangibly here and now, continuity is a flowing *underground* spring sustaining the heirs of the nation.

From Classical times, landed property has been the foundation of economic and, with a lag, political power. Nutini traces seigneurial privileges to the Roman period, and usefully contrasts seigneurial with noble, a rank constructed in the medieval feudal period. Seigneurial privileges include payment for use of the seigneur's land, his administrative power over the communities and persons on his land including local taxation, monopoly on commercial production and distribution in his administration, and the symbolization of the seigneur's primacy by his ritual precedence in public gatherings (Nutini 1995, 118–19). This large arena of power is fixed by the boundaries of the seigneur's landed estate. In the Middle Ages, the exception to the seigneurial system was the bourgs, demarcated urban enclaves administered by the burghers, the bourgeoisie. Burghers drew their economic and political power from movable capital (which allowed manipulation of credit). Were men rational, from the thirteenth century on, mere ownership of land, that straitened source of wealth, would be increasingly disdained. Instead, the burghers signaled their wealth and gradually concomitant power by flaunting aristocratic emblems, especially landed estates (Hobsbawm 1962, 32). Jonathan Oldbuck represents not only the old-fashioned gentleman antiquarian, but more subtly, that haute-bourgeois pride and pleasure in his estate that the bourgeois Walter Scott so passionately fulfilled in his Abbotsford (struggling, as if a born aristocrat, to keep it up regardless of his actual income). Land remained the icon of power.

Physiocrats in the eighteenth century wanted to rationalize—i.e., capitalize and industrialize—agriculture. Adam Smith conceptually separated labor from production and could reject the fixed element, land, in favor of the dynamism of the market. Landowners alienated masses from the land through enclosures and ejection. The more land became a relatively poor source of wealth, the more the populace shifted from the land to factories and the cities, the more romantically educated people loved "the land." Walter Scott, again, is a touchstone, setting so much of his work in rural locales. (Compare with Dickens: colorful characters speaking in rich dialect abound in cities, too.) The land was Motherland, Fatherland. Noble lineages tooks their surnames from their lands. Haute bourgeois could ape: Mr. Oldbuck is called Monkbarns by his familiars. Nobody seems to have referred familiarly to industrialists, such as Friedrich Engels, by the names of their mills " . . . Marx's friend Victoria Mills?" The ideology of industrial capitalism paradoxically naturalized the status quo through organic metaphors, speaking of the "body politic" with physiological terms and of its roots in national soil. Bright young men were encouraged to investigate individual physiology and soil-bound history under the aegis of science, the better to understand contemporary society.

Alike for nationalists chafing under broad empires and for local bourgeois demanding respect, "native soil" became the sacrosanct icon validating what was fundamentally an insistence on autonomy, whether from imperial domination or seigneurial rule. Philippa Levine (1986, 69) noticed that the mid-nineteenth-century enthusiasm for establishing provincial archaeological societies and museums was, in effect, a movement to construct pedigrees for the locality's middle class; Kristiansen finds the same phenomenon in Denmark, perspicaciously aligned with rising democracy by an 1866 source he cites. It would be another half century before the emancipated peasantry caught the notion of recognizing their forefathers in relics (Kristiansen 1985, 27). Initially, in the 1850s and 1860s, simply lying in a local barrow or exposed in a cut, like the Juniper Green burial collected by Chambers and Wilson, was sufficient to elevate an artifact or skull into ancestral status. Stratigraphy was crude, on the scale of Boucher de Perthes' distinction of the wide bands of gravels along the walls of the Somme Valley. Schliemann is cited by Glyn Daniel (1950, 168–69) with "puzzl[ing] his way slowly and laboriously to" understanding the stratigraphy of Hissarlik in the early 1870s; Daniel credits Schliemann's ability to his earlier mercantile career. The stratigraphic column per se did not move into its preeminence in archaeological reports until the last quarter of the nineteenth century. Archaeologists in the preceding quarter century were more excited by comparisons with other artifacts, with elucidating the lifeways of those forefathers in the soil.

That was the original purpose of Daniel Wilson's sequel to *Archaeology and Prehistoric Annals of Scotland*. Committed to monogenesis (a single human species), he took as his guiding assumption a uniformity of human responses to exigencies of survival. Chambers' "Lamarckian and Darwinian views," as he was to circumspectly gloss them in 1878 (147), held that "external physical circumstances" affect the histories of species, with even human "varieties [p]erhaps ... simply types in nature, *possible to be realized under certain appropriate conditions*" (R. Chambers 1844, 283; his italics). "Partly historical, partly ethnological," as Wilson told his friend Blackie in 1860, *Prehistoric Man* would attempt to contextualize Scottish antiquities by collating parallels and seeking to link contemporary and presumed ancient Scottish conditions. The geological model would not be stratigraphy but comparative anatomy, the means through which homologies could be identified and analogies imputed to similar stimuli. Emigrated to Canada, Wilson lacked the library resources for the kind of ethnographic surveys proper for his scheme, and decided to focus on American data. Insensibly, the book turned into an argument against the standard dismissal of American nations as savages. It became a strong ally for Chambers' conclusion, "only when some favourable circumstances have settled a people in one place, do arts and social arrangements get leave to flourish" (320–21). Wilson's experiences traveling on Canada's frontier along the western Great Lakes, in the Old Northwest of the United States, and meeting in Toronto a number of educated Ojibwe and Iroquois Indians, persuaded him of the innate abilities of Indians and the potential benefits of merging the races through intermarriage (McCardle 1980, 127). The net result of his experience was to strengthen ethnographic analogies and blur the archaeological problems.

The 1870s were quite different from the 1840s. The principle of universal non-sectarian education that Combe had championed was generally accepted, if not yet fully implemented, and the notion of universal male suffrage was tenable, if equally distant. The United States had settled, bloodily, the question of agrarian versus industrial domination. Britain had reared three generations of industrial workers, pushing its agrarian era back beyond living memory. Germany and Italy were launched as overtly unified kingdoms poised to compete aggressively with Britain, France, and the United States in industrial enterprises, for exploitable colonies and for markets. Canada gained Dominion status and took over erstwhile Rupert's Land, where another quarter century would see the Hudson's Bay Company replacing its trading posts with department stores. For archaeologists, the issue of poly- versus monogenesis of humans was settled, organic evolution was the reigning paradigm, the comparative method utilizing ethnographic analogy was standard and believed to demonstrate universal cultural evolution toward the Industrial Revolution, and the value of archaeology for nationalistic propaganda well appreciated.

"Prehistory" had been introduced to the English-speaking world in 1851 out of a North Sea consortium of vigorous but marginalized smaller nations. Asserting their patrimonies, they built upon the circumstance that their lands lay at or beyond the Roman frontiers, leaving them a largely prehistoric legacy lending itself to the framework of conjectural universal history extrapolated by Enlightenment philosophes. The early leadership of Denmark and then, briefly, Scotland was overcome in the 1860s by French and English savants enjoying elite support in the great capitals. Wilson's politically liberal, mild progressivism didn't suit; Lubbock's "science boldly predicts" was the ticket wanted. The epitaph for this chapter comes from Henry Adams, remembering his young manhood in the late 1860s:

> He was a Darwinist before the letter; a predestined follower of the tide.... The ideas were new and seemed to lead somewhere—to some great generalization which would finish one's clamor to be educated.... Henry Adams was Darwinist because it was easier than not, for his ignorance exceeded belief.... By rights, he should have been also a Marxist, but some narrow trait of the New England nature seemed to blight socialism.... He did the next best thing; he became a Comteist, within the limits of evolution.... He

never tried to understand Darwin; but he still fancied he might get the best part of Darwinism from the easier study of geology; a science which suited idle minds as well as though it were history.... He felt, like nine men in ten, an instinctive belief in Evolution, but he felt no more concern in Natural than in unnatural Selection.... Natural Selection led back to Natural Evolution, and at last to Natural Uniformity.... Unbroken Evolution under uniform conditions pleased every one—except curates and bishops; it was the very best substitute for religion; a safe, conservative, practical, thoroughly Common-Law deity. Such a working system for the universe suited a young man who had just helped waste five or ten thousand million dollars and a million lives, more or less, to enforce unity and uniformity on people who objected to it; the idea was only too seductive in its perfection. (Adams [1907] 1918, 224–26)

CHAPTER 3

Consolidating Prehistory

Charles Darwin's carefully crafted success in convincing the leading scientists of London that organic evolution fit uniformitarian principles created a framework for prehistoric archaeology. The science of archaeology was there since the 1840s, in Worsaae's work in Denmark and Wilson's organization of Scottish antiquities: It rested on systematic comparison and classification validated by in-situ assemblages. Evolution was a given for human history, fundamental in the eighteenth-century conjectural histories and implicit in the Three-Age ordering. Indeed, cultural evolution could be a model for the concept of the transmutation of species, or as Chambers put it, there can be *one* principle for all organic life, the Law of Development. When Darwin convinced Lyell that populations of organisms, including humans, changed gradually, imperceptibly, and inevitably, the unified science Comte preached was realized.

Archaeology was the one best body of evidence to support the ideological premise of human progress crowned by the Western nations' awesome machines—the railway train in motion, as Lewis Henry Morgan saw it. Proponents of Progress needed evidence, for they were obliged to combat a strong opposite theory, that of degeneration (Chamberlin and Gilman 1985). Degeneration seemed orthodox, clearly following from the Fall of Adam and Eve and the scattering of the nations from the Tower of Babel. Degeneration explained the savages described by Western explorers. Degeneration upheld the eternal suffering that Christian churches threatened to anyone disrespecting the sanctity of the churches' doctors. It was a frightening, fearsome, depressingly pessimistic doctrine that scriptural Revelation disclosed. Against this orthodox theory, rebels and optimists could adduce the Book of Nature's revelations of geological progress from an earth of smoking volcanoes or limitless seas, of steadily more intelligent organisms, and of human technological feats.

Disillusion with conventional Christian doctrine is a feature of the eighteenth-century Enlightenment. The philosophes' conjectural histories used the Book of Genesis as a source of historical data on pastoral societies and simpler kingdoms, usually without directly confronting the discrepancies between verses or openly calling the Fall and Babel myths. Darwin confessed that by the late 1830s he realized that the Old Testament "was no more to be trusted than the sacred books of the Hindoos, or the beliefs of any barbarian" (quoted in Moore 1988, 274). George Combe and Robert Chambers stepped around Christianity to speak frequently of the Creator, providing their hundreds of thousands of readers a sense of happy promise. Orthodox Christians were outraged. Reverend Adam Sedgwick, professor of geology at Cambridge, vehemently attacked *Vestiges* in a long review climaxing in the charge that its "degrading materialism" would damn England's "glorious maidens and matrons" (quoted in Secord 1994, xxxii). Chambers had expected Sedgwick, as a geologist, to accept *Vestiges'* progressionism. The Reverend's choleric outrage bespoke a deeper schism in England than Chambers had foreseen—he knew the Scottish evangelicals would reprehend the book—and pointed Darwin and his secular associates to reticence and a strategy of marshalling volumes of impeccable data.

"Natural theology" was a cover term that had papered over the profound differences between doctrinal orthodox and the materialists. In 1829, the earl of Bridgewater willed £8000 to be disbursed by the president of the Royal Society of London and the Archbishop of Canterbury on the publication of one or more works "on the power, wisdom, and goodness of God as manifested in the creation." Eight tendentious volumes came out in the 1830s, by such worthies as Dean Buckland (*Geology and Minerology*), William Whewell, Peter Roget, and Dr. Thomas Chalmers. George Combe complained to Robert Chambers that his own *The Constitution of Man* fulfilled the Earl's bequest, and deserved to have at least been cited by Chalmers (quoted in Gibbon 1878, I:296). The slight rankled, and by 1847 Combe published a pamphlet "On the Relation between Religion and Science" (he would expand it to book length in 1857). Responding to a letter regarding the essay from the wife of the Archbishop of Dublin, with whom he had been corresponding since 1832, Combe stated:

> The theology of nature, in other words, the exposition of the things which God has instituted in the natural world, of the relations which He has established among them, and of the effects which all of these produce on human happiness, belongs, in my opinion, to the men of science.... The principle for which I am now contending is *new*, and if it shall prove sound,

it will introduce a new epoch in religion. . . . Christianity will stand side by side with it, purified and rendered more and more practical, and more congenial to the highest and best cultivated minds. (quoted in C. Gibbon 1878, II:233, 235)

Combe closes the letter with a "striking illustration" of his arguments for the moral imperative of honoring God's laws for human health, the 1846 figures for mortality in Edinburgh-Leith: mean age at death for "gentry and professional men," $43^1/2$; for "merchants, master tradesmen, clerks, &c," $36^1/2$; and for "artizans, labourers, servants, &c," $27^1/2$.

Combe's 1847 essay appears to have been the first to call explicitly for a "Second Reformation" (Moore 1986, 69). The term was used in 1853 in a *Westminster Review* article by J. A. Froude, and then taken up in 1860 by Thomas Henry Huxley and subsequently by others in the *Westminster Review* circle: George Lewes, Leslie Stephen, and Herbert Spencer. (Robert Chambers also frequented the *Westminster Review* office when he visited London in the 1850s.) George Combe published in the *Review* (in 1854) and Mary Ann Evans (George Eliot), assistant editor of the *Review,* had in 1852 spent two weeks in Combe's house in Edinburgh.[1] Nevertheless, at the *Review,* it was Auguste Comte's Positivism rather than Combe's physiological laws of Nature that stood in for Scripture. Comte's writings were abstractly metaphysical, whereas Combe's empirical style deflected religiosity. Herbert Spencer's prose much resembled a railway train in motion, cars full of baggage barreling along with great snorts and puffs and whistles; many of his contemporaries hailed it as a triumph of civilization. With Harriet Martineau's blessedly condensed translation of Comte's *Cours de Philosophie Positive* paving the way, Spencer gave his compatriots their new creed: "the ultimate development of the ideal man is logically certain . . . man must become perfect" (Social Statics, 1850, quoted in Pollard [1968] 1971, 143).

Spencer's relentless reach gave Victorians *First Principles* (1862), *The Principles of Psychology* (1855), *The Principles of Biology* (1864–67), *The Principles of Sociology* (1876–96), and *The Principles of Ethics* (1891), the set totaling *The Synthetic Philosophy.* A contemporary writing soon after Spencer's death in 1903 is worth quoting at length to give the flavor of his reputation:

The idea of development [is] the great formative idea of the present century. . . . In England it is best known through Darwin. But while Darwin shows its scientific side, the most celebrated of recent English philosophers, Mr. Herbert Spencer makes it the basis of a philosophy. *The Synthetic Philosophy* . . . is distinguished for the vastness of its design, the accomplishment of which gives Mr. Spencer a place among the few encyclopædic thinkers of the world. His philosophy is interesting also because it concentrates and reflects the spirit of the time. No other thinker has so strenuously laboured to gather together all the accumulations of modern knowledge and to unite them under general conceptions. . . . The future only can determine the exact value of this knowledge, for there are grave differences of opinion between Mr. Spencer and some of the leading biologists, like [August] Weismann. . . . Mr. Spencer's unique interest is that he has attempted an exhaustive survey of all the facts relating to the development of life and of society. He does not go beyond that, to the origin of all things; for it is one of his cardinal principles that behind the Knowable there is dimly visible a something not only unknown but unknowable. We are compelled to regard every phenomenon as the manifestation of an infinite and incomprehensible Power. In this the philosopher finds the reconciliation of religion with science. . . .

The Spencerian philosophy is the most comprehensive and ambitious application of the principle of evolution ever attempted. Without showing anywhere that mastery of detail and that power of marshalling facts in evidence which give Darwin's great work its unequalled significance, the *Synthetic Philosophy* yet reaches at both ends beyond the limits Darwin set himself. Mr. Spencer begins by recognising three kinds of evolution, in the spheres of the inorganic, the organic and the super-organic . . . [the last] in the *Principles of Sociology* . . . [which] combines in an unusual measure the best results of ancient thought with full justice to modern individualism. . . . He sees that "the survival of the fittest," and with it progress, are impossible unless 'the fittest' both wins and keeps advantage to himself. Unlimited altruism would be as bad as unlimited egoism. . . . Hence there arises a society which is a balance between the two principles. . . . as society is composed of individuals, a society in which the strongest has no advantage is a society in which progress is impossible, but, on the contrary, deterioration is sooner or later certain. . . .

But whatever its faults the *Synthetic Philosophy* remains unequalled in the present age for boldness of conception and for the solidity derived from its league with science. No other philosophy is so eminently modern in spirit and method. (Walker 1909, 171–74).

And what was his method?

[A] process [which] began by being inductive and ended up being deductive; and this is the peculiarity of the method followed. On the one hand, I was never content with any truth remaining in the inductive form. On the other hand, I was never content with allowing a deductive interpretation to go unverified by reference to the facts. (quoted in Macpherson 1900, 48)

Spencer had assistants copy the facts out of books onto index cards, classify them, and bring them to his desk when he called for facts on a topic (Rumney [1937] 1966, xii–xiii). He disliked reading (Wiltshire 1978, 67, 72; Macpherson 1900, 57) and never produced any primary research, either field or laboratory, although he did follow his father's enjoyment of tinkering and invented a device for calculating the velocities of railway trains in motion (Richards 1987, 247).

That very select little coterie, the X-Club, did not appreciate the enormous difference between the windy metaphysics of the chaste Londoner Spencer and the meticulously supported arguments of Darwin. Huxley, for example, in 1870 referred his listeners to Spencer's *Principles of Psychology* as an authoritative text on "the relation between nerve-action and consciousness" (Huxley [1870] 1887, 296). Darwin, surrounded by hundreds of experiments on plants, on pigeons, on earthworms, by vast arrays of barnacles, and dozens of children, most of them produced by an unusual set of cousin marriages, built his interpretations upon his firsthand observations, judiciously expanded by direct discussion with selected other scientists whom he cultivated as research associates (Secord 1985, 534–35). With great care, Darwin hewed to the principle of actualism[2] articulated by Lyell in those *Principles of Geology* Darwin had read while voyaging on the *Beagle*. It cannot be sufficiently stressed that Darwin worked and wrote as a scientist and Spencer as a philosopher. Cynthia Russett remarked, "If ever ideas sprang full-blown from the brow of any man, that man was Spencer. In fact, his greatest resemblance to Comte may have been in his single-minded absorption in his own thoughts" (Russett 1976, 16). Comte and Spencer worked from ratiocination, Darwin from observation.

From the Great Exhibition to 1873, a generation felt swept along in rapidly accumulating industrialization, the dreary drab muscle-power of humans, horses, and donkeys replaced by machines roaring, belching smoke, darkening the skies like hordes of dragons. Where in myth, Beowulf died opposed to these monsters, now his vaunted Anglo-Saxon descendants commanded these behemoths, bred them in this era of the Super-organic. John Tyndall (1820–1893), one of the X-Club, asserted in his Presidential Address to the British Association for the Advancement of Science meeting in Belfast in 1874:

> The impregnable position of science may be described in a few words. We claim, and we shall wrest, from theology the entire domain of cosmological theory . . . science claims unrestricted right of search. It is not to the point to say that the views of Lucretius and Bruno, of Darwin and Spencer, may be wrong. (Tyndall [1874] 1970, 474–75, 477)

At the end of the century, Alfred Russel Wallace, co-discoverer of the principle of natural selection, suggested that "the establishment of the general theory of evolution ... may be held to be the great scientific work of the nineteenth century" (A. Wallace 1899, 135). "This is, of course, partly due to the colossal work of Herbert Spencer," he admitted, although by 1900 "for one reader of his works there are probably ten of Darwin's" (142). In 1870, the two names were co-equal, as Tyndall indicates. His generation was understandably exhilarated by the rapidity of technological conquest of space and time—railways, steamboats, telegraph. In response to industry's need for literate labor, all Britain was following Scotland's lead in providing public basic schooling, and Combe and his friends would have been pleased at the growing concern to include hygiene and basic science. Britain's 1867 Reform Act extended the franchise, strengthening bourgeois influence, if still principally a haute bourgeoisie allied with the gentry. Capitalism's markets chugged along, enveloping more and more of the working class in consumerism as urbanization and real wages rose (in Western Europe and America), and extracting ever more resources cheaply from the modern colonies seized for their raw materials rather than for plantations.

With the world they saw so wonderfully transforming, the British and American bourgeoisie, even such intelligent members as Thomas Huxley and John Tyndall, could vibrate sympathetically to Spencer's vision of evolution:

> an integration of matter and concomitant dissipation of motion, during which the matter passes from an indefinite incoherent homogeneity to a definite coherent heterogeneity; and during which the retained motion undergoes a parallel transformation. (Spencer [1862] 1891, 396, quoted in Russet 1976, 14)[3]

Note the choice of mechanical terms, echoing the Laws of Thermodynamics formulated at this time by Helmholtz, Clausius, and Lord Kelvin. Spencer deliberately set out, as Comte had, to unify all the branches of knowledge (*The Synthetic Philosophy*). Huxley explained, in an 1870 lecture, that Descartes had thought mind and matter are quite separate, but Huxley told his audience that such a concept was like a plant with two branches, that is,

> monœcious [with] flowers of different sexes, and ... the only hope of fertility lay in bringing them together ... metaphysics and physics ... will never be completely fruitful until the one unites with the other.... I believe that we shall, sooner or later, arrive at a mechanical equivalent of consciousness,

just as we have arrived at a mechanical equivalent of heat. (Huxley [1870] 1887, 295)

Spencer thus gave his comrades a formula for evolution couched in terms that brought it wholly within conventional mid-nineteenth-century science. If Spencer's penchant for postulating a Vital Force, Persistence of Force, "an Infinite and Eternal Energy from which all things proceed" (quoted in Macpherson 1900, 214–15) sound surely *quasi*-scientific to us, it was quite in line with the inclinations of Henry Sidgwick and three other scientific Fellows of Trinity College, Cambridge, who founded the Society for Psychical Research to discover the "higher law" immanent in the ether (i.e., in the ethereal realm) (Wynne 1979).

Spencer was *the* evolutionist for his generation. Charles Darwin described only "descent with modification," the means for the transmutation of species. His 1859 book was "the species book," *On the Origin of Species*. It was Spencer who popularized the term "evolution" to refer to organic development. He used the word in this sense as early as an 1857 essay, and he implied it could be synonymous with Progress. With Spencer, the Victorian bourgeoisie had a unitary science recapitulating Comte's positivist Progressionism in the naturalistic and mechanist terminology befitting a society experiencing, in the 1850s and '60s, real amelioration in living conditions for hundreds of thousands. True, larger numbers of human beings were as squalid, cold, hungry, and exhausted as ever, but those people didn't buy books.

X-Clubbers Tyndall and Huxley earned most of their income from popular lectures and books. Traveling along with Spencer in revealing materialism's promise of complete knowledge in that stage of Progress almost within our grasp, they conferred scientific and, with their Royal Society leadership, social respectability on evolution. Darwin's *Origin* was the capstone, the final piece that made all the observations fit together and make sense, and Darwin's social rank, a gentleman living on private income, lent evolution the imprimatur of class. Now what was needed was *scientific* evidence that human history vouchsafed evolutionary Progress.

Archaeology as an Inductive Science

The evidence wanted to persuade Victorians of the truth of Progress would have to meet the criteria for science. Merely exhibiting stone axes beside Sheffield steel knives wasn't enough, for the degenerationists could argue that the stone tools indicate the degradation of Man after the Fall (slowly to climb back toward godly civilization), and polygenists could insist savages' stone tools prove separate creation of the varieties of humans. Stratigraphy might show stone tools superseded by bronze and then iron, but these strata could result from invasions and conquests rather than evolution, as everyone witnessed in the European colonizations. Evolutionists needed to fit their observations and conclusions to the formula for inductive science enshrined by Professor Whewell of Cambridge, the preeminent philosopher of science.

William Whewell (1794–1866) was the son of a master carpenter in Lancashire. The boy's intellect earned him a scholarship to Cambridge, and his father was sufficiently well remunerated in his trade that he could help with the youth's expenses, for which the son was properly grateful. At Cambridge, Whewell excelled, was elected a Fellow of Trinity College a year after he graduated, professor of mineralogy in 1828, given the chair of moral philosophy in 1838, and finally made master of Trinity in 1841, the year in which he married a woman who, like himself, came from a successful artisan's family. Whewell's learning did not compensate, in the eyes of some undergraduates, for his lack of social polish: In 1838 and again in 1843, students publicly and contumaciously disparaged his manners. His reputation outside Cambridge began with the publication of textbooks on mechanics (1819), on dynamics (1823), and on mineralogy (1828) and grew with essays, the Bridgewater treatise on *Astronomy and General Physics* (1833), and reviews (reviewing Lyell in 1832, Whewell named Lyell's view "Uniformitarian" and his opponents "Catastrophist"). Original scientific contributions included improving crystallography through the use of mathematics, and a quarter-century of observations of the hydrodynamics of tides, assisted by a former student, the third baronet John Lubbock (father of Darwin's protégé) and numerous seaside residents and coastguardsmen.

Whewell coinced the term "scientist" in 1833, considering the earlier "natural philosopher" to be too broad for the audience he was addressing, the meeting of the British Association for the Advancement of Science. In 1837, he published the landmark *History of the Inductive Sciences,* with *Philosophy of the Inductive Sciences* three years later. "Inductive science" referred to interpretation from empirical observations, contrasted with "deductive science"—armchair cogitation. A major contribution of Whewell's mature work was its critical discussion of the "Baconian method" assuming accumulation of observations would furnish the ground for inductive generalization. Whewell emphasized that great minds "superinduce ... some general idea" (quoted in Yeo 1993, 161). Like the good Indo-European speaker he was, Whewell "naturally" divided his narrative in the *History* into three parts: Prelude, Inductive Epoch, and Sequel; a great man's superinductive discovery or principle, in the Inductive Epoch, is routinized into normal method in the Sequel. The original editions of the *History* and *Philosophy* reject any simple narrative of progress, and consider the intellectual beauty of science its central virtue, practical applications its happenstance result. Whewell's 1840 classic definition of science:

When our conceptions are clear and distinct, when our facts are certain and sufficiently numerous, and when the conceptions, being suited to the nature of the facts, are applied to them so as to produce an exact and universal accordance, we attain knowledge of a precise and comprehensive kind, which we may term science. (quote in Morrell and Thackray 1981, 272)

Visiting the Great Exhibition of 1851, Whewell saw "the laws of operative power in material productions, whether formed by man or brought into being by Nature herself" (quoted in Yeo 1993, 228). So cautious a philosopher as Whewell thus could be brought by the evidence before his eyes to perceive a unitary Force such as Spencer rhapsodized over. Whewell would still not recant his insistence, in the *Philosophy*, that science cannot penetrate to "any intelligible beginning of things," leaving us, by default, a Creator. Robert Chambers savaged this wet-blanket in *Explanations*, his reply to *Vestiges'* critics. Dr. Whewell

halts when he comes to consider the origin of language and of arts, the origin of species and formation of globes [note how culture, biology, and cosmology are conflated as historical science]. These he calls palætiological sciences, because, in his opinion, we have to seek for an *ancient and different class of causes*, as affecting them, from any which are now seen operating ... says he, ... "philosophers have never demonstrated, and, so far as we can judge, probably never will be able to demonstrate, what was the primitive state of things from which the progressive course of the world took its first departure ... it becomes not only invisible, but unimaginable." (R. Chambers 1845, 126–27, quoting from Whewell's *Philosophy of the Inductive Sciences;* Chambers' italics)

Chambers thus cogently exposed Whewell's jump from salubrious caution to an unscientific a priori rejection of certain domains of inquiry. The basic issue was uniformitarianism, a principle on which Whewell criticized Lyell. It is important to take account here of Ernst Mayr's deconstruction of mid-nineteenth-century "uniformitarianism" into six components: naturalism (nineteenth-century "materialism"); actualism (explaining the past through processes observed in the present); intensity of causal forces (whether changing in intensity); configurational causes (will factors have different effects if the situational configuration is different?); gradualism; and directionalism (Mayr 1982, 376–79). Of these, the first, the absolute commitment to naturalism, seemed to Whewell and other Bridgewater treatise authors an unacceptably radical position. Whewell abhorred undisciplined speculation, therefore he emphasized the unobservable *must be* "unimaginable." Chambers (who after all did not have to teach undergraduates) accepted without qualm the premise that all the observable world *must be* explained through actualism, however recondite the extrapolation from present processes to past effects. The next generation, Huxley and Tyndall in particular, went one beyond Chambers by eliminating altogether the First Cause he had segregated beyond the world at the beginning of time. British science by 1870 was unequivocably materialist and uniformitarian.

With "inductive science" demarcated by Whewell from the "deductive" speculations of metaphysicians, and uniformitarianism accepted by the leading scientists after mid-century, *pace* Whewell, archaeology modeled on geology could be adduced to demonstrate cultural aspects of Spencer's evolution. Archaeology literally took up where geology left off, in the uppermost Quaternary strata of the Book of Nature. Inaugurated by Thomsen and carried on by Worsaae initially to validate the philosophes' conjectural history, archaeology by 1851 was ready to provide scientific detail to the human facet of evolution.

To make prehistoric archaeology truly scientific, the uniformitarian principle needed to be extended to the identification of artifacts. This was routinely but intuitively done in museum halls, as in Edinburgh, where in the late 1840s the Society of Antiquaries of Scotland exhibited African, American Indian, and South Pacific manufactures alongside prehistoric British and Danish objects (Ash 1981, 103). Daniel Wilson realized the rationale for the practice should be explicated, and the Baconian practice of collecting observations laid under a "superinduced" organizing hypothesis (Wilson 1900 [1878]). Excavation, at this stage, could give only sequences. The hypothesis proposed was that a monogenic human species had progressed from simple and homogeneous to complex and heterogeneous—Spencer's terminology replacing Chambers' Law of Development and Roget's Law of Variety-Production which Chambers had employed in an 1842 *Chambers's Journal* essay. Was the human species monogenic? This would be a precondition for comparing artifacts across time and space. Does a reasoned ordering of artifacts lead by inductive logic to the conclusion that Progress is a quality of human history? And how does the scientist explain the persistence of less-evolved technology in the present? Daniel Wilson grasped that the key to making archaeology scientific was to adapt geological models—not only the method of exposing stratigraphic successions, but the mode of explanation invoking comparative anatomy, adaptation, and that "law of variety-production" that by the time he would publish would be better known as descent with modification.

Had Wilson obtained one of the positions he sought in Scotland, he would have sat in his study eyeballing the exotic objects available in the Antiquaries' collections. Removed to America, to a Toronto rapidly moving out of a frontier stage, Wilson greatly broadened his empirical base with observations of living American Indians, of crania in American collections, and of prehistoric American monuments studied in an extensive tour of the Midwest. These several experiences eagerly sought led Wilson to a more complex and nuanced picture of "Prehistoric Men" than Sir John Lubbock would put into his rival *Pre-historic Times*. In the event, Wilson's version was less attractive to British intellectuals. Wilson's book, by the same token of more nuanced statements, was more useful to American prehistorians. More basically, the priority of Wilson's 1862 *Prehistoric Man*, its presence as Lubbock and Edward Tylor prepared their first books on the topic, means that Wilson's formulation of prehistorians' methodology was foundational. His preeminence over Lubbock, although ignored by the Londoners, was established by his Scottish compatriot Robertson Smith selecting Wilson, not Lubbock, to contribute the principal article on "Archæology" to the highly respected Ninth edition of the *Encyclopedia Britannica* (1878).

Wilson opens with this introduction:

[T]he investigations of the archæologist, when carried on in an enlightened spirit, are replete with interest in relation to some of the most important problems of modern science. The object . . . is to view Man, as far as possible, unaffected by those modifying influences which accompany the development of nations and the maturity of a true historic period. . . . The ethnologist does indeed study man from the same point of view as the mere naturalist. . . . Our aim, therefore, is to look, if possible, on man *per se*. . . . In so far as this is possible may we hope to recover some means of testing man's innate capacity, and of determining by comparison what is common to the race. (Wilson 1862, vii–ix)

To whatever source the American nations may be traced, they had remained shut in for unnumbered centuries by ocean barriers from all the influences of the historic hemisphere. Yet there the first European explorers found man so little dissimilar to all with which they were already familiar, that the name of Indian originated in the belief. . . . Such, then, is a continent where man may be studied under circumstances which seem to furnish the best guarantee of his independent development . . . and however prolonged the period of occupation of the western hemisphere by its own American nations may have been, man is still seen there in a condition which seems to reproduce some of the most familiar phases ascribed to the infancy of the unhistoric world. (x–xi) . . . Here then appears to be a point from whence it seems possible to obtain, as it were, a parallax of man, already viewed in Europe's prehistoric dawn . . . to test anew what essentially pertains to him. (xii) . . . a long obliterated past of Britain's and Europe's infancy . . . was here [in Canada] reproduced in living reality before [the author's] eyes. (xiii) . . .

> Is, then, civilisation natural to man, or is it only a habit or condition arti-
> ficially superinduced ... ? Such questions involve the whole ethnological
> problem reopened by Lamarck, Agassiz, Darwin, and others. (3)

Wilson's guiding assumptions are: (1) Archaeology can address some major
scientific questions, (2) The ethnologist seeking to describe the species
"man" works as a naturalist but is challenged to find specimens unaffected
by non-natural (artificial) factors, (3) Because America is surrounded by
virtually impassable oceans, its humans remained free of civilization's arti-
ficiality, and (4) The "unprogressive" American lives nearly in a state of
nature (only "frail wigwams" and "tiny birch-bark canoes" modify the forest and bay [Wilson 1862, 42]) and so equates with the prehistoric, not yet
progressed, European. Two scientific goals may be pursued with American
data: the definition of the essential characteristics or nature of the human
species, and the depiction of the ancient condition from which European
man progressed.

Essentialism was taken for granted in the mid nineteenth century. Plato
and Kant warned us to beware of superficialities, to seek humbly evidence
of things-in-themselves. Linné and a host of naturalists conceptualized and
collected type specimens. Darwin's breakthrough came in the realization
that variation, not "type," is reality. Wilson did not reach this radical shift,
nor had Chambers in spite of his emphasis on the Law of Variety-
Production; they accommodated evolution by assuming saltational changes,
i.e., from one essential type to another type (see Mayr 1991, 40–44 for an
elegant summary of Darwin's break). Wilson set himself the task of sifting
out the essence of the human species in order to formulate a type, which
then could be premised to characterize primeval humans in earliest prehistory. He would proceed by the comparative method authoritatively established by Baron Cuvier in his *Leçons d'anatomie comparée* at the opening of
the century. This method included dissection into the depths of a specimen
where crucial essential characteristics might lie hidden (Foucault 1973,
226–32); metaphorically, dissection is excavation, and organs exposed
equivalent to artifacts and bones exposed.

One might suppose that Daniel Wilson's second treatise would focus on
excavation procedures, but this was not yet a desideratum. The alliance
with geology proclaimed by Wilson cut two ways, emphasizing uniformitarianism and allowing the relatively gross, eyeballed stratigraphic units
permissible to geological surveys. Following the Crystal Palace's lesson,
Wilson gave as a major premise:

> The idea which associates man's intellectual elevation with the accompani-
> ments of mechanical skill, as though they stood somehow in the relation of

cause and effect; and with the intellectual as the offspring, instead of the
parent of the mechanical element: is the product of modern thought.
(Wilson 1862, 58)

But this popular assumption may be too facile:

The development of speech into language was, I conceive, a fitter and more
needful occupation for primeval man, than anticipating the wants of remote
generations by a premature birth of mechanical arts, as superfluous to him
as the luxuries of modern fashionable life. (Wilson 1862, 59)

Therefore, Wilson's first substantive chapter is on "The Primeval Occupation: Speech"—onomatopoeia, gesture, types of languages.

Next in *Prehistoric Man* is "The Primeval Transition: Instinct."

The only true analogy between the geologist and the archæologist lies in this,
that both find their evidence imbedded in the earth's superficial crust, and
deduce the chronicles of an otherwise obliterated past by legitimate induction
therefrom. The essential and radical difference between the palæontologist
and the ethnologist lies in this, that the one aims at recovering the history of
an unintelligent and purely instinctive division of extinct organic life; the
other investigates all that pertains to a still existent, intelligent being, capable
of advancing from his own past condition, or returning to it. . . . It is not to be
inferred . . . that the whole history of the human race, and each of its separate
divisions, is affirmed to disclose a regular succession of periods—Stone,
Bronze, and Iron, or however otherwise designated—akin to the organic dis-
closures of geology. . . . These prehistoric annals are guides to . . . showing
how deeply the sources of human action lie implanted in the nature of man;
and how essential to the just interpretation of the external life of a nation is
the knowledge of the ethnic elements, and the intellectual germs, pure or
mingled, out of which it has been evolved. For such ethnic elements are not
peculiar to ancient nations, nor have they wrought only in primitive times.
They survive as vigorously and vividly now as when they puzzled the observant credulity of Herodotus, or dignified to Tacitus the chroniclings of
Rome's despised barbarian conquests. (Wilson 1862, 91–93)

Human intelligence gave the "combined labours of many successive generations" a cumulative power wholly different from the promptings of
instinct in "the inferior orders of being."
    Having made his point that human intelligence is not to be compared to
animal instincts, Wilson then, confusingly, employs the word "instinct" as

a simile in the following chapter titles: "The Promethean Instinct: Fire," "The Maritime Instinct: The Canoe," "The Technological Instinct: Tools," "The Metallurgic Instinct: Copper," "The Architectural Instinct: Earthworks," "The Artistic Instinct: Imitation," and "The Intellectual Instinct: Letters." Some of the "instincts" needed more than one chapter, so in addition there are, in this order interspersed with the preceding, "The Metallurgic Arts: Alloys," "The Hereafter: Sepulchral Mounds," "Propitiation: Sacrificial Mounds," "Commemoration: Symbolic Mounds," "Progress: Native Civilisation," "Narcotic Arts and Superstitions," "Primitive Architecture: Megalithic," "The Ceramic Art: Pottery," "Ante-Columbian Traces: Colonization," "The American Cranial Type," "Artificial Cranial Distortion," "The Red Blood of the West," "The Intrusive Races," "Ethnographic Hypotheses: Migrations," and "Guesses at the Age of Man." Expanded topics draw upon Wilson's 1850s field trips, to Lake Superior to view the Indian frontier, and through the Midwest to see many of Squier and Davis' *Ancient Monuments of the Mississippi Valley* (1848) and other mounds, courteously assisted by Dr. Davis himself, Mr. Charles Whittlesey of Ohio, and other pioneering prehistorians. Wilson also made trips to examine collections in Boston, New York, Philadelphia, and Washington, where Joseph Henry, director of the Smithsonian, was helpful. Louis Agassiz at Harvard was another obliging contact. *Prehistoric Man* collates extensive observations, if generally of others' primary investigations, with the overall design of surveying the principal topics deemed essential to human life. If prehistoric man seems to be American Indian, that reflects Wilson's commitment to firsthand observation if at all feasible, or at least examining fieldnotes with their compiler (in the case of the Peruvian collection of J.H. Blake, a civil engineer, in Boston). *Prehistoric Man* is not an armchair exercise.

A second edition of *The Archaeology and Prehistoric Annals of Scotland* came out a year after *Prehistoric Man*. Prefacing the new edition, Wilson stated:

> Now also that the relations of archæological investigations to other scientific inquiries are intelligently recognised, the evidence and speculations embodied in these volumes in reference to prehistoric and pre-Celtic races may acquire a new significance and value. The careful study of the primitive antiquities of Britain led me to the conviction ... that we must look to a much more remote period.... Since then, long residence on the American continent, and repeated opportunities of intercourse with the Aborigines of the New World, have familiarized me with a condition of social life realizing in the living present nearly all that I had conceived of in studying the chroniclings of Britain's prehistoric centuries. The experience thus acquired in

novel fields of ethnological research, have materially aided me in the revision of opinions originally based on purely speculative induction. (Wilson 1863, xiv–xv)

In the course of writing *Prehistoric Man*, Wilson veered from his early plan to compile a picture of primitive life that would vivify and provide organized analogies for prehistoric archaeology. The Allophylian mother with her cradle-board disappears into the primeval forest as readers are given more and more description of what Wilson saw in America. Reviewing *Prehistoric Man* in 1863 for the X-Club's *Natural History Review*, Sir John Lubbock set it with four monographs on American archaeology published by the Smithsonian. This heavy reliance on American data overshadowed Wilson's basic purpose of delineating the essential human. The imbalance strengthens the scientific validity of the book insofar as it derives from Wilson's commitment to direct and replicable empirical observation, noted in the passage above. His audience by and large would not appreciate this nice distinction between his work and that of Spencer, and John Lubbock, if he noticed it, had no interest in lauding the exiled Scot tradesman over his X-Club comrade Spencer.

Substantively, Wilson in his first edition of *Prehistoric Man* concluded that the Americas were settled through three ancient migrations, one through the South Pacific to South America, a second but minor one across the Atlantic past the Azores to the Caribbean or perhaps Brazil, and the most recent across the Bering Strait into northwest America (Wilson 1862, 448–49, 453). "Central America" (what we term Mesoamerica) was the meeting ground of the expansions of the two Mongoloid populations (452). Who the Mound-Builders were, "Aztec or Northern Indian," he would not decide (383), though he leaned toward a Mexican origin. They were a "semi-civilized race" pacific in inclination although with weapons and fortresses to defend their territories. Incursions of northern barbarians very likely overran and destroyed their nascent civilization, parallel to the experiences of Europe (451). As Lewis Henry Morgan would a decade later (possibly biased by reading and corresponding with Wilson?), Wilson discounted the veracity of Prescott's "romantic" history of the conquest of the Mexica, convinced that Prescott exaggerated the amount of bloody sacrifices as well as the magnificence of Tenochtitlán, the refined manners of the nobility, and "the unreserved freedom of woman" (383).

Prehistoric Man, in its finale, states:

There is no endless cycle in which the nations could revolve. Man primeval in a state of nature, and in the midst of the abundance of a tropical region, employing his intellectual leisure, begins that progressive elevation which is as consistent with his natural endowments as it is foreign to the instincts of all other animals. (Wilson 1862, 465)

The book itself did not present man primeval in a state of nature but examples of degrees of that progressive elevation consistent with man's essential nature. Wilson understood that an empirical scientist could not honestly describe the most primitive imaginable humans, for none survived to be observed by literate Europeans. Eventually he dealt with the problem by examining Shakespeare's character Caliban as a visualization of "the missing link," praising the dramatist's extraordinary genius foretelling a "brute-progenitor" so true to the scientific deductions of nineteenth-century biologists (Wilson 1873).

In the event, Wilson's 1862 *Prehistoric Man* fit into the ideology propounded by John Locke in his *Second Treatise on Government* (1690), "In the beginning, all the World was *America* . . . rich in land, and poor in all the comforts of life . . . for want of improving it by labor." (When he wrote the treatise, Locke was secretary to Britain's Board of Trade, and subsequently to the proprietors of Carolina colony. Calm and rational as was his discourse, he had a blatant pecuniary interest in rendering the Indians incompetent.) Half a century after Locke, William Douglass expanded the theme:

> *America* may with much Propriety be called the youngest Brother and meanest of Mankind; no Civil Government, no Religion, no Letters; the *French* call them *Les Hommes des Bois*, or Men-Brutes of the Forrest: They do not cultivate the Earth by planting or grazing: Excepting a very inconsiderable Quantity of *Mays* or *Indian Corn*, and of *Kidney-Beans* . . . which some of their *Squaas* or Women plant; they do not provide for To-Morrow, their Hunting is their necessary Subsistence not Diversion; when they have good luck in Hunting, they eat and sleep until all is consumed and then go a Hunting again. (Douglass, 1755, quoted in Meek 1976, 137)

Nineteenth-century readers expected to see Prehistoric Man in American Indians. Daniel Wilson left many somewhat bewildered at the data he adduced to show that even the hunting peoples were not Men-Brutes. But then, neither were Scotland's "Allophylian" inhabitants: Nothing so primitive as Boucher de Perthes' antediluvian hand-axes or the Kent's Cavern flints lay in Scotland's glaciated land (Wilson 1863, xiv).

There is, incidentally, a subtext to *Prehistoric Man*. Its frontispiece is Wilson's own engraving of a portrait of a "Chimpseyan Chief" (Tsimshian) by his friend Paul Kane. On a "bright day in the early summer" of 1851 a prehistoric grave disclosed to Wilson, led by Robert

Chambers, "undreamt-of affinities between [crania] of the Old and the New World." Wilson

> had been busy with the supposed evidences of pre-Celtic races, as shown in certain strange types of head found in bog and barrow; and had experienced the utmost difficulty in obtaining the needful materials for any adequate test of the theory . . . of the existence of Primitive Races in Scotland prior to the Celtae. . . . The Juniper Green skull['s] . . . occiput was flattened, precisely as in some of the skulls figured in Morton's *Crania Americana*. What if it were traceable to the same cause?
>
> Here was a theme . . . ethnical affinities, evolutionary development, perpetuated peculiarities, backward to the very origin of man. . . . [When Chambers visited Wilson in Toronto years later] we talked again over questions raised by the strange conformation of the Juniper Green skull; and Dr. Chambers entered with all his kindly enthusiasm into disclosures of the condition and habits of Britain's prehistoric races, derived from the study of living tribes of the New World. (Wilson 1878, 140–48).

Prehistoric Man's chapters on "American Cranial Types" and "Artificial Cranial Deformation" represent the adjustment in his crania studies forced upon Wilson by his emigration. He did not forget the source of his original interest, visualizing

> the Allophylian[4] or Turanian mother threading her way through the forest of Drumselch, with her little pappoose strapped in Indian fashion to the cradle-board slung at her back. For in just such fashion the old chief had been nursed, whose flattened skull, recovered from the Juniper Green barrow, disclosed the first traces of the cradle-board among Britain's prehistoric races. (Wilson 1878, 152)

The 1876 edition of *Prehistoric Man* adds the name of the Tsimshian, Kaskatachyuh, to the frontispiece. He is shown full-face and wearing a conical hat; only the reader who knows of Northwest Coast head-flattening would connect this portrait to the seminal discovery Wilson describes in his memoirs published two years later.

Prehistoric Man was not the book English prehistorians awaited. Its detailed descriptions of imposing earthworks and metallurgical skill, the table of achievements in its penultimate chapter (Table I), were disconcerting to citizens accustomed to America as the virgin wilderness. Worse, these accomplishments contradicted the justification for conquest and dispossession so clearly set forth by John Locke. Nor could racists be pleased with Wilson's admiration for the Métis, Canada's "hybrid" of Indian and European, his favorable sentiment joined in by "Mr. Lewis H. Morgan," writing to him that he, too, believed intermarriage would bring "an increase of physical health and strength, and no intellectual detriment" (Wilson 1862, 389–90).

Wilson's book could not serve Britain's need for a straightforward scientific-looking validation of her dominant class' aggrandizement. It could, and did, work as Robert Chambers' *Vestiges* had worked for Darwin, a stalking-horse for Lubbock's and Edward Tylor's 1865 efforts to better serve ideology's demand. Its plan established a framework for the comparative method in cultural anthropology/prehistory. It was a convenient source from which Lubbock could lift material on the Americas, neglecting as he did so to cite scrupulously that source (e.g., Lubbock 1865, 215 compared with Wilson 1862, 361; Charles Lyell accused Lubbock, at this time, of plagiarizing material from his *Antiquity of Man* manuscript [Bynum 1984]). Edward Tylor began a notebook labeled "Primeval Man" in the fall of 1862, when *Prehistoric Man* was selling (Stocking 1987, 158). Tylor and Lubbock would both publish in 1865, coincident with the second, revised edition of *Prehistoric Man*. Wilson would extensively revise his book for a third edition in 1876, making that more overtly a study of American prehistory and widening the gulf between his work and that of the London savants Tylor and Lubbock.

Meanwhile, Lubbock filled the bill with *Pre-historic Times*. Professor Wilson, in an 1865 letter to Lyell pointing out Lubbock's plagiarism from *Prehistoric Man*, bemoaned the inappropriate hyphen. Lubbock explains, in his preface, that the publishers had suggested he reprint in book form the essays in the *Natural History Review*, 1861–1864, on Danish shell-mounds, Swiss lake-dwellings, "flint implements of the Drift," North American archaeology, and "Cave-men." He decided to include "a short course of lectures on the Antiquity of Man" (title of Lyell's 1863 book). What Lubbock will do is "elucidate, as far as possible, the principles of pre-historic archæology, laying special stress upon the indications which it affords of the condition of man in primeval times" (Lubbock 1865, vi). He relies on visits to prominent prehistoric sites—the Danish *kjökkenmöddings* (kitchen-middens), Boucher de Perthes' Somme Valley gravels, Morlot's Swiss villages, and Christy and Lartet's "celebrated bone-caves of the Dordogne." "Ethnology," he opines:

> is passing at present through a phase from which other sciences have safely emerged; and the new views with reference to the Antiquity of Man, though still looked upon with distrust and apprehension, will, I doubt not, in a few years be regarded with as little disquietude as are now those discoveries in astronomy and geology which at one time excited even greater opposition. (Lubbock 1865, ix)

Archaeology should not raise the disquietude that Wilson's ethnology provoked.

Pre-historic Times begins with "On the Use of Bronze in Ancient Times," then "The Bronze Age," "The Use of Stone in Ancient Times" (including subhead "Stone used after discovery of metal"), "Tumuli," "The Lake-habitations of Switzerland," "The Danish Kjökkenmöddings or Shell-mounds," "North American Archæology," "Cave-men," "The Antiquity of Man" (two chapters), "Modern Savages" (three chapters: Hottentots, Veddahs, Andaman Islanders, Australians, Tasmanians, Feegeeans, Maories, Tahitians, Tongans, Esquimaux, North American Indians, Paraguay Indians, Patagonians, and Fuegians), and "Concluding Remarks" on "unity of the human race," "natural selection," the "sufferings of savages" and "blessings of civilisation," "the diminution of sin," and "advantages of science." The first ten chapters, except for "North American Archæology," are based on Lubbock's extensive travels to sites and museums in France, Denmark, and Britain. The last four chapters are literary; Lubbock never saw any non-Western communities firsthand.

Chapter 1 introduces, on page two, Lubbock's original distinction of four, not three, Ages: "that of the Drift ... the 'Palæolithic'"; "The later or polished Stone age ... the 'Neolithic'"; "The Bronze age," and "The Iron age." "Some nations, such as the Fuegians, Andamaners, etc., are even now only in an age of Stone" (Lubbock 1865, 3). In the course of the book, Lubbock several times—nine, according to the index—cites Daniel Wilson, either the *Archaeology and Prehistoric Annals*, second edition, or *Prehistoric Man*; there are also the lines with citation omitted. While Wilson's two books are by no means a major section of *Pre-historic Times*, Lubbock's use of them proves his familiarity with both. His "Concluding Remarks," like Wilson's, draw more from ethnography than strictly from archaeology, no matter the disavowal of this method in the preface. Eliminating all technology limited in distribution, Lubbock presents a lowest common denominator of human life: no pottery, no weapons except spears, knives, and clubs, "rudest possible" boats, "they were naked and ignorant of the art of spinning," unable to count beyond four, no agriculture, no domestic animal but, probably, dogs (475). One would expect Lubbock to repeat the picture of the "Stone age of the Drift," but he seems to have forgotten his own preface.

Ideology rears up like a prancing white stallion at the finale of *Pre-historic Times*. The last paragraph on "Modern Savages" sighs:

> Perhaps it will be thought that in the preceding chapter I have selected from various works all the passages most unfavourable to savages, and that the picture I have drawn of them is unfair. In reality the very reverse is the case. Their real condition is even worse and more abject than that which I have

endeavoured to depict. I have been careful to quote only from trustworthy authorities, but there are many things stated by them which I have not ventured to repeat; and there are other facts which even the travellers themselves were ashamed to publish. (Lubbock 1865, 472)

These trustworthy authorities unhappily shared, as Marvin Harris said, "the thralldom of racial determinism" (Harris 1968, 162). The obverse of the denigration of everyone outside the English gentry/haute bourgeoisie was the Pollyanna outlook on contemporary London, blind to the abject miseries of the urban lower class so horrifyingly chronicled by Henry Mayhew. "Recent improvements and discoveries" in mid-century hardly worked "to bring [man] into harmony with nature" (shades of George Combe!), and that "of the evils under which we suffer nearly all may be attributed to ignorance or sin," is neither likely to "be admitted" as widely as Lubbock supposes, nor would most readers so sanguinely expect science to diminish both (Lubbock 1865, 491). In short, Lubbock failed to meld his firsthand descriptions of European prehistoric sites with his facile compendium of travelers' tales, and his didactic purpose in the Antiquity of Man popular lectures nullified the generalizations derived from the archaeology. *Pre-historic Times* was less scientific than scientistic (Clark 1997), and as usual in these cases, the public was impressed.

Lubbock's father-in-law advanced the scientific basis of prehistory. Augustus Henry Lane Fox (1827–1900), six years older than John Lubbock, was grandson, on his mother's side, of the eighteenth Earl of Morton. He graduated from Sandhurst Military College, was commissioned in the Grenadier Guards in 1845, served in the Crimean War, and then in 1851 was engaged to improve the British Army's musketry practices. Fox minutely examined and tested rifles and developed *Instructions of Musketry*. Like practically everyone else in Britain, he visited the Great Exhibition in the Crystal Palace. The progression in technology there, coupled with the variety of guns he was analyzing—including the regular issue "Brown Bess," a smooth-bore percussion musket—made him keen to collect weapons of all sorts. His wife's aunt was married to Albert Way, director of the Society of Antiquaries in the 1840s (and in this capacity, a correspondent of Daniel Wilson as secretary of the Society of Antiquaries of Scotland). In 1863, Way, along with Henry Christy whose collection of artifacts Fox had studied, put his nephew up to become a Fellow of the Society of Antiquaries. Fox and John Lubbock were both elected in 1864. Three years later, Fox left active military service to devote himself to what had become a massive collection; duty stations in Malta, Turkey, Bulgaria, Canada, and Ireland had facilitated its growth. Apparently he began excavations only in his last station, Ireland. Freed from military duties, he quickly lent his army experience to the International Congress of

Prehistoric Archaeology, serving as its general secretary for its 1868 meeting in England. His friend Lubbock was President of the Congress, and Lyell as well as Huxley and others in the X-Club attended. Fox was powerfully impressed by the Darwinists, realizing that technological developments were strongly analogous to natural selection and artifacts could be arranged in series of gradual "descent" with modification.

By 1874, Fox's collection overstrained his house, especially with Lieutenant-Colonel Fox again on active duty, though posted only to Surrey. A branch of the South Kensington Museum (the Crystal Palace reassembled on a permanent site) accepted the collection, allowing Fox to continue building it. The catalog prepared for the collection in 1874 explicated the principle espoused by Fox:

> Human ideas, as represented by the various products of human industry, are capable of classification into genera, species, and varieties in the same manner as the products of the vegetable and animal kingdoms, and in their development from the homogeneous to the heterogeneous they obey the same laws. (quoted in M. W. Thompson 1977, 38)

The last line betrays Fox's conversion to Spencer's version of evolution, an allegiance heard in his talk at the opening of the collection to public view: "the object of an anthropological collection is to trace out . . . the sequence of ideas . . . and by this means to provide really reliable materials for a philosophy of progress" (quoted in M. W. Thompson 1977, 38). "Really reliable materials"? "[I]mplements have this advantage over written testimony of any kind, that they cannot intentionally mislead us. If we draw wrong inferences from them, the fault is our own." (1869 lecture, quoted in M. W. Thompson 1977, 37)

Along with purchasing artifacts, during his years of inactive military service Fox carried out field excavations in Yorkshire, making the acquaintance there of Canon Greenwell, author of *British Barrows* and fabled fly fisherman. Resuming military duties did not prevent Fox from accepting the honor of presenting a lecture to the Royal Institution, in 1875; he chose the subject "The Evolution of Culture." The next year, his career climaxed with election as a Fellow of the Royal Society, sponsored by the X-Club in the persons of its members and their close friends Darwin, Francis Galton, Prestwich, Tylor, and the archaeologists Augustus Franks, of the British Museum, and John Evans. Already, in 1872, he had been president of Section H, Anthropology, for the meeting at Brighton of the British Association for the Advancement of Science; ironically, a generation earlier the BAAS had refused a hearing to those investigations which most directly tend to throw light on the origin and progress of the human race.... During several annual meetings, elaborate and valuable memoirs, prepared on various questions relating to this important branch of knowledge, and to the primeval population of the British Isles, were returned to their authors without being read. This pregnant fact has excited little notice hereto. (Wilson 1851, xii; see also Morrell and Thackray 1981, 276 n. 185, 284–86, 344)

If it is objected that Daniel Wilson was here glossing over the BAAS' hostility to phrenology, Fox in 1868 was using phrenological terminology (M. W. Thompson 1977, 36).

Unexpectedly, in 1880 Major-general Lane Fox (a rank achieved in 1877) inherited the immense Wiltshire-Dorset estate of his great-uncle Pitt, Baron Rivers. Augustus took the name Pitt-Rivers, his children becoming known as Fox-Pitt. John Lubbock had been widowed in 1879. In 1882, he met the General's second daughter, named Alice after her mother, at Castle Howard and two years later the young woman married her father's friend. That year, 1884, Pitt-Rivers' huge collection was installed in its own museum at Oxford, named after the now-wealthy donor who added a lectureship in anthropology to the gift. (Edward Tylor received the appointment.) Claiming his health was too poor physically to perform fieldwork, General Pitt-Rivers hired assistants to supervise gangs of laborers from the estate, fulfilling his seignorial duty to provide work for his tenants, and as an enlightened patrician he provided also a public museum and recreation ground with a band, attracting thousands annually.

Pitt-Rivers' positivism prompted both the extreme materialism embodied in his collection, its principles and arrangement, and an unprecedented attention to recording detail in excavations. If Jonathan Oldbuck's mercantile mind gave an advantage to his antiquarian pursuits, so Pitt-Rivers' military command transformed archaeological campaigns.

Every detail should ... be recorded in the manner most conducive to facility of reference, and it ought at all times to be the chief object of an excavator to reduce his own personal equation to a minimum.... I ... organize[d] a regular staff of assistants, and train[ed] them to their respective functions after establishing a proper division of work ... they should all have some capacity for drawing in order that the relics discovered might be sketched as soon as found.... Surveying I was able to teach them myself ... no excavation ought ever to be permitted except under the immediate eye of a responsible and trustworthy superintendent. The work of clearing and drawing the skeletons on the ground also required to be done by competent hands, although no skeleton has ever been taken out except under my personal supervision. The calculation of the indices, the classification and sorting of the pottery ... with the care that I considered necessary, involved an amount of labor. . . . I employed from eight to fifteen [workmen] ...

Much of what is recorded may never prove of further use, but even in the case of such matter, superfluous precision may be regarded as a fault on the right side where the arrangement is such as to facilitate reference and enable a selection to be made. . . . Next to coins, fragments of pottery afford the most reliable of all evidence ... pottery [i]s the human fossil, so widely is it distributed. (Lane-Fox Pitt-Rivers 1887–1892, *Excavations in Cranborne Chase* [the Pitt-Rivers estate], quoted in Daniel 1967, 238–43)

The General had his staff cut trenches cleanly along surveyed lines, measure stratigraphy and objects in three dimensions, and illustrate discoveries through cross-section drawings with the objects accurately placed. Every artifact and feature was so recorded, for "The value of relics, viewed as evidence, may ... be said to be in an inverse ratio to their intrinsic value" (as gold or art) (Pitt-Rivers 1892, in Daniel 1967, 243).

Pitt-Rivers translated military hierarchy and principled precision of detail and order into archaeological terms. Science, too, required replicated precision of detail and order. The General's monographs displayed an abundance of illustrations—expense was no hindrance to carrying out his principles—thus exemplifying the virtual witnessing fundamental to modern science. Pitt-Rivers' affinal relationship to Lubbock, commencing soon after Fox came into his property, and patron status to Tylor ensured respect and dissemination of his views. His comparisons of hordes of artifacts in simplistic unilinear evolutionary fashion under biological metaphors (genera, species, varieties) fit well into popular discourse. Daniel Wilson had introduced the term "prehistory," cutting-edge Danish theory, and a systematic comparative ethnographic survey into English-speakers' world. Lubbock had cleansed Wilson's comparative method of both the professor's prolix flights of literary rhapsody and his disquieting attention to the achievements of conquered colonized peoples. Pitt-Rivers added excavation and reporting techniques aligning archaeology with standards of science. The earl's grandson and the banker's heir lived in the circle of power merging Spencer and Darwin into a Whig history of English superiority. The nineteenth century could close with the Crystal Palace's narrative of technological progress naturalized and scientifically demonstrated in archaeological stratigraphy.

Table I

SOUTH AMERICA	NORTH AMERICA	CENTRAL AMERICA
The Quipu	The Wampum	Architecture
Picture Writing	The Totem	Fictile Art
Bas-relief Chroniclings	Picture Writing	Portrait Sculpture
Mimetic Pottery	Mimetic Pipe-sculpture	Hieroglyphics
Metallurgic Art	Metallurgic Art	Numerals
The Balance	Standard Weights	Letters
Agricultural Science	Geometrical Mensuration	
Beasts of Burden	Metallic Currency	
Peruvian Azimuths	The Astronomical Calendar	

(Wilson 1862, 452–53).

CHAPTER 4

America's History

The antiquities of America posed a problem to Europeans. America was a virgin land, a "country that hath yet her maydenhead," promised Walter Raleigh (quoted in Kolodny 1984, 3). It was a New World. "In the beginning, all the World was *America,*" America was the beginning prolonged. It could not have a history.

Several expedients were devised. Britain officially recognized indigenous nations, formalized treaties with them, and purchased tracts of their lands (Dickason 1992, 177–178). Colonizing companies described their territories as wilderness awaiting the farmer's ax and plow. Naturalists supposed the large earthen mounds and embankments they passed must have been built by a semi-civilized race exterminated by the historic savages— America reverted to a beginning after a fledgling history. America did not have a history but it had antiquities.

Daniel Wilson's term "prehistory" was tailor-made for American antiquarians. So long as colonists remained east of the Appalachians, Locke's picture of America as unimproved waste could be maintained; Massachusetts Bay settlers knew they were using fields cleared by Indians recently wiped out by epidemics, but the fields were neither plowed (they were cultivated with hoes) nor fenced (in season, people watched over the crops from platforms), thus they were "unimproved commons." Once the Midwest was opened, travelers could not but view the monumental remains of Indian activities because most routes followed those that Indians had been using for two or more millennia. A series of gentlemen—Henry Brackenridge, Caleb Atwater, Gilbert Imlay, General William Henry Harrison, Secretary of the Treasury Albert Gallatin, President Thomas Jefferson—knew that the Ohio and Mississippi Valleys had been inhabited by nations capable of raising edifices approaching, if not quite rivaling, those Cortés admired in Mexico. The parsimonious explanation was that they were made by expatriate Mexicans, the "Toltecs" whom the Aztecs told Spanish friars had preceded the Mexican empire. The scenario very loosely paralleled that of Britain with its savage Picts in the north, barbarian Bronze Age Britons in England, and Roman conquest. Samuel Drake avoided a pronouncement, in his 1836 compendium on *Indians of North America* ("exhibiting an analysis of the most distinguished, as well as absurd authors"), remarking, "Every conjecture is attended with objections when they are hazarded upon a subject that cannot be settled. To write volumes ... in connection with a few isolated facts, is a most ludicrous, and worse than useless business" (Drake 1836, 45).

Such sound advice, and taken to heart by Joseph Henry when, prodded by Albert Gallatin, he inaugurated in the 1840s the Smithsonian's encouragement of field studies of America's antiquities. Gallatin had been influenced by Alexander von Humboldt when that great geographer visited President Jefferson, he assisted Jefferson in designing Lewis and Clark's journey, and his continuing collegiality with Jefferson made him cognizant of their results and the communications on Cahokia from Brackenridge a decade later (Kennedy 1994, 24–38). The American Antiquarian Society was founded at this time, in 1812, with Caleb Atwater's study of Ohio Hopewell, its first publication, out in 1820. Lubbock stated that ([1865] 1912, 237) "Our knowledge of North American Archæology is derived mainly from" Atwater's monograph and the four published by the Smithsonian: Squier and Davis' *Ancient Monuments of the Mississippi Valley* (1848), Squier's *Aboriginal Monuments of the State of New York* (1851), Lapham's *Antiquities of Wisconsin* (1855), and Samuel Haven's *Archæology of the United States* (1856). He omits Whittlesey's *Ancient Works in Ohio,* from the Smithsonian in 1852. Daniel Wilson sought out the fieldworkers among these authors and frequently they escorted him to view their sites. At the close of the Civil War, there were thus a number of solid research publications, principally on mounds and other earthworks.

A great obstacle to intelligent appraisal of these voluminous data was Anglo America's blind faith in its manifesto to transform a virgin wilderness into God's chosen country. "Manifest destiny," wrote magazine editor John O'Sullivan in 1845, a few months later urging his countrymen "to overspread and to possess the whole of the continent which Providence has given us for the development of ... liberty and federated self-government" (quoted in Weinberg 1935, 145; Stephanson 1995, xi). Even as Frederick Jackson Turner told America that the physical frontier had indeed been overspread, Senator Beveridge rallied voters with a centuries-old vision:

A hundred wildernesses are to be subdued. Unpenetrated regions must be explored. Unviolated valleys must be tilled. Unmastered forests must be felled. Unriven mountains must be torn asunder and their riches of gold and iron and ores of price must be delivered to the world. (quoted in Stephanson 1995, 99)

English-speaking Protestants were apppointed by God to subdue, penetrate, till, fell, mine these New World lands held inviolate for them (Genesis 1:28). Indians were only Men-Brutes that "live of what the Country naturally affordeth from hand to mouth," stated Captain John Smith, forgetting he mentioned that the Powhatan readily delivered five hundred bushels of maize from his granaries to ransom Pocahontas from her Jamestown captors (Smits 1982, 285). Captain Smith the ideologue could demand, like comedian Richard Pryor, "Who are you going to believe—me, or your lying eyes?" (quoted in Gates 1995, 64)

Under the aegis of the American Historical Society in 1931, a historian commented:

> Longfellow sang the song of Hiawatha, the picture of an "extinct tribe that never lived." Scholarly, urbane, he penned only the beautiful in life for the benefit of the Victorian public. He avoided the shadows of reality. He lived in a famed old mansion in Cambridge and taught in the classic halls of Harvard. He was the epitome of all that made conservative New England culture in the nineteenth century. Had Longfellow spent a night with [William] Wood in an Indian wigwam or sat by the side of Governor Hutchinson, of Massachusetts, while a brave buck sat cracking lice with his teeth, the world would have lost Hiawatha. (Hare 1932, 61)

This historian urged readers to ignore the romantic poet and rely instead on the seventeenth-century Puritan missionaries, "sober, observant, unromantically minded men, writing what they knew to be the truth after intimate association with all ranks of Indian life"(Hare 1932, 38). "What *they knew* to be the truth," they who were agents of colonial conquest. Whether the noble red man of a comfortably urban poet's pastoral epic, or the lice-infested buck of colonial governors and their agents, American Indians could not be permitted to flaunt a history marked with monumental constructions.

From the beginning of the nineteenth century—from Jefferson's presidency—American archaeology faced the quandary of data at wide variance from expectations. Wilson's 1851 adaptation of the Three-Age schema could be applied, but his *Prehistoric Man* acknowledged too much evidence for civilizations—metallurgy, monumental constructions, rudimentary writing—to permit placing all North American Indians in the Stone Age wilderness asserted by colonizers. Lubbock's cribs from Wilson included mentioning these "semi-civilized" traits, but explained them away by a final Age "in which man relapsed into partial barbarism" (Lubbock [1865] 1912, 264). Wilson in his third, 1876 edition would have none of this: "CIVILISATION is for man development. It is self-originated; it matures all the faculties natural to him, and is progressive and seemingly ineradicable" (Wilson 1876, 8). Indians suffered "impediments" because they "had been isolated during centuries of preparatory training" in contrast to Britain's "slow maturity in her collision with successive races only a little in advance of herself" (8). Two pages later, Wilson retreated from that liberal philosophy to declare, "the Indian of the American wilds is no more primeval than his forests. Beneath the roots of their oldest giants lie memorials of an older native civilisation." Contemporary Indians are only the "temporary supplanters" of this older nation (10). There is a clear Old World parallel in the "wild nomads" of Asian steppes and Arabian peninsula, some of whose descendants "have gone forth to prove the capacity for progress of the least progressive races; but the great body tarries still in the wilderness and on the steppe, to prove what an enduring capacity man also has to live as one of the wild fauna of the waste" (12).

"Wild fauna," "of the waste," the key labels required by the ideology of Manifest Destiny. Eleven years before Plymouth colony, an English Puritan, Robert Gray, published on behalf of the Virginia Company a sermon describing

> the greater part of [the earth] possessed by wild beasts and unreasonable creatures, or by brutish savages, which by reason of their godless ignorance and blasphemous idolatry are worse than those beasts ... they participate rather of the nature of beasts than men.... Some affirm, and it is likely to be true, that these savages have no particular propriety in any part or parcel of that country, but only a general residency there, as wild beasts in the forest; for they range and wander up and down the country without any law or government, being led only by their own lusts and sensuality. There is not *meum* and *tuum* [mine and thine] amongst them. So that if the whole land should be taken from them, there is not a man that can complain of any particular wrong done unto him. (Gray 1609, quoted in R. Williams 1990, 210–11)

Here is blatant propaganda (the pamphlet is titled "A Good Speed to Virginia"), Gray colluding with John Smith to ignore the clear passages in Smith's, and Walter Raleigh's, reports noting *meum* and *tuum*, settled villages with cornfields and recognized kingdom boundaries for the Powhatan's domain invaded by the Virginia Company (Sheehan 1980, 23).

By the end of the seventeenth century, John Locke had fully established the guiding principles legitmating colonial usurpation. Locke earned his living in the political entourage of the earl of Shaftesbury, tutoring his

grandson and accepting such benefices as the post of secretary to the Board
of Trade of Great Britain (1689) and, later, secretary to the proprietors of
the Carolina Colony. It was during his Board of Trade tenure, when his
patron's sinuous maneuverings had landed his party in power with
William of Orange, that Locke published his *Two Treatises on Government.*
Locke here declared the equation "in the beginning all the World was
America," "wild woods and uncultivated waste." Civilization developed as
men invested their labor in clearing and cultivating land, creating property
through labor value: "As much land as a man tills, plants, improves, culti-
vates, and can use the product of, so much is his Property" (quoted in
Williams 1990, 248). Transforming free land into personal property is of
great general benefit, according to Locke:

> [H]e who appropriates land to himself by his labour, does not lessen but
> increase the common stock of mankind. For the provisions serving to sup-
> port human life, produced by one acre of inclosed and cultivated land, are
> (to speak much within compasse) ten times more, than those, which are
> yielded by an acre of land, of an equal richnesse, lyeing waste in common.
> And therefore he, that incloses land and has a greater plenty of the conve-
> niences of life from ten acres, thus he could have from a hundred left to
> nature, may truly be said, to give ninety acres to mankind. (Locke 1690,
> quoted in R. Williams 1990, 248)

So we can be persuaded that *meum* is ten times better than *tuum* (see Wood
1984 on Locke's agrarian capitalism). Note that Locke shot two unhappy
birds with his stone, justifying both British landlords' enclosure of what
had been peasant commons, and European take-overs of American lands.

Reiterated during the Revolutionary War period to uphold colonists'
"natural law" right to land they themselves (not the king in England) had
"improved," and again in the Jacksonian era to dispossess Indians, Locke's
treatise on government proved, as Locke meant it to prove, foundational to
capitalist political economy. Chief Justice John Marshall held, in *Johnson v.
McIntosh,* 1823:

> the tribes of Indians inhabiting this country were fierce savages, whose
> occupation was war, and whose subsistence was drawn chiefly from the for-
> est. To leave them in possession of their country, was to leave the country a
> wilderness; to govern them as a distinct people, was impossible. (Marshall
> 1823, quoted in R. Williams 1990, 323, n. 133)

"The tribes of Indians" specifically involved as background to the case
were those popularly called the Five Civilized Tribes, substantial farming
nations of the Southeast who had early adopted many practices and crops

from the overseas colonists, and by Marshall's time included owners of profitable plantations worked by black slaves (Weinberg 1935, 85; Kehoe 1992, 195).[1] When push came to shove, the Chief Justice affirmed the ideological position that Europeans had redeemed a wilderness by definition inhabited solely by beasts.

The nineteenth century above all could not retreat from the colonial ideology (Slotkin 1985). From its early decades driving the Five Civilized Tribes out of their fertile valleys, through its middle years of ruthless Indian wars, finally to Grant's "Peace Policy" of missionary agents backed by the military, the United States carried on a crusade to cleanse the New World of infidels. Neither Government nor citizens could afford to recognize Indian attainments, for that would call into question the moral and legal legitimacy of conquest and genocide. British law was supposedly founded on universal principles that logically held for all rational humans, therefore inalienable rights to life, liberty, and the pursuit of happiness could be abrogated only if it were shown that the subjects were irrational or not human. Ergo, in the nineteenth century, women, Africans, American Indians, and radical labor leaders were declared to be without full capacity to reason, and likened to animals—butterflies and little birds if Christian women, savage beasts if men.

The last third of the nineteenth century saw the major shift from agrarian to industrial economies (Goodman and Honeyman 1988, 204). Only after 1870 did steel come to dominate construction, symbolized in the Eiffel Tower, 1889 (180). Steel-hulled, steam-powered ships began to supersede wood-hulled sailing ships, greatly lowering the cost of shipping by increasing cargo space while decreasing the number of crew (162–63). Britain had reversed the market for cotton cloth by mid-century, exporting to India what in the eighteenth century had been imported and de-industrializing Indian production by drastically undercutting cotton prices through the deployment of mechanized spinning and weaving in Britain (138). Other European nations and the United States followed the British lead, aggressively creating mass markets both internally (Loeb 1994, 8) and for export (Goodman and Honeyman 1988, 64), dichotomizing the world into industrial nations and colonies. Even household food came to include mass-produced, mass-marketed commodities in the later nineteenth century (Goody 1982, 170).

"Technology" was the visible sign of the new political economy led by bourgeoisie, fed by proletarian labor. Ideologically, history had to be written to show how contemporary societies had inexorably, naturally grown (an organic metaphor) through the technological output of nameless, faceless proletarians.[2] Industrial capitalism alienated the product from its maker, exactly as archaeologically excavated artifacts are definitively alienated from their voiceless artificers. John Lubbock's *Pre-historic Times* perfectly filled ideology's need, concluding with his dramatic contrast between his readers and unevolved savages. The public bought it, through six editions.

How could American archaeologists proceed, given the implacable premise of wilderness upon which the civilized colonists built their nations? Antiquities were there, "natural law" was still much touted (Weinberg 1935, 196), the model of Mound-Builders overcome by savage nomads resolved the challenge to the principle of colonialism. Still, in 1813 Henry Brackenridge correctly hypothesized that American Indians may have suffered an "astonishing diminution in numbers immediately before we became acquainted with them" (quoted in Kennedy 1994, 184), and in 1845 Albert Gallatin sagely concluded that the Midwestern constructions must be "proofs, not only of a more dense and therefore agricultural population, but also of a different social state" (quoted in Kennedy 1994, 38). Friends of Jefferson though they both were, their views did not prevail. Cyrus Thomas' exhaustive official *Report on the Mound Explorations of the Bureau of Ethnology,* published for the Smithsonian in 1894, established professional opinion confirming Gallatin's and Brackenridge's judgment that no evidence divorces the great earthen constructions from ancestors of historic Indians. Withall, the import of Gallatin's inference of "a different social state" did not sink in: moundbuilders having been acknowledged to be Indians, colonialist ideology reduces them to the social state of the decimated nations battling European invasions on three extended fronts.

Daniel Wilson saw as did Brackenridge and Gallatin, "a populous district abounding with military, civic, and religious structures . . . [of] imposing proportions" (Wilson 1876:I, 316, on the Alligator Mound near Newark, Ohio). His 1876 edition compared American Indians to "The fierce Dane and Norman [who] seemed to offer equally little promise of intellectual progress in their first encroachments on the insular Saxon." "That among races who had carried civilisation so far [as Cortés' description of Mexico], there existed the capacity for its further development, independently of all borrowed aid" he believed could not be gainsaid (I, 336). *Prehistoric Man*'s first edition, 1862, already veered from Wilson's initial plan to seek analogies to British antiquities. Field visits in the Midwest and personal acquaintance with a few Indians in Ontario moved Wilson to write positively of impressive earthworks and of Indians' arts. A dozen more years, more field visits, and particularly more examination of artifacts in collections, readings, and discussion with other American observers confirmed his conviction that American antiquities merited substantial description. The 1876 edition refocuses, centering on American prehistory. Wilson states, for example (I, 81), "In the [Ohio Valley] collections . . . the examples of flint and stone implements number many hundreds, and would require a volume not less ample than Mr. John Evans's comprehensive monograph of *The Ancient Stone Implements, Weapons, and Ornaments of Great Britain.*" On the page is a drawing of a fine Middle Woodland Snyder (Hopewell) biface. Wilson's focus made this edition a comprehensive textbook on American prehistory.

The 1876 edition of Wilson's work begins forthright with an "Introduction" opening with "The Influence of the Discovery of America," and the argument that the "wild nomads" of Eurasia (Tartars and Arabs) who are kin to the civilized Turks, Magyars, and urban Arabs prove that all races may be presumed to have the innate capacity for civilization and simultaneously the possibility of retaining a nomad existence in other circumstances. The next chapter, "The Primeval Transition," suggests that the development of Toronto may be a model to elucidate the development of ancient cities. Most of this chapter is given to a review of the argument for the antiquity of humans inferred by the association of stone artifacts with extinct mammals, in America as well as in Europe. The topic of "drift" (Paleolithic) artifacts continues in chapter 3, "The Quarry," highlighted by his description of the Flint Ridge, Ohio quarries he visited in 1874. Bone and ivory artifacts, including Magdalenian carved and engraved bone, are surveyed in the next chapter, with a note that the animals face left as a right-handed artist is likely to have drawn them—Wilson was left-handed and over the years compiled notes for a book on handedness. Again Wilson points to "evidence of latent powers" in the fine carvings of the Esquimaux (Inuit). The chapter concludes with a survey of discoveries of shell middens and of the use of tropical marine shells in Oceania and America, with the inclusion of conch shells in Ontario ossuaries noted as evidence of long-distance contacts.

Chapter 5 describes "Man" as "peculiarly fire-using ... the *fire-using animal*" (Wilson 1876, I:135–36). Wilson points out the interesting fact that Esquimaux maintain only a small oil lamp in their huts, rather than roaring fires, "depending for warmth on his fur clothing, and ... the heat-producing blubber and fat which constitute so large a portion of his food" (I:136). Fuegians' fire-making with pyrites and flint leads him to dispute the notion that these peoples are "degraded ... savages;" their weapons "exhibit considerable ingenuity" (I:137). Two pages later, this observation is forgotten in stating, "The aborigines of Australia rival the Fuegians alike in physical and intellectual degradation." Wilson's field excursions suggest to him that "fire may have been valued as a protection against the noxious insects" of glacial periods, in common with the American North (I:141). He ends the chapter, after reviewing sun worship, with this firsthand account of fire-making:

> when camping out with Chippewa guides on the Lake of Bays, in Western Canada. We had struck our tents, and were making our way down the river,

when a steady rain set in, which continued throughout the day. We had to
pass several long portages, involving in each case the unloading, and carrying over them, our canoes and baggage; and on one of these occasions, finding myself alone with my Indian guide at the foot of a portage where we
must necessarily be detained a considerable time, I suggested to him by
words and signs, whether it were possible to kindle a fire. Rain was falling in
torrents, the trees were dripping, and the grass and fallen leaves resembled a
soaked sponge. But Kineesè set to work in Indian fashion, hunted out a
pine-knot, such as are of common occurrence in the Canadian forest....
Having secured this, and a piece of half-burned wood from under the
remains of an old camp-fire, he next stripped off the bark from the lee-side
of a birch tree, and collecting a heap of the dry inner bark, thin as paper, he
carefully disposed it under a cover of pine-bark, and placed over all a pile of
chips cut with his axe from the center of a pine log. All being now ready, he
frayed a handful of the birch bark into the consistency of tow, and placing
this on the charred wood, he made the hard point of the pine-knot revolve
in the wood by means of a cord, while his bent position, pressing the other
end to his breast, protected it from the rain. In a surprisingly short time he
blew the tinder into a flame, applied it to the pile he had prepared, and
nursing this with chips and dry twigs, we were able to welcome our companions to a blazing log fire. (Wilson 1876, I:148–49)

From a portage to chapter 6, "The Canoe," coming round through a
discourse on humans' "tool-using instinct" which, he quotes from his
brother George's inaugural lecture as professor of technology, Edinburgh,
is tied to our "heritage of nakedness" compared to other animals. "In this
view of the case, the canoe of America is the type of a developed instinct
pregnant with many suggestive thoughts for us," for example that from
underneath the modern Clyde shipyards of Scotland, ancient dugout
canoes have been recovered (Wilson 1876, I:156). Much of this chapter is
taken up with Polynesian canoes, leading to the comment, "We must not
be misled here, any more than in our estimate of possible Atlantic voyagers, by the undue contempt with which the European is apt to gauge the
capacity of primitive island mariners" (I:164).

"Tools" are the topic of chapter 7. The reader first suffers a homily on
God's Intelligent Design, the "capacity for moral degradation" that is "an
inevitable attribute of the rational, moral free-agent man" (Wilson 1876,
I:172). Wilson explains that the universality of the "subdivisions of the
archæologist designated THE STONE PERIOD, THE BRONZE PERIOD, and
THE IRON PERIOD . . . must be regarded only as a hypothesis" although one
as well founded as the periods of the geologists (I:173). After discoursing
on the manifestations of craft skills along with "savage vices" among "rude
peoples" such as the Fijians, the Huns, and the Norse, Wilson concludes:

Passive and naturally submissive races, like the Malay or the Negro, survive the intrusion of a dominant race, and are protected by their docility, as the natural serfs of the intruders. But an energetic people, who find their chief employment in war and the chase, can be subjected to no useful servitude. . . . [W]hen such extreme social conditions are abruptly brought into contact as stone and iron periods aptly symbolise, the tendency is towards the degradation and final extinction of the less advanced race. (Wilson 1876, I:196–97)

Chapter 8 continues, under the title "The Metals," the material drawn from Wilson's own field experiences "tracing out the evidence of ancient occupation of the shores of Lake Superior, [where] I have, on repeated visits, coasted its shores for hundreds of miles in canoes; and camped for weeks in some of its least acessible wilds" (Wilson 1876, I:200–01). This is detailed description and history of the copper lodes of Lake Superior, which the Chippewa Wilson spoke with denied working. Illustrations include a number excellently drawn from specimens, presumably by Wilson since no credit is printed. From contemporary denial, Wilson inferred considerable antiquity for the aboriginal copper extraction, and a possible connection with the vanished Mound-Builders who "were greatly more in advance of the Indian hunter than behind the civilised Mexican" (I:226).

"Alloys" continues the discussion of metal through chapter 9, taking Wilson into histories of the Inca and Aztec, with consideration of their probable forerunners, and back to comparison of early European and American bronzes by means of two tables of metallurgical analyses of specimens. From the variations, he deduces that the artisans in both hemispheres discovered by trial that one-tenth tin to copper made the most serviceable bronze implements; neither a single common origin for all bronze, nor great scientific accuracy in alloying, is warranted by the data. The chapter ends reiterating, "the America of the fifteenth and sixteenth centuries was literally another world [from Eurasia], securely guarded from external influences" (Wilson 1876, I:255). The impressive voyages of Polynesian canoes could not dislodge that canonical principle from Wilson's mind.

With chapter 10, Wilson can at last focus on "The Mound-Builders." Their relics "disclose to us proof that this vast area [the Midwest] is not now rescued for the first time from the primeval forest, with its wild fauna, and still wilder savage man" (Wilson 1876, I:256). The Hopewell "sepulchral mounds . . . appear to be unsurpassed by any known works of their kind" (I:257), and he distinguishes Hopewell from Mississippian mounds, and "ENCLOSURES" from "MOUNDS." All "afford indisputable evidence of a settled and industrious population" (I:258). Details are continued through chapter 11, "Sepulchral Mounds," chapter 12, "Sacrificial

Mounds," and chapter 13, "Symbolic Mounds" (effigy mounds), leading
to the conclusion that the "marked diversity between the truncated, pyramidal mounds of the states on the Gulf, the geometrical enclosures of
Ohio, and the symbolic earthworks of Wisconsin, indicate varied usages of
distinct communities" and "separate states" rather than a single empire
(I:320–21). To better evaluate the Midwest antiquites, chapter 14 charac-
terizes "Native American Civilisation" by reviewing Mexico and Peru.
Volume I ends with a chapter of "Art Chroniclings," comparing Mound-
Builders' art, particularly effigy pipes, with that of Mexico, Peru, and the
Northwest Coast.

Volume II opens with chapter 16, "Primitive Architecture," moves to
the Maya, who are described as evidencing "true native architecture" in
contradistinction to the Mound-Builders whose earth-pyramids lack "the
decorative design" that raises structures to "fine art." Wilson invokes John
Stephens at Copán, emphasizing that Stephens' firsthand familiarity with
the ruins of Egypt and Petra lends weight to his awe before the Maya constructions. One minor observation Wilson particularly points out (Wilson
1876, II:4), the flattened foreheads depicted on a bas-relief at Palenque;
chapter 21 will be devoted to "Artificial Cranial Deformation," and the
frontispiece to Volume II is a colored engraving of a Flathead (Salish)
woman with her infant beside her bound in its cradleboard, a thick pad
tied over its forehead. Wilson evaluates Mayan art and architecture (known
to him primarily through Catherwood's drawings) as "akin to that of
Europe's thirteenth and fourteenth centuries" (II:12), and accepts its
refinement as supporting the Aztec histories chronicling their intrusion
into the realm of the more civilized Toltecs. Somewhat of a parallel tran-
spired in the Andes, Wilson writes (II:17), with the conquest-era Incas
creating their imposing architecture after the earlier Tiaguanaco (Tiwanaku), whose Titicaca Basin ruins are "the only truly primitive architecture
of the New World," i.e., simpler and earlier yet still evidencing artistic
design. From the visible massive rude architecture of Tiwanaku, Wilson
infers the possibility that it may have been "a possible centre from whence
that intellectual impulse went forth, pervading with its influences the
nations first discovered in the sixteenth century on the mainland of
America."[3]

Chapter 17, "Ceramic Art," argues that "the real progress of a people is
recorded with more graphic minuteness, where the traces of taste and skill
are found in combination with the appliances of daily life." "Fictile art"—
pottery—is therefore to be appreciated as much as "architectural remains
... among the materials of archæological history." Wilson's engravings
from his own drawings for this chapter testify to his own considerable
skill. A quarter-century before William H. Holmes' massive Smithsonian
monograph on American aboriginal ceramic types, Daniel Wilson outlined

as ceramic provinces the Great Lakes, the Southeast, the Mississippi Valley, Mexico, Central America, Brazil, "Chili," and Peru, while west of the Rockies, closely woven baskets substitute for ceramics. Of Northeastern American ceramics, Wilson remarks (1876, II:19), "the incised patterns ... often present a curious correspondence to the simple linear devices on the ancient sepulchral pottery of Europe," a correspondence noticed also by Stuart Piggott in the 1950s when he was Abercrombie Professor of Archaeology at Edinburgh. Wilson describes the few complete examples of Mound-Builders' vessels as fine productions, pointing out that absence of a potters' wheel does not preclude use of a manual turntable (II:25).

After listing the museums holding collections of American ceramics and lamenting the dissipation of other collections, Wilson comes to the occurrence of Greek key ("frette" is his term) designs on Mexican sherds.

> Alike in the works of the Peruvian modeller and sculptor we find evidences of their adoption of ornaments familiar to the artists of Etruria, Greece, and Rome. To the ethnologist, this independent evolution of the like forms and devices among nations separated equally by time and space, is replete with an interest of a far higher kind than any that could result from tracing them to some assumed intercourse between such diverse nations. They are evidences of an intellectual unity, far more important in its comprehensive bearings than anything that could result from assumed Phoenician, Hellenic, or Scandinavian migrations to the New World. (Wilson 1876, II:30–31)

Then Wilson jumps to the other side, exactly as Alfred Kidder will in his 1936 essay for the Kroeber festschrift:

> But while such is the conclusion forced on the mind when required to account for these recurring coincidences, it is otherwise when we find the ornamentation of Peruvian pottery reproduced as a prominent feature in the architectural decorations of Central America and Yucatan. (Wilson 1876, II:31)

Finally, thinking of Schliemann's relics from Troy, Wilson realizes a mediating possibility:

> The points of resemblance are too numerous to be summarily set aside as accidental. It may be that through ancient Trojan, Assyrian, and Mongolian art, along with evidence of other kinds hereafter referred to, the old footprints may be so identified as to place beyond doubt an Asiatic migration to the continent of America, in southern latitudes, and by way of the Pacific. But if so, it was at a period so remote as to allow the primitive colonists of

the New World abundant time to develop specialities of their own. (Wilson 1876, II:43–44)

I shall return to these kernel statements.

"Letters" is the topic of chapter 18. Hieroglyphs—Mayan and Egyptian—Peruvian quipus, runes, ogham, and Upper Paleolithic bone objects with apparent engraved tallies are discussed until we come round again to picture-writing, Algonkian and Aztec, and mnemonics such as wampum belts. This chapter concludes Wilson's survey of artifacts.

Chapter 19 opens by comparing 1492 to Caesar's invasion of Britain, each inaugurating history. Wilson discourses at length on the Norse discovery of America according to Rafn's 1837 monograph *Antiquitates Americanæ, sive scriptores septentrionales rerum ante-Columbiarum in America,* from the Royal Society of Northern Antiquaries. With his usual prolixity, Wilson suggests the boastful Norsemen should have left runic inscriptions in America, and arrives at Dighton Rock near the Massachusetts coast. "No more confused and indistinct scrawl ever tried the eyes of antiquarian seer," Wilson confesses of his examination of a cast of the Dighton engravings exhibited at the 1856 American Association for the Advancement of Science meeting, in Albany (Wilson 1876, II:97). He similarly examined a wax impression of the engraved disk from the Grave Creek Mound, on the Ohio River in West Virginia, and decided it is "notorious" that the disk is mentioned only when the excavator began charging tourists admission to view the site; a description sent to Samuel Morton said nothing about a remarkable alphabetic inscription. The following pages of chapter 19 could be a review of Barry Fell's *America B.C.* (1976), ur-text for Celtiberian, Libyan, runic, and ogham inscriptions in eastern North America. Daniel Wilson could only conclude that the Norse who touched North America, whom he did not doubt, were remarkably transient.

With chapter 20, Wilson could indulge in that pursuit that first intrigued him on that May, 1851 walk to Juniper Green with Robert Chambers. "The American Type" was defined, says Wilson, by Samuel Morton, quoted by all subsequent scientists. Wilson himself endeavored to see Morton's "American type" in Indian crania he obtained in Canada, and could not accept Morton's generalizations. The vexing question of the Mound-Builder race occasioned even more dubiety. Wilson reports he was present at the excavation of a mound near Newark, Ohio, and that there as in other mounds in the region, human bones were so decayed that no measurements could be taken (Wilson 1876, II:131). On page 133, Wilson presents a table of his own measurements of crania found in mounds and Midwestern caves, from Morton's and other collections, and concludes that the paucity of good specimens precludes definitive statements on the Mound-Builder race. The chapter contains sixteen more tables from

Wilson's measurements, on Peruvian brachycephalic and dolichocephalic, Mexican ditto, "American" ditto (Creek, Choctaw, Dacota, Pawnee, etc.), New England, Iroquois, Algonquin, Algonquin-Lenapi, Chukchee, and Eskimo crania, with a final summary of the means of the preceding tables. One comment of Wilson's is that his data do not bear out Morton's claim of clear distinction between Eskimo and all other American crania.

The ready acceptance by scientists of such repute as Agassiz of Morton's single American type "may deserve," Wilson avers, "a place among the curiosities of scientific literature" (II:199). Wilson is proud that he "challenged this dogma," in 1857 at the AAAS (published later that year in the *Canadian Journal of Industry, Science and Art*). He further insisted:

> [T]he results of such attempts at a comparative analysis of the cranial characteristics of the American races go far beyond [Morton's dogma]. They show that the form of the human skull is just as little constant among different tribes or races of the New World as of the Old; and that ... there are ... a tendency of development into the extremes of brachycephalic and dolichocephalic forms, and of many intermediate varieties.
>
> The legitimate deduction from such a recognition ... is, not that cranial formation has no ethnical value; but that the truths embodied in such physiological data are as little to be eliminated by ignoring or slighting all diversities from any predominant form, and assigning it as the sole normal type: as by neglecting the many intermediate gradations, and dwelling exclusively on examples of extreme divergence from prevailing types. (Wilson 1876, II:200–01)

Here, rejecting the high road of essentialism, Wilson's strong grasp of scientific method is revealed.

Chapter 21 has to deal with "Artificial Cranial Distortion," so frequently illustrated in the preceding chapter, not to mention the frontispiece. Wilson opens with refuting another of Samuel Morton's dogmas, that the Americas are characterized by the custom of interring corpses in a sitting position, and that this is "peculiar" to the Americas. Not at all, answers Wilson, sitting posture is found in all manner of British entombments, Europe, Asia, Africa, and the Pacific—"it takes up the least room, and ... the smallest amount of excavation." Nor is the custom universal in the Americas, where "nearly every ancient and modern sepulchral rite has had its counterpart in the New World" (Wilson 1876, II:206), and he gives us his engraving of a Chippewa birchbark gravehouse. The apparent digression on variations in burial practices develops into a prolegomena on cranial deformation, its worldwide occurrence from prehistoric through Classical periods into the present (nineteenth century) in several provinces

of France. Attila and his fellow Huns' "hideous" appearance is attributed
to their head deformation. Some archaeologically recovered crania seem
deformed because of posthumous pressures; most deformations were,
however, due to the plasticity of infants' skulls, sometimes "owing to the
mother being able only to suckle at one breast" (II:225). The Juniper
Green skull was probably flattened occipitally by its cradle (II:227).
Readers' curiosity is finally assuaged by the direct observations, in the
Pacific Northwest, by Paul Kane and Horatio Hale of Flathead infants
undergoing head deformation: The babies seem not to suffer while bound
(though they cry when released), and the process does not stunt their mental powers, for the Flatheads, "acute and intelligent, generally drive a hard
bargain in the sale of their furs" (II:235).

In chapter 22, Wilson reiterates the Asiatic origin of American Indians,
their isolation from the Old World once they had migrated through the
Arctic, and their extirpation after 1492. Detailed perusal of the Old
Testament, and European history, indicate that what is happening to
American Indians is neither extraordinary nor limited to inferior races.

> It is impossible to travel in the far west of the American continent, on the
> borders of the Indian territories, or to visit the reserves where the remnants
> of displaced Indian tribes linger on in passive process of extinction, without
> perceiving that they are disappearing as a race, in part at least, by the same
> process by which the German, the Swede, the Irish, or the Frenchman, on
> emigrating to America, becomes in a generation or two amalgamated with
> the general stock.... I was particularly struck with this during my first visit
> to Sault Ste. Marie ... in 1855.... Nor are such traces confined to frontier
> settlements. I have recognized the semi-Indian features ... in the halls of
> the Legislature, among the undergraduates of Canadian universities....
> And this is what has been going on in every new American settlement for
> upwards of three centuries. (Wilson 1876, II:250–52)

Specifically, Wilson points to the preponderance of men colonists, so that
"the native women help to restore an equality in the proportion of the
sexes" (Wilson 1876, II:256). Ten pages follow on the excellence of the
Métis of Manitoba. A letter solicited from Lewis Henry Morgan states
that Morgan agrees that intermixture is common in the United States,
although Morgan does not know of any source for statistics on the matter,
and warns of considerable range in skin color among Indian nations
unlikely to have yet much admixture. Wilson made an effort to visit a variety of eastern Canadian Indian settlements and to obtain statistics on population, economy, education, etc., from government and mission agents.
This survey, reported in detail and including notes on the Cherokees and
other slave-holding agricultural groups earlier in the century, demonstrates

his inference that the extinction of independent tribes is not to say the extermination of Indians but rather their transformation into segments of the Canadian population, some achieving higher social status especially when "recognized" by upper-class colonist fathers, most settling into villages exhibiting variations on regional rural patterns.

The final two chapters, on "Intrusive Races" and "Migrations," continue chapter 22's argument for assimilation, carrying it to the more fundamental issue of mono- versus polygenesis, still a question in the 1870s. "Do the subdivisions which ethnography clearly recognises in the human family, partake so essentially of the characteristics of distinct races among the inferior orders of creation, as to be incapable of permanently perpetuatng an exotic life, or transmitting fertility to a mixed breed?" (Wilson 1876, II:303). The negative reply, Wilson identifies as "inimical to the theory of permanent triumph as the destiny of the Anglo-American colonists of the New World" (II:304). A second question is whether a race bred in a particular geographical climate can survive transplantation to another. This question does not affect Manifest Destiny because the ideology pictures Anglo America as a temperate land closely similar to Europe.[4] Wilson discusses the involuntary transplantation of Africans to America as an "undesigned scientific experiment" that unfortunately cannot yield indisputable results because its "consequents" cannot be separated "from its incidental political and social bearings" (II:304) which Wilson then expounds: Denial of education or training for citizenship and its responsibilities, privation exacerbated in the cases of fugitive slaves who became the majority of Canada's small "coloured" population, "caste" structure in Canada as in the United States that maintains African Americans segregated and in the lower class, and encourages those who can "pass" to disappear into the Anglo caste, removing them from the gaze of the social scientist. The Republic of Haiti is a similarly tainted experiment, subjected to "the instability of a government founded on insurrection and revolution" as well as the burden of unpreparedness borne by summarily freed slaves; neither the aboriginal Indians nor the African ex-slaves "could escape the malign elements by which man mars every paradise into which he is admitted" (II:315). "It is something to say of such a people that their government has not proved less stable, nor less compatible with the progress of the community, than the republics established by the descendants of the Spanish discoverers and depopulators of Hispaniola" in the other half of the island (II:313).

Accepting the capacity of humans, including those of mixed parentage, to survive and reproduce in new climes, Wilson examines the variety of "races"—what biologists now term *demes*—he can see even in the island of Britain. "It is in such minute ethnology that the truths of the science must be sought. The simplicity of such systems as that of Blumenbach, with his five human species ... is exceedingly plausible and seductive" (Wilson 1876, II:332) and thereby appeals to students who would escape the laborious research from which empirical actuality can be inducted.

Wilson compares the constant formation of new minute races to the "process of degradation and reconversion" by which languages arise out of trade jargons and creole patois. The bulk of his last chapter considers the relevance of American Indian languages to the problem of the origin of human languages, a problem that Wilson shows to be multifarious and admitting of only one really firm proposition, that the capacity for complex, abstract speech is inherent in humans. Language similarities can be adduced to supplement physical characteristics in tracing populations and migrations, which leads to an interesting hypothesis, proposed by Albert Gallatin, that some of the founding populations of the Americas were Polynesian, sailing across the Pacific; that the Bering Strait was not the only route of entry (Wilson 1876, II:343–47). Settlement of the Caribbean by colonists from Cape Verde, the Canaries, and the Azores is a third perhaps probable hypothesis (II:347–49).

Finally, Wilson raises an even more fundamental issue. Other ethnologists have stated that "mankind is governed by the same zoological laws which regulate animals generally," but

> those are propositions which I am not prepared to admit with considerable qualification [for] apart altogether from the question of unity or multiplicity of [the human] species, this fact is overlooked, that man's normal condition is that of domestication, which for all other animals is an essentially artificial one. Take man in what is popularly called a state of nature, such as the Red Indian of the American forests or prairies. He lives in a community controlled by many binding, though unwritten laws; he selects his food, and modifies it by artificial means; ... he clothes himself ... according to the changing climate, and also according to fashion, taste, and prescriptive usage. (Wilson 1876, II:318)

The human "is a clothing, cooking, fire-making, tool-using animal ... distinguished from all other animals by certain characteristics which seem to point to civilisation as his normal condition."

Daniel Wilson was able to segue from this major premise to a chapter conclusion that parrots the conquest ideology:

> the intrusion of the vigorous races of Europe ... are to replace scattered tribes living on in aimless, unprogressive strife ... races who accomplish so imperfectly every object of man's being. If the survivors can ... be admitted to an equal share with the intruding coloniser, in the advantages of progressive civilisation: then we may look with satisfaction on the close of that long

night of the Western World, in which it has given birth to no science, no philosophy, no moral teaching that has endured. (Wilson 1876, II:339–40)

The key is his last three words. Through two volumes he has demanded acknowledgment of the accomplishments of American Indians and of their physical capacities. But neither their archaic civilizations nor their populations have endured the onslaught of European conquest. Indians are fully human and in the isolation of their continent realized to a degree humans' natural state of civilization. In the event, they could not absorb immigration as Britain had her waves of Roman, Angle, Saxon, Danish, and Norman conquerors over a thousand years (Wilson 1876, II:313).

The first edition of *Prehistoric Man* concluded with a chapter, "Guesses at the Age of Man." Charles Lyell's 1863 *The Geological Evidences of the Antiquity of Man* made such a chapter superfluous. The third edition of *Prehistoric Man* ends with a recapitulation of the hypothesized three routes of original entry into the Americas and the summary table of the 1862 edition (Table I of my chapter 3), deleting "Picture Writing" from South America and "Standard Weights" from North America. Without quite saying so, Wilson gives the reader to understand that *Prehistoric Man* has not been able to delineate its subject as he once had hoped, for his firsthand exposure to living American Indians and to their ancestors' products has convinced him that his project was based on "what has been inaccurately regarded as a state of nature" (Wilson 1876, II:386). No observable humans can be premised to illustrate our earliest origins. In the beginning, all the World was different from *America*.

Prehistoric Man's third edition was radically different from its 1860s predecessors, both Wilson's and Lubbock's. The fruit of twenty years' field visits and collections study made the 1876 volumes an introduction to American prehistory. Antiquarians now had a reasoned overview of issues and comparative notes. The antiquities of America were shown to include works of art and of technological finesse, the history of America to have encompassed nations sufficiently civilized to be worthy of a place in the narrative of the ancients. The American archaeologist should be no handmaiden to European prehistorians but a scholar with his own disciplinary area. This area could share methods with Europeanists because both worked to recover knowledge from the undocumented past of the human species.

CHAPTER 5

Positivists of the New Frontier

During the half-century between the full establishment of industrial economies, in the 1870s, and the final consolidation, with the extension of the franchise to women, of liberal democracy based on universal suffrage, ideology gave the principle of possessive individualism a most peculiar spin. The "New Frontier" proclaimed by Turner spawned rugged individualists charting unknown territories by psychology rather than on foot. Industrialists and their confrères, the mass-market merchants, inundated the country with advertisements showing individuals, addressing individuals, promising their products would enhance each individual's well-being. While the ads promoting individual consciousness deluged the country, merchants displayed piles of identical items and industrialists transformed manufacturing so that each worker was looked upon as an interchangeable cog in the factory and forced to work by clock discipline. Amongst themselves, the bourgeois leaders discussed "crowd psychology" (Bush 1991), how to influence the greatest number of consumers to want mass-produced objects.

We might call this the Age of Metonymy, the epoch of the part—the individual purchaser—standing for the whole, the mass of consumers who fueled the national economy and voted in its legislators. Archaeology reflected its age, excavating a few individual artifacts that were made to stand for whole societies. The same attributes of surface, shape, size, and material that advertisements emphasized were noted by archaeologists for the ancient artifacts.

To a deeper degree, archaeology conformed to the peculiar usage of the epoch's advertisers who relished a "female form which was but scantily clothed in the shining garment of Truth" (quoted in Ewen 1976, 72). "Truth in Advertising" was the slogan adopted by the Associated Advertising Clubs of the World, meeting in Britain in 1924. In his *Successful Living in the Machine Age,* 1931, department-store magnate Edward A. Filene made clear the need to teach consumers to recognize "facts" and nothing but "facts." These facts were to be read in advertisements. That "facts" are transparently so was assumed.

Though it may seem frivolous to link prehistoric archaeology with advertising, each is a visible aspect of the society that its practitioners share. Mass consumerism with its mass advertising was integral to the industrial capitalism dominating America after the Civil War. Advertisers mirrored the preoccupations of the citizenry, often in a veiled manner— for example, literally picturing the home as the abode of sweetness and light during the economic depression of the last quarter of the nineteenth century when hundreds of thousands feared losing their homes. Overtly, advertisements were to kick-start businesses; covertly, they meant to excite fleetingly, then assuage the populace, and their aping of evangelists' motifs and styles reveals the conflation between salvation and consumption (Loeb 1994, 100–03).

Archaeologists' fixation on artifacts had its roots in the cabinets of curiosities collected by antiquarians, and the drive to *classify* artifacts comes out of eighteenth-century science, but twentieth-century American archaeology can be understood only as a positivist science practiced in a Protestant industrial-capitalist imperialist nation. American archaeologists could illuminate the continent's prehistory only so far as Manifest Destiny would allow: "no science, no philosophy, no moral teaching that has endured ... races who accomplish so imperfectly every object of man's being" (Wilson 1876, II:340). Daniel Wilson demonstrated the humanity of Indians and the propriety of studying their past in the same manner as the prehistory of the Old World. Thus furnishing a paradigm for American archaeologists, he limited the American past to Stone and Copper Ages, precluding the presence of cities or states north of Latin America's archaic Bronze-Age civilizations. American data could not be interpreted sui generis, the recognition of its inhabitants' humanity set them firmly within the Enlightenment's ethnocentric European universal history.

Positivism

Positivism was the name of the game for a century, from Comte's maturity to the breakdown of modernism in the 1960s. At the outset it must be understood that Comte initially presented his *Cours de philosophie positive,* in the 1830s, as a major treatise in synthetic philosophy unifying mathematics, astronomy, physics, chemistry, biology, and "sociology" (social sciences), each of these building upon the one preceding. The 1838 *Edinburgh Review* praised "his absolute freedom from all personal and national feelings" (quoted in Hawkins 1938, 5). In time,[1] Auguste Comte believed himself to have achieved so lofty an understanding that he proselytized a Religion of Humanity, Humanity taking the form of a Goddess and himself her High Priest; devotees could memorize *The Positivist Catechism.* A radical community, Modern Times, founded in western Long Island in 1851 by Josiah Warren and Stephen Pearl Andrews, attracted Henry Edger, an English immigrant who became a convert to the Religion of Humanity upon reading George Henry Lewes' 1852 account of Comte's work (Hawkins 1938, 114ff.). A fully contextualized account of positivism should not neglect the later excesses of faith epitomized by Edger's worship, for some of the power of the original *Cours* comes from Comte's prophetic style and extraordinary breadth of vision. Still, Modern Times and its freethinking, free-loving residents are extraneous to archaeology. Reference to positivism here is limited to the allegedly purely scientific version.

Comte expounded seven meanings of the word "positive." These were explained by a disciple in the English periodical *Positivist Review,* published between 1893 and 1906.

> ... *real* as opposed to what is imaginary or miraculous. "Real" comes from the Latin word for "thing," and it is used for all thoughts about things built up from material supplied from our own experience ... we take one phenomenon or fact from the bundle of facts in which we find it, and examine this fact and others like it so as to discover their laws or the properties which they hold in common. (Bridges [1915] 1974, 199)
>
> Elimination of superfluous truth is of the very essence of science.... The second meaning of the word *Positive* is *useful.* (202) ...
>
> To deal with real things, and with important things, is not enough ... unless we are able to say about them what is true and certain.... The origin of the chemical elements, ... the origin even of the Greek race—these things, whether from the weakness of our faculties or from the destruction of evidence, are inaccessible to us, and are perhaps destined to remain for ever uncertain.... They are not within the range of Positive thought. The third meaning of *Positive* is *certain.* ...
>
> A further feature distinguishing scientific knowledge from common knowledge is that it is not only certain, but also *precise....* There is a degree of precision attainable and appropriate in each inquiry, and this it is that the man of scientific genius aims at. (203–04) ...
>
> We have now discussed four meanings of the word *Positive—reality, utility, certainty, precision* ... other meanings yet remain. One of these is that Positive teaching is *organic* ... it is living, not dead, not stereotyped, not immutable. Contrast the body of truth of which any science consists with

the Westminster Catechism or [other religious dogmas] . . . scientific truth is in course of perpetual evolution. (205–06) . . .

Life is the mutual action and reaction of organism and environment . . . the life of relation. . . . Positivism . . . implies relativism. . . . There is a definite relation between a given stage of civilization and the political institutions adapted to it . . . thus we see that in every department of thought Positive doctrine is *relative,* not *absolute.* (207–08) . . .

Positive doctrine . . . is not merely real, useful, and all the other things of which we have spoken. It is also *sympathetic.* It lifts man above himself into communion with Humanity, through whom he lives, for whom he works. [Footnote: This seventh meaning was given to the word by Comte in 1854.] (209)

In another essay, this disciple explained that "speculations as to the origin of the universe and of life would be discouraged . . . on the grounds which exclude theological speculation. . . . They dissipate intellectual energy, of which the world has none too large a stock" (Bridges [1915] 1974, 179).

Comte was the scintillating tip of the iceberg of empirical science slowly floating through the sea of philosophy from the sixteenth to the twentieth century (at the end of which it is melting in global warming). James Clerk Maxwell in 1874 summed it up in doggerel, "There is nothing but atoms and void, all else is mere whims out of date" (quoted in Basalla, Colemen, and Kargon 1970, 437). John Tyndall told the British Association for the Advancement of Science that year:

the physical theories which lie beyond experience are derived by a process of abstraction from experience. . . . Every meal we eat, and every cup we drink, illustrates the mysterious control of Mind by Matter. . . . The Human Understanding . . . is itself a result of the play between organism and environment. (in Basalla, Colemen, and Kargon 1970, 468–69, 473)

With a touch of malice, Tyndall assured his audience that "you ought to know the environment which, with or without your consent, is rapidly surrounding you, and in relation to which some adjustment on your part may be necessary" (477).

American philosophers added their own finesse to the basic strong empiricism dominant by the 1870s. C. S. Peirce is now known as the father of semiotics, but in his own day, thanks to his Harvard colleague William James, he was associated with the pragmatist idea that the actual effects, or lack of effect, of a proposition should be the overriding determinant of its truth-value. A Comtean would nod, pointing out that the Grand Pontiff of Humanity had included utility as one of the seven meanings of positivism.

In the 1920s, positivism was welded to symbolic logic under the label "logical positivism." According to Herbert Feigl, one of its original members, the Vienna Circle hammering out logical positivism was founded and led by Moritz Schlick. Schlick held a visiting appointment at Stanford University in 1929 and then and on other occasions promulgated in America as well as Europe the philosophy of science his group worked out (Feigl 1969, 4–5). "Meaningfulness" was narrowly defined by the Vienna Circle to "separate factual questions and propositions from metaphysical pseudoproblems and pseudosolutions of such problems," member Herbert Feigl explained (5), no doubt winning many hearts with so generous a view of everyone but them. (Carnap had published *Pseudoproblems in Philosophy* in 1928, setting the keynote for the Circle.) "Verifiability," more exactly "testability" was demanded of propositions, a demand that pulled the Circle into operationalism, the requirement that true knowledge depended upon replicable means for observation or mensuration. Feigl states the Circle accepted David Hume's insistence that "regularity in the sequence of events [be] recognized as the only testable cognitive content of the principle of casuality" (7), or in simpler words, that to speak of a cause meant repeated, observed correlation between events—neither more nor less than that.

Archaeology became a discipline under the regime of positivism. Focus on artifacts was perfectly congruent with positivists' restriction of knowledge claims to instances of things. Indeed, prehistoric archaeology is a very good science for positivists: purporting to discover "the past," it discovers only tangible measurable mementos. Conventional prehistory published reams on commonplace sherds and stone blades as if these measurable things constituted the past. Statements describing "Clovis," "Beaker folk," "megalithic builders" describe only those index things assigned to particular time-and-space coordinates. Archaeologists such as Gordon Childe who ventured in popular-style publications to derive a picture of a society from a suite of contiguous things were exceptions.

Archaeology also maintained the positivists' notion that good science, in being above all objective, is value-free. The archaeologist in a dusty trench far from the madding crowd was in a kind of ivory tower, as removed from the clamor of propaganda as a hermit. No one became rich from the practice of scientific archaeology, no one was likely to garner votes by proclaiming himself an archaeologist or even to be solicited for his vote. Archaeologists didn't need to become skilled in dialog, they gave orders to their workmen and read dry technical papers to their colleagues. Archaeologists *chose* to disengage from politics, money-grubbing, socialite smoozing; out there in desert or jungle or cornfield, they could epitomize the dedicated selfless seeker after objective knowledge. Therefore, the results produced by archaeologists were highly unlikely to be tainted by jingoism, racism, or any other kind of ideological bias. It is the thesis of this book that quite the opposite has been the case.

American Archaeology on the New Frontier

Archaeologists exploring the prehistoric past were charting a territory, like the legendary frontiersman carving a known out of a virtual wilderness. There was no question that the past lay there pregnant with data. Samuel Haven, Increase Lapham, Henry Brackenridge, Charles Whittlesey, Edwin Davis, and Ephraim Squier had amassed volumes of observations and measurements of American antiquities. Their successors after the Civil War had a model for synthesis in the concept of an American Stone Age *cum* aborted archaic civilization, the Mound-Builders.

The generation of American archaeologists active in the last quarter of the nineteenth century—Frederic Ward Putnam, Stephen Peet, William Henry Holmes, Cyrus Thomas—worked more at systematizing than at straight recording. In Thomas Kuhn's term, they now had a normal science within which they could solve puzzles. Putnam from his position as Curator of Peabody Museum, Harvard, arranged for fieldwork addressing outstanding questions on Eastern prehistory and the possibility of Pleistocene Americans. Holmes' *Aboriginal Pottery of the Eastern United States* (1903) and eventually *Handbook of Aboriginal American Antiquities: The Lithic Industries* (1919), and Thomas' *Report of the Mound Explorations of the Bureau of Ethnology* (1894) provided classifications for managing data and deriving generalizations. The German archaeologist Max Uhle worked on shellmounds in San Francisco Bay (*The Emeryville Shellmound*, 1907), introducing state-of-the-art stratigraphic interpretations that bewildered A. L. Kroeber. Nels Nelson, who excavated Bay shellmounds after Uhle without apparently absorbing the lesson of Uhle's method, then learned stratigraphic excavation from l'Abbé Breuil in Spain and introduced it, to much acclaim, in the Galisteo Basin of New Mexico in 1913. Alfred Kidder had learned the value of stratigraphic excavation from his Harvard professor, the Egyptologist George Reisner, and selected Pecos to investigate because it promised stratigraphic sequences (Browman and Givens 1996, 83–87). By World War I, methods and major interpretive surveys reflected the formalization of the discipline of American archaeology.

Frederick Jackson Turner's famous 1893 American Historical Association address on the closing of the geographic frontier in America, channeling adventuresome Americans into explorations of the mind, markets, and scientific fields, suggests the orientation of many of the first generation of professional archaeologists. With an end to government-promoted homesteading, the United States felt established, in being rather than becoming. Searching out—not merely surveying—the country's past was appropriate. Coincidentally, an unprecedented influx of non-English-speaking immigrants seemed to threaten the nation's Anglo culture. "American history" was defined as the documented history of European colonists, leaving the undocumented past beyond a disciplinary frontier.

The politics, not to say ideology, behind the 1890s declarations of the domain and role of history underlie the contemporary practice of American archaeology. Charles W. Eliot, president of Harvard University, chaired an 1892 Committee of Ten organized by the National Education Association to meet in the Progressive Movement capital, Madison Wisconsin, to make recommendations on "History, civil government, and political economy." Woodrow Wilson was one of the ten. "History" was specified to be that of the United States, England, Greek and Roman "with their Oriental connections," and France (Kehoe 1989, 204). In 1908, a committee of the American Historical Association published guidelines advocating that American Indians, George Washington, Thanksgiving Day (the Pilgrims), and Memorial Day be studied in the first two primary grades; from third grade on, U.S. history and "civics" should occupy students. By the 1920s, it became standard for children to study American Indians in the primary grades and their state's Indians in fourth grade. On such an elementary level, "Indians" were presented as primitive precursors with no history of their own. Throughout an American student's years of texts and lectures, American Indians consistently existed beyond the frontier.

Spencerian evolutionary Progress imbued American history. Eliot admired Spencer's ideas to the degree that he wrote the introduction for a 1910 American edition of Spencer's *Education*. Spencer's opinion that education ought to be pragmatic preparation for living fit Progressive tenets, fruiting in a 1918 National Education Association pronouncement that the "main objectives" of secondary education should be "health, command of fundamental processes, worthy home-membership, vocation, citizenship, worthy use of leisure, and ethical character" (quoted in Cremin [1961] 1964, 93). These objectives echo Comte's conception of education as "mental hygiene" (Bridges [1915] 1974, 49–50). For positivists,

> Science ... inspires resignation, and gives confidence and precision to action. Whirled helplessly onwards in the machinery of the solar system, our days and nights and years are appointed for us.... All we can do is wisely to guide our action in accordance with these resistless laws ... believing in the laws of social evolution. (Bridges [1915] 1974, 49)

Citizens impelled by Manifest Destiny need not waste time on vanishing races. W. J. McGee, Powell's chosen heir at the Smithsonian's Bureau of American Ethnology and, said his colleague Holmes, "the strongest man in

Anthropology today in America, if not in the world" (quoted in Hinsley 1981, 249), assured the nation that "the budded enlightenment of Britain" had by 1899 flowered into the "full-blown enlightenment of America" (quoted in Rydell 1984, 161).

Renounced by historians and professional educators, the study of America's undocumented past not only used principles from geology but seemed quite allied to that science. Put another way, American archaeology was discouraged from considering itself a branch of history, and relegated to the realm of the natural sciences. There it could march with its fellow sciences collecting and classifying what lies out there to be observed, confident that its labors would solidify the grand history of evolutionary Progress. Because positivism laid as a major premise the repudiation of metaphysical questions, natural scientists including American archaeologists could ignore philosophers' debates on epistemology. A continent had been won, a continent lay inviting explorers on the frontiers of science.

Pragmatist, positivist, seeing all about them abundant demonstration of the power of their own civilization, American archaeologists around the turn of the century increasingly formulated research agendas, although there continued to be initial surveys of unknown regions such as Harlan I. Smith's in British Columbia. The Bureau of American Ethnology supported some archaeological work, but more was financed by wealthy patrons, or carried out by independently well-to-do scholars. Adolf Bandelier, a Swiss-American businessman and correspondent of Lewis Henry Morgan, was commissioned by the Boston-based Archaeological Institute of America to sort and date Anasazi ruins; Boston heiress Mary Hemenway and Phoebe Hearst of the newspaper-owning family both paid for projects of Frank Hamilton Cushing. Best known for trying to live as a Zuni in Zuni Pueblo, Cushing delved for Zuni history in abandoned locations near the pueblo town and learned, or figured out by experimentation, to replicate a variety of ancient and "primitive" objects (for a Zuni view of their very eager guest, see Hughte 1996). Cushing exemplified to the nth degree the combination of romantic temperment, positivist onslaught on data, and pragmatist predilection for utility that was common among his peers.

Cushing illustrates the ambiguity about American Indians that lurked in anthropology for a century. On the one hand, he enthusiastically participated in Zuni activities and escorted several leading men of that nation on a tour of the East; on the other hand, he presented the Zunis as childlike (Hinsley 1989) and his command of the language was never as great as he made it seem (Ladd 1995). Curtis Hinsley (1989, 172–75) locates the work of Cushing and other Southwestern researchers of his period in the controversy between Lewis Henry Morgan, insistent exponent of unilinear social evolution, and Hubert Bancroft, chronicler of the historic encounters between *conquistadores* and Indians. Bancroft wrote of the magnificence of Aztec Tenochtitlán, of its aristocratic ruler and formidable army. Morgan would have none of that, accusing Bancroft of naïvétè. For Morgan, no American Indian ever reached a degree of civilization comparable to that of even early-sixteenth-century Europe. The cramped adobe apartment blocks of the historic Pueblos were the best architecture achieved by Indians. There is a direct connection between Morgan's opinions and the development of professional American archaeology in the early twentieth century: The preeminent archaeologist of that generation, Alfred Vincent Kidder, was born in Marquette, Michigan, to a mining engineer who had assisted Morgan in his study of the beaver and who had Morgan's books in his library (Givens 1992, 1). Kidder devoted the major part of his field career to excavating Southwestern pueblos.

America's Indian past was constrained within the poor existence of the decimated, conquered nineteenth-century Indians: "an American Indian tribe is a very simple as well as humble organization" (L. H. Morgan [1877] 1985, 112). Major Powell, founder-director of the Bureau of American Ethnology, followed Morgan's declarations (Vincent 1990, 42, 52):

> When civilized man first came to America the continent was partially occupied by savage tribes, who obtained subsistence by hunting, by fishing, by gathering vegetal products, and by rude garden culture in cultivating small patches of ground. Semi-nomadic occupancy for such purposes was their tenure to the soil.
>
> On the organization of the present government [United States] such theories of natural law were entertained that even this imperfect occupancy was held to be sufficient title. (Powell 1881, xxvii).... The attempts to educate the Indians and teach them the ways of civilization have ... disappointed their enthusiastic promoters.... The great boon to the savage tribes ... has been the presence of civilization, which, under the laws of acculturation, has irresistibly improved their culture by substituting new and civilized for old and savage (xxviii).... The industries and social institutions of the pristine Indians have largely been destroyed, and they are groping their way to civilized life. (xxx)

This American ideology continues to blind archaeologists. In the third, 1993 edition of their *A History of American Archaeology,* Gordon Willey (Bowditch Professor of Mexican and Central American Archaeology at Harvard) and his former student Jeremy Sabloff acknowledge that Bruce Trigger "has argued that an anti-Native American ethnic bias on the part of North Americans in general caused archaeologists of that area to ignore the possibilities of long-term culture depth and change in the native archaeological record. . . . [W]e are hesitant to accept . . . this interpretation

... without more explicit evidence and substantiation" (Willey and Sabloff 1993, 92). What better evidence than these annual statements of the government's director of anthropological research?

Archaeologists March On

Professionalism organized archaeology as it did other disciplines between the 1880s and 1920s (Kehoe 1998, Patterson 1995, 48–53). The majority of those who published scholarly archaeology came to be salaried employees of universities, museums, or research foundations. (Harvard had its independently wealthy gentlemen scholars [Willey 1988].) To be a *recognized* archaeologist, a person was expected to have graduated from a reputable college and preferably to have earned the doctorate. These criteria excluded persons who could not afford or would not usually be admitted to reputable colleges—lower class, African American, Asian, American Indian, and Jewish men and nearly all women, or in other words, the great bulk of Americans. A handful of scholarships and a quota for Jews played to the American ideal of free opportunity. Colleges allied with museums and a few philanthropic research foundations, e.g., the Carnegie Institution, to preempt research, channeling it to their credentialed staff and the graduate students being credentialed under the staffs' direction. Universities' faculties published scientific journals and monograph series, guaranteeing to the credentialed the power to legitimate, to give their imprimatur to those adhering to accepted models and to assign to oblivion those who would not respect the models. Professionals jealously assert the autonomy of their discipline, claiming they and they alone have gained the expertise required to perform in their field (Freidson 1984). The long selection process instituted by professions under the guise of education instills a sensitivity to what is normal practice and what is tabooed.

Professional archaeologists used the concept of culture areas developed by Otis Mason of the Smithsonian and Franz Boas, popularized especially by Clark Wissler in handbook guides for the American Museum of Natural History (Wissler 1917 et seq.). Boas must not have anticipated that the culture-area concept would uphold racism. Positivists held, as noted above, that "Life is the mutual action and reaction of organism and environment." Tyndall had reiterated that in 1874; even in 1939 a committee of prestigious educators advising the World's Fair laid down the dictum, "As science is the best use of the human intelligence to study and improve the environment of human living, so education is, broadly speaking, the effective adjustment of the individual to his environment" (quoted in Rydell 1993, 113). Not quite: Comte's Religion of Humanity capped its calendar of celebrations[2] with the Festival of Inventors, "many of them workmen, very few of them either philosophers or capitalists, who, possessing a few elements of theoretical knowledge, large practical experience, and vigorous imagination, devise new forms of applying and economizing force, and thus help mankind forward to the mastery of the world" (Bridges [1915] 1974, 369). The bourgeoisie *actively* engaged with their environment, overcoming its limits—for example, in rapidly transporting millions of people over the ocean and across North America.

For a full century, bourgeois anthropologists upheld this powerful guiding assumption:

> Contrasted with these major civilizations, there have always existed other civilizations, those of aboriginal peoples, where societies were fundamentally stable, where no basic internal social-economic crises occurred. . . . Here we have an amazing antithesis which it is of fundamental importance to remember if we wish to understand the civilizations of aboriginal peoples and to see them in their proper perspective. (Radin 1953, 7–8)

A widely used anthropology textbook taught that for "aboriginal peoples"

> the primary local unit of culture is numerically small . . . isolated geographically . . . patterns set in a rigid frame . . . cut off from its own past . . . tradition soon passes into myth . . . the elders are in the saddle . . . They stand for established routine, a fearful avoidance of the new. . . . The individual here is but a miniature reproduction of the group culture. . . . Nor does this exhaust the factors which stand for conservatism. . . . Here every breath of cultural life is dominated by natural things and events. . . . Under such conditions the economic adjustment is taken almost as a fact of nature. It may be sorely inadequate, but it works after a fashion and is accepted as final. (Goldenweiser [1937] 1946, 407–10)

Major Powell had said it, between aboriginal peoples and the civilized there is a "difference so profound" that the aborigine can never understand "his cultured brother" (Powell 1896, xxiii).

Notice that the absolute dichotomy premised between aborigines (primitives, tribal people) and their civilized observers is not demanded by unilinear evolution. Saltational jumps were in fact repudiated by evolutionists in the natural sciences, where Lyell's gradualism reigned prima facie (G. Simpson 1970). It was the ideology of imperialism, not simply evolutionism, that constituted the conquered nations opposite to the bourgeoisie in every valued characteristic (Kuper 1988, 9). Anthropologists were employed to discover these differences, ostensibly to enlighten administrators, implicitly to validate the denial of citizens' rights to those adjudged deficient in understanding. Archaeologists no less than ethnologists assumed a priori that trans-frontier societies had the primitive traits enumerated above by Goldenweiser.

Customary archaeology is well displayed in the major textbook *Indians Before Columbus,* by Paul S. Martin, George I. Quimby, and Donald Collier. All three were curators in the Department of Anthropology of the Chicago Natural History Museum (Field Museum). Collier was a son of the reformer John Collier, Commissioner of the Bureau of Indian Affairs in Roosevelt's New Deal. He had worked on the Upper Columbia in the Northwest, Martin was a specialist on the Southwest, and Quimby on the northern Midwest. Published in 1947, *Indians Before Columbus* summarized three generations' investigations into the prehistory of America.

Like Daniel Wilson, Martin, Quimby, and Collier organize chapters around the data of archaeology: "Objects of Stone," "Objects of Copper," "Objects of Bone and Shell," "Pottery," "Basketry and Cloth," and "Trade and Commerce" (evidenced by objects). Following this extended section on "Arts and Industries," they outline archaeologically known "cultures" by culture area, for which the endpapers are culture-area maps. Each "culture" is summarized for "Area," "People" (classification according to Earnest Hooton's "Racial Types in America," 1933, with Georg Neumann's preliminary work for the East), "Language" (seldom indicated), "Houses and/or villages," "Livelihood," "Pottery," "Metals" (seldom), "Basketry and weaving," "Wood-working," "Tools, utensils, and weapons," "Pipes," "Travel and transportation," "Costume," "Cradles" (another seldom category), "Musical instruments," "Ornaments," "Games," "Art," "Burials," and "Conjectures" (on temporal placement and relationships to other "cultures"). The uneven geographical coverage indicates where archaeological research had been concentrated in the previous half-century, the Southwest and Eastern Woodlands taking three-fifths of the book.

Introducing the volume, Martin, Quimby, and Collier state that their experience indicates "interested laymen and beginning students ... want to know about archeology:

1. How long have the Indians been in the New World?
2. Who built the mounds, shell middens, cliff dwellings, etc.?
3. How long ago were they built?
4. What became of the builders?" (Martin, Quimby, and Collier 1947, v)

It would seem that the American public had only the questions discussed a century earlier, and by Wilson.

Martin, Quimby, and Collier explain, regardless of the laypeople:

[W]e are attempting to reconstruct the history of the Indians [hence their title, *Indians Before Columbus*] ... we are forced to deal exclusively with material remains ... and our first task is to build up histories of material culture.... But many readers will wonder why we are eager to investigate the life of the ancient Indians. In short, why dig up dead Indians? (Martin, Quimby, and Collier 1947, 3–4)

They offer a startling non sequitur:

We are living today in a very sick world. If civilization is to endure, we must push forward the study of man in every way possible.... In our particular culture science has permitted man to bring some of the physical world under control. This knowledge may be used for good as well as for evil. At present much of our scientific knowledge is being used for destructive purposes. Many people blame science for this state of affairs.

Actually this is an uninformed point of view. The present chaotic condition of the world is not new; it is only worse than ever before.... What the atomic bomb will do to us, no one knows; but everyone is agreed that the study of nuclear physics, if man chooses to make it so, may be beneficial to him.

If through anthropology we can understand all the facets of life in a relatively simple culture, if we can discover the whys and wherefores of such a culture, then we are better able to understand and attack the greater and more complex problems that must be solved if we are to attain real knowledge of man in the modern world....

Thus, digging up dead Indians has a very real significance and holds possibilities that stagger the imagination.

Furthermore, the study of the history of the Indians is important because they have made contributions to our own history and civilization ... : corn, pumpkins, maple syrup, tobacco, pipe- and cigarette-smoking, succotash, beans, moccasins, toboggans, snowshoes, corncribs, and canoes. (Martin, Quimby, and Collier 1947, 4–5)

American archaeology was not about Indians per se, it was an extension of the quest for the alchemy to transform humanity. Why, indeed, would anyone bother with the history of people whose greatest achievements have been succotash and corncribs?

Martin, Quimby, and Collier carried out a prodigious task combing through and systematizing the archaeological literature plus unpublished data from seven of the country's most productive archaeologists (Philip Drucker, Charles Fairbanks, James Ford, James Griffin, Robert Heizer, Richard MacNeish, and Will McKern). They and these seven were all salaried professionals employed by universities or museums. They had been among the organizers of the Society for American Archaeology, the principal professional association, in 1935. The overall framework and presentation of *Indians Before Columbus* represents the standard for the discipline from about 1913 to the 1960s.

The strong positivist and progressive tone set in the introduction pervades the book. Page after page in declarative style impresses the reader with the amount of data retrieved by archaeologists. "Probably," "possibly," "may" sprinkle many sentences, lending an air of scientific caution in the face of recalcitrant objects. Basically, the volume is a compendium of trait lists fronted by pseudo-ethnographic observations such as "Burial customs [of Hopewell] indicate a preoccupation with death" (Martin, Quimby, and Collier 1947, 236). (Aren't burial customs *by definition* preoccupied with death?)

Some of Martin, Quimby, and Collier's statements reveal assumptions soon to be rejected radically. Their dating, of course, is way off: With tree-rings in the Southwest the only means of establishing elapsed time, they divide American prehistory, like Caesar's Gaul, into the magic number of three parts, Archaic from ¿B.C.–A.D. 900, Intermediate from A.D. 900–1300 and Late Prehistoric from A.D. 1300–1600. Initial immigration over Bering Strait having been governed by glacial advances (Martin, Quimby, and Collier 1947, 81), "¿B.C." is on the order of twenty thousand years. Two thousand years is the maximum they consider indicated for the development of Indian cultures beyond the initial Archaic hunting and gathering nomadism. "The Indians' ... culture remained more or less unchanged for thousands of years. With the introduction of agriculture and pottery, the process of becoming more sophisticated was greatly accelerated" (94). Maize agriculture was introduced from Mexico, five hundred years earlier in the Southwest than in the Eastern Woodlands, and pottery into the Southwest from Mexico, but into the Northeast from Asia across Bering Strait (in the Holocene) (518–19). The Late Prehistoric period in the Mississippi Valley and Southeast "was a time of intensive hoe agriculture, sedentary village life, fortified towns, and the use of the bow and arrow" (237). "Village-states" wherein "larger villages were probably ceremonial centers for smaller communities surrounding them" are suggested by the mound-and-plaza ruins (237).

What of the noble goals of Martin, Quimby, and Collier? They figured out (page 160) that "Pueblo culture ... was smashed by the advent of the Spanish conquerors. This invasion was almost as devastating to the simple Pueblo culture as the atomic bomb may be to our own culture." But (page 197) the "Hohokam-Salado towns" of southern Arizona were already abandoned at the Spanish entradas. In the Mississippi Valley, Marksville "was probably part of the Hopewell culture. It is not hard to imagine that the agricultural South and the industrial North [Hopewell] were not on the most cordial terms even in Burial Mound II times, and it is possible that the farmers of the Marksville culture were 'cussing out' (in a friendly way) the 'damyankee' Hopewell manufacturers in Ohio . . . [and] the Hopewell traveling salesmen" (Martin, Quimby, and Collier 1947, 278). Such insights notwithstanding, the great question remains:

> Why do societies develop along certain lines, accept or reject innovations, become advanced, and then collapse? These are a few of the questions anthropologists are wrestling with and attempting to answer. When these and other more complicated [*more* complicated?] questions are answered, the science of human behavior will have a wider scope and a greater accuracy. (Martin, Quimby, and Collier 1947, 197)

The introduction to *Indians Before Columbus* unwittingly illuminates the authors' failure to realize their lofty aspiration. "How the Archeologist Works" tells the reader that "Usually, the archeologist arbitrarily decides that each layer shall be, for example, six inches thick." Only "sometimes" can the archaeologist work through visible "natural" strata. Field excavation entails laboratory classification: "The archeologist sorts his materials, placing like with like, and then makes comparisons with other similar or identical materials from near-by sites. . . . In this way, the excavations yield a historical record" (Martin, Quimby, and Collier 1947, 7–9). Recalling that actual stratigraphic succession was the only reliable means of inferring chronology for these data, the term "historical" seems inappropriate for the results of the exercises described. The veneer of science becomes yet thinner when we read that "The only way one can learn to classify this material is by doing it under the supervision of a competent archeologist" (8). Learning by ostension (that is, by showing the student what is referred to) is part of the bedrock of positivism, and the positivists' faith in the unproblematic relationship between words and their ostensible referents is precisely where Wittgenstein and later critics cracked their grand structure of science (Toulmin 1969, 38–39).

One year after *Indians Before Columbus,* the archaeologists complacently marching beyond the frontier were ambushed. Paul Martin would be grievously wounded, in his final years groveling before his affronters. Quimby and Collier, lacking Martin's ambition, went on, unconcerned, with their jobs. Neither the initial nor later attacks, oddly, were propelled by any Wittgensteinian penetration of the positivists' Dance of the Seven Veils. Quite the contrary, the archaeologists' critics castigated them for too little positivism. Guy Gibbon sees the attacks to have been "an urgent defensive measure to protect entrenched positive social science" (G. Gibbon 1989, 140). The fate of our world, after all, depended upon archaeologists making the objects of the past into a historical record.

CHAPTER 6

Petrified
Puddle Ducks

One year after *Indians Before Columbus* recapitulated the field of American archaeology, a Harvard dissertation came out from the American Anthropological Association attacking the discipline. Walter W. Taylor had written *A Study of Archeology* in 1942 and revised it for publication in 1946 after army service overseas during World War II. Taylor had been encouraged, egged on, by his professor at Harvard, sociocultural anthropologist Clyde Kluckhohn. Kluckhohn, John Bennett who had turned from archaeology to cultural anthropology, and Julian Steward who conducted both ethnographic and archaeological research in the Great Basin, all criticized American archaeologists' focus on typology instead of behavior (Kluckhohn 1940; Bennett 1943; Steward and Setzler 1938; Steward 1942). Heedless of protocol, Taylor's bare-knuckled onslaught beat on the most prominent Americanist archaeologists.

Petrified puddle ducks, Taylor said they were, the revered Alfred V. Kidder, Emil Haury, Frank H. H. Roberts, William Webb, William Ritchie, James B. Griffin. Page after page, he tears apart their reports to argue disjunctions between avowed goal and actual performance. Neither before nor since has there been such merciless exposure of cant, braggadocio, formulistic pronouncements, and naive or unthinking procedures. Blood flowed in torrents from a host of gored oxen, and their bellowing could be heard throughout the land.

Behind Taylor stood Clyde Kluckhohn (R. Woodbury 1954, 295). Kluckhohn was a self-consciously brilliant anthropologist fighting to raise his colleagues' consciousness of the central importance of theoretical positions, the subject of his 1936 Ph.D. dissertation (for Harvard). In the

1950s, he taught the Harvard anthropology graduate students' required course on theory, pacing like a caged lion back and forth across the front of the classroom. In the 1950s, he drew on linguistics theory and methods, in his opinion the most sophisticated of the anthropological sciences, urging especially the archaeology students[1] to incorporate such research design in their work. Kluckhohn knew whereof he spoke: In 1937, he and Paul Reiter directed the excavation of the small ruin Bc 50–51 in Chaco Canyon, opposite the large Pueblo Bonito and Chetro Ketl buildings. Publishing the report on this work in 1939, Kluckhohn found that the simple little building Bc 51 could not be comfortably fitted into the standard Pecos classification schema. He sharply criticized Kidder and Roberts for the "unilinear and limited set of categories of the Pecos classification. ...We must remember," he reminds his peers, "as [Alfred North] Whitehead has so often reminded us, that a classification is, at best, 'a halfway house'" (Kluckhohn [1939] 1962, 85–86).

Walter Taylor obtained his undergraduate degree from Yale University in 1935, and worked there as a laboratory fellow the following year. At Yale, Cornelius Osgood impressed him with the importance of close attention to the range of material culture and its relationship with environment (Taylor 1948, 10). Osgood had worked in Alaska with the Ingalik (Deg Hit'an), producing an exemplary set of studies on their "Mental ... ," "Material ... ," and "Social Culture," and carried out archaeological excavations in Cuba and Venezuela (all published by Yale). Taylor then went to the Southwest, attending the 1938 Chaco Conference and presenting a paper at the 1940 Conference (R. Woodbury 1993, 135, 141). Ethnologists as well as archaeologists participated in these conferences, albeit in fewer numbers than the archaeologists, attempting to interpret the archaeological remains through ethnographic observations of contemporary Pueblos, Pima-Papago, and Navajos. Kluckhohn argued his interpretation of Bc 51 "in terms of what we know about Pueblo cultures" (Kluckhohn [1939] 1962, 83). Underlying Taylor's deconstruction of Southwestern archaeology is the dehumanizing effect of archaeological practice; deeper yet is the tension between humanities and science.

Reviewing contemporary statements on the nature and purpose of American archaeology, Taylor sees that the discipline is subsumed within anthropology and at the same time, believes its aim is "reconstructing history." "What has history to do with cultural anthropology?" asks Taylor (1948, 27). Neglect of this question has been, to Taylor, a serious weakness in the discipline. The obverse of the neglect has been claim that anthropology, or history, "is *the* Master-science which is to synthesize the totality of human experience ... historians and anthropologists ... are ... not philosophers and should not aspire to write Universal History or alone to pursue the Study of Man" (30). Returning to his question, Taylor is convinced that historiography logically includes ethnography (i.e., there is no compelling break between past and present), and this "construction of cultural contexts" must be preliminary to, yet is distinct from, the search for generalizations that is the matter of cultural anthropology (41). The answer to the question? Archaeology is neither history nor anthropology but a set of techniques for retrieving data (43–44).

Having reduced his colleagues to the status of technicians, Taylor examines the adequacy of these technicians. Lest his caustic words be suspected to rise from personal animosities, he declares that the subjects of his critique are "men whose influence in academic and professional circles has been of the highest," and that he will limit himself to their published statements and work (Taylor 1948, 45). (With the criterion of "highest influence," Taylor can only consider men, since no women would be considered to be within that circle [Parezo 1993, 29]). First among the first-rank was Alfred Vincent Kidder, convener of the first Pecos Conferences, author of *An Introduction to the Study of Southwestern Archaeology,* 1924, and the standard-setting *The Artifacts of Pecos,* 1932, and chairman of the Division of Historical Research for the Carnegie Institution— the "dean of American archaeology" (N. Woodbury 1996, 9). Kluckhohn had already excoriated Dr. Kidder in the critique he contributed to *The Maya and Their Neighbors* (Kluckhohn 1940). Kidder's work, both his own researches and those he sponsored through Carnegie, focused on describing artifacts, defining specimen classes, and delimiting the classes in space and time relative to others in the region. Surely these are necessary steps in any study of remains. But, shouts Taylor, in Kidder's principal publications on Pecos, "*there is neither any provenience given for the vast majority of artifacts nor any consistent correlation of these specimens with the ceramic periods*" (Taylor 1948, 48; his italics). Kidder, Haury, Roberts, and other respected leaders in the discipline only occasionally mention quantities of artifacts in their classes or support inferences with quantified data, and failure to consistently provide proveniences prevents readers from rectifying the lack. These failures disable anyone who wishes to proceed past the preliminaries to "reconstruct"—better, construct[2]—Pueblo cultural contexts and, thereby, history.

Part II of Taylor's *Study of Archeology* presents his prescription for the discipline, the "conjunctive approach." The good archaeologist will focus on the site itself instead of seeking comparisons in space and time. He will excavate and record according to natural or artifactual units (e.g., rooms, refuse layers) rather than the arbitrary segments such as six-inch levels favored by American archaeologists (cf. Martin, Quimby, and Collier 1947, 7). *All* phenomena bearing human imprint, whether whole or fragmentary, will be recorded, along with what was, or was not, utilized in the local environment. Subvention of the costs of specialist analyses of recovered material is recommended through the creation of a "central agency or clearing house" for American archaeology (Taylor 1948, 201). Illustrations of the conjunctive approach are taken from Taylor's 1940–41 U.S. National Museum project in caves in central Coahuila, Mexico, and his 1939 season as Assistant Archaeologist supervising Bc 51 in Chaco Canyon—the same ruin excavated by Kluckhohn and Reiter in 1937. Outcry from the "deaf men answering questions which no one has asked them," men "tatting endless taxonomic rosettes out of the same old ball of 'material culture'" (Taylor 1948, 95), was of course immediate and loud. Calm, reasonable Richard Woodbury was selected to write the review of *A Study of Archeology* for *American Antiquity*. Woodbury felt that Taylor had underestimated the achievements of Kidder and the Carnegie employees, while conversely, Taylor himself "repeatedly falls far short of his own goals" in Part II. The Bc 51 section is particularly bad, Woodbury states, tedious, difficult to follow, lacking proper map and scale drawings (what is given is schematic)—in short, "horror" (R. Woodbury 1954, 295). Let him who is without sin throw stones; Taylor lives in a glass house.

Taxa Versus Culture

Taylor's barrage of stones somewhat obscured the crux of his essay, "What has history to do with cultural anthropology?" That Kidder, Roberts, Haury et al. failed to describe and document their data in enough detail to facilitate others' full use is secondary to the basic question of the purpose of American archaeology. Woodbury's review slights the conflict Taylor identifies between "chronicles" and universalizing generalizations. United States archaeology in the 1930s had been drafted to fight in the Great Depression. Requiring little capital investment and able to utilize hundreds of uneducated laborers, archaeology attracted the attention of the Works Progress Administration. The result of dozens of excavation projects was a conglomeration of data the professional archaeologists overseeing the projects felt compelled to assimilate. A series of conferences produced a beautifully constructed scheme to bring order out of the chaos: the Midwestern Taxonomic Method. Most archaeologists called it the Midwestern Taxonomic System, the MTS, or the McKern System. The McKern System was so much on everyone's mind after 1939 that neither Taylor nor Julian Steward (1942) had to explain they were attacking it when they deplored "taxonomy."

Will McKern believed that "In men's affairs, chaos does not reduce itself to order without a plan. The accomplishments of science stand as a monument to planned orderliness" (McKern 1939, 303). The method he devised is monumental: it could order *all* archaeological data into its hierarchical system (Kehoe 1990). Its inspiration was no less than the

Linnaean biological taxonomic system, although its nomenclature was independent. To McKern, the situation in the 1930s was this: Inauguration of a steadily increasing number of college and university archaeological training programs, expansion of state historical society and geological survey field identifications of sites, and authorization of grants-in-aid from the Smithsonian (1928) and, through the Rockefeller Foundation, the National Research Council (1929) caused rapid proliferation of archaeological data in the Eastern United States (Guthe 1952, 3-5). In the Southwest, tree-ring dating along with recovery of a number of stratigraphic sequences provided a temporal framework interdigitating regional collections. East of the Rockies, building logs were not preserved and there appeared to be a remarkable paucity of stratification in excavated sites (3). How to weight observations of regional co-ocurrences and broader similarities was a principal procedural problem.

According to the man who served as his field assistant in 1929, McKern fretted in camp over how best to label the components of the Stoddard site near Trempeleau, Wisconsin (Fisher 1987). At the time, Stoddard was the only site known in the state to exhibit stratigraphic succession of Hopewell and Oneota ("Upper Mississippian"). McKern felt the upper component (Oneota) was qualitatively different from the material in a lower stratum, differences greater than he would have expected from mere chronological succession. Sherds from the lower stratum strongly resembled classic Hopewell burial mounds in the central Midwest; upper stratum sherds resembled those associated with platform mounds. Sure, the components could be seen as different "cultures." The practice in the eastern half of the country was to label archaeological collations according to historic Indian occupations, e.g., Algonquin or Iroquoian, or even Chiwere Sioux or Iowa. This cannot be supported, for there is seldom direct attestation that particular objects or sites were produced by historically known communities, and the supposition that some artifacts may be centuries or thousands of years old increases the improbability that historic labels should accrue to archaeological objects (McKern 1939, 302–03). Those Hopewell sherds separate from and underlying the Upper Mississippian should not be facilely labeled Algonquin.

The student assistant, Alton Fisher, suggested that the situation was analogous to that facing Carl Linné when he undertook to systematize organisms. Linné had loosely defined geographical regions, he did not know the temporal relationships between populations of organisms, and he had no particularly compelling principles of classification. He realized that it is not easy to recognize the "true" essential characteristics of a class, therefore the student must beware of "factitious" or "artificial" definitions and be prepared to discuss "natural" definitions including all characteristics that might distinguish classes. Selecting attributes related to

reproduction in plants proved a workable (and logically defensible) principle for botanical classification. The animal kingdom was more intractable,
and many of Linnaeus' genera were seat-of-the-pants classes intuited from
observation rather than rigid principle (Mayr 1982, 176–79). Overall,
Linné's simple nested hierarchy of classes resting on morphological attributes enabled researchers to bring consensual order out of chaos. A century
later, the Linnaean system could accommodate Charles Darwin's great
principle of evolution, descent with modification, opening it up to temporal ordering.

Debating pros and cons of a Linnaean-type method of ordering,
McKern saw young Fisher's point about a system that did not demand
time or space coordinates. Above all, the method of ordering must require
only *archaeological* data (McKern 1939, 303). Questions of historic affinities or linguistic affiliation needed other data. McKern developed a system
of orders ranking from most general to limited particulars, and by early
1932 was ready to share his method of reducing chaos (note: he proposed a
method that *uses a system*, the system itself less important than the method).
The first engagement of the method came in a May, 1932, symposium at
the annual Illinois State Academy of Science meeting, in Chicago. Here,
reports James Griffin (1943, 327), "the promiscuous use of the word 'culture' emphasized" the necessity of a finer-grained ordering method. In
October, 1932, Carl Guthe, chairman of the national committee on state
archaeology surveys, circulated a mimeograph of a version of McKern's
paper modified by comments from the Chicago symposium participants.
Returns were discussed at the University of Chicago in December 1932
and revised mimeographs circulated April 1933 and August 1934. These
presented McKern's analysis of Wisconsin data to illustrate the application
of the method. James Griffin was (by his account) the first to employ
McKern's method on new data, in 1935. Thorne Deuel, William Duncan
Strong, Waldo Wedel, Paul Cooper, and William Ritchie hastened to jump
on the bandwagon.

The "MTS" had archaeologists begin with the artifacts and records of
occupation strata in specific sites. Each stratum (or if no strata can be discerned, the site) is premised to constitute the detritus of a human community. These "natural" assemblages are the minimal unit, the "component,"
in McKern's system. Because components are considered natural con-
glomerations, strictly speaking (said McKern) they are not part of a classification but preliminary to one. The lowest class, sensu stricto, is the
"focus," a recurring set of culturally significant traits. To claim a focus,
the archaeologist must test the validity of the assemblage of traits from one
site or stratum by replicating it at another site. Thus components are the
raw material of foci. A component may be the refuse of human behavior
but only if its traits are replicated elsewhere can it be inferred to have con-

stituted a distinct cultural phenomenon—in spite of disclaiming any necessary correspondence between focus and "local tribe" (McKern 1939, 308), McKern was looking for ethnic identity markers.

Next above foci are "aspects." Foci with "a preponderating majority of [cultural] traits and trait elements" but some dissimilarity in details should be grouped into an aspect. Aspects are grouped on the basis of general traits into "phases"; shared technology variously manifested are a suitable trait to present as a phase determinant. A few "broadly general traits" shared across phases allow those phases to be grouped into a "pattern." A pattern is a "reflection of the primary adjustments of peoples to environment, as modified by tradition." Finally, the most general similarities "such as pottery, sedentary tendency, and, possibly, horticulture" form the "base" (McKern 1939, 308–10). The Stoddard site's Oneota component is classed into the Mississippi Pattern, its Hopewell into the Woodland Pattern (primarily on ceramic traits) and both provisionally in a Horticultural-Pottery Base.

The bottom line, Walter Taylor decried, is that McKern's Method is one of adumbrating "cultures" through a laundry-list of observations ("traits"). Similarity is a matter of presence or absence of a trait. McKern's discussion of quantification is not, Taylor fulminated, of ratios of traits within components but of counting how many traits are similar between foci, aspects, or phases. Taylor rightly bemoaned obscuring the difference between an assemblage with, say, a couple of shell-tempered sherds and hundreds of grog-tempered, and one with the reverse ratio. Far more tendentious is the presentation of traits as self-evident (Taylor 1948, 150). This positivist premise opened the door to two abuses, lumping or splitting observed attributes to engender traits to list, and the creation of arenas where more confident egotistic professionals could dominate cautious, insecure, or philosophically astute workers (Kelley and Hanen 1988, 115–17; R. Woodbury 1993, 93). Every Midwesterner will immediately think of James B. Griffin's virtuoso performances labeling sherds by type, skill honed by decades of experience supervising the ceramic collections of the University of Michigan's Museum of Anthropology, yes: but in the final analysis, the ceramic types he could name so facilely exist primarily through his rule-making and the deference he enjoined.

If McKern's Method led to a system of weighting and engathering similarities, it was neither chronicling nor the similitude of anthropologically conceived cultures. The Kidder classification for the Southwest, created through a 1927 conference hosted by Kidder at his field camp at Pecos, was meant to be a chronicle of aboriginal history in the Southwest. It collated architectural, ceramic, and other artifacts apparently used in communities residing in the sites, or in a few sites within a series of strata, designating "cultures" according to the presence or absence of pottery, evidence for or postulation of agriculture, and building techniques and forms. From an anthropologist's perspective, both classification systems obliterated the sense of living communities that might be gleaned from the artifacts. This sense Taylor desired to restore through his ballyhooed "conjunctive approach."

The "conjunctive approach" (defined, Taylor 1948, 7, explicated in ch. 6) conjoins all the evidence observed in a component. The destruction entailed in archaeological excavation makes it imperative, Taylor reminded readers (page 155), to record fully every phenomenon visible in the site. Beyond the moral obligation to preserve data, the archaeologist should see his[3] work as paleo-ethnography (not Taylor's term), asking every phenomenon to tell him of the past community's life. Taylor seems to slight interpretation of the "natural matrix" of the community in favor of positing cross-cultural generalizations, á là those produced by Yale's George Peter Murdock (172–74). Beyond these, he is very open to inferences on aesthetic values of the community, drawing upon striking asymmetries in Coahuila mat and basket designs to contrast them with the highly symmetrical baskets pictured in Kidder's reports from northeastern Arizona, and contrasting Coahuila cordage with that in Lovelock Cave, Nevada (159–63). These examples bring out another aspect of the standard procedure, lack of concern for fiber artifacts (49–50, 77–78, 134–37). Desert Coahuila's dry caves provided Taylor with a relative abundance and variety of textiles for which he found, when he came to compare his pieces, an insufficiency of analyses in other archaeologists' publications. The conjunctive approach forced Taylor to work in detail on his textiles, whereas the standard procedure privileged stone and ceramic artifacts. Taylor laid himself open to the opprobrium of his peers by ignoring Kidder's innovative and exemplary presentation of bone artifacts, extending even to cut-marks on food bone, in *The Artifacts of Pecos,* 1932. The upshot of Taylor's "conjunctive approach" seemed to be, to quote Willey and Phillips' (1958, 2) paraphrase, that "archaeology is anthropology or it is nothing." No one quite grasped that Taylor's strident insistence on the importance of the site in toto, the data literally as givens, opened up a major epistemological issue unseen by positivists: data as syntagm, interpretation as paradigm. The distinction came to the fore with Thomas Kuhn's 1962 *Structure of Scientific Revolutions* but remains esoteric to mainstream American archaeologists. When Walter Taylor embarked on his dissertation, he faced a Southwest ordering system that his mentor, Kluckhohn, had found painfully inadequate for either chronicling or cultural "re"construction, and an Eastern system that held in abeyance both chronicling and culture in the anthropological sense. Imbued with Cornelius Osgood's strong sense of the reality of Dené groups' culture, and Kluckhohn's exasperation at muddling through, Taylor the young bull charged through the potsherds shop goring the gentlemen tending their tables. The rampage made Taylor's name, made it anathema. Everyone agreed that taxonomy for its own sake is mere scholasticism, and that the existing systems, Kidder's and McKern's, were far from ideal; everyone agreed, also, that Taylor hung himself by his own petard whenever he presented his own work in the monograph. The provisional and, in McKern's case, hermeneutic nature of both the major systems was admitted at the same time that the brash challenger was declared out-of-bounds. Taylor would find employment thanks to the revolutionary expansion of universities in the 1960s (and the attraction, to provincial former normal schools, of an upper-class Eastern background), but he found himself non grata in the profession.

Polemics aside, *A Study of Archeology* illuminates fundamental problems in the discipline of archaeology. Chronicles or societal reconstruction? History or universal generalizations? How can objectivity be enhanced? How to deal with poor comparability between sites, due to uneven preservation, varying extents of excavation, more versus less complete description in publications? These are up-front issues. Profound matters such as the arrogation of the American past by WASP professional men did not appear. For all his upstart air, Walter Taylor accepted the preeminence of positivist science and the privileged role of its practitioners in the generation of knowledge. Indians lived only to produce data by which anthropologists could discover the laws of human behavior.

Processualism

Progressivism fell back under the body blows dealt by World War I and the Great Depression. Enlightened pragmatists could not overcome either mankind's depraved lust for violence, nor capitalism's heedless pursuit of profits. Did these blows sap respect for science as the road to effective knowledge? Not for most citizens, although populist leader William Jennings Bryan did see Darwinian evolution undermining Christian morality (Numbers 1992, 41). Social scientists decided they had to delve deeper to discern the forces affecting humans, to pay more attention to natural processes. Doing so, they melded history and the study of nature (Ross 1991, 317–19). Put another way, the development of historiography in the nineteenth century raised consciousness of the biases and obfuscations in historical records, leaving observations of nature apparently more straightforward, amenable to replication, true. Positivist science soldiered on while Comte's positivism expired.

During the 1930s, people yearned for the restoration of order in society. Displaced workers, bankrupt banks, homesteads buried in swirling dust betokened chaos. Depresssion measures, especially the WPA, directly

affected archaeologists (Quimby 1979; Lyon 1996), favorably in the immediate sense but disturbing insofar as it demolished the old verities of hard
work makes the man. Fascism was a response to public perceptions of
chaos. The country needed a strong leader to put people to work and make
the trains run on time; democracy had had its opportunity and proved
ineffectual. When Will McKern proferred a means to bring order out of
chaos through a scientific method, his message resonated against the cho-
rus of families on the dole, hobos, Okies, tent cities of protesters. Managing the masses of data accumulting through state surveys and federal
relief projects stimulated the 1930s conferences to order the field, but
longing for order was pervasive in the 1930s.

The Science of Man in the World Crisis came out in 1945, climaxing the
call to responsible citizenship stimulated by the Depression and then
another Great War. Ralph Linton, professor at Columbia University but
previously at the University of Wisconsin, edited the volume. Concluding
his introduction "The Scope and Aims of Anthropology," he reiterates the
word "order":

> The phenomena of human existence and especially of human behavior are
> exceedingly complex and the work of reducing them to intelligible order has
> only begun.... this does not mean that such phenomena are without
> order.... The aim of this science is the same as that of all sciences. It seeks
> to ascertain the processes and continuities involved ... with a view to the
> prediction of events and ultimately to their control. (Linton 1945, 17) ...
> [Anthropologists] are attempting to arrive at certain generalizations, "laws"
> in common parlance, which will make it possible to predict the course of
> events and ultimately to control it. (11)

The same goal appears a few years later in sociologist Bernard Barber's
Science and the Social Order. "The social sciences, like all science, are primarily concerned for analysis, prediction, and control of behavior and values" (1952, 259). The 1933 Chicago Exposition had condensed the
American ideal into the slogan, "Science Finds—Industry Applies—Man
Conforms" (in Goldman 1989, 294). Linton and Barber, and McKern,
who would have no truck with political Fascism, nevertheless sought
order, laws, conformity. Where they diverged from Fascists was in repudi-
ating a strongman in favor of Science—the community of scientists.

Against this backdrop of Science on a throne, Walter Taylor's championing of the human communities particular to the past sounds anachronis-
tically humanistic. He writes of deriving generalizations from a large body
of such studies, but not of predicting and controlling human behavior. His
mentor, Kluckhohn, wrote contrary to the tenor of the time, urging cul-

tural relativism and stating, "all talk of an eventual peaceful and orderly world is but pious cant ... unless there are, in fact, ... some codes or canons that have or can obtain universal acceptance" (Kluckhohn [1952] 1962, 286–87). "Unless some have or can obtain," a decidedly skeptical tone. Kluckhohn and Taylor held a maverick position, one closer to Boas than to the postwar trend (Taylor 1972, 31). Geographers realized the trend, per se, more clearly than did archaeologists: After a decade of discussions over whether or not geographers deal in unique historical facts, thereby precluding law-like generalizations, the issue was joined in a pair of papers in the *Annals of the Association of American Geographers*, 1965–1966. "Process" conceived as generalizations about human behavior won a strong position in geography (Bird 1993, 11–13, 129).

Mainstream scientists returning to their research after the stark disruption of war yearned to find continuity in spite of the deranged state of the world. "Process" somehow appealed widely, from sociology to philosophy and theology (Lucas 1983). Two horrible wars and the economic fragmentation between them punched at the solar plexus of faith in Progress. Time had betrayed us. A few diehard Marxists refused to renounce historical materialism, among them Leslie White whose lopped-off evolutionism (Peace 1993) would become, for younger veterans of World War II, what Darwinism had been for Henry Adams in the aftermath of the Civil War. More mature scholars back in mufti simply wanted to forgo time, to forget the dreadful meaning of history. Julian Steward, Gordon Willey, and Philip Phillips formulated versions of universal history that relegated time to an epiphenomenon of process. Their two major publications of the 1950s, each with trial drafts in the *American Anthropologist* (Steward 1949; Willey and Phillips 1953, 1955), bridged the halves of the twentieth century.

Steward can be more briefly discussed here. His disengagement from time was rooted in traditional ethnography. During the 1930s he worked on a portion of A. L. Kroeber's Culture Element Distribution survey of the intermontane West. *Basin-Plateau Aboriginal Socio-political Groups*, 1938, published when he was employed at the Bureau of American Ethnology, detailed Shoshoni and Gosiute communities remembered by older members of these nations. Before he had completed the ethnography, he had published a model of primitive nomadic social groups in the 1936 *festschrift* for Kroeber. The indigenous people of the Great Basin did not live in the patrilocal bands he had premised to be fundamental to human life, nor even in the "composite bands" he thought up to explain observed irregularities through historical breakdown and ad hoc aggregations. In his monograph (Steward 1938, 258), he was reduced to admitting the discrepancy between expectation and data, and laid it to the extreme poverty of the desert environment. "Families" (households) were the only social units feasible for the Numa, he explained, because low density and fluctuations of food resources prevented establishing persistent communities.

After editing the B.A.E.'s massive multivolume *Handbook of South American Indians*, Steward felt he could carry culture-area theory into an evolutionary framework. Unilinear and universal evolution schemes (his distinction) are untenable; "multi-linear" evolution lifts the babies out of the gray bathwater of conjectural histories and sets each young human into its own geographical arena. Back in 1748, Montesquieu had pointed to "the nature of the terrain" governing human social development (Jones 1992, 746). Darwin's principle of natural selection seemed to give natural surroundings a powerful role in organisms' fates. Steward (1955, 89) distinguished a "cultural core" representing a society's adaptation to its environment, from "secondary" cultural traits independent of environmental constraints or stimuli. Historians could trace intersocietal contacts and group movements in the secondary traits, anthropologists could compare culture cores in a search for the factors governing societal development, or lack of development.

The glaring flaw in Steward's mid-century work was a continuing acceptance of the postulate that non-Western groups were less evolved than their conquerors. Progress from savagery through barbarism to civilization remained the implicit model. This being so, Steward's *Theory of Culture Change* did not threaten the petrified puddle ducks. Younger archaeologists happily joined anthropologists describing regional subsistence regimes to fit societies into the rechristianed developmental classes, now "levels of sociocultural integration." Although Steward did not emphasize "processual," he used "process" and "processual" often enough (e.g., 1958, 21, 93) to fit the zeitgeist.

"Cultural ecology" claimed not to be old-fashioned environmental determinism—climate or resources do not mysteriously generate kinds of cultures. The sweet thing about cultural ecology was its synchronic frame. Practitioners enlisted natural scientists to prepare pictures of local environments, highlighted resources used by humans in the locale, and figured out rationales accounting for the observed societal practices. This looked not so very different from Walter Taylor's conjunctive approach, especially given the common American desert setting for Steward's and for Taylor's fieldwork. Except for Paleo-Indian studies, defined as research into the Pleistocene era, twentieth-century environments were generally assumed to characterize prehistoric habitats and postconquest territories to represent earlier resource areas. This led to the cogent criticism that in *Basin-Plateau Aboriginal Socio-political Groups*, Steward gave lip-service to changes introduced by "the White man" but did not grapple with the fact that the Mormons had colonized the Great Basin nearly ninety years before his fieldwork. All of his informants, and their parents and grandparents, adapted above all to that invasion. So did the indigenous fauna and flora. There was a direct influence from Steward's monograph to archaeology when Jesse Jennings validated his "Desert Culture" drawn from his Danger Cave data, by reference to Steward's picture (Jennings 1994, 173–74; see Ranere 1970 and Thomas 1983 for informed critiques).

Cultural ecology was a form of functionalism. In this it partook of midcentury's dominant mode of sociological explanation. Societies were premised to incorporate mechanisms for maintaining homeostasis (if an organism model was envisioned) or equilibrium (a mechanical model). Baldly stated, stability was the goal and ideal condition of societies. Would one expect any other ideal from men buffeted by the upheavals and dislocations of the 1920s and '30s? Functionalism was highly compatible with positivism because it asked researchers to take observed behavior and posit no more than that surviving societies must have means to fulfill the survival needs of their members. If some observed behavior, let us say Roman Catholic High Mass, seems recondite from that point of view, no problem, man differs from animals in using symbols rather than headbutting to keep everyone in the group. When an anthropologist such as Anthony F. C. Wallace, son of a historian and himself soaked in two hundred years of Iroquois history, tried to account for observed societal changes, he constructed a paradigm that began and ended with posited homeostasis, though the middle "periods" did make up an elegant model (A. Wallace 1956).

American archaeologists had been willing to neglect directly studying culture change but they couldn't ignore it. Even in McKern's system, the differences between phases, aspects, and foci implied an assumption that societies had been changing. In the late 1930s, James A. Ford began seriating collections of sherds until he could draw bell curves of types' rising and diminishing popularity (e.g., Ford 1936, and co-authored works such as Phillips, Ford, and Griffin 1951). Ford's colleague Gordon Willey remarked, "With the continuous depositional record of a site occupation before his eyes, the archeologist could not help being impressed with the evidence for culture dynamics" (Willey 1953, 365). Functionalism looked at social change from the premise that human actions, and the "institutions" constituted from actions, are integrated or linked so that a different action here causes a readjustment there; Nancy Lurie put it, "function is used in a mathematical sense. As one angle of a triangle is changed, at least one other must change to retain the triangular structure" (Lurie 1968, 291). There's not much useful in that for archaeologists, and functionalism's popularity in social anthropology was one factor alienating American archaeologists.

Willey and Phillips, in their magisterial *Method and Theory in American Archaeology* (1958), propose the term "processual interpretation" for what in their trial formulation they had called "functional interpretation." The two Harvard professors explain that their "processual" term, trendy in the 1950s, covers "what is vaguely referred to as the culture-historical process" and that, in turn, "implies an attempt to discover regularities in the relationships given by the methods of culture-historical integration" (Willey and Phillips 1958, 6). Such attempts are proper for American archaeology, they state, because it

> is anthropology or it is nothing ... [and] anthropology is more science than history.... [A]rchaeology ... is compelled to[ward] ... an actual convergence with cultural anthropology and the possibility of an eventual synthesis in a common search for sociocultural causality and law. (Willey and Phillips 1958, 2, 6)

"'Processual interpretation,'" they say, "might conceivably cover *any* explanatory principle that might be invoked" (Willey and Phillips 1958, 5; my italics). Lurking behind these hegemonic statements is the guiding assumption that "for pre-Columbian America there is in effect no such history [as] the record of events in the past" (Willey and Phillips 1958, 1). Locke's dictum is reversed: In the world, *America* is the beginning. Instead of conceptualizing American archaeology as a parallel to the work of metahistorians such as the French *Annales* school constructing the past of commoner Europeans out of material culture, Willey and Phillips chose to blank out the American Indian past. The arrogance of this move is poignant considering that both Gordon Willey and Philip Phillips conducted their fieldwork in regions producing portrait art and tombs of great persons—Peru, Mesoamerica, and the U.S. Southeast. Both scholars knew quite well the art historian Tatiana Proskouriakoff who was about to publish her identifications of historic individuals in Maya narrative art (Proskouriakoff 1960). Instead of urging their colleagues to keep in mind that the artifacts they dug up were made by men and women whose descendants are fellow-citizens, whose nations faced Europeans for centuries across bloodily contested frontiers, Willey and Phillips starkly divorced American archaeology from history. The direct historical approach was receding as radiocarbon chronometry demonstrated greater temporal complexities to American prehistory than had been assumed, and rather than accept a challenge to forge more sophisticated modes of research, Willey and Phillips said, "In sum, it looks as though the present chances are against archaeological phases having much, if any, social reality, but this does not prevent us from ... act[ing] as if they did have" (Willey and Phillips 1958, 50).

Method and Theory in American Archaeology presents a specious American past loosely coordinated into five "historical-developmental" stages:

Lithic, Archaic, Formative, Classic, and Postclassic. These are emphatically not temporal periods or eras (Willey and Phillips 1958, 65). Clarifying the existing confusion between chronological sequences and alleged developmental schemata, Willey and Phillips co-opt the propositions of their competitors Julian Steward and Alex Krieger (1953). To build up the regional sequences they cross-cut with developmental stages, they modified McKern's units into "component" and "phase" (replacing focus), linked spatially by "horizons" (a concept introduced by Max Uhle in 1913 as "horizon style") and temporally by "traditions." The result is a grand synthesis of all the archaeology of the Americas, dominated by the implicit premise of a single trajectory that climaxed in the first millennium A.D. in Mesoamerica and Peru. In the Americas outside Mesoamerica and Peru (i.e, the Incas' Tawantinsuyu empire), no society achieved the quality of art and architecture earning the label "Classic." Tellingly, not one American nation was seen to have *maintained* such quality into the protohistoric epoch. All fell into "militarism and secularism . . . standardization and mass production" (Willey and Phillips 1958, 193) about when the Norse first sighted America.

Neither Willey and Phillips nor Steward escaped the straitjacket of Eurocentric universal history. That imperial conceit vitiated the analytic advances they did make. It remained for Emma Lou Davis, a woman who in middle age moved into a career as an archaeologist, to show the Mono Lake Paiutes' sophisticated exploitation of their territory that recasts Steward's data (excellent as far as it went) and makes it quite credible that one of their relatives in the Walker River Valley, Jack Wilson (Wovoka) thought it reasonable to propose acting as President of the West, complementing President Harrison in the East (Hittman 1990, 153; Davis 1963). Willey and Phillips could not jettison the a priori conviction that "there are but two broad divisions of a fundamental technological and economic nature: hunters-gatherers and agriculturists" (Willey and Phillips 1958, 72). They acknowledge McKern's critique of their trial paper's placement of Northwest Coast societies in the Archaic stage, say they feel uncomfortable discussing these "marginal" regions, but retain their traditional dichotomy (135–37). Lumping Northwest Coast nations with early Holocene archaeological manifestations dramatically underscores that Willey and Phillips' "historical-developmental stages" are neither historical nor developmental (Kehoe 1992, ch. 8 esp. p. 440); they make up a retrospectively conjectural unilinear evolutionary schema.

Gordon Willey adroitly moved back and forth between the domains of science, as exhibited in *Method and Theory in American Archaeology*, and humanities, per papers such as "The Early Great Styles and the Rise of the Pre-Columbian Civilizations" (1962) and "Mesoamerican Civilization and the Idea of Transcendence" (1976). Philip Phillips devoted years to a catalogue raisonné of motifs in shell engravings from the Mississippian site of Spiro (Phillips and Brown 1978). Of course, they laid out the position that "any explanatory principle that might be invoked" will be "processual interpretation." Perhaps the key word was "might." The rich legacies of the Maya and Mississippian kingdoms might not oblige any invocation of explanatory principles.

The two great 1950s syntheses, *Method and Theory in American Archaeology* and *Theory of Culture Change*, each reaffirmed the original Wilsonian paradigm for American archaeology, that (following Locke) America exhibits Prehistoric Man. The utility of archaeological excavations in the Americas, under this paradigm, lies in amplifying our picture of Europe's forebears. Especially the third, final edition of Wilson's *Prehistoric Man* delineated richness and diversity in America's aboriginal past, and both Fifties books grant civilization to the principal historic empires of the New World. Their impact nevertheless was to sterilize their data, expunging the flavor of humanity carried by Wilson's Victorian verbosity. The two syntheses enshrined supposedly objective dessicated summaries, spurning Taylor's plea for fully contextual studies. Willey and Phillips never got to any explanatory principles, only classification. Steward did integrate archaeological and ethnographic data in the "common search for sociocultural causality and law" Willey and Phillips (1958, 7) advocated, but in what sense his expositions are "processual" is not evident.

Down to Epistemology

Under the big guns of the Willey and Phillips and Steward syntheses a battle of considerable significance raged. Albert Spaulding, of the University of Michigan, reviewed James Ford's 1952 "Measurements of Some Prehistoric Design Developments in the Southeastern States." This was a series of histograms of percentage frequencies of ceramic types within excavated arbitrary or visible layers in mounds and middens. From the dark days before radiocarbon chronometry, the histograms were converted into curves and these matched to give population trends for the ceramic types, then translated into relative chronologies. In this way Ford attempted to correlate a number of sites into regional sequences. The procedure has been standard since Flinders Petrie taught it in Egypt, at the end of the nineteenth century, and Kroeber employed it on Zuni sherds in 1916. Spaulding tore into Ford as Taylor had torn into Kidder, insisting "the study reveals . . . serious methodological deficiencies . . . fundamental misapprehensions of scientific method" (Spaulding [1953a] 1972, 85). While he was at it, Spaulding wrote an "exceedingly astringent letter" to Willey and Phillips, telling them that their "vague and sweeping talk" about components "leads to methodological obfuscation" (Willey and Phillips 1958, 15–16).

Ford replied. In *American Antiquity* (1954a), he explained that statistics are meant to describe variation and probability. Spaulding's expectation that statistically derived clusters will represent "real" (i.e., actual) norms or templates held in a particular community perverts the exercise. Then (1954b), Ford felt compelled to discuss the misapprehensions more formally in the *American Anthropologist*. Archaeologists' types are heuristic "working tools," he stated. Researchers may play around with sorting an assemblage to see whether attributes seem to cluster into discernible natural types, *or* they may deliberately select attributes that seem to follow temporal or spatial clines in order to delineate chronology or spatial units: Researchers' goals determine the varying significance of attributes. Kelley and Hanen (1988, 119) support Ford's contention that ceramic types are tools for archaeological interpretation. Their exposition of the distinction between "discovery" and "justification" (40–41) clarifies Spaulding's misunderstanding of Ford's procedures. The word "discovery" occurs four times on the first page of Spaulding's 1953(b) paper in *American Antiquity*. Ford, however, was engaged in justifying[4] his hypotheses (derived from limited stratigraphic occurrences) on regional chronologies and relationships.

Spaulding's faith in cabalistic statistics to uncover actuality stemmed from the essentialism that dominated European philosophical thinking since Plato. It was he who taught that the real world holds discrete unvarying essences (*eide*) imperfectly manifested, so that we see variations rather than the true form. It follows that the natural philosopher (renamed "scientist" in the nineteenth century) will survey the variations in order to perceive their common characteristics, the clue to the truly real *eide*. Spaulding expected one could accomplish this by counting characteristics and correlating them statistically, which makes good sense *if* variations are indeed imperfect realizations of underlying types. The astute biologist Ernst Mayr has only scorn for faith in statistics. The gist of Mayr's denunciation is that to make observations tractable to mathematical handling, the scientist selects those features that *seem* to be most highly significant. The scientist is a cowboy cutting off at the pass real phenomena that don't pass muster. Impersonal statistical manipulations are no better than overtly subjective evaluations of phenomena of the organic world, because the inevitably subjective reification of attributes is prior to their manipulation. Charles Darwin realized that conceptualizing organisms as types had crippled biology; he did not seek to use mathematics and spent his time charting variations visible in actual populations. Thus he was able to see natural selection. Means and tendencies appear in populations due to an inordinate number of circumstances and happenstances, fixed in the moment of our view like a stopped film frame (Mayr 1982, 37–47, 58).

Richard MacNeish says of James Ford, "he could brilliantly discuss theory" (MacNeish 1978, 243). Ford spent the greater part of his professional life working in museums, unlike Spaulding who taught in doctorate-granting university programs. Comparing Ford and Spaulding, Ford performed far more fieldwork and artifact analysis, and published many more monographs based on primary research. Spaulding schooled many more students. A cohort of the students he shared with Leslie White took fire, embracing the transcendentally mechanistic worldview the two men proselytized, a world where the essence of life is harnessing energy—in measurable K-cals—and counting and statistical formulae will reveal true entities. Ford's world was profoundly more complex, mutable, and difficult. It had no cutting edge, no marked frontier, no railway trains in motion, no microwavable instant dinners; it wasn't the American world that hailed an official document titled *Science—The Endless Frontier* (England 1982, 21–23). Ford's indeterminacy, his understanding of the construction of concepts, did not appeal to ambitious younger Americans. Spaulding and White were their white knights.

CHAPTER 7

The New Archaeology

1968 was *the* year that *the* New Archaeology staged its putsch. *Mein Kampf* had been published in *American Antiquity* six years earlier under the title "Archaeology as Anthropology" (Binford 1962). Lewis Binford had come out of the hills of Virginia, and a stint in the U.S. Army occupying Okinawa, to study anthropology at the University of North Carolina. Appreciating the value of temporal as well as ethnographic cross-cultural comparisons, Binford decided to work in archaeology and pursue a doctorate at the University of Michigan. There he admired the crisp logic in Leslie White's and Albert Spaulding's mathematical style of discourse, contrasting it with James B. Griffin's unrelentingly empirical presentations. Griffin's incomparable familiarity with potsherds in the eastern United States permitted him, he averred, to recognize affiliations and discontinuities among assemblages; he taught students by flashing before them photograph after photograph, drawer upon drawer of sherds, those in the Museum of Anthropology and those in dozens of other laboratories to which he chauffered the students. Binford could not duplicate Griffin's feats of association, and the master's scorn was a constant irritant. In contrast, Al Spaulding disdained merely recognizing artifacts: statistically demonstrated relationships within archaeological data were the proper goal of researchers. Binford had found his métier (1972:3–6).

"Archaeology is anthropology or it is nothing," Willey and Phillips said, then they classified by the same seat-of-the-pants familiarity with artifacts that infuriated Lewis Binford. He took up their challenge, sat down at his typewriter and in one night, wrote his manifesto. It would be the platform from which he could slaughter not only Griffin, but the other tweed-jacketed gentlemen of archaeology who wouldn't concede Lew's genius. (All these emotions are recounted in the autobiography he published ten years later at age forty-two [Binford 1972].) Binford exhorted archaeologists to "accept a greater responsibility in the furtherance of the aims of anthropology ... [which are] the solution of problems dealing with cultural evolution or systemic change." Archaeologists who don't contribute to the solution of these problems are "retarding the accomplishment of these aims" (Binford [1962] 1972, 31). Graduate students in his classes at the University of Chicago were "excit[ed] ... enthusiastic;" he names "Stuart Struever, Bill Longacre, Robert Whallon, James Hill, Leslie Freeman, James Brown, for a time Richard Gould, Kent Flannery, and Sally Schanfield" (who became one of his wives) (10).

The new party went on the hustings with a symposium Binford organized for the 1963 Society for American Archaeology meetings. Not many attended, and one who did was so stupid he asked Longacre, at the finish of his paper, to tell them the date of the Carter Ranch material he had spoken about. Next push was a symposium for the 1966 American Anthropological Association; this one was scheduled for a large room, the room was completely filled and the audience "began rising to their feet clapping their hands" for Binford, who "was choked up and wondered if Huxley had ever cried" (Binford 1972, 13)—yes, Lewis Binford felt he was to Leslie White and Albert Spaulding as Thomas Huxley was to Charles Darwin, their bulldog. The symposium papers were published in 1968 as *New Perspectives in Archeology*. That summer, six younger archaeologists including Fred Plog from the University of Chicago and Mark Leone, from Arizona, introduced a formal symposium on theory at the Pecos Conference (R. Woodbury 1993, 304–05). In 1972, Binford could write, "The original 'Mafia" have all now received their degrees and are off teaching at universities all over the country. The 'New Archaeology' is taken seriously and the field is changing" (Binford 1972, 13). A dramatic story, touching in the hero's casting of himself as Huxley when he was more the Darwin of archaeology breaking open a new, scientific paradigm.

Paul Martin, he of *Indians Before Columbus*, was thunderstruck by this powerful mind a few blocks away from the Field Museum. "The Revolution in Archaeology" was, Martin confessed, "a far cry from what I did in earlier stages of my career ... digging up sites ... classifying pottery and tools ... dating places and things" (Martin [1971] 1972, 9). He recalled he had had four goals: environmental reconstruction (with the assistance of natural scientists); exploring poorly known areas to fill in spatial and temporal distribution gaps; relating historic Hopi and Zuni to prehistoric data in their region; and working out a chronology of archaeologically identified traits. At the time, 1961, that Binford launched his putsch in Chicago, Martin had come to visualize his data in terms of "cultural ecology" and to try to relate his eastern Arizona sites to the prehistoric culture patterns "Anasazi" and "Mogollon" (Martin, 12-13).

Oddly, it escaped Martin's memory that in 1950 he and John Rinaldo had made quite a stir with a monograph on Mogollon in which they used George Peter Murdock's 1949 *Social Structure* generalizations to infer social organization and to postulate causes for changes assumed to be evidenced in the sequence of occupations in the Pine Lawn Valley of western New Mexico. Martin explicitly asked, "What principles of culture growth and change could be established?" (Martin [1950] 1972, 52). It is true, Martin had not been "concerned with contemporary problems in behavioral science" (9), but he certainly was making "probabilistic predictions" about Mogollon societies (11). Julian Steward was assuredly doing that, and specifying method, in his 1955 *Theory of Culture Change: The Methodology of Multilinear Evolution*. The "revolution in archaeology" touted by Martin was not a matter of making generalizations, of linking into cultural anthropology, of stating hypotheses and seeking validation for them; all these practices can be seen, cautiously ventured, even in that bland textbook *Indians Before Columbus*.

This article of faith underlay the trumpeted revolution in archaeology through which Paul Martin was born again:

> Human behavior is patterned ... and if the patterning has not been disturbed by erosion, plough, or pot-hunters, it can be recovered by proper techniques of *limited* excavation (sampling). Most of the data relevant to all parts of the extinct sociocultural system are preserved ... a systems approach to culture permits us to view a site at a single point in time. When one system is compared to another, we perceive process at work—that is, change with or without continuity. By process, I mean the analysis of a system at one point in time and at one place, and how it is transformed into a different system in the same area at a later time. (Martin [1971] 1972, 11; my italics).

Heretofore, the immensity of the globe and of time, and the virtual infinity of data from the past, humbled archaeologists. However much digging might be done, we would be barely sampling portions of the human past; however many sherds and blades might be recovered, the imperishable data are a pauperized record of deceased lives. There was consensus that Walter Taylor's conjunctive approach was impractical in its demand for intensive studies of all recoverable data. The crux of Binford's "new paradigm" was his promise that *limited* sampling would be sufficient to discover all we want to know about past societies.

The Knowable Past

How could Lewis Binford warrant archaeology to produce true knowledge of human behavior? On the superficial level, he asserted that systems theory is the key to reconstructing the past. More deeply, he believed Spaulding's statistics drew out significance otherwise inchoate in data, and therefore not previously seen. Deeper yet, he held a picture of science that merged 1920s logical positivism with a Fundamentalist conviction that the Book of Nature lies before us, its truths awaiting those who have been taught how to read it.

You can take the boy out of the hills of Virginia, but you can't take the hills-south thinking out of the boy. Binford admits that his "hills-south, hard-working, coal-mining father's side and ... mother's side which lived in the nostalgic world of the antebellum south" strongly colored his reactions to academia. Consciously, the angry revulsion he felt toward the ostensibly upper-class Robert Braidwood at Chicago drove him to defy the man and denigrate his achievements (Binford 1972, 340). Binford did not reflect upon the intellectual orientation he absorbed in Virginia, as a child and during his undergraduate studies in forestry and wildlife conservation at Virginia Polytechnic Institute in Blacksburg, 1950–52. Leaving VPI for army service, Corporal Binford, assigned to the U.S. occupation of Okinawa, investigated shellmounds below and pithouses above a cliff near the village of Uebaru. According to an interview published in *Pacific Stars and Stripes*, March 16, 1954, "Binford theorizes that the world flood, mentioned in religion and verified by geologists, was responsible for the mass migration to the Ryukyus and for the high location of the [pithouse] holes" (*Pacific Stars and Stripes* 10(74):8). World flood? Five years after Binford left Viriginia Polytech, the school hired Dr. Henry M. Morris to chair its civil engineering department. Morris studied for the Ph.D. in hydraulic engineering (at the University of Minnesota) the better to study the relics of the universal deluge his Bible described. When he took up his appointment at VPI, Morris was working on the book that would earn him fame and power among Fundamentalists, *The Genesis Flood* (1961, with John C. Whitcomb, Jr.). As early as 1946, Morris had published *That You Might Believe* "in which a scientist from a secular university advocated recent special creation and a worldwide flood" (Morris quoted in Numbers 1992, 194). Morris remained at Virginia Polytechnic until 1969, finding many compatible evangelical Christians among the faculty, in the community, and in nearby towns such as Lynchburg where Jerry Falwell became an associate (212). Although Lewis Binford left too soon to meet Dr. Morris, Blacksburg did not challenge the home beliefs brought by the boy from southern Virginia.

Scientific Creationism and American New Archaeology touch more profoundly than merely in the person of a naïve Corporal Lewis R. Binford. Both uphold an obsolete model of science that premises a real world out there awaiting discovery through human reason; a corollary premise is that humans have the capability to comprehend fully this world, if they use proper methods of discovery and interpretation. Scientific Creationists hark back to the concept of a Book of Nature presented by God, alongside the Book of Scripture. Spaulding, Binford, and their disciples left God out of the matter. Scientific Creationists and New Archaeologists are positivists insofar as they assume data exist in a pure state, and it is the task of scientists to recover these uncontaminated and offer unvarnished interpretations hewing closely to the observations. A maxim of Christian Fundamentalists, including Scientific Creationists, says, "When the plain sense makes common sense, we seek no other sense" (Kehoe 1995, 17). New Archaeologists would amend this to, "When statistical results make common sense, we seek no other sense." Neither Scientific Creationists nor New Archaeologists considered their use of a natural language, i.e., English, fraught with culture-bound categorizations. Vienna Circle logical positivists of the 1920s had been deeply concerned with the fuzziness of natural languages, although not the inheritance of particular cultural traditions embedded in a language. The Vienna philosophers tried to substitute symbolic logic and the New Archaeologists took over a liking for lines that look like algebraic equations, without noticing that the philosophers had bowed to their erstwhile comrade Ludwig Wittgenstein's radical deconstruction of that enterprise.

It is easy to show that scientific creationism is not science because it goes outside the domain of science with its proposition that a preternatural Being created the world. It is non-scientific in proposing a priori that no observation or interpretation can be valid if it seems to contradict Scripture,[1] and in accepting unique preternatural events (miracles) in its universe of discourse. Ironically, a conference of philosophers and historians of science to discusss science versus "pseudoscience" was held at Virginia Polytechnic Institute in 1982, sparked by the Arkansas federal court case that year debating whether "creation science" could be taught in public schools as science. There in Blacksburg, the conferees avoided directly confronting the issue of "creation science" (Laudan 1983). The upshot of the meeting was that criteria for good science are notoriously difficult to define unambiguously today and have shifted through the centuries.

A social-science perspective illuminates the unexpected attraction of science to fundamentalist religion evangelicals by examining not only the worldview expressed by American Christian Fundamentalists (Kehoe 1983; 1985; 1995) but the parallel case of Islamic Fundamentalists declaiming:

> that all scientific ideas, concepts and even formulae are to be found in the Quran. Thus [university science students'] role as Islamic scientists is to study the Quran and reveal these scientifc concepts and formulae for the public to know, abide by and learn to apply. (Shamsul 1995, 125–26)

The Malaysian anthropologist Shamsul says that the "Western, rational, positivistic scientific method" learned by bright Malaysian science students was applied, in their religious study groups, to the fundamental question of whose Truth—Western, Islamic, or secular Malaysian— should guide one's life and that of one's nation. Positivism's assurance that certain knowledge can be discovered through rigorous methods sustains hegemonic moves whether fascist, religious fundamentalist, Marxist, or careerist. Paradoxically, as Shamsul exhibits for Malaysia, science provides "positivistic, scientific analytical tools" to confirm "revealed knowledge" structuring a political agenda (Shamsul 1995, 132).

New Archaeology and scientific creationism glimmer alike reflecting the nineteenth-century American version of Scottish Common-sense Realism. This American version is obsessed with the Second Law of Thermo- dynamics as stated in the mid-nineteenth century by the German physicist Rudolf Clausius: "Die Entropie der Welt strebt einem Maximum zu." Foreboding as that sounds, it refers only to the tendency for heat energy to transfer from hot to colder bodies and in the process, lessen energy avail- able for work; entropy is the term for measuring this unavailable thermal energy. Clausius' example is the dissipation of thermal energy from stars into interstellar space. The host of American entrepreneurs inventing and implementing ways of more efficiently transforming mechanical energy into work cared very much about the Second Law of Thermodynamics, especially the potential loss of energy. Hundreds of thousands of machines were contrived to minimize entropy and thus maximize profits. Scientific Creationists stress the alleged incompatibility between the physical "law" that entropy tends to increase (i.e., thermal energy is dissipated) and evo- lutionists' interpretation of increasingly complex organisms: From one- celled organisms to mammals, birds, and the more recent plants, the amount of thermal energy available *increases* (entropy decreases). For a Scientific Creationist, this contradicts a Law written in the Book of Nature and therefore organic evolution is impossible. For the vast majority of Christians, and others, no problem exists because Clausius described a *ten- dency* or regularity, not an immutable condition. For anthropologist Leslie White, Lewis Binford's revered teacher, the Second Law of Thermo- dynamics was at the core of evolutionary Progress: Harnessing energy for work was the theme of evolution, the principle through which organisms and societies became capable of more efficiently and effectively surviving and reproducing. Scientific Creationists say only God can interdict the Second Law of Thermodynamics, Leslie White said evolution overcomes it,[2] both mirror the capitalist culture they imbibed as bourgeois Americans.

Lewis Binford presented a lecture on evolution to faculty and graduate students at the University of Chicago in 1960. "This was my big chance; archaeology's Huxley was on the move," he records. What happened? "There was practically a riot.... I was not allowed to finish my presentation.... [L]ate at night, I decided to fight" (Binford 1972, 9–10). "Archaeology as Anthropology" was the published punch, cunningly framed as a constructive response to Willey and Phillips. The 1960 lecture was finally published nine years later, obscurely in the U.C.L.A. graduate student journal and then in 1972 in Binford's collected works cum autobiography. This manifesto opens with a long quotation from Leslie White:

> The second Law of Thermodynamics tells us that the cosmos as a whole is breaking down structurally and running down dynamically ... but in a tiny sector of the cosmos, namely in living material systems [note the term for "organisms"], the direction of the cosmic process is reversed.... Life becomes a building up process.... All life is a struggle for free energy. Biological evolution is ... a movement toward greater organization, greater differentiation of structure, increased specialization of function, higher levels of integration, and greater degrees of energy concentration. (L. White 1949, 367)

Archaeology's Huxley, like Darwin's, loved Spencerian evolutionism. Thomas Huxley campaigned for "a new professional authority at the call of an imperial nation" (Desmond and Moore 1991, 472). So did Leslie White at the University of Michigan. Spencer, Huxley, White, and Binford were spurred by the conviction that progressive evolution explained the organic world and enjoined them to enlighten everyone else.

Leslie White

Leslie Alvin White was born on the American frontier, Salida, Colorado, in 1900, the son of a railroad civil engineer (cf. Beniger 1986, 213–19). Alvin Lincoln White, the father, kept the three children after he divorced their mother in 1905, and in 1907 brought them to a farm in Kansas, then in 1914 to one in Louisiana—a quintessentially American boyhood for Leslie, except for the separation from his mother. Leslie White, like Henry Adams, served his country in a devastating war. When White entered college in 1919, he, like Adams after the Civil War, thirsted to discover how such horror could have been unleashed (Peace 1993, 126). White studied history, then political science, psychology, and finally sociology and anthropology, receiving his degree in the last discipline in 1927 from the University of Chicago. Although White had attended Columbia, he never took a course from Franz Boas. In New York, he had been introduced to Alexander Goldenweiser's version of anthropology—Boasian in its emphasis on cultural relativism and the non-importance of race, but still retailing the concept of living primitives (Kehoe 1983, 59–61; see Goldenweiser 1937)—and in Chicago had taken coursework from Fay-Cooper Cole and Edward Sapir. Late in 1925, Sapir recommended White to Boas' wealthy colleague Elsie Clews Parsons, who financed his research at Acoma and subsequently at Taos pueblos, and paid for the publication of his several monographs on the pueblos (Zumwalt 1992, 271–73, 279 n. 153, 325 n. 37). Parsons intended to prepare White for his first fieldwork during a meeting she scheduled for June in Chicago, but he left for the field in May, breaking the appointment and going off "rather half-cocked," Parsons remarked (272). His dissertation, "Medicine Societies of the Southwest," was drawn from his 1926 fieldwork at Acoma Pueblo financed by Parsons.

White's first job, obtained with his brand-new Ph.D., was teaching at the University of Buffalo. Though he stayed only three years, it was crucial in that residence near the Tonawanda Seneca prompted White to read Morgan. In 1929, White visited the U.S.S.R.[3] and began reading Marx and Engels, in whose work Morgan received praise. Another writer who had been favorably impressed by Morgan was Daniel DeLeon, founder of the U.S. Socialist Labor Party (Peace 1993, 128) and a Columbia student in the 1880s (Ross 1991, 259). Leslie White, using a pseudonym, published in the Socialist Labor Party's weekly paper between 1931 and 1946 (Peace 1993, 144, n. 8). Reading Marx and DeLeon reinforced White's certitude that "cultural processes grind steadily on . . . [to] the next stage of political evolution" (129, quoting White, New Masses 6:14–16, 1931). Uniformitarian progressive evolutionism seduced White as it had young Henry Adams after the previous Great War.

When White accepted, in 1930, the position at the University of Michigan that became his permanent post, he brought with him two mainstays of his popularity, undergraduate courses on "The Evolution of Culture" and "The Mind of Primitive Man." White was physically unprepossessing but lit up with what Carneiro (1981, 219) calls an intellectual charisma, fueled by unwavering conviction of the value of the ideas he argued. Service, who "knew him well" (1981, 30), characterizes White as "by inclination an essayist-debater and short-tempered polemicist" (30). Equally embattled (Carneiro 1981, 220–21) as "God's Angry Man" (Service 1981, 30) against "the Boas school" (White 1966, 2–3; Barrett 1989, 996) and against the Popery his Protestant ancestors had rejected,

White impressed his Michigan students as "a dragon-slayer" (Binford 1972, 6, quoted by Carneiro 1981, 220–21).

The antagonism between Leslie White and Franz Boas had many facets (Pinsky 1992). America's ideal pathbreaker in the wilderness (Hinsley 1981, 153; Bruce 1987, 69) looked like an unwashed bumpkin before Boas' commanding commitment to the stringently critical methodologies recognized by the profession of scientists (Lesser 1981, 4). In that era when the agrarian republic disappeared under urban industrialization built upon millions of immigrants, Boas personified, to White, the urban immigrant destroying the cherished Jeffersonian America. Boas, the immigrant, was a usurper arrogantly challenging the legitimacy of America's own beneficent leaders. "Racism, sexism, and anti-Semitism still pervaded all the academic professions" in the 1920s when Leslie White completed his doctorate (Ross 1991, 392). Not himself overtly anti-Semitic, White charged that Boas discriminated against "American-born gentiles" (L. White 1966, 16).

Carneiro (1981, 224) says of his Michigan cohort, "We students had the feeling that we were being armed with powerful intellectual tools with which to go out and conquer the world for evolution and culturology . . . it was Michigan against the field. . . . We never doubted for a moment that our views (White's views) . . . would ultimately triumph" (1981, 224). The dragon that Leslie White, "brazen" (Kohl 1987, 27), fought was the historical particularism he associated with Boas. From Marx, White obtained assurance that actual history is epiphenomenal. From Morgan, he obtained not only basic Spencerian progressive evolution but an enthronement of technology as prime mover and also two key elements of American exceptionalism, that the continent was, if not a virgin land, mired in mud huts and bark wigwams when Europeans invaded, and that the liberal society was "sometime in the future" (Ross 1991, xiv). White's narratives of cultural evolution (1949, 1959), abjuring particularism, are ahistoric. In this, as in their rhetoric of control, they are firmly within American social science (Ross 1991, 472). White adorned Morgan's ideological construct with the scientistic "window-dressing" (Mayr 1982, 850–52) Ross (1991, 406) identifies as a feature of twentieth-century American social science.

White's addendum to his predecessors' evolutionism was to specify that by harnessing ever-increasing quantities of energy, humans' technology carved out a realm in nature whose laws would inexorably determine a pattern of development. This principle remarkably conforms to the American ideological dictum "Technology begets power." Writing out his version of evolution, White aped the algebraic-looking mode popularized by the Vienna Circle:

Culture, as a thermodynamic system . . . the control and expenditure of energy by instrumental means in order to serve some need of man. We may, then, think of the culture process ... by the simple formula, ExT$\Rightarrow$P (L. White 1959, 40). ... Culture will vary, therefore, as the variable determinant varies. Thus, in the formula ExTxV$\Rightarrow$P, in which ... V stands for environment, ... P, the total product, or degree of cultural development, will then vary accordingly. (White 1959, 49)

At the turn of the century, Karl Pearson had reiterated the promise that Baconian empiricism, *the* scientific method, would inevitably yield the natural laws dominating the world (Ross 1991, 156–57). "Science allowed them to speak with the voice of universal rationality, while bestowing special authority on its elite class of practitioners" (62). Working in New Mexico among the conquered pueblos, the fieldwork method Leslie White learned from his patron Parsons embodied an attitude of lordship, of the anthropologist as scientist of eminent domain, ferreting out data regardless of the communities' wishes, even at the real risk of informants' lives (Zumwalt 1992, 245, 256, 272). (Boas, in contrast, had during his year of fieldwork in Baffinland painfully learned to respect the Inuit men and women in whose hands his own life rested [Cole 1983].) White's views, and those of so many American archaeologists, constitute an interesting demonstration of the deterministic role White himself attributed to what he called "culture ... as the culture, so the experience; as the experience, so the philosophy"(L. White 1959, 273). It is almost too neat, White's WASP descent and appearance "like a postmaster in a small Midwestern town" (Binford 1972, 7), his sole parent a frontier railroad engineer and Midwest farmer, his philosophy celebrating a central tenet of American Christian Fundamentalism—in the words of the Scientific Creationists' favorite theologian, "God himself had told mankind to have dominion over nature" (Schaeffer 1976, 140).

The New Archaeology, and Geography, and Ecology of the 1960s

Two members of White's Michigan group, Marshall Sahlins and Elman Service, carried the torch by burning Julian Steward. Presented by Sahlins at the 1959 Central States Anthropological Society annual meeting and published in 1960, their essay argued that a *general* evolutionary progress—that is, Spencerian evolution although they did not so identify it—is wholly compatible with the *specific* adaptive histories posited by Steward as multilinear evolution. Where Steward in 1955 struggled to save a remnant of the Spencerian model of progressive complexity in spite of his understanding of the Darwinian principle of natural selection, Sahlins hierarchized the competing concepts, making the Spencerian unilinear trajectory subsume historical instances. Specific evolutionary narratives, merely illustrations of general stages, lost any import.

Binford rejected the Sahlins and Service hierarchy, accusing them of failing to go beyond description:

> If ... we never ask explanatory questions or venture explanatory propositions, our study will never be evolutionary.... Concern with evolution is concern with the operative processes.... The major gulf between White and Steward ... is rooted in fundamental incompatible positions with regard to epistomology [*sic*] and the logic of science. (Binford 1972, 110–11)

Binford references Carl Hempel's 1966 *Philosophy of Natural Science* to guide archaeologists. The Spaulding-Ford debate seemed to be resolved in favor of Ford: "Units are relevant insofar as they can be justified as informative observational referents for measuring the behavior of certain specified variables" (Binford 1972, 113). Inductive and deductive methods are said to be complementary so long as they remain "in the context of theory." Only Leslie White worked in the context of theory, in Binford's opinion; Steward did not, Sahlins and Service did not, one must say Ford did not by Binford's criterion.

How could Binford make such a sweeping indictment? Julian Steward's 1955 opus is titled *Theory of Culture Change*, he used the word "theory" frequently and was quite aware of a distinction between theory and description: "The past eighteen years of reseach will modify the substantive but not the theoretical aspects of the material," he noted in reprinting a 1937 paper (Steward 1955, 151). Ford may not have explicated "theory" in so many words but no one who knew him—and Binford himself could have sought Ford out for discussion—doubted his sophisticated grasp of theory (Willey 1988, 51; MacNeish 1978, 243). No wonder Robert Braidwood advised the University of Chicago against tenuring Binford on the grounds that he was "incompetent" (Binford 1972, 11). Clearly, Lewis Binford was staking out a territory, stalking down Main Street with both guns blazing.

Walter Taylor had trod that Main Street earlier, his guns rat-a-tat-tatting, and it had been "suicidal" (Watson 1995, 685). The crucial difference was that 1948 was a catch-up phase in American archaeology, dozens of men released from armed forces service returned to their positions, everyone in the country trying to resume lives rosy in the nostalgia nursed through the War. An internal, second factor was that in 1948, establishing chronology through stratigraphic sequences and estimates of duration remained a necessary task for archaeologists. Twelve years later, radiocarbon dating had radically reduced the immensity of this task. Far more significant, the United States in 1960 saw itself as stable, its economy stronger than any other nation's, its citizens were completing high school and a large number going on to college (Caplow 1991, 76). The bourgeoisie expanded to include most of the working class (v–vi).[4] Hindsight thirty years later perceived 1960 to be a critical year, climax of postwar solidity and beginning of revolts against the mid-century status quo (ix). Lewis Binford engineered his putsch in this year ripe for revolts and, conversely, intent on preserving that status quo.

The single most influential factor in Lewis Binford's success was the Cold War. The United States was severely jolted by the Soviet Union's launch of Sputnik around the globe in October of 1957. The U.S.S.R. sent a dog into space before the U.S. even got its first tiny satellite into orbit in 1958. Millions of Americans watched the Soviets' Sputniks, bright little lights transgressing our skies. The Government beefed up the National Science Foundation, founded in 1950. Its funding went from eighteen million to one hundred thirty million dollars in the decade after Sputnik; money was made available for archaeology beginning in 1954 (Yellen and Greene 1985, 332). Meanwhile, the Missouri River Basin Survey (most massive of the Inter-Agency Archeological Salvage Programs) that had funded the country's major archaeological projects from 1946 was winding down after 1960. The River Basin Surveys aimed to recover as many data as possible from sites scheduled to be drowned or destroyed—tedious work, much of it repetitive of others' labors (Jennings 1985). The National Science Foundation offered big bucks (averaging one-and-one-half million dollars per year, exclusive of dissertation support) for projects of the investigator's choosing, free of time and bureaucratic supervisors' pressure. Two tracks opened in American archaeology, CRM jobs for people who just wanted to dig and sort sherds and points, and the National Science Foundation for ambitious academics. The primacy of NSF for the ambitious is reflected in a correlation reported by the Foundation's Anthropology Program director: more than four-fifths of American archaeologists cited several times in Willey and Sabloff's *History of American Archaeology* for projects carried 1954–1983 were granted NSF support (Yellen and Greene 1985, 341).

To win a National Science Foundation grant, a researcher needed to frame his proposal as basic science. It had, of course, to be positivist, since the term "basic science" is meaningless outside a positivist worldview. NSF staff expected proposals to be clearly structured, to explicate the contribution of the proposed project to general scientific knowledge, and to demonstrate the investigator's familiarity with state-of-the-art science. Initially, the Foundation restricted its investments to "basic" research in the "objective" sciences, i.e., laboratory research into principles underlying non-human phenomena. President Lyndon Johnson and his Congress in

1968 directed the Foundation to include social sciences if they could meet standards of "objectivity, verifiability, and generality" obtaining in the physical sciences (England 1982, 350; Lomask 199–200). Implicitly, NSF favored projects that might strengthen the United States in the Cold War; this hope selected for projects resembling those that had been significant in World War II, such as the systems theory utilized in the development of computers. One early response to NSF domination was Willey and Phillips' *Method and Theory in American Archaeology*, the two Harvard professors supporting their students' proposals by codifying method and theory. Poor Willey and Phillips! slipping into humanistic discourse with terms like "tradition" and "horizon," they couldn't make the grade.

No such gentlemanly background in the arts handicapped Lewis Binford. His unsuccessful assays at the Michigan Ceramic Repository presided over by Griffin, played out against Spaulding's statistics and White's cutting logic, had honed his sensibility for what he liked to call "mysticism," the propensity to rely on personal experience rather than articulated principles. Recall that Martin, Quimby, and Collier advised readers, "The only way one can learn to classify ... material is by doing it under the supervision of a competent archeologist" (Martin, Quimby, and Collier 1947, 8). National Science looked for mathematical precision such as had built the atomic bomb, not fuzzy impressions of "tradition" or "horizon." Up to 1960, only Leslie White among anthropologists wrote anything like $E x T x V \Rightarrow P$. White talked about systems. He selected a measurable quantity, the harnessing of energy, for the principle of evolutionary development. His book was titled *The Science of Culture*. White's science and Spaulding's statistics could outfit Binford and his students to win National Science Foundation grants.

The power of the National Science Foundation to mold disciplines can be seen in the interesting parallels between archaeology, geography, and ecology. All three disciplines spawned a "New" movement in the 1960s (Bird 1993, 1; McIntosh 1982, 26–28). British geographer David Harvey, who moved to Johns Hopkins in 1970, pushed for the same philosophers of science engaged by Binford: Hempel, Nagel, Carnap, and Braithwaite, for the hypothetico–deductive method of proceeding in science and the deductive–nomological model of explanation (Paterson 1984, 56). Harvey published a major book, *Explanation in Geography*, in 1969 before veering off into Marxist discourse during the 1970s. Independent of Harvey, other British and American geographers called for much greater use of statistics and explicit models, systems theory and the derivation of scientific laws from geography (21). Similarly, ecology had its charismatic leader with "infectious persuasiveness," Robert MacArthur (Mertz and McCauley 1982, 232–33). MacArthur wowed colleagues with mathematical expression and impressed upon them the paramountcy of theory. Hypothetico-deductive method (H-D), quantitative data, and systems theory were here, too, stridently preferred. MacArthur differs from Binford, and Harvey, in having died untimely in 1972. So each discipline appears to have had its genius, each purportedly revolutionizing his field by exposing the inadequacy of all that had gone before and shilling statistics, systems theory, and H-D. Well, what have we but a case illustrating A. L. Kroeber's simultaneous inventions arising from common culture (Kroeber 1952, 7–8)! Simberloff and McIntosh attribute the primacy of the ecosystem in ecological research from the 1960s to U.S. Government support, initially the International Biological Program and then within the National Science Foundation. Ecosystems analysis, in Simberloff's eyes, possesses "the glamor of turning ecology into a space-age science, replete with the terminology of engineering and physics." Under the glamor is a two-thousand-year-old biddy, Plato's essentialism, crooning the lullaby of an ideal, tidy balance in nature. Adam Smith's invisible hand manages ecosystems (Simberloff 1982, 84, 89–90). In line with essentialism, the messiness of actual observation sets is taken to indicate the imperfections, the unfortunate skewings, of the perverse natural world (Mertz and McCauley 1982, 233–34). Bernard Barber's dictum that science is "concerned for analysis, prediction, and control of behavior and values" (1952, 259) is the key to the Government's across-the-board endorsement of research promising to reduce the world to managed systems.

Principles of the New Archaeology

Mark Leone's summary in his 1972 reader, *Contemporary Archaeology*, is generally accepted as a valid statement of the New Archaeology of the 1960s. Leone propounds three principles: (1) systems are self-regulating; (2) evolutionary adaptation is based on the existence of variation, and (3) cultural systems adjust autonomously by selecting from the variability available to them (Leone 1972, 18). Leone allows that evolutionary theory is not new to archaeology, citing V. Gordon Childe, and that Grahame Clark's "cultural ecology" (Leone's term—it was really environmental archaeology) was the other principal forerunner of the New Archaeology. Childe being dead and Clark devoted to his rose garden in England, Leone could adduce them as forebears without jeopardizing his claim he was staking for New Archaeology; nowhere does he mention Julian Steward whose true cultural ecology was the Binford group's real competitor for hearts and minds.

Were it not for the seductive pull of the magic of three for speakers of Indo-European languages, Leone could have subsumed his third postulate under his first. The New Archaeology, drawing upon White and Spaulding, was figured by White's unilinear evolutionism and the use of statistics; whether or not Leone realized it, White's evolutionism, being Spencerian rather than Darwinian, ignores the existence of variation in populations. On another plane, the statistics taught by Spaulding assume as a precondition a bounded universe seldom presented in archaeology. Blalock's *Social Statistics*, the most popular text on statistics used in anthropology in the 1960s, is quite clear on that problem (e.g., Blalock 1960, 110–11; incidentally, Blalock was teaching at the University of Michigan). Binford discussed the theory of sampling at some length without raising the basic problem of how to calculate *unrecovered* data (Binford 1972, 139–42, originally presented at the 1963 Society for American Archaeology meeting). There is also the issue of whether the probability calculus assumed by Spaulding is appropriate for archaeology (Kelley and Hanen 1988, 242–46); an experienced field archaeologist could sense that possibility even from Blalock's caution on nonprobability sampling (Blalock 1960, 410).

Unpacking Leone's presentation, the core is the concept that sets of data should be analyzed as if they constitute systems. To place systems theory coeval with evolution, as Leone did, implies that systems are an inherent property of populations rather than aides-mémoire, models based on a metaphor. Such a mistaken attribution of actuality to metaphor is a prime flaw in positivist science. Binford has identified the source of his, and thereby his disciples', commitment to systems models in White's description of organisms as "living material systems," from which they can approach the world as materialists, a good solid American stance. Parallel to the New Archaeology, ecologists grabbed systems theory from engineering and, as with White, looked at organisms and populations as energy-processing systems (McIntosh 1982, 34–39). Instead of testing whether and in what way components of an assemblage may have interacted as a system, New Archaeologists set components out as a system and asserted that change in one feature affected the rest (Kelley and Hanen 1988, 322–24). Along the same line, the notion of adaptation was bandied about as prime mover, oblivious of its powerful implication of multiplicities of change on scales from minute to geological. Natural selection was indistinguishable from Adam Smith's invisible hand managing human affairs.

It is necessary to go back to Leslie White to comprehend the popularity of the New Archaeology in the 1960s and '70s. White, in turn, is symptomatic of the cultural milieu of America around 1960; the allure of his work comes from its mirroring of social themes. *The Science of Culture* came out in 1949, the year the Soviet Union detonated its first atomic bomb. Physicists renewed their efforts to construct a hydrogen fusion bomb, achieved in 1952. Influential Americans seriously discussed "preventive war," a blitz destruction of Russia. Citizens were torn between patriotic pride at American know-how and horror at the annihilation of Hiroshima and Nagasaki. Leslie White, like Henry Adams, dealt with the demons of destruction by taking refuge in Spencerian evolution flavored with unacknowledged (in White's case, covert) Marxism. The physicists and the government that funded them were, to White, borne on the crest of the wave of Progress, a "culturological" instinct impelling them to create extrasomatic means of adaptation to their environment, selecting for survival those men and nations able to harness the greatest amount of energy. For was not the efficient capturing of ambient energy the very essence of life? The "living material systems" called Edward Teller and the Livermore Lab were the climax of evolution. Teller himself commented, "the atomic adventure ... was great and it was inevitable" (quoted in Easlea 1983, 137).

Leslie White had declared in his manifesto, published in 1943, reprinted after the War and repeated in his 1959 *The Evolution of Culture*, "Culture advances as the proportion of nonhuman energy to human energy increases" (L. White 1959, 47). Culture was, for him, the sum total of all human extrasomatic creations; societies, nations, or epochs are illusory divisions. Technological evolution is the *vera causa* of social evolution (L. White 1959, 19–26), and technological evolution boils down to the harnessing of energy. In 1943 he wrote, "The great wars of the twentieth century derive their chief significance from this fact: they are the means by which an old social order is to be scrapped. . . . The tremendous forces of the Power Age are not to be denied" (L. White [1943] 1996, 251). Just what atomic-age America wanted to hear: in 1947, White was selected to represent all the social sciences in the NBC radio series, "The Scientists Speak," broadcast Sunday afternoons in the intermissions of the New York Philharmonic Society concerts.

The popularity of Leslie White's evolutionism lies in its extraordinary packaging of the principal themes of American ideology. Materialist to the *n*th degree, it celebrates nameless tinkerers' ingenuity, it bestows upon the tinkerers all the laurels, it assures Americans that the energetic must and shall prevail over stodgy, benighted primitives and effete class-bound aristocracies. This is Manifest Destiny brought up to date for a nation overreaching its continental shores, exploding a thousand suns over its rivals. Add to this All-American rhetoric a personal intensity and predilection for titillating polemic, and Leslie White's attraction for students is not to be wondered at.

White's embodiment of American ideology was the perfect standpoint for proposals to the National Science Foundation. His mechanistic materialism (Diamond 1964, 34) fit perfectly the Cold War policy of overwhelming the Communist countries with shows of firepower and consumer goods, capital-intensive operations that filled many a pork barrel. If his conjectural history of mankind could be demonstrated objectively,

America's dominance would be assured. Hence, New Archaeology proposals to uncover human "systems" linking technology, environment, and Cultural Progress sounded sweet to Uncle Sam's ears. "Hard science" had won World War II, hard science was the best bet to win the Cold War, and from White's perspective, archaeology no less than any other of man's extrasomatic appurtenances could be hard science. Binford may not have thought any of this out; his was the variation that was selected for in the environment of 1960.

None of the New Archaeology was really different from standard American social science in the twentieth century. What was new was the inclusion of archaeology among the sciences benefitting from national funding. Heretofore, archaeology was a humanities area related to history, offering when needed a means of salvaging patrimony about to be destroyed by technological Progress. The niche that Binford colonized had always been there, witness both Daniel Wilson's explicitly scientific books and his lead article in the Ninth *Britannica*, and the flurry of papers in the early issues of *American Antiquity*, in the late 1930s. McKern's Taxonomic Method was explicitly scientific. Positioning archaeology in the middle of an aggregate of natural sciences was the heart of Taylor's conjunctive approach, though the goal was humanistic. The "New" element at the end of the 1950s was National Science Foundation big bucks, hanging like ripe fruit over archaeologists watching the River Basin Surveys run dry.

New Archaeology was a bandwagon carrying a standardized package of theory and techniques, as sociologist-of-knowledge Joan Fujimura discusses this model (1992; "bandwagon" and "standardized package" are her terms). Fujimura asked how it happens that researchers using a variety of theories and approaches come to commit themselves to a single standardized theoretical view and methods. A "package" contains protocols, research tasks, and operations procedures readily performed after conventional training; the training imparts the tacit knowledge learned in apprenticeship, a precondition for picking up the package's cookbook models (Fujimura 1992, 179). One element facilitating adoption of a standardized package, that is, climbing on the bandwagon, is ambiguity in theoretical concepts. Ambiguity allows a greater range of phenomena to be inscribed through the package's protocols and procedures. Popular packages construct "nature" in such a way that a variety of topical and local interests fit within the ambiguous concepts and these, in turn, appear to justify procedures that are relatively easy to perform and readily funded (203–05).

"Objectivity, verifiability, and generality" were the catch-words for NSF support. The Foundation's policy directed funds to social-science projects that most closely mimicked physical science (Lomask 1976, 205). Binford's early exposure to the simplistic Baconian science in the Fundamentalist hills of southern Virginia pre-adapted him to meet the

Government's need to favor projects that looked like most Americans' (read, "Congressmen's") picture of true science. The fact that Leslie White had been chosen as *the* social scientist for NBC's radio network clued Binford to the saleability of White's mechanistic materialism. Binford affirmed, in his presentation of his standardized package the "New Archaeology," that "one striking feature of traditional archaeological method ... has been the lack of any rigorous means of testing." He called for a "shift to a consciously deductive philosophy, with the attendant emphasis on the verification of propositions through hypothesis testing" (Binford [1968] 1972, 89–91). Regarding "generality," he stated "we must deal with the full range of determinants which operate within any sociocultural system, extant or extinct" (95). Positivist physical science model?

> Propositions concerning any realm of culture—technology, social organization, psychology, philosophy, etc.—for which arguments of relevance and empirically testable hypotheses can be offered are as sound as the history of hypothesis confirmation.... We can anticipate that progress toward achieving the goals of archaeology will be marked by ... the development of more accurate and less multivariate scales for measurement.... Many kinds of variation will be shown to be the result of the normal functioning of internally differentiated cultural systems; others may document evolutionary changes within cultural systems. Still other kinds of variation may reflect changes in content within an essentially stable cultural system. In our search for explanations of differences and similarities in the archaeological record, our ultimate goal is the formulation of laws of cultural dynamics (Binford [1968] 1972, 95, 98–100).

The year this declaration was published, one of Binford's students announced to the Pecos Conference, "Archeologists must ... formulate their research problems in such a way that they are relevant to current anthropological, sociological, and economic problems" (F. Plog quoted in R. Woodbury 1993, 305).

CHAPTER 8

The Philosophy of the New Archaeology

For the New Archaeology, Carl Hempel was Moses, Lewis Binford his Aaron. On the rock of Hempel's rules for science the discipline would stand. When Leslie White advised Lewis Binford to read philosophy of science, in the late 1950s, he meant, as a matter of course, what Wesley W. Salmon now terms "the old consensus" or "the received view" promulgated by Hempel and Paul Oppenheim in their 1948 paper "Studies in the Logic of Explanation" (W. Salmon 1989, 3, 8). The old consensus, crafted out of the Vienna Circle's logical positivism, is known as logical empiricism because it emphasized to a greater degree the validation of truth claims by observation. The key word here is "degree": The primacy of logic statements remained a principle.

As luck would have it, the old consensus crumbled just when Lewis Binford had absorbed it. Logical empiricism went stale. Philosophy of science in the 1960s sparkled from the rockets' red glare detonated by Thomas Kuhn and Paul Feyerabend, as Karl Popper sputtered and Imre Lakatos rumbled. Over on the edge, Stephen Toulmin was trying to see how it looked from more or less a biological standpoint. Pledging allegiance to Hempel in that decade was betting on the dinosaurs—but let us not forget that extinction of an entire taxon is an extraordinary occurrence (Mayr 1982, 619). Outside the ivory towers and medieval quadrangles, there is still an enormous population never doubting that *the* scientific method consists of collecting facts, putting them into categories, and discovering the universal laws hidden in the categories (Bell 1994, 143–44).

Twentieth-century positivism is a lovely example of a species evolving under natural selection. First, it cut its apron strings from the embarassing late Comte, High Priest of the Goddess Humanity. The knife was Bertrand Russell and Alfred North Whitehead's *Principia Mathematica,* 1910–1913, an extraordinarily meticulous exposition of the logic that can support such empirically derived propositions as $1 + 1 = 2$. Then, the Vienna Circle of the 1920s carried the ball, defining "The Scientific Conception of the World" (Sintonen 1989, 280 n.34). Hitler drove most philosophers of science out of Vienna. Forced to engage more directly with English-speaking philosophers, they realized that their movement was as much a confrontation to ordinary language as to *Geisteswissenschaft.* Their denunciation of metaphysics encompassed discourse that failed to rigorously define every term and the relationships between terms (W. Salmon 1989, 6, 35–36). With *Principia Mathematica* for their model, they held out the promise of exquisite clarification of empirical experience (hence, "logical empiricism"). Hempel and Oppenheim delivered on the promise, invigorating the species. The 1948 paper expounded the deductive-nomological form of explanation, which appeared, from lack of any further discussion in the paper, to constitute the only acceptable form of scientific explanation. Wesley W. Salmon, an American philosopher of the logical empirical school, summarized the critical portions of the Hempel-Oppenheim paper:

> The general conditions of adequacy are . . . logical and empirical. Among the logical conditions we find
>
> > (1) the explanation must be a valid deductive argument,
> >
> > (2) the explanans [premises] must contain at least one general law,
> >
> > (3) the explanans must have empirical content.
>
> The only empirical condition is: (4) the sentences constituting the explanans must be true. (W. Salmon 1989, 12) . . .
>
> Hempel and Oppenheim introduce a formal language in which scientific explanations are supposed to be formulated. It is a standard first order functional calculus without identity, but no open sentences are allowed. All individual variables are quantified, so generality is always expressed by means of quantifiers. Two semantical conditions are imposed on the interpretation of this language: First, the range of the individual variables consists of all physical objects in the universe or of all spatio-temporal locations; this ensures that requirement (2) on lawlike statements—that their scope be unlimited—will be fulfilled, for there is no limit on the range of the variables that are universally (or existentially) quantified. Second, the primitive predicates are all purely qualitative; this feature . . . is . . . a direct reflection of the fourth requirement on lawlike statements (17) . . . [that] implicit reference to particulars is excluded. . . . As Hempel and Oppenheim are fully aware, the prohibition against reference to particulars they impose is extremely stringent. Under that restriction, neither Galileo's law of falling bodies (which

refers explicitly to the earth) nor Kepler's laws of planetary motion (which refer explicitly to our solar system) would qualify as laws or lawlike statements. (14)

Part of the appeal of the Hempel-Oppenheim position must lie in the teasing thought that someone who can meet their strictures surpasses Galileo and Kepler.

Leslie White could be comfortable with the Hempel-Oppenheim rules because he, too, disdained actual particulars. His savage attacks upon Boas were couched in scorn for Boas' commitment to piling up particulars, Boas' position that anthropology could not formulate general laws until the discipline had collected vastly more data. Premising general laws in "universal form, their scope ... unlimited, ... not contain[ing] designations of particular objects, and ... contain[ing] only purely qualitative predicates" (W. Salmon 1989, 13)—Hempel's four properties of lawlike sentences— was exactly what White liked to do. His algebraic aphorisms such as E x T x V $\Rightarrow$ P look like babytalk symbolic logic. For archaeology to fit into Hempelian terms, it would need to be subsumed into general anthropology *as Leslie White conceived it.* This Binford recognized: so, "Archaeology as Anthropology" (1962) is his opening gambit.

Here is where context must be heard, the context that by moving archaeology from its lackadaisical positivism to the Hempel standardized package, Lewis Binford and his students could prepare funding proposals conforming to the expectations of the National Science Foundation (Adams and Adams 1991, 271). Not that the NSF staff explicitly espoused Hempel's package: the overt link lay in physics, the model science for positivists and the science that Hempel consciously held as normative for all that would be called science (M. Salmon 1989, 385). The Hempelian package made archaeological proposals look scientific by forming them in the mold that Hempel drew upon.

Perhaps it would be enough, for National Science Foundation staff, to expect proposals to look like those in the physical sciences simply because the Foundation had grown from a physicist's plan to maintain wartime technology research into peacetime (England 1982, 1). But physical sciences as model science draws upon the deeper current of positivism, a philosophical position that developed with modern Western states and played a role in the secularism strengthening them vis-à-vis their early opponent the Church. Philosopher Joseph Agassi bluntly said, "positivism, inductivism, pure rationality, scientific proof, and all that, are parts of a myth" legitimating the modern state (Agassi 1981, 386). Positivism has the effect of supporting the status quo (Bird 1993, 45, 56–58). Herein lies its utility to government-sponsored research, and its attraction for persons desiring the government's bounty.

Limiting discourse to that which can be subject to replicable observations privileges the tangible and excludes non-measurable conditions such as "ethically good," "damnable," "oppressive," "amiable." Social scientists of course have worked very hard to figure out how to measure betterment and worsening; the point is that translating "feeling good" into a brain-scan lighting up certain neural synapses may fulfill the logical empiricists' criteria of worth but it does not link to any political action. Positivism holds that scientists, qua scientists, are contaminated by political advocacy (Hempel 1969, 175). Putting government money into positivist research protected the political arena, divorcing scientists from policy-makers.

Externally, the consequence for archaeology of embracing Hempelian "pure science" was to capture a goose laying golden eggs. Universities were expanding, normal schools and local colleges upgrading into universities during the 1960s—to meet the social-class revolution triggered by the G.I. Bill—and academia was a sellers' market. With NSF funds, graduate students could mount impressive dissertation projects that, furthermore, were explicitly explained in the common language of science familiar to many hiring officers. The two-step move of announcing archaeology to be anthropology and then anthropology to be tantamount to a hard science discovering universal laws, assured archaeologists of comfortable positions with time and laboratories for research and their own students to carry on the research.

Internally, the scene was staged like Mozart's "Magic Flute," Hempel/Sarastro solemnly leading the princely neophyte through purifying flames. Paul Martin was an overaged Papageno and Patty Jo Watson took up the role of the loyal, obedient Pamina. Binford had the good sense to speak in generalities of the woeful inadequacies of his elders' work, rather than name them and specify their faulty performances as Walter Taylor had; on the other hand, Binford's followers "—the louts—made a point of leaving the room when the old conservatives got up to do their papers. For shame!" (Hawley Ellis quoted in R. Woodbury 1993, 307–08). Established archaeologists continued their projects funded during the 1950s, perhaps leading their own research program as Gordon Willey did with settlement archaeology (focusing on local and regional assemblages, rather than traits, on the premise assemblages reflected prehistoric societies). Annual meetings of the American Anthropological Association and the Society for American Archaeology provided arenas to showcase the New Archaeologists' programmatic declarations and preliminary results. Established archaeologists dismissed these as "term papers," one of them remarking that "Paul's [Martin's] boys are involved in methodology—not research" (quoted in R. Woodbury 1993, 315). Since no one becomes a professional archaeologist because they want to pursue the philosophy of science, very few in the New Archaeologists' audiences felt qualified to critique their version of science.

The direct effect of the New Archaeology assaults was to force practicing archaeologists to at least briefly consider how they would characterize their research strategies. Pressure for this might have occurred without Binford as catalyst as the River Basin Surveys were nearing completion, closing four decades of governmental sponsorship of patrimony salvage (Jennings 1985). A few younger archaeologists publicly challenged the New Archaeology's Hempelian model; one major paper was by Donn Bayard, in *American Antiquity* in 1969.[1] Bayard took a position in New Zealand and dropped out of the debate arena. A Canadian undergraduate on the crew excavating Fort Walsh, a pioneer North West Mounted Police post in southwestern Saskatchewan, became intrigued by the debate and its underlying issues and went on to a doctorate in philosophy of science. Once she completed her dissertation, "Positivism and the New Archaeology" (1982, 1985), Alison Wylie could speak authoritatively, counterbalancing assertions from Binford and his group's spokespersons on philosophy, Patty Jo Watson, her philosopher husband Richard Watson, and their friend Merrilee Salmon, a member of the Hempel school. It should be noted that Wylie's influence comes in part from her championing women in the discipline, exposing the real-world inequities ignored by the ivory-tower scholasticism of Hempel's advocates (Nelson, Nelson, and Wylie 1994).

By the time Wylie reached professional standing, the Hempelians themselves had found their extremely stringent program fatally flawed (W. Salmon 1989). Their friends offered the "consolation" of pragmatist schemata (Sintonen 1989, 253–54). For archaeologists, Wylie's steady succession of papers and the books by Guy Gibbon, a practicing archaeologist who spent a sabbatical studying philosophy of science at the London School of Economics, and Kelley and Hanen—collaboration between an archaeologist and a philosopher of science—unpacked the Hempelian package and set out reasonable alternatives (G. Gibbon 1989; Kelley and Hanen 1988). The years required to prepare these thorough, clearly written studies had the effect of placing them like cairns on a trail no longer much used by runners. The late 1980s saw the pot of gold moved from National Science Foundation to National Endowment for the Humanities (NEH) (Yellen and Greene 1985, 340).

Taking the Binford package as it was presented in the 1960s, the crux of its problem for archaeology lay in one sector of the Hempel-Oppenheim model, the rule that the explanans must include at least one general law. This premise takes one side of the highly controversial question whether general laws can be validly articulated for human behavior. Questions have even been raised, whether general laws can be discovered for the behavior of sentient organisms, let alone humans, or for the apparently highly complex situations of real-world environments. In the late 1950s, the issue was not yet well debated in print. After 1963, Binford was either naïve or unprincipled to ignore Kuhn, Dray, and Simpson. Each of these had published major statements. Kuhn (1962) wrote that "normal science" is an elaborated model that sooner or later will come to be so riddled with anomalies that it will be rejected in favor of a radically different model (a scenario played out with the Hempel model of philosophy of science [W. Salmon 1989]). After Kuhn, conviction that there is one eternally correct model of science can be seen as faith in divine revelation not much different from that of Scientific Creationists. Dray (1957) published a philosophy for historians explicitly disagreeing with Hempel, who as early as 1942 had declared it incumbent upon historians to follow the one true road to knowledge: science. Historians wholeheartedly agreed with Dray that Hempel peddled scientism, not well-founded science (Novick 1988, 397–99). Simpson, doyen of paleontologists, prepared a position paper for the journal *Science* (G. Simpson 1963), following it with a magisterial essay in the *festschrift* for the geneticist Dobzhansky (G. Simpson 1970). He scornfully rejected "hypotheticodeductive explanation," or as he alternatively termed it, "Hempel-explanation," and said it is "quite inacceptable in the practice of historical science" (G. Simpson 1970, 86).

David Hull, a philosopher specializing in the study of biology, asked, "Why do genuine scientific laws continue to elude the sciences of 'man'?" (Hull 1984, 17). His answer shows contempt for "those permanently wedded to the covering-law model of scientific explanation": They fail to realize, he argues:

> [T]hose putative theories and laws limited *necessarily* to a single species [*Homo sapiens*] . . . are at most true descriptive statements, possibly theory-laden, but not themselves laws or theories. They lack the requisite generality and extrapolatability. (Hull 1984, 33, his italics)

This is exactly what Hempel said about the limitations of the conclusions of Galileo and Kepler. Why did not Binford, Watson, and Merrilee Salmon perceive this limitation?

The New Archaeology is an American product. Its proponents have been Americans. Coincident with the New Archaeology, British researchers were excited by the incisive exposition of systems theory published in 1968 by the Cambridge archaeologist David L. Clarke. Clarke, like Binford, bemoaned the absence of explicit theory underpinning archaeological practice and meant to revolutionize that practice, yet his book backgrounds theory in favor of meticulous explication of statistics in archaeology. His readers come to understand the powers and the limitations of statistics. Humble before the complexities of real societies, Clarke emphasized *trials* rather than promising definitive interpretations; his work was summarily dismissed as "not sufficing" by Watson and her junior authors (Watson, LeBlanc, and Redman 1971, xi). Significantly, Clarke ends his preface saying, "To my College, Peterhouse [Cambridge], I owe the academic frame which has enabled me to live in and exploit the atmosphere of opportunities which circulate in a great University" (D. L. Clarke [1968] 1971, xv). The serene walled gardens of Cambridge protect a fortunate few. Such exclusive privilege is repugnant to Americans.

Joseph Henry's aspiration for a democratic science echoes in the "explicitly scientific" slogan of the New Archaeologists. Philosopher of science Steve Fuller (ironically, at Virginia Polytech University) notes:

> [T]he important sense in which the methods of science are "objective" is not that they provide direct access to the truth (for they do not), but that they provide public access to the knowledge production process itself.... For ... the positivists ... science works by methods that are detachable from the particular people using them.... [T]he fixation on method ... paves the way for the *democratization* of scientific authority. (Fuller 1992, 394; his italics)

Henry was very much aware that the Baconian method, *the* scientific method under popular Common-sense Realism in the mid-nineteenth century, opened science to the citizen. American democratic science enables the National Science Foundation to operate, premising both that every citizen should have the right to be a candidate for federal tax funds, and that public scrutiny is appropriate. Science is American as apple pie:

> Sell more SCIENCE.... Who can object to teaching more science? What is controversial about that? ... Speak only of science.... YOU are for science; anyone else who wants to censor scientific data is an old fogey and too doctrinaire to consider. (*Bible-Science Newsletter* quoted in Numbers 1992, 249)

There was enough congruence between Baconian and Hempelian science that the proposals of Binford, Watson, and their group appeared to move archaeology from *National Geographic* exotica to mainstream American business, just one side of quantitative sociology. Laid out, Hempelian science seems the reverse of Baconian science:

BACONIAN SCIENCE	HEMPELIAN (H-D) SCIENCE
Observation	Hypothesis formulation
Classification	Deduction of prediction
Generalization:	Observation:
Generalizations come by induction from the observations.	If prediction confirmed by observation, hypothesis validated.

This apparent difference disappears in practice. No one "observes" without some notion of *why* attention should be paid to these phenomena, and conversely, no one can create a hypothesis without having some prior experience (observation) of phenomena. "Old fogey" archaeologists collected and classified observations lent significance by the unarticulated hypothesis that the phenomena were caused by human communities, a hypothesis that predicted ruined structures, potsherds, lithic blades and flakes, etc. Similarly, the New Archaeologists formulated the hypothesis of human communities, et seq., after absorbing anthropology classes and experiencing fieldwork. To take another instance, although Scientific Creationists say they follow Baconian science, they begin with the hypothesis that Genesis describes actuality, predict natural kinds (species) and geological evidence of floods, and go out and observe what they have predicted, validating the truth of Genesis.

Contrast, or competition, between induction and deduction is a dinosaur concept. Merrilee Salmon (1982, 33–34), Watson, LeBlanc, and Redman (1984, 60), Kelley and Hanen (1988, 33–34, 39), Gibbon (1989, 101–02), and the Adams brothers (1991, 281) all patiently explain that the classic contrast—*in*ducing generalizations *from* observed phenomena versus *de*ducing what phenomena ought to appear *if* a general statement (hypothesis) is true—is about the closest to splitting hairs a practicing scientist can get. Watson and her junior authors tell readers that real archaeologists go back and forth, or in their words "iterate," between a "question" (hypothesis) and observations; the authors do admit that their first edition and their colleagues' writings were not as clear on this praxis as might be (Watson, LeBlanc, and Redman 1984, 60). Given the recherché character of the distinction between induction and deduction, Hempel's hypothetico-deductive method can hardly stand as *the* scientific method. What is left, and it was not negligible, was the *rhetorical* advantage gained by emblazoning it on banners waved before the NSF, academic administrators, and competitors. The narrow, "rigorous," "explicitly scientific approach"—*their own* term—propounded by the New Archaeologists was a strategic maneuver simultaneously dissociating them from less-valued historically oriented archaeologists and affiliating them to the mainstream science that 1960s Americans believed had "made the world safe for democracy," i.e., won the war for our side.

Principles of Historical Science

Paleontology is a historical science. It excavates its data, and studies organisms and populations of organisms. These parallels make it eminently suitable to illuminate archaeological method and theory. Paleontology has attracted several first-rate minds with broad outlooks, most notably George Gaylord Simpson and Stephen Jay Gould. The obvious common ground of paleontology and archaeology recommends paleontological discourse to the attention of archaeologists.

George Gaylord Simpson distilled his decades of practice and reflection into a major statement submitted to honor his colleague Dobzhansky. He first disentangled the principle of actualism from the assumption of uniform rate, two concepts previously conflated in Lyell's foundational presentation of "uniformity." Having rejected any necessity to assume uniform rate (and thereby opening the field for Gould and Eldredge's punctuated equilibria model, published two years later), Simpson declared:

> Actualism ... necessary for successful research into history.... We ... observe present configurations and from them infer configurations that preceded them. The principle of actualism is essential for such inferences. Historical inference depends less on projection into the past of the immanent, construed in a static sense, than on projection of processes, which of course do depend upon immanent characteristics. For the most part, these processes are recognized and characterized as they occur in the present....
>
> In the total study of ... any history, there are three phases:
>
> (1) obtaining and studying the historical data, ...
>
> (2) determination of present processes, ... and
>
> (3) confrontation of (1) and (2) with a view to ordering, filling in, and explaining the history. (Simpson 1970, 81, 84–85)

Both Simpson and his equally eminent, and reflective, colleague in biology, Ernst Mayr insist that the biological sciences are not in the business of formulating universal "laws" (Mayr 1982, 37–43). Their strongly empirical approaches aim to clarify relationships among data rather than address metaphysicians' grand questions. At the same time, they, like Gould, avoid positivists' tendency toward naive reification whether of natural-language categories, scientific taxa, or statistical orderings.

The fundamental difference between anthropology and physics lies in the scale of phenomena studied. Biology fits between these two fields, embracing some phenomena (e.g., viruses, bacteria, fruit flies) closer to the molecules of the physicist and other phenomena (e.g., elephants) closer to that of anthropologists. Biologists grapple with the complexities of scale-dependent analyses (e.g., O'Neill et al. 1986). Edwin Ardener, a British anthropologist, made the point in his 1971 Malinowski Memorial Lecture, "The New Anthropology and Its Critics" (the 1960s made everything "new," it seems). He allowed that positivism might be "powerful ... for the examination of causality in systems on a *non-human* scale" (his italics). Observing humans, the observer is on the same scale as the observed and becomes, as it were, Maxwell's Demon. Like the physicist's fantasy of a being as tiny as the gas molecules around him trying to make sense of Brownian motion, "he cannot command the information to map the system of which he is a part." For this reason, "predictivity fails at the only moment at which it is truly important" (Ardener 1971, 456).

Ardener introduced a semiotics approach drawn from linguistics, the field that Kluckhohn had been recommending to students in his last courses. Already in 1958, Jean-Claude Gardin, a French archaeologist, had drawn Kluckhohn's attention by utilizing semiotics. Gardin has been the leader of a group of archaeologists at France's Centre National de la Recherche Scientifique (C.N.R.S.) who present their work in formal logic. To do so forces them to subject their interpretations to stringent analyses: what is the initial proposition? what are the consequents? the terminal proposition? These are usually laid out as sequences of statements. The virtue of Gardin's approach is that it is praxis, not programmatic; real assemblages of excavated data are being prepared for reports. Empirical in action, the method clarifies labels, premises, and classifications. Gardin published an English version of his text on his method, *Archaeological Constructs,* in 1980 but received little attention from English-speaking archaeologists.

Edwin Ardener's proffered "new anthropology" had no more success. His method drew upon Louis Hjelmslev's paired terms "syntagm" and "paradigm" to clarify the difference between empirical data and their recognition. For Hjelmslev, paradigms are the "necessary premiss" for comprehending observed expression (Hjelmslev [1943] 1961, 39). Syntagms, from the Greek *syntaxis,* meaning "arrangement" or "layout" (as of soldiers on a battlefield), are what is actually observed. (The terms parallel Saussure's distinction between *langue* and *parole.*) Ardener was ahead of his time, social anthropologists' worry over "writing culture" versus "objective" observation needing another decade and a half to fruit. Archaeologists seem to have failed to notice Ardener's Malinowski Lecture—Ian Hodder's students invited Edwin and Shirley Ardener to be discussants at a 1980 Cambridge conference on "Structuralism and Symbolism in Archaeology" but there was no discussion of the syntagm/paradigm concept.[2]

Returning to Simpson's procedure for historical sciences, "obtaining the historical data" and "determination of present processes" will be explicitly scientific only insofar as they are actualistic. That demands utmost care in labeling, lest thoughtlessly applied terms distort recognition of the empirical content. An obvious example is the casual application of the term "projectile point" to pointed stone blades. The "syntagm"—that is, assemblage—in which most stone blades occur is a human occupation area, frequently one containing hearths and food debris. A large percentage of stone blades are asymmetrical near the tip, one side straight and sharp and the opposite side slightly convex and often lightly ground; these are the attributes of small kitchen knife blades. Projectiles with these ill-balanced blades would not fly straight. Given these features, and the syntagmatic relationship of such blades to hearths, food debris, and other evidence of habitation, the label "household knives" encompasses the association of attributes better than does "projectile points." It is inference to the best explanation. Labeling the blades "household knives" fits them into a "paradigm" of family/household/community instead of "hunting party" and predicts a variety of other data consonant with household living.

A suite of properties goes with each of the contrast pair, syntagm and paradigm:

SYNTAGM	PARADIGM
percept	concept
signifier	signified
contiguity	similarity
combination	selection (from a substitution set)
metonymy	metaphor
indexical	iconic
marked	unmarked
Grundbedeutung	*Gesamtbedeutung* (Waugh 1976)

Applying the contrasts to archaeology, it can be seen that most archaeologists take the syntagm first and figure out what it seems similar to, what is signified by it (house? camp? shrine?), in short, what concepts it can reasonably be associated with. Unexpected syntagma demand that paradigms be stretched or even new paradigms postulated. The New Archaeologists' espousal of Hempelian H-D procedure meant they would begin with a paradigm (source of hypothesis) and seek data fitting it. This easily becomes tautological, and tends to leave unexpected syntagma dangling as anomalies (e.g., Service's [1962, 94–107] "anomalous" Shoshone and Eskimo). It certainly is not conducive to expanding our universe of knowledge of human behavior.

Spaulding stimulated one foundational tenet of the New Archaeology that in Binford's handling became another intriguing parallel to scientific creationism. To use the statistics Spaulding advocated at the University of Michigan (Spaulding 1985, 307), an archaeologist needed to define the "universe" of data. Binford addressed the issue in his 1963 Society for American Archaeology session, and published it the next year in the Society's journal, *American Antiquity*. He provided detailed procedures for sampling correctly. In his view, an archaeologist meets only two kinds of sampling universes, the region and the site (Binford 1972, 148). Each is to be defined spatially; once this was done, random sampling techniques could be employed. David Clarke did not agree, calling sampling "exceedingly difficult" for archaeologists (D. L. Clarke [1968] 1971, 550). He worked on, but only illuminated, the problem by studying reports on ethnographic populations such as California Indians, for whom Kroeber and Driver had published Culture Element Surveys (374–88). The root of the difference between Binford and Clarke is Binford's refusal to consider the archaeologically recoverable record of the past inadequate to understand fully the human past. His manifesto:

> The practical limitations on our knowledge of the past are not inherent in the nature of the archaeological record; the limitations lie in our methodological naiveté, in our lack of development for principles determining the relevance of archaeological remains to propositions regarding processes and events of the past. (Binford 1972, 96)

Such a remarkably counterintuitive claim makes sense only if one believes a Book of Nature has been placed before men designed to be able to read it.

Real Science

Every action has an equal and opposite reaction. Logical empiricists tinkered manfully with their rigorous propositions, only to find each delicate adjustment too fragile. The more adamantine their position, the more discomfiting it became to historians of science; gradually, a real discomformity opened. The breakthrough was the publication, in 1979, of Latour and Woolgar's *Laboratory Life*. The book was not proscriptive but ethnographic, chronicling ordinary working scientists' actual days. Bruno Latour, the senior author, had trained in philosophy, then anthropology, with field experience in French Africa. That anthropological background sensitized him to the distinction between "real" and "ideal," the reality of both in social interaction, and a Whorfian appreciation of the subtle paradigms in natural languages. Coupled with Steve Woolgar's unabashed iconoclasm (Woolgar 1988), the ethnography stood science studies on their head.

Even before ethnographic demonstration, thoughtful scientists had come to realize, as the physicist John Ziman put it, "The objectivity of scientific knowledge resides in its being a social construct" (Ziman 1978, 107). Latour and Woolgar's study was followed by Karen Knorr-Cetina's *The Manufacture of Knowledge,* in which ethnography in a chemistry laboratory led to the conclusion:

> Scientific enquiry [is] ... constructive ... in terms of the decision-laden character of knowledge production, [is marked by] indeterminacy and ... contextual contingency—rather than non-local universality—[and by] analogical reasoning which orients the opportunistic logic of research. (Knorr-Cetina 1981, 152; her italics)

Informed by these contemporary ethnographies, Steven Shapin and Simon Schaffer analyzed records of the Royal Society, its aristocratic members and commoner outsiders, to argue that "Matters of fact" are established within "a disciplined space, where experimental, discursive, and social practices were collectively controlled by competent members" (Shapin and Schaffer 1985, 39, 51–72, 78).

Jolting as were these radical accounts of actual science practice, groundwork for their interpretations had been laid by the sociologists Berger and Luckmann in their *The Social Construction of Reality,* and by philosophers Norbert Russell Hanson (1971) and Mary Hesse (1980, esp. ch. 4). Hanson emphasized that an observation is not a fact until someone recognizes it and states it to be one; the key word is *re*-cognize, to perceive that certain sense-impressions match existing mental constructs (Hanson 1971, 9–10). Hesse urged the operational importance of analogy and metaphor, exactly what struck Latour, Woolgar, and Knorr-Cetina. The power of mediating natural language has been well discussed by George Lakoff, whose work builds upon that of Sapir and Whorf in the first half of the century (Lakoff 1987; Lakoff and Johnson 1980).

The sociology of scientific knowledge crystallized in the 1980s. One component was the "interests" group lodged at Edinburgh University's Science Studies Unit, led by Barry Barnes. His associates included Steven Shapin and David Bloor, whose dissertation setting forth a drastically suspicious "Strong Programme" riled up the field. South in England, Harry Collins and Michael Mulkay contributed more ethnographic observations. Ostensibly, sociologists of scientific knowledge searched to identify the class, faction, or individual benefitting from decisions taken in the pursuit of science, i.e., in whose "interest" did this decision fall? Unspoken in most of the work, but emanating from the reports filling their bookshelves, the fear of a nuclear holocaust galvanized sociology of science studies. The image of an Edward Teller tenaciously building a hydrogen bomb hovers around these investigations into *how* research gets funded, *who* gets funded, the rationales for funded projects, and especially, what ideology justifies them? Barnes and Shapin had eased into the work with Edinburgh students examining the organic metaphors dominating nineteenth-century science, then engaged more overtly with issues in technology and society including the damning analysis by Donald MacKenzie, *Statistics in Britain, 1865–1930: The Social Construction of Scientific Knowledge.*

Behind all the social constructionist and "interests" interpretations stands that pregnant moment in the history of knowledge, Heisenberg's statement of the indeterminacy principle. Since 1927, no well-informed scientist could insist that humans can achieve truly objective, exact, and complete descriptions (Kitcher 1989, 449; Novick 1988, 138–40 describes the impact of physicists' indeterminacy upon historians). In the absence of certainty of descriptions, how could universal laws be formulated? Physicists fall back on statistical regularities, for which reason Wesley Salmon devoted much of his life to analyzing the defensibility of this position. Taking Ardener's point about us anthropologists being so many Maxwell's Demons in the Brownian motion of actual ongoing societies, the impossibility of our obtaining numbers of observations comparable to those physicists make on submicroscopic particles underscores the incommensurability between the physical and human sciences. The sociology-of-scientific-knowledge approach has the grace to save the New Archaeologists from the charge of indefensible stupidity, by shifting the question from "Does this method derive from physics, the pure queen of the sciences?" to "What pragmatic interests were served by professing the New Archaeology in the 1960s and '70s?"

Kent Flannery skewered three decades of archaeologist cohorts, sharply characterising the "interests" propelling them. In 1973, he labeled archaeologists like patent medicines; in 1976, he created three interlocutors, the Great Synthesizer (he could only be Gordon Willey), the standard archaeologist who digs "telephone booth"-shaped holes into sites, and the jargon-spouting Graduate Student contemptuous of both old fogies; and in 1981, he delivered an address nostalgically recalling the River Basin Survey guys with the High Plains squint and the trusty Marshalltown thrust through the back of the belt of their khakis. Neither the self-proclaimed philosopher nor the Machiavellian careerist who forced out the oldtimer, gilding his beloved trowel, should call himself an archaeologist, Flannery implied (1982). Flannery's identifications of the "interests" within American archaeology are no less accurate for being clothed in caustic wit.

After all the rhetoric, not much really changed in field archaeology. Sites continued to be recognized by surface features and scatters of artifacts, to be laid out in rectangular grids—1-meter squares instead of 5-foot squares was a sop to international science—and excavated by layers, still often arbitrary levels in much of American archaeology. A new technique was flotation, to recover minute data overlooked in troweling, and an increasing number of laboratory procedures using chemistry, physics apparatus, and computer imaging. None of these could be said to represent new "paradigms," either in Ardener's sense or Kuhn's—particularly not in Kuhn's; they enriched existing paradigms. The only new paradigm appeared in the 1980s, that of explicitly conceptualizing gender roles from archaeological data.

The practice of archaeology did change substantially in America during the 1970s and 1980s. The catalyst was the Moss-Bennett Bill, Public Law 93-291, the Archeological and Historic Preservation Act of 1974. Originally brought by Carl Chapman and Charles R. McGimsey, III, to McGimsey's Senator Fulbright, of Arkansas, in 1969, the legislation was formally introduced to the Congress under the sponsorship of Senator Moss of Idaho and Representative Bennett of Florida. McGimsey and Chapman, assisted by other archaeologists, lobbied each senator and representative and monitored each step of the five-year legislative process until President Nixon signed the bill. In effect, Moss-Bennett supplanted the advisory Committee on the Recovery of Archeological Remains that had overseen the River Basin Surveys; due to oversight in its drafting, it did not supersede the 1966 National Historic Preservation Act, a fault that led to a series of amendments (McGimsey 1985; see Knudson 1985 for details on the legislations). The federal mandate to recognize America's patrimony shifted American archaeology from academic discipline to private enterprise, tremendously increasing the number of jobs while decreasing the academic preparation they required. By the 1990s, a majority of archaeologists were employed, full time or on contract, in Cultural Resource Management (CRM) (Pape 1995; Zimmer, Wilk, and Pyburn 1995, 10).

CRM rationalized American archaeology as no philosopher could. Federal and state agencies wrote regulations and the latter named State Historic Preservation Officers (SHPOs) to supervise adherence. To demonstrate that a contract had been satisfactorily performed, an archaeologist planned and reported a project to fit bureaucratic guidelines, not "deductive-nomological" but inductive-particular. A parcel of real estate, legally titled, is threatened with alteration, and the CRM archaeologist must determine whether evidence for human occupation exists within the legally-defined boundaries, if so what historic significance seems probable to accrue to that parcel of land, and how best to conserve the patrimony, through changes in development plan or salvage of the evidence. Empirical evidence and interpretations must be documented in such a way that they can be verified by government officers and developers' legal advisors. Thus CRM strengthened positivism in archaeology. Many of the procedures dear to the New Archaeologists, such as random sampling of a defined universe, became routinized not on philosophical grounds but because they lend themselves to bureaucratic format; it became secondary whether a defined area did or did not wholly match prehistoric occupation zones, the definition was by legal title.

As hundreds of thousands of citizens discovered they needed to hire an archaeologist before they could proceed with construction, from highways and shopping malls to a new little pier at the lake cottage, government officials realized they had to persuade the public that the expenditure was reasonable. Public outreach, formerly usually limited to disgruntled response to collectors carrying arrowheads who somehow found one's office, suddenly became a mission when Secretary of the Interior Manuel Lujan announced, in March 1990, it must be addressed by each branch of his domain. Lujan directed the federal agencies to exchange information on archaeological sites, to educate the public, and to organize opportunities for the public to participate in archaeology on federal lands (Jameson 1991). A month later, the Society for American Archaeology created a Public Education Committee chaired by a Federal Bureau of Land Management employee. Within a year, an Office of Environmental Education was ready to disburse federal funds for local public education and for university projects and training in public education.

The Public Education Committee worked quickly, putting out the first issue of a substantial quarterly newsletter, *Archaeology and Public Education,* in September 1990. Five years later, seven thousand five hundred copies of each issue were mailed, the majority to schoolteachers. Members of the committee organized workshops, sessions, and poster presentations at the society's annual meetings. Private consulting archaeologists began offering workshops to teachers in the regions where they worked, and a few certified teachers experienced in archaeology found employment developing and presenting programs and curricula. (One of the first was appointed by the Alberta Archaeological Survey in 1985. Other Canadian archaeology education efforts earlier than the U.S. federal mandate include the City of Toronto's archaeologist-educator working with its schoolchildren, and the Saskatchewan Archaeological Society, an organization of avocational archaeologists in the province, which included education outreach among its director's duties.) One immediate effect of the sudden sanctioning of public education was the visibility of women, not only those trained to teach in K–12 schools, but also women archaeologists who had accepted positions few men would take. At the 1991 planning conference of the Formal Education Subcommittee of the SAA's Public Education

Committee, the Committee's burly, bearded chairman bemusedly found himself the lone male professional archaeologist in a roomful of female colleagues.

In 1991, the National Park Service anticipated publishing an anthology of discussion and suggestions to be titled *Digging for the Truth: The Public Interpretation of Archaeological Sites* (Jameson 1991, 4). The same time this expectation was advertised, one hundred forty archaeologists met at David Clarke's college, Peterhouse in Cambridge, to discuss interpretations in archaeology. Clarke himself died in 1976, unexpectedly during surgery, but the conference sought to continue his "radical and reflective thought" (Hodder et al. 1995, 1). The editors of the conference volume concluded that "there is no final and definitive account of the past as it was . . . we can therefore expect a plurality of archaeological interpretations suited to different purposes, needs, desires" (Shanks and Hodder 1995, 5). More than an ocean separated archaeologists. A decade earlier, the young Cambridge archaeologist Ian Hodder bid to unseat Lewis Binford as Main Man in Archaeology. Hodder and his successive sets of graduate students proclaimed processual archaeology and its positivism unreal. Binford and his cohort, once his students, scoffed at the subjectivity exhibited by the Cambridge "postprocessualists." The conflict would seem unresolvable, except that sociologists of scientific knowledge pull off the masks of intellect to let us view the "interests" at stake, endowed professorships, adulation, yes even young women.

Change is trumpeted, not much changes. In the mid-1980s, decreases in National Science Foundation allocations from Congress prompted a decline in grant proposals from archaeologists markedly greater than the actual decreases in available funds (Yellen 1991, 10). "Interpretive strategies," "reflexivity and reflection" became the hot topic in general anthropology. "Interpretive" projects appeared more saleable, to the National Endowment for the Humanities, to Department of the Interior agencies and to local historic enterprises looking for tourists. With the quincentennial of Columbus' voyages, 1992 saw many conferences bemoaning the cruelties of inexorable fate and capitalist Europeans. The year over, the moans petered into pianissimo. Money for archaeology, and jobs, had come to be so largely within CRM that "the regs" (regulations) had far more impact upon American archaeology than any academic ploy. In the 1980s, American archaeology really became a democratic science, populated for the first time by thousands of ordinary Americans earning their bread.

CHAPTER 9

Cahokia:
Hidden in
Plain Sight

Roger G. Kennedy is a historian who was director of the Smithsonian's Museum of American History and then director of the National Park Service. He says that in 1991 as he was exploring a cave in Indiana, he came upon an Indian's sandal and torch more than half a mile from the entrance. The mute evidence that he followed an ancient adventurer stimulated Kennedy to inquire into the prehistory of the Midwest. To his surprise, he learned of monumental cities hidden in plain sight, recorded by Thomas Jefferson's associates and then unremarked. How could a historian become director of the preeminent Museum of American History without being aware of America's medieval and Classical cities?

Kennedy answered that question with a book, *Hidden Cities: The Discovery and Loss of Ancient North American Civilization.* He contrasts the sober readiness of Jefferson, Albert Gallatin, and many other early nineteenth-century politicians and entrepreneurs to take at face value the monumental Indian architecture of the Midwest, with the "obscurantism," as Kennedy calls it, of later Americans. Kennedy writes of the "anxious imperium" wrought by Americans' Manifest Destiny ideology, seeking to purify the nation's soul by rejecting the humanity and accomplishments of its African and American Indian residents (Kennedy 1994, 239). There was good Biblical precedence for this in the Israelites traducing the Canaanites they had invaded, not to mention John Locke's treatises for England's conquests. Stone and MacKenzie, editors of the volume *The*

Excluded Past, make a significant parallel with the neglect of prehistory in British education, arguing that curricula that equate history with literacy lump Europeans' long millennia of prehistory with contemporary nonindustrialized societies and by teaching that the former is hardly worth studying, extend contempt to present-day peoples excluded from power (MacKenzie and Stone 1990, 2–3). David Hume, known for his hardnosed skepticism in philosophy, gave his opinion in 1753,

> There never was a civilized nation of any other complexion than white, nor even any individual eminent either in action or speculation. No ingenious manufactures amongst them, no arts, no sciences. (quoted in Bracken 1984, 62)

That a mind as sharp and questioning as Hume's could hold such blatant prejudice is testimony to the blinkers fastened on by privilege.

American archaeologists were subject to the same indoctrination that let historians perpetuate the myth of America the virgin wilderness. Schools recognize an obligation to prepare children for citizenship, interpreted as patriotic pride in the nation as it exists as well as faith in the principles of democracy (Novick 1988, 71–72). Once compulsory schooling was established in the latter nineteenth century (deemed necessary to produce a citizenry competent to maintain industrial and mercantile capitalism), professional historians lobbied to make their discipline central to American education. In 1892, President Charles W. Eliot of Harvard chaired an eminent Committee of Ten that

> *Resolved.* That history and kindred subjects ought to be a substantial study in the schools in each of at least eight years [few students went beyond grade eight until the 1920s] ... [and] That American history be included in the program ... That English history ... that Greek and Roman history, with their Oriental connections ... That French history be included.... (quoted in Rumpf 1974, 18)

Four years later, the American Historical Association appointed its own Committee of Seven to recommend a curriculum, and in 1905 a Committee of Eight that prescribed study of American Indians only in the first two primary grades. George Washington, Thanksgiving, and Memorial Day were the other portions of history the committee considered proper for beginning grades, i.e., the formal study of history began with indoctrination in American civil religion. Woodrow Wilson, one of the Committee of Ten, advocated teaching "the common thought ... of the uncritical and conservative rather than of the educated classes" (quoted in Novick 1988, 71). Eventually, the National Council for the Social Studies budded off the

National Education Association and constructed a "scope and sequence" guide picturing a child learning in a series of widening circles, from "home and self" in kindergarten, "neighborhood" in Grade 1, "communities" in Grade 2, and so forth. American Indians come in Grade 4 as part of state history and world geography (Kehoe 1990, 205).

After twenty or more years of formal education in which American Indians are studied exceedingly briefly, for part of Grade 4 and then probably once in college under the rubric of Anthropology area courses, it is no wonder that archaeologists and historians tend to follow the national party line that Indians were of little account. The pernicious effects of so many years of indoctrination masked as simple silence—a speaking silence—is most clearly seen by studying research on Cahokia, one of the largest monumental constructions in the world. Roger Kennedy remarks,

> The astonishment of [Henry] Brackenridge ... "When I examined it in 1811, I was astonished that this stupendous monument of antiquity should have been unnoticed by any traveler" ... was justified. But it is even more amazing that after the Cahokia complex was registered in its magnitude by Brackenridge [to Thomas Jefferson in 1813], many Americans were still so trapped in a European point of view that they responded with a yawn.... [Brackenridge wrote,] "The philosophers of Europe, with a narrowness and selfishness of mind, have endeavored to depreciate every thing which relates to ... the antiquity of America." (Kennedy 1994, 185)

Cahokia

Cahokia lies in the floodplain of the confluence of the greatest rivers of North America, the Mississippi, the Missouri, and the Ohio. Like its successor on the opposite bank of the Mississippi, St. Louis, it commanded the intersection of the continent's principal transportation systems. In the center of Cahokia stands the third largest structure in preindustrial North America, the pyramidal Monks Mound, 316 meters N–S, 240 meters E–W, and 30 meters high (Fowler 1989, 90). Only the Great Pyramid at Cholula and Teotihuacán's Pyramid of the Sun are larger; the Egyptian pyramid at Gizeh is smaller than Monks Mound.

Monks Mound dominates an area of 83 hectares, delimited along its eastern side by a bastioned palisade (Fowler 1989, 195). In front of Monks Mound is a constructed plaza 300 meters N–S by 400 meters E–W (198). Seventeen additional mounds border the Grand Plaza and the smaller plazas flanking Monks Mound to the east and west. Within 1 kilometer of the central 83-hectare area are six additional plazas with mounds (202). Five clusters of mounds lacking apparent plazas are within a 5-kilometer radius from Monks Mound although outside the 1-kilometer zone (201–02).

Five more mounds lie regularly spaced along the south bank of Cahokia Creek, north of the central complex (205). Altogether, 104 mounds in the Cahokia section of the floodplain have been mapped (198), and 1992 work revealed the extensive East St. Louis mound group, west of the Cahokia complex and closer to the Mississippi River, was contemporaneous with Cahokia. At least forty more mounds were observed in the present St. Louis area, across the Mississippi, in 1811 (205). In 1811, *monticulos*, to use the Mayanists' term for small raised household buildings' foundations, covered the land between the mound groups (8). These, and many of the mounds, were destroyed before archaeologists could record them.

Mississippian culture appears at Cahokia in the Sponemann phase, dated A.D. 925 in Hall's (1991, 10) calendar-years calibration (the FAI-270 Project publications of major recent American Bottom excavations do not as a rule calibrate radiocarbon dates). Full Mississippian, Lohmann phase, is recognized at A.D. 1075 (10), the climactic Stirling phase at A.D. 1100 (10), decline is noted with the Moorehead phase, A.D. 1200 (10), the marked decline of Sand Prairie a century later (1275:10]), and replacement of Cahokia Mississippian by Oneota at A.D. 1350 (10). Cahokia correlates closely, in time, with the Early Postclassic of Mesoamerica.

Ethnohistorian William Swagerty compared Cahokia to its contemporaries in Europe: assuming a population of forty thousand for Cahokia at AD 1100 (Milner 1986, 227; Fowler 1974b, 20; Fowler 1989, 191–92 demurs, preferring thirty thousand), only Constantinople and Seville were larger, Venice and Milan were comparable, and London, Paris, Cologne, and Novgorod were smaller (Swagerty 1989, table "Select Cities"). Among American cities, somewhat earlier in the Late Classic, Tikal had perhaps eighty thousand people (Schávelzon 1990, 74), Dzibilchaltún perhaps forty-two thousand (Marcus 1983, 197; but see Schávelzon 1990, 71), while in the medieval-era Early Postclassic, Tula in Hidalgo—possibly but not certainly Tollan of the Toltec kings—had around forty thousand (Diehl 1983, 59–60).

Thanks—ironically—to a federal interstate highway expansion along the American Bottom, as the Cahokia floodplain is called, an unprecedentedly thorough archaeological research program investigated a long, narrow section of the district from 1977 through the 1980s. A series of reports on these FAI-270 mitigation projects documents the occupations of the highway corridor and its borrowpits. These reports complement earlier and contemporary investigations of the central Cahokia area. The FAI-270 reports pertain *only* to the highway corridor and associated borrowpits (e.g., Fortier, Maher, and Williams 1991, 453): strictly delimited by non-archaeological criteria, the FAI-270 project is *not* comparable to the settlement study projects at Tikal (Haviland et al. 1968) or Dzibilchaltún (Kurjack 1979). In fact, because highway planners were obligated to avoid heritage destruction if possible, the FAI-270 corridor was designed to *minimize* contact with major archaeological sites, and hit only a small portion of one large Mississippian town (the Lohmann Site) (Jackson and Hanenberger 1990, 8). A century and a half of deep plowing and construction disturbances of the American Bottom floodplain obliterated the *montículos* that would have constituted basic settlement data for comparisons with Maya Lowlands investigations. To compensate, FAI-270 stripped the plow zone, exposing postmolds and wall trenches within the corridor. FAI-270 corridor occupations usually lie on natural levees and sand ridges in the floodplain, and are bordered by the sloughs, oxbow lakes, and wet swales created by the Mississippi's meanders.

Occupations recorded for the American Bottom begin with the Middle Archaic, around 4500 B.C. Ceramics appear about 600 B.C., inaugurating the Early Woodland Marion phase. Middle Woodland begins around 150 B.C., Late Woodland A.D. 300, and Emergent Mississippian at A.D. 750 in FAI-270 chronology, with the Sponemann phase, or A.D. 925 in Hall's (1991, 10) calendar-years calibration (see Braun [1987, 153] on the seventy-five-year forward shift recommended by the 12th International Radiocarbon Conference). Full Mississippian, Lohmann phase, is recognized at (uncalibrated) 1000 (A.D. 1075 [Hall 1991, 10]), the climactic Stirling phase at (uncalibrated) 1050 (A.D. 1100:10]), decline is noted with the Moorehead phase, 1150 (A.D. 1200 :10]) (but see Lincoln 1985), the marked decline of Sand Prairie a century later (A.D. 1275:10]), and replacement of Cahokia Mississippian by Oneota at 1400 (A.D. 1350:10]) (Fortier, Maher, and Williams 1991, xxiv).

To put Cahokia in full context, let us recall that the Late Archaic Labras Lake and Prairie Lake phases in the American Bottom coincided with Poverty Point downriver. Poverty Point, 1500–1300 B.C., comprised a large and complex set of impressive earthworks at the confluence of the Arkansas and Mississippi Rivers (Saunders and Allen 1994, 471). It used stone from the Ohio and Mississippi Valleys, Tennessee, and Oklahoma for its large knives (Motley "points"), although most of the ordinary knives were made of local cherts, and used copper presumably from Lake Superior in sheet and wire form, as well as beads. Pottery was uncommon, but there are a few fiber-tempered sherds from the St. John's River, northeastern Florida, and Middle Stallings Island from adjacent Georgia (Jenkins, Dye, and Walthall 1986, 548). Steatite vessels were somewhat more common, and the source of the steatite was the Georgia-Alabama piedmont (548) A Mexican-style trough metate and loaf-shaped manos, small clay female figurines, much use of small stone blades, and extraordinary skill in fine lapidary work in exotic and semi-precious stones suggested to Clarence Webb and James Ford, the principal excavators at the site, that Poverty Point was a trans-Gulf outpost of Olmec trade (Neuman

1984, 90–112, with references). More recent work in Florida and Louisiana, for example at Hedgepeth Mound A (6 meters high, 50 meters in diameter) in north-central Louisiana, dated several earthen mounds to the Late Archaic, late fourth millennium B.C., establishing a long history of mound building in the Lower Mississippi Valley and Gulf Coastal Plain (Saunders and Allen 1994). Nothing remotely resembling Poverty Point has been recognized in the American Bottom, nevertheless trade to Poverty Point must have passed through the floodplain.

During the Middle Woodland period (Mesoamerica's Protoclassic), the American Bottom seems to have been less important than the lower Illinois River Valley to the north (Griffin 1989, xvii). That is to say, characteristic Hopewell burial mounds have been tested and identified along the Lower Illinois but none are definitely known in the American Bottom. A relatively large Middle Woodland site (McDonough, unexcavated) lies northeast of Cahokia, with two conical, possibly Hopewell, mounds overlooking it from the adjacent bluff to the east, and four smaller Middle Woodland sites lie within a kilometer or two of it (Fortier et al. 1989, 8). FAI-270 crews excavated seven round pole-framed houses associated with Middle Woodland artifacts at one of these sites, named Holding. Its radiocarbon dates cluster around A.D. 100 (485). Five houses seemed to have been built around an open area that the excavators tentatively termed a courtyard and compare to a similar pattern at the contemporary Millville site in southwestern Wisconsin (Fortier et al. 1989, 121–23). The site plans published by Fortier et al. are not particularly convincing on this interpretation, especially given the limitations on excavation imposed by the mitigation plan and some unscheduled destruction (Fortier et al. 1989, 52). Subsistence at Holding appeared to conform to the general Hopewell base of cultivated indigenous grains—maygrass, goosefoot (Chenopodium), knotweed, and little barley—and cultivated sunflower and squash, plus wild grapes, pawpaws, berries, and nuts (450–63), deer, waterfowl, fish, squirrel, raccoon, rabbit, woodchuck, beaver, and mussels (466–82). There were a few kernels, cobs, and cupules of maize (461), the very limited presence of maize characteristic of Middle Woodland (Riley et al. 1994; Riley, Edging, and Rossen 1990, 527).

Although Holding is described as a small village, it contained the finer as well as coarser types of Hopewell ceramics (Griffin 1989, xx), including some resembling Marksville from the Lower Mississippi Valley, clay figurines, Hopewell blades, and artifacts made from typical Hopewell exotic materials: obsidian, mica, schist, copper, galena, and fluorite (Fortier et al. 1989, 7). Modest as the FAI-270 corridor settlement seems, it participated in the civilization we term Hopewell, that raised at Portsmouth, at the mouth of the Scioto in Ohio, twenty miles of embankments in three groups of huge figures (Squier and Davis 1848, 77–82), around Newark raised a set of works covering 4 square miles, with some embankments 30 feet high, raised numerous circles enclosing 50 acres, and at least five precise rectangles each 1080 feet on a side (Squier and Davis 1848, 48–49). Roger Kennedy comments, "The person who does not wonder at this will not wonder at anything" (Kennedy 1994, 51).

Mesoamerica's Classic period was, inversely, the period in the central United States lacking impressive sites or art. It may be significant that the Late Woodland period seems to coincide with a cooler, drier climatic episode that may have adversely affected maygrass and marsh elder crops (Braun 1987, 168–69). Supporting the inference that a climate shift affected the central Middle Woodland is the more consistent development of populations in the Lower Mississippi Valley, e.g., Troyville-Coles Creek (e.g., Neuman 1984, 169–217). One may note that this period, A.D. 450–950, is termed the Dark Ages in temperate Europe, a parallel dissolution of larger polities (Hodges 1982, 139).

Whatever the reason monumental construction and extensive trade in exotic materials fell into abeyance, reversal of the situation correlates with a warmer climate and also with a powerful change in subsistence from the indigenous grains favored by Middle and Late Woodland to a reliance on maize. This is a twelve-rowed Midwestern maize distinct from the historic and Oneota hardy eight-rowed Northern Flint. Riley et al. (1990, 528–29) suggest Midwestern twelve-rowed was introduced from Gulf Coast Mexico, although they admit a possibility that it came from the U.S. Southwest where a similar twelve-rowed race seems somewhat earlier. Mississippian cornfields were laboriously constructed in ridge-and-furrow form (Riley 1987), on the principle of raised beds typical of eastern Mexico (Riley, Edging, and Rossen1990, 529); Cahokian-dominated Middle Mississippian used a stone hoe on these fields, while other societies used scapula hoes (Riley 1987, 298–99). Both the abundance of maize in Mississippian storage pits and isotype analyses of Mississippian skeletons testify to the dominance of maize in the diet during this period. Squash continues in the Mississippian as, contrasted to maize, it had been part of Middle Woodland subsistence. Sunflowers and marsh elder also continued to be raised (Fortier, Maher, and Williams 1991, 412–19). Riley et al. make the interesting observation that although Mexican domesticated beans are common in non-Mississippian Ohio Valley and Eastern Late Prehistoric sites, e.g., Fort Ancient, they have not been recovered from Middle Mississippian sites (1990, 530–31). This difference might indicate Middle Mississippians may have obtained relatively more meat, with less dependence on vegetable proteins.

In the Middle and Upper Mississippi Valley, extensive building of platform mounds correlates with the shift from indigenous grains to intensive maize cultivation. Toltec Mounds, in central Arkansas on the floodplain below the point at which the Arkansas River emerges from the interior highlands, has the earliest dated Mississippian platform mounds (Smith 1990, 5), c. A.D. 800 (Rolingson 1990, 34). Construction of Monks Mound at Cahokia is believed to have begun in the late tenth century (uncalibrated, presumably) (J. E. Kelly 1990, 136), although the Grand Plaza was constructed, with 75 cm. of fill to level this huge area, slightly earlier (Woods and Holley 1989, 230). Fortier et al. claim that "Mississippian emergence ... seem[s] to appear overnight" in the Patrick phase in the FAI-270 investigations (1990, 452). Patrick is radiocarbon dated A.D. 600–750 (uncalibrated), followed by the shorter Sponemann phase radiocarbon dated c. A.D. 750 ± 70 uncalibrated, or calibrated according to the twelfth Radiocarbon Conference Stuiver and Pearson curve, at c. A.D. 800 (Fortier, Maher, and Williams 1991, 444). Patrick includes semisubterranean houses in villages with large courtyards, arrowpoints, hoes, spades, discoidals (chunkey stones), pipes, and tobacco, but no significant amounts of maize appear (452) until the following Sponemann phase (458), when it is found with ceramics that seem to indicate admixture of local American Bottom with Upper Mississippi stylistic traits, leading Fortier et al. to suppose the maize was introduced from the north (461; contrary to Riley, Edging, and Rossen 1990, 528).

Full Mississippian culture is recognized with the remains designated Lohmann, A.D. 1050–1100 (calibrated). For 10 kilometers from the East St. Louis Mound Group near the confluence of Cahokia Creek with the Mississippi River, eastward to Monks Mound, there appears to be continuous occupation (Woods and Holley 1989, 231), although intensity of habitation declines west of Powell Mound (Fairmount City), 2.5 kilometers west of Monks Mound (230–31). Because there are only a few mounds between the west bank of Canteen Creek, at its confluence with Cahokia Creek, and Monks Mound, it has been assumed that there was little occupation of the area eastward from Monks Mound, and relatively little investigation was conducted, "so data on nonmound utilization of the Cahokia site is skewed to the western portions" (Fowler 1989, 215). The FAI-270 corridor, it should be remembered, runs north-south *east* of Cahokia (Fortier, Maher, and Williams 1991, 453). North to south, habitation evidence has been discovered from Kunneman Mound, along Cahokia Creek's north bank, southward 3 kilometers to Rattlesnake Mound; Kunneman and Rattlesnake Mounds are at the ends of a straight line passing along the west side of Monks Mound (with the spectacular burial site Mound 72 on this line) (Fowler 1989, 202).

The Range Site, 11-S-47, 20 kilometers south of central Cahokia, is a 10-hectare occupation zone along the edge of the Prairie Lake meander slough near the Illinois bluffs (Kelly, Ozuk, and Williams 1990). Although only the eastern portion of the occupation zone came within the FAI-270 excavation parameters, the Range Site data represent the most intensively studied habitation areas of the American Bottom. At the Range Site, structures were assigned to Dohack or to Range phases on the basis of ceramic traits present, the radiocarbon dates for Dohack phase clustering around A.D. 950 (uncalibrated) at both Range and two other sites, contrary to estimated assignment at a century earlier (282), and Range dates also around A.D. 950, again fifty to one hundred years later than projected (531).

Dohack phase structures lay on a lower elevation, Range structures on a 5-meter-higher elevation bordering Dohack on the north, both phases on a point bar overlooking what is now a marsh (Kelly, Ozuk, and Williams 1990, 320, 553). FAI-270 analysts postulate a rise in water level forcing Range-period people to build on the highest area of the locality. Dohack structures were oriented northeast-southwest along the point bar, Range structures (on the higher elevation) were oriented northwest-southeast, otherwise the structures of the two phases (or sectors of the site) were quite similar (320). Range phase structures had more material imported from a distance (Madison County shale tempered jars, Mill Creek chert tools, *Anculosa* snail shell beads), and fewer from the adjacent bluff uplands (54). Range phase and Dohack phase ceramic assemblages were distinguished primarily by intuitive weighing (387) of the presence of the ceramic type "stumpware" and more bowls than jars in the Range phase structures.

In a seminar paper ignored by, but not unknown to, FAI-270 archaeologists, Charles Lincoln extrapolated the approach he had taken for dissertation research at Chichén Itzá. Lincoln focused upon the "range" (i.e., standard deviation spread) rather than average of radiocarbon dates to demonstrate that Lohmann, Stirling, and Moorehead phases strongly overlap (seen also in Hall's [1991, 10] chart). Lincoln then proposed that the differences between these phases *premised* to represent chronological change, may instead indicate socioeconomic status differences (Lincoln 1985, 8). This hypothesis is tenable because "the *only* well-documented, continuous stratigraphic sequence for the entire occupation of the Cahokia site area" (Fowler 1989, 39; my italics) is a deep section excavated in 1971 below an east "lobe" (slump) of Monks Mound; this section showed a sequence from Patrick through Sand Prairie phases (106). Lincoln's interpretation, he remarked (1985, 7A), is similar to James Porter's suggestion, in a 1983 FAI-270 petrographic analysis report, that functional rather than chronological significance be inferred from the differences between such FAI-270 sites as Edelhardt and Robinson's Lake.

In both Dohack and Range phases at the Range Site, structures were grouped around open areas termed "community squares," with Dohack "squares" marked by four pits usually around a central post (Kelly, Ozuk, and Williams 1990, 302), and Range "squares" by the same, by a center post without pits, or in one instance by a "screen," a short line of five posts

(385, 535). There were six clusters around "squares" for Dohack (281), and five for Range (534). Excavators discerned one rectilinear structure in each cluster to be larger than the others. Ordinary structures seem to be often paired, sometimes in sets of three (e.g., Kelly, Ozuk, and Williams 1990, 309–10, 372, 378, 381–82, 385).

Artifacts from the Range Site Range phase include a variety of ceramic jars, bowls, and cups (Kelly, Ozuk, and Williams 1990, 390). Stone includes "projectile points" (small knife blades and arrowpoints; no edge-wear examination is reported [456]), larger bifacially flaked knives and ovals (use unknown) (461), hoe blades (461), celts, adzes, a gouge, perforators (464), denticulate scrapers, wedges (469), gravers, two disks of unknown use (471), seven discoidals that may have been chunkey stones, a pipestem (475), hammerstones, anvils, manos, trough metates, and grooved abraders (478). Bone was used for fish gorges, antler tine flakers, awls, flat shuttles and a spatulate tool, a needle, and deer phalanges possibly used in the cup-and-pin game (500-506). *Anculosa* (freshwater snail) shell beads, mussel shell hoes, and a possible shell spoon were recovered (507). Textiles were not reported in spite of the number of "cordmarked" sherds recovered (cf. Drooker 1989, 234; 1992, 177; Voorhies 1989, 196). Dohack phase artifacts from the Range Site are closely similar to those of the Range phase, the principal criterion of difference being ceramic (Kelly, Ozuk, and Williams 1990, 553).

Marked increase in twelve-rowed maize, recovered from three-quarters of the pits in the Dohack and Range phase occupations (Kelly, Ozuk, and Williams 1990, 279, 521) while the Woodland indigenous grains maygrass, knotweed, and goosefoot are *relatively* less frequent, indicates a major shift in subsistence economy in the American Bottom. Fowler (1969) published aerial photos from the Lunsford-Pulcher Mounds site 10 kilometers south of Cahokia and the Texas Site on the Kaskaskia River, at the southern end of the American Bottom, indicating ridge-and-furrow raised planting fields. Mississippian chert hoes and hoe fragments occurred on the surfaces of these areas. Fowler (1969, 370–71) trenched the Texas Site, finding ridges a meter wide separated by swales 2.5–3 meters wide. These measurements fit within the ranges given by Gallagher and Sasso (1987, 145) for (Late) Mississippian ridged fields; these extensive ridged fields required considerable investment of labor. Faunal remains are similar for Dohack and Range phases at the Range Site, reflecting utilization of the broad resources of the American Bottom and bluffs, from fish and waterfowl to small mammals and deer (Kelly, Ozuk, and Williams 1990, 511). Artifacts indicate processing the variety of subsistence resources at the Range Site.

I have given so much detail from the Range Site because so little has been recovered, much less published, from habitation in central Cahokia.

Wall-trench houses dominated in the tracts sampled just west of Monks Mound (Hall 1975, 20, 24–25); they may represent upper-class residences contrasted with pole houses (cf. Lincoln 1985, 35–37). One interesting datum is that the *only* FAI-270-reported (McElrath and Finney 1987, 182, 390) replacement of a post house (Feature 223) by a wall-trench house (Feature 334) was discovered at the George Reeves Site (11-S-650), 3 kilometers south of the Range Site, in the phase termed Lindeman on the basis of ceramics but on other evidence preferably termed Lohmann (390). (Three [uncalibrated] radiocarbon dates for "Lohmann" at George Reeves are A.D. 1000 ±130, A.D. 1005 ±75, and A.D. 1145 ±75 [7], encompassing the Range, George Reeves, Lindeman, Lohmann, and Moorehead phases; as Hall [1991, 9–10; cf. Toom 1992] insists, these uncalibrated dates run in the early 1980s must not be treated as calendar dates.)

Porter described the Mitchell Site (IAS# Ms-30), 10 kilometers north of Cahokia; it and Lunsford-Pulcher equidistant southward are held to mark the boundaries of the Cahokia-dominated American Bottom (Porter 1969, 156). Mitchell had eight mounds, four around a central plaza, and in its day, the twelfth century, it controlled the confluence of the Mississippi and a creek in a meander that probably gave access to Cahokia. The Mississippi narrows at Alton, overhung by the great bluff inscribed with the Underwater Panther ("Piasa"), are as far north of Mitchell as it is of Cahokia (151). Excavations at Mitchell exhibited "houses ... the wall trenches clear in the base clay ... widely distributed (with some apparent plan) ... scattered living units" (143). Though Mitchell seems to have been more important than the Range Site, the similarities between its features and those at the Range Site, coupled with the similarities between Mitchell and the excavated tracts west of Monks Mound in Cahokia, support the hypothesis that the Range Site is representative of commoner habitation in Cahokia, too (Mehrer 1995, 142).

Sites touched by the FAI-270 corridor seemed to vary from farmsteads, through villages such as the Range Site, to communities with buildings apparently serving as local temples, the Lohmann, Sponemann, and BBB Motor Sites. Lohmann, south of central Cahokia, had a single mound and the limited excavation at the site revealed a Mississippian-period structure both larger and oriented along its long axis parallel to, rather than at an angle to, the ridge of the site as are the smaller, apparently residential, buildings. A cache of at least fifty formed but unfinished diabase celts had been discovered by commercial surveyors near the Lohmann mound years ago, and the archaeologists note that caches of igneous-rock celts seem to be associated with mound centers (Cahokia, East St. Louis, Lohmann) in the American Bottom (Esarey and Pauketat 1992, 157–58). Sponemann and BBB Motor did not have mounds, so far as is evident, but excavation at Sponemann showed a cluster of eight buildings on the east edge of the site ridge, with one building, 4 by 4 meters, containing fragments of three intentionally broken fire-clay figurines of women with plants and/or serpents. Other houses in the cluster contained red cedar posts and hearth wood, a human effigy pot, one with little bear effigies on its handles, and a small white-slipped pot that seems to have been modeled to represent a conch shell, and tobacco seeds. The unusual amount of red cedar, a symbol of life in many historic Eastern North American societies, and the clearly symbolically significant tobacco and effigies suggest this cluster of buildings at Sponemann was the scene of ceremonies. A second excavated cluster of four buildings at the site is interpreted as residential (Jackson, Fortier, and Williams 1992). BBB Motor Site Stirling-phase excavations revealed two sets of paired buildings with burials (eight with one set, eleven with the other) to the west or southwest of the buildings (Emerson and Jackson 1984). Broken fire-clay female figurines, one with serpents and plants, lay in these buildings as at Sponemann. One figurine at BBB Motor (Keller figurine) and one at Sponemann (Willoughby figurine) had a woven box or, in the Keller case, possibly a free-hanging-warp loom. Both the Sponemann and BBB Motor Sites are on the northeastern edge of Cahokia, and are less than a mile apart, i.e., they could have been portions of one town.

Contrasting dramatically with the dispersed farmsteads, clusters of houses with storage pits and outbuildings, and simple temples revealed through the FAI-270 mitigation work, is central Cahokia with its truly enormous Monks Mound and Grand Plaza, and serried ranks of satellite mounds and plazas. Huge cypress posts marked points in the geometry of the central city, and may have served, perhaps with sightlines along mounds, to observe solstice points on the horizon. One of the small mounds, Mound 72, lies due south of one long side of Monks Mound and its long axis is oriented northwest-southeast between summer solstice sunset and winter solstice sunrise (Fowler 1989, 1991). Mound 72 turned out to be a tomb; how many other mounds at Cahokia contained burials, no one will ever know, given the number destroyed, the size of many that remain, and a commendable reluctance to disturb them.

Melvin Fowler's 1967–1971 excavations in Mound 72 unveiled another spectacular display of raw power. The mound was a 2-meter high oval 43 by 22 meters, oriented 30° north of east, 850 meters directly south of the southwest corner of Monks Mound and contemporary with it. The excavator distinguished six phases of construction of the mound; these may well be serial acts in a single event, since no sets of burials intrude upon another, although Fowler (1974a, 22) assumed a few years separated each event from the others. Taking Mound 72 as a single performance in a theater of power, it included the placement of a large post marking the north-south line from Monks Mound; a rectangular building free of habitation debris, dismantled and covered with earth in which twenty-one bodies, some inhumations and some bundle burials, were interred; burial pits prepared east and south of the structure and filled with at least sixty-five bodies; an offering pit with pottery, "projectile points" (arrowheads or knives, is not clear), and shell beads prepared just west of the south burial pit; another post directly in a line 21 meters southeast from it; halfway between the first set of burial pits and the southeast post was a rectangular pit with the bodies of fifty-three young women, and on a low platform on the line, just northwest of the maidens, were four men lacking heads and hands. The two posts were removed and a low platform constructed in the southeast sector, on which was laid a mantle covered with twenty thousand shell beads forming the shape of a falcon or hawk. On this glittering mantle was placed a man; under the mantle was a second man. Bundle burials and partly disarticulated bodies were laid near the principal, plus six complete bodies accompanied with fifteen chunkey stones, a copper-sheathed staff, sheet copper and sheet mica, and sets of fine arrows, about eight hundred altogether, with points chipped from stone imported from Wisconsin, Oklahoma, Tennessee, and southern Illinois. (O'Brien [n.d., 8] suggests these sets of imported arrows represent tribute from the four corners of the Ramey empire.) A pair of parallel long-rectangular burial pits was prepared along the middle of the southwest side of Mound 72 and in one, fifteen individuals were laid, nine of them on litters; two more individuals were in an oval pit next to this one, and thirty-nine bodies thrown into the second long pit. After all these, and a few more, bodies—a total of two hundred sixty-one (Rose [1973] n.d., 20)—were in their places, the final cap was spread to form the permanent mound (Fowler 1974a, 20–22; 1989, 148–54). The magnitude of human sacrifices in Mound 72 is hardly matched even in Mesoamerican and South American pre-Columbian cities.

Cahokia, in its immensity, is a beautiful example of the city as theater of power. It fits very well the model of traditional capital cities outlined by Amos Rapoport. He emphasizes that *relative* density of population would be

impressive, although the actual sizes and populations were small by present-day standards.... Moreover, their populations were heterogeneous.... Size was reinforced (i.e., redundancy increased) through the use of city walls, towers, gates and moats [a massive log palisade was built near Monks Mound in the Stirling phase], the latent function of which was at least as important as their defense function.... Capitals achieve strong control through *redundancy*, the use of multiple means of control. Traditionally, a capital is a center of roads, communication, education and literacy; of excellence, so that anyone aspiring to success had to be there; of culture—art, crafts, lifestyle, speech, fashion, etc., hence a center of style from which diffuse intellectual, religious, social and aesthetic standards; of rituals and cere-

monials, specially those significant for the entire society, legitmating and
fortifying the ruler and reinforcing cohesion; a center of justice and law; of
continuity with the past, through the site, name, myths of origin, tombs,
etc.... A capital is thus a center of symbolism, of culture-specific expression of grandeur, elaboration, sacredness, resources invested. (Rapoport
1993, 33)

Rapoport, like Arensberg (1968), refers to "two morphologies of capitals
... : dispersed—where the center stands alone (cf. some Maya, Monte
Albán) and the more common compact variety;" in either type, "the built
environment [has] its role as a communicator of high-level meanings....
In preliterate societies, or where literacy was limited, the built environment was the only medium for encoding group memory over time"
(Rapoport 1993, 39). The capital city is the axis mundi where the cosmic
order flows into territorial order. The capital is a "theatre of power"
(Rapoport 1993 [quoting Cohen 1987]).

The theater of power we call Cahokia was plausibly the capital of a
state. First Guy Gibbon (1974) and, more recently, Patricia O'Brien (1989;
1991) have argued that Cahokia must have been the capital of what they
call "the Ramey state" (Ramey was a Cahokia landowner whose name is
given to a mound and to the fine ceramics found at Cahokia and Midwestern towns contemporary with it). Gibbon

proposed ... that the American Bottoms [*sic*] ... was a region of secondary
urban generation displaying interrelationships beween environmental,
demographic, and sociocultural variables sufficiently similar to Teotihuacan
... to consider it an example of the same cross-cultural type ... induced
indirectly from Mesoamerica.... [D]uring the Stirling phase ... the extension of Cahokia's influence outside the core zone became a major factor in
promoting change in other Midwest groups ... the extension of the Ramey
symbiotic-extractive exchange system into a variety of ecological niches outside the core zone ... traced by the distribution of a complex of traits, generally labeled Mississippian, that includes shell-tempered Ramey Incised
and Powell Plain pottery, flat-topped pyramidal mounds, ear plugs [ear-
spools], discoidals, and elements of the "Southeastern Ceremonial Complex" (e.g., ... forked-eye motifs, Long-nosed God ear pendants of shell).
(Gibbon 1974, 133–34)

O'Brien (1994) adduces falcon/thunderbird and pecked cross-in-circle
petroglyphs to delimit the Ramey heartland as a large oval roughly 350 by
150 kms., an area of 5.2 million hectares with prime agricultural land, deer
parks, fish-rich streams and ponds, timberlands, valuable chert, sandstone,
galena, hematite, and salt sources, and of course the hub of the conti-

nental river system. Mapping the occurrence of platform mounds, O'Brien discovered a strong correlation between Mississippian mound sites and locations controlling access to hinterlands. This had not been so clear until her archival research revealed many mounds leveled a century ago for railroad bed construction. The territorial dominance implied by these Mississippian town locations (inferred also by Lathrap and Porter [1985, 70]) leads O'Brien to postulate both trade and tribute in the Ramey political economy. She notes that at 52,000 sq. kms., the Ramey state was significantly larger than Lagash in Sumer or fifteenth-century Florence, and similar to the largest Hausa state. Robert Hall also (e.g., 1991) has consistently emphasized the trade expanse centered in Cahokia, although he has demurred from using the name "Ramey state."

Gibbon, Patricia O'Brien, and Hall would seem to be following a straightforward positivist inductivism inferring a political state from unambiguous field data of multiply redundant monumental architecture, sacrifice of over two hundred persons including dozens of young women in a single entombment, and quantities of fine ceramics and artifacts from a wide range of relatively rare raw materials, found both in Cahokia and in towns along its principal transportation routes. To turn the procedure around to make it hypothetico-deductive, should an archaeologist posit a state in the Late Prehistoric Midwest, he or she would predict such data to confirm an inference of the presence of a state. Nevertheless, the "Core System" (Kelley and Hanen 1988, 111, 118–19) of archaeologists working in the American Bottom—Melvin Fowler and the FAI-270 members—follow the University of Michigan school's lead and label Cahokia a "chiefdom." Nearly all contemporary studies of other Mississippian societies similarly label them "chiefdoms" (The United States thus is seen to be the first and the only *state* to exist on the American continent north of Aztec Mexico.

Mainstream American archaeologists' inability to perceive, to comprehend, the sheer magnitude of Cahokia, is a marvelous demonstration of the power of ideology. Nineteenth-century archaeologists realized that the massive mounds of the Midwest, most of them larger than any prehistoric mounds in Europe, could not be accommodated in a scenario of virgin wilderness inhabited by Men-Brutes not providing for To-Morrow. The popular resolution was to assume the Mound-Builders had been invaded and conquered by savages, the ancestors of historic Indians. At the height of Manifest Destiny in the 1890s, with Indians reduced to wards of the United States, these peoples could be looked upon benignly, a vanishing race soon to be merged in the mists with the Mound-builders who may as well be their ancestors. For half a century, archaeologists and the public relaxed. Conquered nations were primitives and their descendants our contemporary ancestors (Service 1962, 8). Relatively little archaeology was conducted at Cahokia and its preservation neglected. Even after World

War II, the State of Illinois widened its highway straight across the Grand Plaza at the foot of Monks Mound, and a subdivision of ranch-style homes with backyard pools was constructed along the east side of the Plaza. Cahokia was hidden in plain sight.

That last surge of positivism and its Siamese twin unilinear evolutionism in the 1950s aftermath of another Great War spawned a theoretical construct that perpetuated the de facto colonization belying the touted independence of Third World countries. Primitive societies could be bands, tribes, or chiefdoms; their status as primitives indicates they did not evolve into states. This gospel truth was encoded by University of Michigan professor Elman Service in his 1962 *Primitive Social Organization*, still the standard reference among American archaeologists. Echoing Major Powell seventy years earlier, Service declared:

> the most profound division that can be discerned in the total evolution of culture, particularly in terms of the social criteria used here, is that between the primitive, or *societas*, kinds of cultures (including chiefdoms) and civilization. (Service 1962, 174)

Service noted that "The stages of Bands, Tribes, and Chiefdoms were characterized with what may have seemed like an air of confidence," asking rhetorically whether he might, similarly confidently, "bridge the gap theoretically between our comprehension of primitive culture [note the singular] and the beginnings of civilization." His answer is, "No."

The term "chiefdom" was adopted by Service from a 1957 paper by Kalervo Oberg, an ethnographer experienced in lowland South American Indian societies. Oberg made no claim that the term was new, indeed it was already given in even the Concise Oxford Dictionary; Oberg's contribution was to argue that societies are "social organism[s] . . . somewhat comparable to a biological organism which is studied and classified by biologists." He asserted, "social organisms of this kind do exist and . . . they can be classified in terms of their structures" (Oberg 1955, 472). So strongly positivist an approach must appeal to persons convinced that nations can be dichotomized into the unbridgeable contrast primitive/civilized. Oberg also accepted a unilinear evolutionary model, singling out "population density and . . . a food surplus above subsistence needs" as the factors creating increasingly more complex social organisms (473). The northern lowland Colombian Calamari, Quimbaya, Tolú, Cenú, and Mompox and the Taino of Hispaniola are Oberg's examples of "politically organized chiefdoms," which differ from the next more complex Feudal Type States in lacking "the palace and the temple" (484–85). (This explicit criterion should exclude Mississippian mound towns from the category "chiefdom.") Archaeological applicability of the term "chiefdom" was tested for northwestern lowland South America, reasonably close to Oberg's region, by Warren DeBoer, who backcrossed, as it were, to Welch's 1991 monograph on Mississippian Moundville and concluded in regard to the Ecuadorian site of La Tolita:

> In terms of all the stigmata of chiefdoms—chiefly elites, settlement or administrative hierarchies, sumptuary goods restricted to the elite, craft specialization and so on, the preliminary evidence is either uncertain or negative. (DeBoer 1996, 207)

If Oberg's classificatory term isn't helpful to an archaeologist working in the Intermediate Area (between Meso- and South America) where Oberg considered it historically justified, surely it should not be assumed appropriate for Mississippian societies. DeBoer ruminates, "How do we imagine a past that may have been different?" (DeBoer 1996, 207)

Service's definition of "chiefdom" is based on Karl Polanyi's marking the political economic practice of redistribution from central collections (the reference Service cites is his student Marshall Sahlins, rather than Polanyi directly). Service offers "chiefdom" for the heretofore undistinguished cultural-evolutionary stage that is neither still *societas,* i.e., "familistic, egalitarian . . . without private property . . . or a market," nor yet *civitas.* Chiefdoms are non-egalitarian and have central (chiefly) "direction" but still no private property or markets; ranking but no socioeconomic classes. Redistribution of resources through the chief is (following Polanyi),[1] although "unfamiliar and unnamed as a distinctive form of economic organization," common enough in the Americas, Asia, Africa and Oceania to merit categorizing as a stage in cultural evolution, according to Service (1962, 172–73, 152–54). Notice that no examples of chiefdoms are given from Europe.

A strange thing happened on the way to the forum. Morton Fried, editor of the series in which *Primitive Social Organization* was published, persuaded Elman Service that "tribes" are not ancient indigenous social formations but arise as resistance against encroaching empires, or are governmental units designated by conquerors. Service accepted Fried's argument, then decided to drop "band" from the evolutionary scheme, on the grounds that ethnographically known bands are broken remnants of preconquest societies. That line of thought led to dropping "chiefdom," the ethnographic examples being too involved with colonial empires to represent pristine types. In place of "band," "tribe," "chiefdom," and eventually "state," Service proposed the Egalitarian Society, the Hierarchical Society, and Archaic Civilization or Classical Empire (Service 1971, 157). This recantation of the 1962 formulation is ignored by mainstream American archaeologists.

"We now know that most early historic period societies in the Southeast were of the sort identified as chiefdoms by Elman Service.... Within the past few years, more and more anthropologists and archaeologists have come to realize that both prehistoric and historic period societies in the Southeast were operating as chiefdoms ... i.e., Mississippian societies" (DePratter 1991, 8, 14). In other words, Service's obsolete *Primitive Social Organization* furnishes the label and paradigm under which archaeological and ethnohistorical data will be subsumed, an example being DePratter's dissertation collating historical observations, principally from Swanton's compendia, into headings taken from Service's description of "the chiefdom." One obstacle stands in the way of routine emplacement of data in the model: sixteenth- and early seventeenth-century documents describing the "kingdoms"—not "chiefdoms," although that word was available—of the Southeast.

Hernando De Soto invaded the Southeast in 1539, a generation after Spanish conquests of the Caribbean islands and Aztec Mexico. The Southeast may already have felt repercussions of these wars, economic disruptions, and the smallpox epidemics of 1518 in Hispaniola and 1520 in Mexico, and measles in 1530 (McNeill 1976, 207–09). De Soto's chroniclers apparently referred to the heads of the societies they visited as *caciques* (Smith and Hally 1992, 100); Hassig (1985, 34) says the [Arawak] word *cacique* "was used by the Spaniards to refer to the native rulers ... [Nahuatl] *tlatohqueh* (sg, *tlahtohqui*, also *tlahtoani*)." John Smith, in Virginia, used the English word "king" when referring to the werowances of that country (Lemay 1991, 122), and was keenly aware of the difference in status between himself, an English commoner, and the Powhatan's daughter Pocahontas, charging that his enemies falsely accused him of courting the maiden that "hee would have made himselfe a king, by marrying Pocahontas" (quoted in Lemay 1991, 126). De Soto's officers and John Smith, citizens of late-Renaissance European kingdoms, easily recognized the American equivalents of the kings they knew. We today think of seventeenth-century rulers, Louis XIV or Charles of England, as typifying "king," forgetting that in the medieval period, European kings were the comparatively petty lords of Shakespeare's historical dramas, jockeying for power against brothers and cousins. Just as medieval American cities ought to be compared with medieval European cities, not late-nineteenth-century Paris or London, so medieval American rulers and their domains ought to be compared with medieval European rulers: the word "king" seemed appropriate to John Smith, and we can respect his judgment of equivalence (Vincent 1990, 130).

Refusing to use European or Mesoamerican terminology—"kings" or *caciques*—for Mississippian leaders severs American Indians from world history. This has been Anglo colonial policy from Locke to the 1960s

(Feuchtwang 1973, 79–86); in 1937, the Royal Anthropological Institute declared the "subject races" of America, Africa, the Pacific, and India to be "tribal peoples" "where [administrators] did not find personnel of a class which they could readily associate with themselves in the formation of the legal administrative institutions of the country" (Lord Hailey, 1944, quoted by Feuchtwang 1973, 88). Feuchtwang, following Peter Worsley, saw "a surreptitious evolutionism, unworked and unquestioned except as a matter of fact, has continued" in anthropology (1973, 77). Supported by imperial governments, anthropology was charged to discover "how systems of stability and internal cohesion worked," and found it could do so only when constricting its models to "small scale tribal divisions of [actual historical] systems" (90).

Willey and Sabloff affirm that "evolutionary thinking had been rejuvenated" in the late 1950s United States, and as a result, "American archaeology stands poised for a great stride forward . . . : Inquiries into the whys and wherefores of the development of cultural complexity" (Willey and Sabloff 1993, 313–14) must be "developmentally inclined—that is, evolutionary." Explanations featuring intersocietal contacts "—that is, culture-historical" are "primarily diffusionistic" and "Such theories did not explain culture change" (207–08), though the authors do not inform us why, for example, the invasion of North America by Europeans does not explain the subsequent culture changes observed among indigenous nations. Gordon Willey and Jeremy Sabloff being two past presidents of the Society for American Archaeology, their pronouncement in each edition of their textbook history of the discipline carries weight.

According to the dominant group of American archaeologists, "Mississippian" is "an adaptive system" of intensive maize agriculture in major river floodplains (Smith 1978, 486; Griffin 1967, 189). An adherent of this school of archaeology insists that Mississippian societies are

> of anthropological interest *primarily* as an example of the transformation of acephalous tribal organization to hierarchical social organization. Most, and by some definitions all, Mississippian societies were . . . simple chiefdoms. (Welch 1990, 197; my italics) . . . The emergence of Mississippian culture . . . involved change in two distinct cultural subsystems, i.e., subsistence and social integration. . . . The subsistence change . . . was a rational response to subsistence stress. . . . [S]imple chiefdoms develop by two constrasting mechanisms . . . by an extant sanctified role acquiring political and economic functions. Alternately, a central political and economic role may acquire sanctified authority. (218–19)

Another contributor to the same symposium stated, "The Mississippian

chiefdoms . . . of the southeastern United States . . . evolved without stim-
ulus from state societies" (Scarry 1990, 227). Such flat denial presumes
knowledge more detailed than history ordinarily can deliver, much less
archaeology, and particularly so when "The subject of intergroup trade
holds a minor place in Mississippian period archaeology" (Brown, Kerber,
and Winters 1990, 251).

The positivist evolutionary approach prompts questions along the line
of "How can one hope to understand the distribution of chiefdoms in the
Southeast without a thorough knowledge of the nature of these chiefdoms
and the limitations placed upon them by biological, cultural, and climatic
variables among others?" (DePratter 1984, 16). Demurring from the
expectation that archaeology and sixteenth-century chronicles will yield us
"*thorough* knowledge of the nature of these chiefdoms," or of any polity
half a millennium past, we may reflect upon George Gaylord Simpson's
delineation of historical sciences and follow the principle of actualism
rather than nineteenth-century armchair ratiocination.

Cahokia in particular calls for comparison with the capital city built in
historic times upon its western edge: St. Louis. The late-eighteenth-
century jockeying for control of the Mississippi by France, Spain, Britain,
and the United States, culminating in the Louisiana Purchase and the development of St. Louis, demonstrate the power accruing to the polity controlling the American Bottom and the waterways debouching into it, and the
Mississippi south of it. The principle of actualism, not to mention Occam's
Razor, posits Cahokia to be a market hub, and one that was likely to ship
goods downriver. Downriver from Cahokia leads into the Gulf of Mexico
and the ports of the Huastec and Maya. Huge platform pyramidal mounds
constructed around great plazas—the central theater of power signaled by
an imposing wall—neighbored by relatively well-constructed (wall-trench)
houses with a variety of finely polished open bowls, cups, and jars, amid
miles of hamlets among raised fields of maize and squashes? This form for a
metropolis was standard in Mesoamerica. No archaeologist can demonstrate
that not one tenth-century person from the American Bottom saw, and
returned from, Mexico, nor that not one Mexican ever traveled up the
Mississippi. The parsimonious hypothesis is that Cahokia's pyramidal
mounds and plazas and "green city" farmsteads and hamlets, which replicate the general Mesoamerican pattern of the urbs, embody architectural
conceptions originating in Mexico (e.g., Marcus 1983; Arnold and Ford
1980, 724; cf. Kostof 1989, 121–27). This is not to claim wholesale migrations, but instead the common comings and goings, up and down river,
around and across the Gulf, sometimes on foot across country, so amply
observed historically (J. C. Kelley 1955). It is highly implausible, it is
contrary to the principle of actualism, to deny contacts between persons

surrounding waterways; these ordinary human contacts would have occurred over the millennia, occasionally forays to seize territory, most often trading ventures and the quests of youths for new experiences. Whenever an ambitious provincial lord ordered his capital to be enhanced, the image he sought was not novel but well known, if only from tales. It is a fact of geography that Cahokia lies on the northern border of the Gulf Coastal Lowlands.

In the tenth century, a nation called the Tolteca conquered many others in Mesoamerica (Hassig 1992, 110–21; Conrad and Demarest 1984, 16–19; López Austin 1988, 84). Like the Aztecs after them, the Toltecs' jaguar and coyote lords (Hassig 1992, 114) demanded tribute be brought to its capital from the many *tlatocayotk* (principalities) of Mesoamerica. The Toltecas' dominion lasted only two centuries, collapsing by 1200 (traditionally, A.D. 1179 [Hassig 1992, 119]). Our accounts of the Tolteca all come from their heirs in the Valley of Mexico (D. Kelley 1987), nations who saw the northern lands as one vast wilderness of dog-people (*chichimeca*). That the Tolteca may have traded, perhaps via nations in the Huasteca (Hassig 1992, 115–16), across the Gulf and up the Mississippi lacks hard evidence (other than filed human incisors [Lathrap and Porter 1985, 77]), but hard evidence for Highland Mexico itself in this period is relatively limited (Molina Montes 1982; Hirth 1991, 211–12 on transportation) and subject to much debate. If the Tolteca did trade with Cahokia, the hub of trans-Gulf America, what might they have taken? Slaves (and *tlamenes* [Smith and Hally 1992, 103] and mercenaries)? Mantles? Velvety, superbly tanned deer hides such as those that Southeastern Indians produced commercially in the early colonial period? No hard evidence of any of these could be recovered.

Evidence for contacts, for shared conceptualizations, does exist in similarities between Early Postclassic Mexico and contemporary Mississippian (e.g., Carlson 1981; Hall 1984; Gillespie 1991). Some of the strongest parallels are in iconography (especially if mound-and-plaza architecture is counted as iconography). Philip Phillips of Harvard conducted a study of engraved conch-shell cups from the principal tomb at Spiro, a Late Mississippian town (J. Brown 1996), to evaluate iconographic parallels between these and Mesoamerican art. A colleague explained:

> Phil [Phillips] ... has always been rather conservative in the methods and conclusions that he has applied to such broad-ranging stylistic comparisons ... not that he abjured such integrations, he just insisted that one do a properly detailed analysis before leaping to conclusions of similarity. (Williams 1978; Foreword)

During his analysis, Phillips consulted "an acknowledged expert" on Gulf of Mexico shells and was told by this expert:

[T]he Spiro shells ... must have come from either the Huastecan area or the Florida Keys. Since a practically identical tradition of shell carving existed contemporaneously at Spiro and in the Huasteca, I think that cultural exchange between these areas must have been strongly developed. (quoted in Phillips and J. Brown 1978, 26–27)

The Harvard "acknowledged expert" failed to deliver the proper opinion. Phillips contemptuously commented, "a good deal of hard evidence is needed to prove it ... an individual who knows both his shells and his archaeology, if such a prodigy exists" (Phillips and Brown 1978, 27). Phillips' tenacity in rejecting Mississippian-Mesoamerican contacts even when evidenced on Gulf of Mexico shells transported to eastern Oklahoma, is a strong example of the power of core beliefs in this discipline (Kelley and Hanen 1988, 278–79, 302–03, 316).

Cahokia was not a Toltec creation. It was on the north-central border of Early Postclassic Mesoamerica, as Chaco, with a remarkably similar history (Windes 1991, 126–27; Trombold 1991, 155), was on its northwestern border. Development of secondary states on the frontiers of imperial expansion is a historically observed process, and therefore to be preferred, in a historical science, to invoking unobserved processes such as the evolution of pristine chiefdoms (Kopytoff 1987, 78; McGuire 1992, 150–55; Southall 1991, 79–80, and 82: "We should pay more respect to the terms which the people themselves use"). Actualism favors the hypothesis that "Toltec" empire-building was the opportunity, and perhaps impetus, for a lord in southern Illinois to expand his power, locking into the distant, avaricious, southern kingdom and constructing his own awesome seat on the model of the cities of Mexico. The Lord of Cahokia, like the little kingdoms of Britain at the brink of Roman conquest, may have exported slaves, hides, corn, and such minerals as copper, silver, and galena.[2] When the Tolteca fell, they brought down the Lord of Cahokia, too. His western *tlatocayotl*s moved up the Missouri (Toom 1992), his northern *tlatocayotl*s formed the protohistoric culture area we call Oneota, and the precariously independent Southeastern kingdoms were strengthened. When the Aztecs finally achieved power in central Mexico a century and a half later, no one there remembered the Ramey State.

CHAPTER 10

Burrowing Through the Chiefdom

A historical representation will be ideological ... if ... : first, the historical account employs an interpretative framework or set of assumptions that are covert and neither justified nor argued for in the account; second, the framework or assumptions express the shared values and position of a particular community ...; third, the main function of the framework or assumptions is to justify the shared values and position rather than to realize the principal value of recovering the past; and finally, the historian's interpretations and arguments serve chiefly to justify the framework and thus the values. (Richards 1992, 175)

Or in Lewis Feuer's aphorism, contemporary ideology is a "myth written in the language of philosophy and science" (Feuer 1975, 17). There is no question that Enlightenment conjectural universal histories were ideological (Meek 1976), nor that their persistence in the nineteenth century reflected ideological pressures (Stocking 1987, 228, 237; R. Williams 1990). A Canadian official of the time openly derived policy on Indian affairs from principles of unilinear evolution he read in *Bible Teachings* in Nature (Carter 1990, 15). More sophisticated Americans such as John Wesley Powell were inspired by Lewis Henry Morgan's version of unidirectional technological evolutionism (Vincent 1990, 39; Kehoe 1985). Powell knew very well he served the interest of the United States government in providing rhetoric to justify displacing, dispossessing, and subjugating the indigenous nations whose lands were being given to citizens of European origin.

The unilinear cultural evolutionism that dominated anthropology in general until Boas' campaign, and then persisted in mainstream American archaeology, fit competitive capitalism like a glove. Even in 1996, one of Leslie White's students stated, "cultural evolution replaced organic evolution as the primary means by which human beings prevailed in the struggle for existence," admittedly a Spencerian view not accepted by biologists (Carneiro 1996, 271–72). Spencerian evolution allows for "retrogression" from "higher" to "lower" form (273), inching very close to the nineteenth-century debate on whether humans, or at least the primitive ones, degenerated from what God originally bestowed. Whether devolved or never much evolved, those who had been conquered by (self-identified) higher civilization fell into the category of primitive, and it is the nature of categories to be marked by defining attributes. Within the Lockean political philosophy of "possessive individualism" (C. B. MacPherson 1962), conquered people—lower, primitive, compared to their conquerors—cannot, must not possess attributes of the superior class. Lewis Henry Morgan:

> The Iroquois confederacy is an excellent exemplification of a gentile society . . . in the Lower Status of barbarism; . . . the institutions of political society [are] founded upon territory and upon property, with the establishment of which the gentile organization would be overthrown (L. H. Morgan [1877] 1985, 148–49) . . . the rule in the Lower Status of barbarism . . . [was] that [property] should be distributed among the gentiles . . . or agnatic kindred of the deceased owner. (75)

Only when personal property was inherited by the children of the deceased, and not by other kin, would a society advance to the Upper Status of barbarism, a status achieved by the Greeks early in the first millennium B.C. (L. H. Morgan [1877] 1985, 216). Personal possessions were not property unless inherited exclusively by a man's children. Similarly, American Indian societies, "tribes," *appeared* to possess territory on page 112 of *Ancient Society*, "the area of their actual settlements, and so much of the surrounding region as the tribe ranged over in hunting and fishing, and were able to defend . . . Without this area was a wide margin of neutral grounds." Eleven pages later, "gentile society," "tribes," did not possess territories in any *significant* sense: Morgan now explained, "A state [*civitas*] must rest upon territory and not upon persons, upon the township as the unit of a political system, and not upon the gens which is the unit of a social system [*societas*]." He reiterated after his extended discussion of the Aztec, "Until the idea of property had advanced very far beyond the point [the Aztecs or Iroquois] had attained, the substitution of political for gentile society was impossible" (214).

Prescott's 1840s histories of the conquests of Mexico and of Peru had informed Americans of indigenous empires ruled with pomp, fabulous cities, and elaborate political hierarchies. These exciting chronicles of heroic invaders prompted readers to wonder why United States Indians seemed to lack marvelous empires. Morgan had the answer, and it was breathtaking in its audacity: The Aztecs and Incas had been grossly misrepresented! His chapter on "The Aztec Confederacy" in *Ancient Society* is subheaded "Misconception of Aztec Society," and begins:

> The Spanish adventurers, who captured the Pueblo of Mexico, adopted the erroneous theory that the Aztec government was a monarchy, analogous in essential respects to existing monarchies in Europe.... A terminology not in agreement with [Aztec] institutions came in with this misconception which has vitiated the historical narrative nearly as completely as though it were, in the main, a studied fabrication.... The histories of Spanish America may be trusted in whatever relates to the acts of the Spaniards, and to the acts and personal characteristics of the Indians; in whatever relates to their weapons, implements and utensils, fabrics, food and raiment, and things of a similar character. But in whatever relates to Indian society and government, their social relations, and plan of life, they are nearly worthless, because they learned nothing and knew nothing of either. We are at full liberty to reject them in these respects and commence anew; using any facts they may contain which harmonize with what is known of Indian society.... The remarkable spectacle presented [to Cortés] so inflamed the imagination that romance swept the field, and has held it to the present hour.... Certain facts remain of a positive kind from which other facts may be deduced; so that it is not improbable that a well-directed original investigation may yet recover, measurably at least, the essential features of the Aztec social system ... simply a confederacy of three Indian tribes, of which the counterpart existed in all parts of the continent.... The Aztec monarchy should be dismissed from American aboriginal history, not only as delusive, but as a misrepresentation of the Indians, who had neither developed nor invented monarchical institutions. The government they formed was a confederacy of tribes, and nothing more; and probably not equal in plan and symmetry with that of the Iroquois. (L. H. Morgan [1877] 1985, 186–88, 196)

Substantive grounds for these overarching assertions are that the Aztecs wore breech-cloths, "this rag of barbarism ... the unmistakable evidence of their condition" ("Montezuma's Dinner," *North American Review* 122:293, 1876, quoted in Bieder 1986, 238).

Morgan continues his systematic denial of the chronicles written by Cortés' associates and two succeeding generations of sophisticated Spaniards dealing for years in the administration of Central Mexico.

Indian chiefs are described as lords by Spanish writers, and invested with rights over lands and over persons they never possessed. It is a misconception to style an Indian chief a lord in the European sense, because it implies a condition of society that did not exist. A lord holds a rank and a title by hereditary right.... On the contrary, an Indian chief holds an office, not by hereditary right, but by election from a constitutuency, which retained the right to depose him ... no analogy exists between a lord and his title, and an Indian chief and his office. One belongs to political society, ... while the other belongs to gentile society. (L. H. Morgan [1877] 1985, 202)

Elman Service doesn't reference *Ancient Society* in his *Primitive Social Organization,* but the relevance of Morgan's construction of a chief to Service's chiefdom is obvious.

Joan Vincent, in *Anthropology and Politics,* carefully lays out the development of Morgan's avowedly scientific anthropology. His first work, *The League of the Ho-de-no-sau-nee, or Iroquois* (1851) preceded, as she points out, not only Darwin's *Origin* but Herbert Spencer's books. Over the next quarter-century, Morgan reframed his enterprise, from a description of a foreign nation to a universalizing science that can explain how contemporary America came into existence—and in explaining, counsel how America and her institutions might continue. We needn't look far to figure out Morgan's interests: he was a lawyer and prominent citizen among the bourgeoisie of a provincial city, an investor in railroad and mining ventures on the Old Northwest frontier, and a candidate for the New York legislature from the new Republican Party during the 1860s. Equally important, Morgan's closest friend (and to Curtis Hinsley, his "mentor" [Hinsley 1981, 47]), was Josiah McIlvaine, a Presbyterian leader steeped in Scottish Common-sense Realism and the conjectural histories of Adam Smith, Ferguson, Kames, Monboddo, and their compatriots in Edinburgh and Glasgow (see Slotkin 1965, 412–60 for a generous sampling of what Noll [1994, 84] terms the "didactic Enlightenment"). This school of philosophes sat in the very archetype of the Industrial Revolution, where capital-intensive industry replaced mercantile and agricultural wealth (Goodman and Honeyman 1988, 142; Crafts 1989, 39). Their engagement to understand that radical shift in political economy spoke directly to Morgan's sensibility, a century later, that America's post-Civil War industrialization cried out for a social charter.[1]

"The origin myth of Western capitalism," Vincent calls the Scots school of conjectural history (Vincent 1990, 36). It was called "history" because by the late Enlightenment, Hayden White notes, "historical reflection ... serve[d] as the very paradigm of realistic discourse ... constituting an image of a current social praxis as the criterion of plausibility by reference to which any given institution, activity, thought … can be endowed with the aspect of 'reality'" (H. White 1987, 101–02). Morgan writes forthrightly of the irrelevance of actual Indians to his conjectural history; after condescending toward the Iroquois to establish that they are not outside the bounds of humanity, he explained that they

> were [note past tense] a vigorous and intelligent people, with a brain approaching in volume the Aryan average … they counted in their ranks a large number of able men.… Our own remote forefathers passed through the same conditions.… However little we may be interested in the American Indians personally, their experience touches us more nearly, as an exemplification of the experience of our own ancestors … in the Lower Status of barbarism (L. H. Morgan [1877] 1985, 148–49).

Unilinear cultural evolutionism exiled American Indians to remote antiquity; it distanced them more effectively than their reservations on marginal lands along the frontiers. At the same time, it flattened their past so that American archaeology either contented itself with culture-area delineations or premised mysterious Mound-Builder races.[2]

Ancient Society is a tour-de-force of mystification, inscribing, in utmost detail, a deductive, logical typology for human societies, rhetorically decked out with ethnographic minutiae. Like Comte and Spencer, Morgan asserted the inevitability of Progress from the unutterable Otherness of primitives, i.e., non-Western peoples, through the corrupted history of Europe to the American crucible where "the next higher plane of society" is nascent. Feuer comments:

> An ideology is never content with the narrative of the [social charter] myth; the drama must be shown to be deducible from the laws of existence itself. As such, every ideology attaches to itself some combination of philosophical unit-ideas; the mythological drama, is regarded as derivable in some fashion from the latter. (Feuer 1975, 17)

A coalescence, in late nineteenth-century America, of "northeastern gentry and the new capitalists" looked to "call upon the authority of modern science … to speak with the voice of universal rationality, while bestowing special authority on its elite class of practitioners" (Ross 1991, 61–62). Morgan had achieved a position in that class. *Ancient Society* was its elaborated manifesto, complete to the *de rigueur* finis invoking liberty, equality, and fraternity.

Having published his *Grundrisse* in 1871—the scrupulously scholarly looking lengthy tables collating kin terminology from nations across America and Asia—Morgan was confident that *Ancient Society* would be received as a work of scientific authority. That it was indeed so taken, by Major Powell and thousands of other Americans, by Friedrich Engels and eventually by Leslie White, is testimony to Morgan's genius in perceiving and fulfilling industrial America's need for an ideological charter. Perhaps through his long discussions with theologian McIlvaine, Morgan utilized what a recent historian has called "the catch-phrases of nineteenth-century mechanistic scienticism," centering on typology as the foundation of scientific method:

> the collecting, scientifically arranging, comparing, exhibiting, and defending of *all* facts from any and every source . . . great time-periods . . . fall into a well-defined order . . . as the blueprint to the builder or the chart to the mariner. . . . Contemplation of the doctrine of human conduct belongs properly to a science which purports to discover, classify, and exhibit the great doctrines. (Lewis Sperry Chafer, 1947, quoted in Noll 1994, 127–28).

That these catch-phrases come from a work entitled *Systematic Theology* makes the point that in late-nineteenth-century America, the taken-for-granted domination of the Protestant bourgeoisie erased even the Constitutional separation of State and Church. *Ancient Society* came out at the height of enthusiasm for President Grant's Peace Policy allocating the agencies on Indian reservations to twelve Protestant denominations and the Catholic Church (seven out of seventy-three) (Prucha 161).

Had Morgan not trashed the Aztecs and their Spanish chroniclers, a reader might see virtue in the more-or-less straight ethnographic information on a variety of American Indian social structures, but that chapter on the Aztec should have signaled to readers that the book is a traducement of scholarship. Pure racist prejudice fueled Morgan there; not Stephens and Catherwood's Maya volumes, nor Edward Tylor's *Anahuac,* nor Daniel Wilson's *Prehistoric Man*—all known to Morgan—are cited, for their sober descriptions of Indian achievements would have vitiated his grand vision of Aryan supremacy. That impassioned disregard for scholarly circumspection sold the book. Discussing Protestant Americans' postbellum slide into the dogmatic scientism that eventually gave us Scientific Creationism, Noll outlines:

> nineteenth-century traits that . . . undercut the possibility for a responsible intellectual life. These included a weakness for treating [data] as pieces in a jigsaw puzzle that needed only to be sorted and then fit together to possess a finished picture of . . . truth; an overwhelming tendency to "essentialism," or the conviction that a specific formula could capture for all times and places the essence of . . . truth for any specific issue concerning God, the human condition, or the fate of the world; a corresponding neglect of forces

in history that shape perceptions . . . ; and a self-confidence, bordering on hubris, manifested by an extreme antitraditionalism that casually discounted the possibility of wisdom from earlier generations. (Noll 1994, 127)

These qualities are components of the "engineering ideology" (Rosenberg 1976, 267; D. Noble 1977, ch. 10) admired by the American bourgeoisie.

The crux of the power of *Ancient Society,* as of *Primitive Social Organization* and the rest of that ilk, is the abyss created between bourgeois Westerners and all others whom we are obliged to count as human. America has long faced a real dilemma. As a republic boasting that it honors the self-evident truth that all men are endowed with unalienable Rights including those to Life, Liberty, and the Pursuit of Happiness, the United States should not harbor men denied these Rights. No sooner had the dissonance raised by slavery been resolved, than the final conquests of Indian nations revived the specter. Most Americans accepted monogenesis, the doctrine that there had been a single creation of humans; this doctrine undergirded Christian evangelicalism as well as liberal political philosophies. Dichotomizing humans into primitive and civilized, *societas/civitas* if a scientistic term was wanted, neatly solved the dilemma: all men may have been endowed with unalienable Rights but the benighted heathens alienated *themselves* into gens instead of townships, imposed upon themselves the poverty of the commons. Morgan's erudite explanation glorifying the great breakthrough supposedly achieved by the Classical Greeks allayed his compatriots' discomfort.

How did this fundamental dualism affect American archaeology? With the principal synthesizing works coming out of Powell's Bureau of American Ethnology, "the past," Kroeber remarked later, "is felt not as a receding stereoscopic continuum but as a uniform nonpresent" (Kroeber 1952, 151). B.A.E. archaeologists' hard line against recognizing great time depth to American prehistory was a consequence of the ideology of aborigines stuck in the Lower Status of Barbarism; it was definitely not for lack of either data or of familiarity with the principles and methods by which European archaeologists inferred immense time depth for their ancestors (Trigger 1989, 121; also 1980). Not archaeologists, but paleontologists forced acceptance of evidence for humans in Pleistocene America (R. Woodbury 1993, 10).

Beginning in the 1890s, archaeological research in Latin America shifted toward constructing a glorious patrimony for the regimes suffering dependency status vis-á-vis the European and North American powers. Although their contemporary, and very substantial, Indian populations were denigrated, the regimes uncovered and exhibited the monumental architecture and aesthetic gems of the preconquest past to contend mutely the potential might of these disrespected lands. Much of the archaeological work was performed by American archaeologists, supported by American corporations (Carnegie, United Fruit) (T. C. Patterson 1995, 60); recognizing ancient civilizations in distant peripheral countries was no threat to Manifest Destiny, in part because the story persistently read out of the ruins was the story of collapse. Collapse was discussed for decades about the Maya in particular, creators of much of the finest art and of the most developed literacy in preconquest America; seldom did scholars emphasize that Maya flourished all around when cities in the southern lowlands of the Yucatán peninsula were abandoned.

Published a year before *Ancient Society,* Daniel Wilson's third edition of *Prehistoric Man,* available on many a library shelf, was a reasonable guide to the antiquities of the Americas. Morgan's contumely on the Aztecs could not withstand the onslaught of impressive data from Mesoamerica, once Latin American regimes and their American sponsors came to see the collapsed glories of indigenous civilizations as symbol of the weakness of their successors, global capitalism's dependent states. America's past became a flat place ornamented with many white towers and massive fortresses. For two-thirds of a century, American archaeologists labored to fill museums and books with the crafts and building plans of the vanished races of each culture area delimited by ethnologists. There was little discussion of theory because there was so much work to be done collecting data—and the Baconian science so generally accepted in America let theory flow from accumulated data.

"Normal science" in American archaeology from the 1890s into the 1950s remained very much within nineteenth-century America's Baconian science. Artifacts lie out there in nature, to be collected, collated, and classified; a classification that works has revealed the essential attributes of the specimens fit into the class. Sorting specimens by spatial occurrence and depth (arbitrary measured levels, obviously more scientific than messy natural strata) clusters artifacts into components, phases, foci, and traditions. The American version of Baconian science decried "speculation," inanely repeating Newton's "hypotheses non fingo," confident the Book of Nature can be read as it were by phonics, sounding out each observation like a letter. The emphasis on collecting facts looked similar to Franz Boas' insistence on amassing quantities of data but differed in a vital aspect: Where Boas was thinking in terms of populations and range of variance, most American scientists well into the mid-twentieth century thought in terms of types and type specimens. Archaeologists were therefore content with the kind of limited sampling from "telephone booth"-shaped test pits (as Kent Flannery called them), and created "cultures" from these samples. That all indigenous American "cultures" belonged in the "primitive" side of the Great Divide was a given.

Baconian science was just right for the burden laid upon archaeologists in the 1930s, to help alleviate Depression unemployment through excavations putting to work as many hundreds of the rural proletariat as could possibly be managed. Mounds were ideal, huge amounts of dirt to be trenched through and a very low proportion of artifacts or features (to be logged in by the educated supervisor) for the volume of mass. After World War II, River Basin Surveys continued the good fit of Baconian science, now because the purpose was to lift out of the condemned river valleys all their archaeological data; crews were smaller and mostly college boys, but with the Corps of Engineers hovering near, no time could be allotted to sitting and reflecting on the work. Whether in the Thirties or the Fifties, American archaeologists were being paid to collect data and hand in reports pigeonholing artifacts and features according to chronologically and geographically delimited types. Since about 1930, "the stereotype of the American archaeologist has somehow come to be a pretty dull sort of clod, with most of his gray matter under his fingernails" (Wauchope 1956, v).

In 1954, the Carnegie Corporation, major sponsor of excavations in Mesoamerica and of state archaeological surveys before the War, granted the Society for American Archaeology money for a set of seminars on "problems of a broad or theoretical nature. The Corporation . . . believed," its grant organizer stated, "that certain matters of cultural dynamics and human relations can be uniquely illuminated through archaeological techniques" (Wauchope 1956, v). Twenty-four archaeologists were invited to meet in four seminars. Sixteen of these were associated with universities, three with research institutions, three with museums, one with a small private foundation, and one with the National Park Service. The topics chosen were: An Archaeological Classification of Culture Contact Situations; An Archaeological Approach to the Study of Cultural Stability; The American Southwest: A Problem in Cultural Isolation; and Functional and Evolutionary Implications of Community Patterning. The first constructed a logical matrix of "site-unit intrusions" and "trait-unit intrusions," exemplifying the categories with references to archaeological cultures. The second concerned itself with "the concept of tradition . . . a socially transmitted cultural form which persists in time" (Thompson 1956, 39); Albert Spaulding and Walter Taylor were both, oddly, members of this group of seven concentrating on that staid conventional topic. The third seminar meant by "problem," the fact that "Southwestern relationships to cultures lying north, south, east, or west, either early or late in time, have been for many years ignored, blandly dismissed, or categorically denied. When they have been recognized, these relationships have not been explained or studied" (Jennings 1956, 67). Of the eight members of this group, only one, James B. Griffin, did not work in or on the borders of the Southwest. One of their conclusions was the need for "Attempts to sort out or identify an archaeological reality corresponding to each of such concepts as 'influence,' 'migration,' 'colonization,' 'trade,' 'religious movements'" (120). The final seminar, with six members, paralleled the first in constructing a logical matrix, in this case of seven degrees of sedentism from the ethnographically unattested "Free Wandering" to "Supra-Nuclear Integrated," plus three types of pastoral nomadism. The total ten types were related to the (postulated) evolution of food production (Meggers 1956, 151–53). The one substantive-question report, on the Southwest, is twice the length of any of the purely theoretical reports.

Taking the four seminars as representative of questions and approaches mainstream in American archaeology in mid-century, the domination of essentialist typology is apparent. Equally clear, in three of the four, is the universalizing, the presumption that logical categories ought to be applicable wherever a category's few diagnostic attributes can be identified. This presumption was termed "etic" the year the seminars grant was approved, 1954; the next decade would see heated debate among cultural anthropologists over the validity of presumptively universal classifications. They of course derive from the Western cultural tradition, the academic tradition of formal philosophy and the patterns of Indo-European languages. Since no articulate human can be free of his or her enculturation including the patterning of natural languages, it does not seem possible for any human to construct universal categories unbiased by a particular living society. No one in the three theoretical seminars seems to have worried over this, and it may well be none had yet read Kenneth Pike's *Language in Relation to a Unified Theory of the Structure of Human Behavior* (1954, Summer Institute of Linguistics).

Mainstream the Seminars in Archaeology were in 1955, but they had a short use-life. The conclusion of the seminar in which Spaulding participated urged the development and greater use of quantitative techniques, and emphatically declared it had "presented our statements about cause and effect in terms of hypotheses . . . [a] major area for future work is the testing of hypotheses" (R. Thompson 1956, 55). Lewis Binford referred only once, and disparagingly, to the 1955 Seminars in his major 1960s papers establishing the New Archaeology (Binford 1972, 88). The seminars frequently faltered when they adduced exemplars for their logical constructs; they set up universal categories but held back from announcing discovery of universal laws or principles. Fundamentally, the seminars' overall tone of genteel caution was inappropriate for the new era of Big Science funded by the National Science Foundation.

The 1955 Seminars and the New Archaeology had in common Morgan's standpoint, "However little we may be interested in the American Indians personally, their experience touches us . . . as an exemplification of the experience of our own ancestors . . . in the Lower Status of barbarism." Whether the tone be one of gentlemanly discretion or in-your-face prescription, the attitude is identical: sites and artifacts are raw sources of data for scientific theorizing. When the data come from Anglo-America, they come from primitives unrelated to us, in whom as persons we have very little interest indeed.

Chiefdoms and Indians

The literature on "chiefdoms" comes out of this attitude of disengaged observation in which the data are significant only as means to construct models serving to dichotomize the civilized West from the rest of humanity. One would suppose that anthropologists, including archaeologists, wishing to understand the formation of more complex societies would focus on analyzing text-documented Classical Greece, the Roman republic and later empire borders, and post-Roman Europe. One would suppose that two classes of rich data, text and archaeological, ought to be more fruitful than archaeological data alone. Few American anthropologists, fewer archaeologists look into these data, and those who do are not recognized as mainstream (e.g., Viana Muller and John Gledhill, both in Patterson and Gailey 1987; Patterson overtly positions himself against the mainstream). *In the absence of any discussion of principles for exclusion,* omitting European history from discussions of the formation of structurally complex societies feeds the ideological message in traditional anthropology.

Classical Greece had more than two hundred city-states, many of them ruled by tyrants and none of them democratic in a modern sense. Where are they in Service's band-tribe-chiefdom-state classification? He refers to "the Greek and Roman Empires" as "'archaic' or 'classical' civilizations of the order of dynastic China and Mogul India" (Service 1962, 175). The Greek city-states are apparently more evolved than the "primitive states" of Ashanti and the Inca (175–76), although these empires, in contrast to the Greek polities, controlled large—in the case of the Inca, truly vast—terrritories and populations. Service makes no mention of either Europe beyond the Roman Empire or Europe after the Roman Empire. How should we classify the tribes, the principalities, the tiny kingdoms (four, for example, in medieval Wales) and the elaborate but fragile empires? He tells us only, "Chiefdoms are chiefdoms and states are states" (173).

Within political anthropology, Service's *Primitive Social Organization* and his "chiefdom" type have failed to prevail as they have in American archaeology; indeed, Yoffee, himself an archaeologist but one working on early Mesopotamian states, remarks that "the subject of 'chiefdoms' is light-years away from anything that modern anthropologists study" (Yoffee 1993, 64). Claessen, van de Velde, and Smith in their series of edited volumes on the nature and formation of states discuss Service among a number of authors of conceptual schemata; they argue that Service's typology is too simple to accommodate the range of data they and their contributors adduce (M. E. Smith 1985, 97; Claessen and van de Velde 1985, 132–37, 1991, 4; Townsend 1985, 143). Vincent contrasts the 1960s "neo-evolutionary paradigm" presented by Service, "a popular and simple taxonomy ... that gave offense to few," to the politically aware work on real-world complexity being conducted in the same decade by such anthropologists as Eric Wolf. She notes that by the end of the decade, the terms "primitive" and "social control" dropped out of anthropologists' vocabularies, and some attempted to sensitize colleagues to the pain and legal setbacks suffered by new or dependent nations when they were characterized as "tribes" (Vincent 1990, 312–13, 330–31). A theme running through Vincent's masterly study of political anthropology is the contrast between focus on "timeless universals" versus historicity. Among those highly sensible of the fundamental importance of historically grounded models is Igor Kopytoff, who concluded his review of African data:

> In the harsh light of ethnography, bands do not grow into chiefdoms, nor do most chiefdoms grow out of bands.... As we have seen, small polities arose not out of archaic bands rooted in pre-history but were produced out of the entrails of existing functioning societies, of which some were small polities and some were large and mature states. (Kopytoff 1987, 78)

This is actualism.

Compared to political sophistication displayed by so many social anthropologists, mainstream American archaeologists have been petrified puddle ducks. The spate of archaeological treatises on Mississippian polities ignore most of the contemporary social-anthropological literature on states and their precursors (e.g., on Mississippian polities, Anderson 1994, DePratter 1991, Mehrer 1995, Pauketat 1994, Welch 1991, Williams and Shapiro 1990). The one exception that contrasts with the norm is the volume *Lords of the Southeast* (1992), edited by Alex W. Barker and Timothy R. Pauketat, both obliged at that time to tread with care, for they were newly hatched Ph.D.s seeking posts. Barker and Pauketat's "Conclusion" uses the word "lord" rather than "chief," omits the term "chiefdom," and tellingly opens with a passage from Shakespeare's *Henry V*: Shakespeare's historical dramas are extraordinarily rich pictures of small kingdoms that may well be our very best documents for understanding class-stratified polities not caught within Wallerstein's modern-capitalist world-system.

Mainstream Mississippian archaeology is illustrated by Bruce Smith's paper interpreting the "woodhenges" at Cahokia. The paper is positivist in

Smith's uncritical acceptance of the excavator's 1969 interpretation of incomplete circles of large wooden posts; Smith labels them "solar circles" or "solar calendars, unique in eastern North America" (B. Smith 1992, 18). The "woodhenge" idea was initially presented soon after much ado in the world of archaeology over Gerald Hawkins' postulation of several astronomical alignments in England's Stonehenge. A site with large concentric circles of wooden posts in the same county and general time period is called Woodhenge. Cahokia's incomplete circles do not much resemble the site in Wiltshire, and only very superficially the stone "medicine wheels" of the Northwestern American Plains (Kehoe and Kehoe 1979; Brumley 1988). A parsimonious interpretation would be that these arcs of great posts represent a temporal succession of ritual structures seen in much reduced form in the Sun Dance and Okipa lodges of nineteenth-century Siouan-speaking nations of the prairies, societies with geographical contiguity and probable linguistic ties to the Cahokian state. Smith makes no reference to Siouan, Muskogean, or Caddoan ethnographies; his universalizing "scientific" stance can ignore historical particularities.

Smith mentions quincunxes and circles divided into quadrants in Mississippian art, assuming they are iconic representations of "the fourfold [seasonal] division of time . . . derived from the sun itself." Widespread use of these cosmological symbols in Mesoamerica across the Gulf is disregarded, thereby closing off any understanding derived from comparisons with better-documented Mexican iconography. Extending his inference, Smith supposes a "solar-derived authority of the elite . . . the direct link between the sun and the chiefly elite" (B. Smith 1992, 28). Model for this supposition must be the classic descriptions of the Natchez (DePratter 1991, 57), but Smith omits referencing a source, implying the "solar-derived authority" is self-evident or universal. A final point is that Smith repeats the ideological line that the leadership of Cahokia was "kinship-based" (B. Smith 1992, 17). This interpretation wholly lacks archaeological foundation at Cahokia, where the poor preservation of bone in Mound 72 precluded anthropometric testing for genetic relationships. In sum, this senior archaeologist at the Smithsonian not only accepts without discussion an inadequately supported label for the archaeological data of arcs of wooden posts at Cahokia, but constrains his entire interpretation within the received type "chiefdom," perpetuating Morgan's insistence that all American Indians were caught in *societas,* never *civitas*—that is, never more than primitives cut off from the historical world.

This dominant ideology can be truly pernicious. William Sturtevant of the Smithsonian reminded the 1979 meeting of the American Ethnological Society that anthropologists are summoned to courts of law to deliver expert opinions on Indian nations' claims for land, compensation, or federal benefits (Sturtevant 1983). A 1987 volume by ethnologist Allen

Johnson and archaeologist Timothy Earle, *Evolution of Human Societies,* seems oblivious of the real-world implications of the unilinear cultural evolution they present:

> Foragers[3] diversify and gradually adopt agriculture; villages form and integrate into regional polities; leaders come to dominate and transform social relationships.... Subsistence intensification, political integration, and social stratification are ... observed again and again in historically unrelated cases [this statement of nullity is nowhere demonstrated, merely premised] ... population growth and a chain reaction of economic and social changes underlie cultural evolution ... population growth provides the push, technological change the pull. (Johnson and Earle 1987, 4–5)

This position is a blueprint for American ideology (Staudenmaier 1985). That it is ideology, not a working hypothesis, for Johnson and Earle is evidenced by their neglect of the effect of the devastating post-Columbian epidemics on societies they use as illustrations of stages of evolution. Events in time are without significance; space stands in for time, in the manner of Lubbock's and Morgan's ethnocentrism, the most distant peoples representing the earliest stages (McGuire 1992, 151–55). Earle, not incidentally, has been a leading exponent of the use of the classification "chiefdom" in archaeology (e.g., Earle 1987; 1991).

The Kwakiutl (Kwakwaka'wakw) of the eastern North Pacific are one of Johnson and Earle's exemplars of "The Corporate Group and the Big Man Collectivity," societies "'less evolved' ... when compared to their neighbors on the continuum [of unilinear cultural evolution]" (Johnson and Earle 1987, 314). These "Indian Fishermen of the Northwest Coast," they say, have a "competitive, entrepreneurial, and *seemingly 'capitalistic'* economy" (161; my italics).[4] In spite of the "seemingly capitalistic economy," they describe the Kwakwaka'wakw as no more than "subsistence-oriented producers [with a] Big Man [who] is a *local* leader" (160; their italics). The classification under which Johnson and Earle discuss the Kwakwaka'wakw and neighboring nations is "The Local Group" (contrasted with the "Regional Polity") "... headed by Big Men ... a strong charismatic leader ... [whose] power is dependent on his personal initiative" (Johnson and Earle 1987, 20; for a contrary, ethnohistorically informed discussion see Boxberger and Miller 1997). Debate may continue on how to best translate our data on Eastern North Pacific "houses" into European terminology (Lévi-Strauss 1982), but that these American nations had formally institutionalized societal stratification epitomized in *inherited* titles regulating resource dominion has never been in doubt. Seguin in her monograph on the Tsimshian summarized (1985, 95), "Chiefs had to be descended from Chiefs [and] elevated by distributions of property"; they controlled demarcated territories. Adams in his 1981 review stated, "the facts of class, residence and citizenship . . . together produce a society consisting essentially of *an oligarchy of chiefs and their clients*" (J. W. Adams 1981, 385; his italics). Among the Tsimshian, north of the Kwakwaka'wakw on the British Columbian coast,

> surpluses of salmon and many other abundant resources supported a complicated class structure with a basic distinction between freemen and slaves. The freemen were further classified along several axes into noble lineages and non-noble lineages, into titleholders . . . and commoners, and into graded ranks determined by the relative importance of each title. Titleholders . . . were individuals of wealthy heritage, trained to their positions. . . . This system of governance has survived and contemporary Tsimshian leaders use the principles . . . in their struggles for self government within the Canadian political order. (J. McDonald 1994, 156)

In the Seguin-edited volume, George MacDonald established through archaeology that at least one Skeena district fortress dates from the seventeenth century, well before European intrusions, and combined these data with oral history, epics, and documentary history to clarify the politics and economics recorded in Gitksan sagas (G. MacDonald 1984; see Moss and Erlandson 1992 for expansion of these data). Seguin also (1985, 96–97) describes the continuing Tsimshian use of formal feasts to publicly establish houses' territories in claims before Canadian courts.

Johnson and Earle put "slaves," like "capital" and "wealth," in quotation marks, and insist (Johnson and Earle 1987, 171) "Slavery . . . was not an institution in the sense of being a regular part of the economy. . . . Slave-owners, even wealthy Big Men, did the same work as their 'commoners' and slaves. . . . Slaves never amounted to more than a tiny fraction of the population." Yet in January 1984, three years before Johnson and Earle published, Donald Mitchell had stated in *Ethnology,* "Slaves were present among all groups, sometimes in considerable numbers . . . [and] the necessary work undertaken by slaves [leads one] to conclude their paramount importance as captive labor . . . [and] objects of wealth" (Mitchell 1984, 39). Mitchell was drawing upon a decade of published work by himself and Leland Donald (e.g., Donald 1983). The issue of slavery as an institution had been central in a 1900 monograph, Nieboer's *Slavery as an Industrial System: Ethnological Researches,* considered by Joan Vincent (1990, 87–89) to be a milestone in anthropological methodology. Two decades after Nieboer, Robert Lowie asserted the primacy of "democratic individualism" (Vincent's term [172]) throughout Native North America. "Thus," remarks Vincent, "was the Native American tribe shorn of both its historicity and its provenance. . . . Reified, it became the conceptual unit the sociological comparative method required."

A listing of Johnson and Earle's cited sources[5] reveals they favored traditional colonialist discourse and scanted twenty years of more recent scholarly research and discussion on eastern North Pacific nations. Marvin Harris (1994, 73) called Johnson and Earle's book representative of recent theory "based on vastly improved and expanded research methods." They chose to base their picture of "[Northwest Coast] Social Organization" (165) on a 1957 unpublished Master's thesis titled "An intergroup collectivity among the Nootka," by one P. Newman,[6] ignoring John Adams' 1981 *Annual Review of Anthropology* "Recent Ethnology of the Northwest Coast." Johnson and Earle make no mention of Lévi-Strauss' important comparative discussion of eastern North Pacific "houses" in his 1982 *Way of the Masks,* nor of two easily accessible landmark edited volumes published in 1984, Miller and Eastman's *The Tsimshian and Their Neighbors of the North Pacific Coast* and Seguin's *The Tsimshian.* Johnson and Earle's research method is the same hoary ideological mythologizing as Sir John Lubbock's, "exemplary of Victorian ethnocentrism, racism, and shamefully sloppy science" (Stevens 1996, 1089).

Wanting illustration of their conceptual unit the Big Man Collectivity, they thrust the Kwakwaka'wakw into their model, disregarding both the active scholarship on Northwest Coast history and indigenous political economies, and the present contests between these Indian nations, British Columbia, and the Dominion of Canada. Their parrotting of long-outmoded ethnology to make an evolutionist type undermines the Kwakwaka'wakw nation's claim to self-rule in our contemporary world. George Speck, a Kwakwaka'wakw, said, "Anthropologists and lawyers that present Indian people purely in terms of traditional ways of life are setting us up for a kick in the ass" (quoted in Dyck and Waldram 1993, 177).

Indians and Archaeologists Outside the Mainstream

Outside the mainstream, there is a long tradition of archaeologists seeking to work with actual Indian nations. A disproportionate number of these atypical archaeologists have been women. Marginalized because they are women, these archaeologists seem to have been more sensible of that other marginal class, Indians. It took the Native American Grave Protection and Repatriation Act, 1990, to persuade many male Euroamerican archaeologists to recognize whose history they work in.

Memoir Number One of the Society for American Archaeology inaugurated a series that, as a whole, is significant for the history of American archaeology. Perhaps because the new society was an untried venue for monographs, its first memoir was not by an established practitioner but by a young woman, Dorothy Keur. A doctoral dissertation directed by William Duncan Strong at Columbia, Keur's *Big Bead Mesa* followed the direct historical approach promulgated by Strong in his research on Pawnee sites in Nebraska (where he had been employed, 1929–1931). Her task was to find and test Navajo sites to elucidate the settlement of Apacheans in the Southwest. Big Bead mesa, in northern New Mexico, had Navajo and some Pueblo material dating to the later eighteenth century; sites in the Gobernador region farther north in the state exhibited Navajo materials from the earlier eighteenth century. "Scant attention has been given to the archaeology of so inconspicuous a group as the nomadic Navajo in a land where great and imposing pueblos dominate the archaeological scene," Keur noted (1941, 15). Keur wanted to examine acculturation, a fashionable topic in late-1930s anthropology, from archaeological data, and to tie these to historical and ethnographic information. Her field identifications were aided by her crew of Navajo laborers and the Navajo herder who reported the mesa sites. "[H]ere you were in an entirely different cultural milieu," Keur recalled of this fieldwork with Navajos, "That was the great appeal." A number of other women archaeologists who worked in the Southwest echoed this sentiment (Fox 1993, 308). Keur spent her professional life teaching heavy loads of undergraduate courses at Hunter College, and after World War II turned to pioneering ethnographic research in collaboration with her biologist husband John. *Big Bead Mesa,* in spite of its circulation by the Society for American Archaeology, has been virtually ignored, receiving mention in the histories of archaeology by Willey and Sabloff and by Trigger only because John Bennett cited it, and Madeline Kneberg's Tennessee research, in a 1943 paper on "the Functional Interpretation of Archaeological Data," a paper deemed worth a paragraph in each history. (Bennett, like Keur, worked in social anthropology after World War II.)

Other thoroughly professional women archaeologists who conducted ethnographic research in conjunction with archaeological projects include Florence Hawley Ellis, Frederica de Laguna, Clara Lee (Fraps) Tanner, Isabel Kelly, Jane Holden Kelley, Ruth Gruhn, and Nathalie F. S. Woodbury (whose ethnography is in the service of applied anthropology).[7] Hawley Ellis cooperated with eight Pueblo nations in support of their court claims to land and water rights; de Laguna published monographs on Southwestern Alaskan Yupik, Dene, and a tour-de-force on Yakutat Tlingit; Isabel Kelly carried out ethnography with Paiute before moving to Mexico to concentrate on archaeology; Jane Kelley produced a poignant and historically important study of Yaqui women: all work deeply valued by the First Nations involved. All except Woodbury carried heavy teaching loads, like Keur, although the youngest of these women, Kelley and

Gruhn, have directed doctoral students as well as undergraduates. Tanner was Gordon Willey's first instructor in archaeology, "a comely young lady ... attractive Miss Fraps" he mentions in his reminiscences (Willey 1989, 10)—and that, it seems, was that, for the workhorse of the University of Arizona's Department of Anthropology.

The methods and rationales for marginalizing these and other excellent scholars are well discussed by Nancy J. Parezo (1993). Women archaeologists' tendency to be aware of, concerned with, and comfortable with Indians was viewed by many male archaeologists as weakness, a distraction from pure objective science and surrender to Woman's emotional pull toward personal relationships. Dismissing women archaeologists' appreciation of the rich data and mind-stretching experience gained by respectful cooperation with Indian communities served to maintain the traditional ideological dichotomy between the primitives and the civilized scientists who studied them. These women's insistence on the validity and necessity of placing investigator and laborer on the same plane, of experiential knowledge absorbed through participant observation, subverted the discipline's role in presenting American Indians as the vanished race, doomed by its cultural retardation to conquest and domination.

CHAPTER 11

The Taboo Topic

The nineteenth-century construction of American archaeology as a science bequeathed two principles, the dichotomy between research object, that is to say American Indians, and its observers, and the notion that a proposition in science is validated by replication. This element of Baconian science led anthropologists to seek independent cases to confirm postulates on human behavior and cultural evolution. Assuming that no voyagers had crossed either ocean before Columbus in 1492 gave these would-be scientists a whole continent of tests of cultural development hypotheses. Transoceanic voyages prior to 1492 would negate the independence of American instances.

Daniel Wilson's position was that the human species is so imbued with instincts for developing civilization that some independent development was inevitable, regardless of contacts. His discussions in Canada with traders, Indians, and particularly the artist Paul Kane, who traveled across the country painting scenes of Indian life in the 1840s, gave Wilson an appreciation of the capacities of "primitive" boats such as bark canoes and Aleut baidarkas. He realized that the settlement of Polynesia proved the ability of canoes—at least those with outriggers—to traverse oceans (Wilson 1876:I, 161). It then seemed reasonable to suppose that the Polynesian migrations had ended in South America, that the settlement of mid-Atlantic islands (the Canaries, the Azores) had sent a second wave of colonizers eventually into the Caribbean, and that the migrations over Bering Strait were the last of three to populate America (II, 385). The principal point, for Wilson, was that all humans have, and exhibit to varying degree, ability to invent the arts of civilization. He was concerned to argue both for monogenesis of the human species and for Indians' capability to assimilate into Canadian citizenship.

John Lubbock, on the other hand, lacking firsthand experience outside Europe, considered "the Van Diemaner [Tasmanian] and South American are to the antiquary what the opposum and the sloth are to the geologist," living fossils (Lubbock 1912, 408); his descriptions of Fijian and Polynesian canoes are limited to their manufacture and appearance. Where Wilson felt the dynamics of history, Lubbock wished to impress his readers with the dichotomy that relegated all the less-clothed nations into the sink of savagery: his table comparing "savages" includes Fuegians, Bushmen, Hottentots, Andamanese, Australians, Esquimaux, North American Indians (one class, divided into West and East sub-classes), Fijians, Maori, Society Islanders, and Friendly Islanders. The last four have "Very good" canoes, Western North American Indians "Bad" ones, Eastern North American Indians "Middling" ones (528). The question of pre-Columbian transoceanic contacts was precluded, for Lubbock, by his conception of American Indians and Polynesians as living fossils.

Independence of the Americas became a dearly held tenet once the Mound-Builders were accepted as ancestors of historic Indians. So long as it was premised that the forebears of the contemporary Indians overran a Mound-Builder race, Indians could be adduced as unredeemed savages destined for conquest by civilized Christians. Identify Indians with the Mound-Builders, and they gain a discernible, if foggy, history. The task before early twentieth-century American archaeologists was to conform to the dictum Lubbock stated, "Savages may be likened to children" (Lubbock 1912, 545) and differ only from the effects of living in one or another climate (526). American antiquities could be accommodated within Lewis Henry Morgan's stages of Savagery and Barbarism without contradicting Lubbock's doctrine, thanks to Morgan's firm dismissal of Latin American Indian nations as anything more than the poverty-stricken Iroquois villagers he knew. Childlike savages could never have voyaged across oceans, nor could they have received foreign voyagers before Columbus, for events beginning in 1492 demonstrated that contacts with civilized men had enormously destructive impact upon the native races. A happy corollary of this obvious truth was that American Indians must constitute independent tests of the Enlightenment universal history Dugald Stewart had labeled "conjectural."

Initially, for the first half of the twentieth century, American prehistory was framed parallel to that of Eurasia, a Nuclear America center from Mexico to Peru sending out ideas and inventions as Mesopotamia and Egypt were believed to have sent out civilization in Eurasia. "Nuclear America" had been articulated in 1917 and codified in 1928 by Herbert Spinden naming an "Archaic" Mesoamerican cradle of civilization based on irrigated maize agriculture accompanied (and archaeologically marked) by little female figurines (Spinden [1928]1943, 63–64). Kroeber stated the same year, "practically all American students, seem in agreement . . . [on] a radiating transmission" (Kroeber 1928). Kidder declared, in the Thirties, "I am not a polygenist as regards American culture. I believe it had a single point of origin, though this tenet, I grant, is illogical in view of my strong feeling that civilization sprang up independently in the Old and New Worlds" (Kidder 1936, 151). In mid-century, Gordon Willey published "The Prehistoric Civilizations of Nuclear America," and Duncan Strong considered the assumption of "radiating transmission" out of Mesoamerica to still characterize his colleagues' perspective (Willey 1955; Strong 1951).

The illogic Kidder admitted was dramatically confronted by the 1951 American Museum exhibit of trans-Pacific similarities presented by the Austrian scholar Robert Heine-Geldern and the American Museum's Mesoamericanist, Gordon Ekholm (Heine-Geldern and Ekholm 1951; Heine-Geldern 1966). Alfred Kidder looked, refused to change his opinion, and confessed, "doubtless because of the obstinacy of increasing age and hardening of mental arteries, I am still one hundred percent American"(Kidder 1951, 222). Phillip Phillips stood with Kidder, and engaged to rebut the Heine-Geldern-Ekholm postulation of pre-Columbian contacts (Phillips 1966). He hoped to discover, with the assistance of a 1964 graduate seminar he led at Harvard, a method for drawing out stylistic distinctions casting doubt on alleged strong resemblances.

Phillips' seminar failed to work out a satisfactory means of refuting claims of contacts. It did draw Phillips' attention to the wealth of Mississippian engravings on shell, especially conch-shell chalices, that lie scattered in dozens of museums and had never been systematically compared. Sending a series of women out to make rubbings of the shells, Phillips and his younger colleague James Brown closely examined the reproductions and discerned two "schools" of Mississippian art evidenced in the tombs at Spiro, Oklahoma (on the Arkansas River at the border of the Mississippi Valley lowlands) (S. Williams 1978). Phillips and Brown published the results of their study through Harvard's Peabody Museum in a set of sumptuous volumes; it is not incidental that Phillips enjoyed an inherited private income.

Assaults by the New Archaeologists against established leaders of the discipline, battles that may be viewed from Patterson's delineation of an Eastern Establishment vis-á-vis a Core Culture west of the Appalachians, buried the old concept of Nuclear America (T. C. Patterson 1995, 106). Phillips had

> firmly disallowed . . . seeking stylistic and iconographic parallels in areas outside of the Southeast. . . . Our far from thorough attempts to establish stylistic connections between Spiroan and Huastecan art in shell seemed to yield no prospects of success, and it was this perhaps, rather than the excuse

of insufficient time and space, that prompted our decision to dodge the question altogether. (Phillips and Brown 1978, 128)

Ingenuousness may be a mark of men so securely ensconced socially no one dares to shout at "our far from thorough attempts," "our decision to dodge the question," or Kidder's "illogical" belief. The Spiro and Huastecan art referred to includes iconographically similar complex figures carved in the same difficult medium, *Busycon* shell from the Gulf of Mexico. The shell *must* have come from the Gulf of Mexico (Florida Keys through Veracruz, possibly as far as Yucatán) (Phillips and Brown 1978, 26–27). Phillips' arbitrary decision to disallow comparisons beyond the U.S. border lent a cachet of responsible scholarship to a closure his own meticulous publication showed to be intellectually unjustified. Phillips' prewar willingness to discuss Mesoamerican-Southeast connections made his 1960s and 70s attitude appear to indicate weakness in data, although his own words suggest merely disinclination to enter the large, complicated, and rapidly expanding field of Mesoamerican archaeology (Phillips 1940). The Gulf of Mexico became, conceptually, part of the Great Oceans isolating Anglo American prehistory from history. Coincidentally reinforced by the New Archaeologists' cultural-evolutionary disregard for actual history, mainstream archaeologists working in Anglo America dismissed Mesoamerica. Ekholm's predecessor George Vaillant had told a young Gordon Willey in 1939, when Willey asked his advice about starting a book-length study of Mesoamerican-Southeast ties, "Don't wait until you're old, and have a family, and are worrying about things like money and your career!" Willey got the hint and wrote a paper on Southeastern chronology (Willey 1939, 112). After mid-century, any archaeologist worried about money or career avoided looking at pre-Columbian contacts across saltwater.

Kelley and Hanen use the issue of transoceanic "diffusion"[1] to illustrate the effect of the social position of the idea and its proponent upon its acceptance. They choose Paul Tolstoy's advocacy of the hypothesis that barkcloth and paper-making spread from Southeast Asia, probably the Celebes, through Polynesia to America (Tolstoy 1963). The case is apt because Tolstoy advances his hypothesis through unusually explicit consideration of scientific method and probability, "commendable rigor" in the opinion of Kelley and Hanen (1988, 299). They conclude that Tolstoy's failure to persuade stems more from his peripheral status—he teaches in a French-language university in Quebec and excavates for fine-grain stratigraphic control on the rim of the Basin of Mexico—than from flaws in his argument for the transoceanic spread of barkcloth making. Exacerbating the situation, Celebes archaeology and the process of barkcloth and paper-making are unfamiliar to most American archaeologists, who are therefore uncomfortable assessing Tolstoy's argument. If Tolstoy aggressively socialized with mainstream American archaeologists, which he does not, then perhaps his hypothesis would be more easily accepted, or if he discussed lithic or ceramic technology perhaps it would be more easily understood, Kelley and Hanen imply (1988, 300–03). Being "explicitly scientific" but in a mode not congruent with the Binford-Watson version of logical positivism hinders Tolstoy's effort to establish a reasonable case of transoceanic borrowing.

The metaphor of a mainstream flowing with the ideological current and a marginalized periphery is the strongest explanation of the general rejection of hypotheses of transoceanic contacts before European invasions. Gordon Ekholm and Paul Tolstoy gained solid respect for their highly professional excavations in Mexico, but their interpretations of evidence for foreign contacts are not seriously discussed. David H. Kelley (parenthetically, Jane Kelley's husband) gained a leading position among Mayanists, but his exhaustive and brilliant research demonstrating a high probability of relationship between Mesoamerican and Asian calendar systems is ignored. Their colleagues in geography, George Carter and his students Stephen Jett and Carl Johannessen, similarly are not given judicious hearings for their provocative yet carefully documented hypotheses on the trans-Pacific spread of chickens, maize, organic dyes, and artifacts such as the blowgun. Although there seems no doubt that the sweet potato, an American domesticate, was found throughout Oceania by the first European voyagers, the observation does not lead to studies of the cultivar's history or probable processes of diffusion. Recognition of extensive seafaring, trade, and societal dynamics among Lubbock's designated primitives would directly counter Manifest Destiny; the discomfiting fact of pre-Columbian kingdoms on the Pacific islands is wrestled into the straitjacket Stage of Barbarism. The black comedian Richard Pryor wasn't really being funny when he asked, "Who are you going to believe—me, or your lying eyes?" (quoted by Gates 1995, 64).

Joseph Needham and the Question of Transpacific Contacts

Nothing so well explodes the positivist myth that Truth prevails through careful scientific method, as the refusal of American archaeologists to heed the work of Joseph Needham. Needham (1900–1995), a fellow of the Royal Society since 1941, Sir William Dunn Reader in Biochemistry at Cambridge University, master of its Gonville and Caius College, and finally director of the East Asian History of Science Library (now the Needham Research Institute), was described in *Nature*, on the occasion of his ninetieth birthday, as "probably the world's greatest living scholar . . . a genius almost without parallel in our time" (Temple 1990, 591). His first major work, the definition of the field he developed in his Cambridge laboratory, was *Chemical Embryology* (1931); then came *A History of Embryology* (1934) and *Biochemistry and Morphogenesis* (1942), all reprinted decades later. In 1966, Needham formally retired from biochemical research to work full time on the history of science and technology in China. From this enterprise came the multivolume collaborative, ongoing series *Science and Civilisation in China*. Needham was a great biochemist and unique as a historian of science, unmatched in his "facility of seeing both the wood and the trees at the same time," as he himself realized.

In his own words, Needham had "a love of little concrete things, and facts, the building-stones, the 'brass tacks', without which the grandiose generalisation will not reveal itself with relative certainty" (Needham quoted in Lu 1982, 37). This strong empiricism always playing into theoretical principles and questions was polished in his decades directing a major experimental laboratory drawing postdoctoral students from all over the world (23). When he turned fulltime to the history of science in China, he and his associates undertook to comprehend the texts they studied through hands-on experiment (Butler 1982). Firsthand, physical experience of data was critical in the task Needham set, providing him the Chinese title he delightedly created, *Shêng Jung Tzu*, "the Victorious-over-Confusion Master." To this end, Needham traveled widely.

Volume 4, part 3, of *Science and Civilisation in China* appeared in 1971. A major section (pages 540 ff.) addresses the issue of transoceanic voyages and pre-Columbian contacts with America. Consistent with the series, every statement is meticulously documented and practical, physical aspects carefully considered. David Kelley and I waited for Americanists to read and discuss this weighty contribution to our field. Nothing happened. Noticing that Dr. Needham was in his seventies, we decided after five years that the onus was on us to ensure that his unprecedented expertise and superb scientific mind were brought to bear on the important question of the premised isolation of the Americas. Lita Osmundsen, then Director of Research for the Wenner-Gren Foundation, agreed that ours was a valuable project and recommended it for funding; the Ford Foundation matched her grant, and the Coca-Cola Company assisted with the expenses of Needham and his principal collaborator, Lu Gwei-Djen. (Coca-Cola was at that time negotiating for a franchise in the People's Republic of China.) We arranged for Needham and Lu to spend two weeks in Mexico in 1977, visiting major sites and collections, accompanied by archaeologists who had been principal investigators in the areas. Thus our key participants could visually compare actual artifacts and sites in Mesoamerica against their wide field experience in Asia and their incomparable knowledge of scientific and technical texts. Queries on the material they were examining would be answered directly by Mesoamericanists. Gordon and Marguerite Ekholm and Paul Tolstoy came along (each with significant archaeological experience in Mexico, of course), and to ensure wide and open discussion, we included Paul Wheatley, author of the treatise on Asian urban geography *Pivot of the Four Quarters* , Donn Bayard, an American archaeologist working in Thailand and New Zealand, and agricultural history expert David Harris. Of the participants, Kelley, Tolstoy, the Ekholms, Needham, Lu, Mexican archaeologist Yolotl González Torres, Gordon Whittaker, an Australian who had just completed a Yale dissertation on early Monte Albán, and myself believed pre-Columbian transoceanic contacts merited serious consideration.

The outcome of the two-week peripatetic conference was to be a volume presenting both pro and con papers on trans-Pacific contact. Needham and Lu would author the opening chapter. Needham even proposed a working title, *The Smoking Mirror: A New Look at the Ancient Asian and Amerindian Civilisations,* and outlined a balanced volume before the group on our last evening. Needham and Lu finished, in good time, a reconsideration of the transoceanic section of volume 4, part 3 of *SCC.* The Ekholms, Kelley, Tolstoy, and González Torres prepared drafts of the papers they had volunteered. Not one of the participants who had come to the conference opposed to recognizing "diffusion" would write on the subject, no matter how often we assured them an exposition of their "con" views was necessary to the projected volume. Either these well-established scholars feared losing their reputations by association with the tabooed topic, or they could not marshall good arguments for their position. In the end, Needham and Lu published their contribution as a slim book with World Scientific, of Singapore (Needham and Lu 1985).

The Smoking Mirror title came from the Aztec fourfold deity Tezcatlipoca, whose black obsidian mirror is an instrument for penetrating beneath surface illusions into hidden truths. Joseph Needham characteristically identified the actual referent of the symbol, "a burning mirror for igniting tinder" (Needham and Lu 1985, 1). He surely smiled as he wrote those words, knowing how inflammatory the topic of transoceanic contacts can be. Trying to defuse the controversy, they emphasized, "We often know very little of how transmissions took place, but as in all other fields of science and technology, the onus of proof lies upon those who wish to maintain fully independent invention" (13). Two criteria, collocation and time, should be invoked in assessing the probability that contact was the source of innovation. The collocative criterion, similar to early-twentieth-century Austrian anthropologist Fritz Graebner's criterion of quantity, weighs number, specificity, complexity, and patterning of apparently similar traits or elements in two or more cultures. The time criterion notes the time differential between the two or more occurrences of the traits. Graebner had "form" as his second major criterion, allotting greater significance when neither raw material nor function seem to have dictated form (Lowie 1937,

158; Lucas 1978, 35–44); this criterion falls within Needham and Lu's collocative criterion (Needham and Lu 1985, 12).

The real force of Needham and Lu's study comes from the authors' years of tracing contacts and influences throughout Eurasia. Again and again, they and their erudite collaborators were able to demonstrate derivation across distance and time, often in the face of the most stringent barriers to diffusion of knowledge (as in the spread of gunpowder technology out of imperial China [Needham 1986]). The converse of demonstrating diffusion, marshalling reasons to postulate independent invention, was a devil's advocate constantly beside them. Ranke's famous call to write history *wie es eigentlich gewesen* dominates *Science and Civilisation in China*. Interdisciplinary to the max, welcomed by eminent scholars throughout the world, thoroughly ingrained with the practice of scientific method, Needham and Lu were capable as no one else to evaluate postulates of intersocietal contacts.

Among the similarities between Mesoamerica and Eastern Asia discussed by Needham and Lu after our 1977 conference are a number that comfortably meet both collocative and time criteria. These include a large suite of traits related to calendar astrology, which in itself is an unnatural, fantastic notion: that the movements of stars correlate closely with human events. In order to divine fate, Asian and Mesoamerican societies supported astronomers highly skilled in mathematics; only in China, India, and the Maya nations did these mathematicians compute with a sign (small circle) for zero, earlier among the Maya than on the Asian side of the Pacific (Needham and Lu 1985, 38). On both sides of the Pacific, a millennium or more before Columbus, people divided the night sky into lunar mansions and the year into repeating sets of named days, all these associated with animals, colors, Nine Lords of the Night, and benign or malign fates. On both sides, people saw a rabbit in the moon that pounds plant extracts in a mortar to make liquor. Needham reminds readers that Alexander von Humboldt published a lengthy, detailed exposition of these similarities in 1814.

Technology similarities are another class. Gordon Ekholm published a description, in *American Antiquity*, 1946, on finds in Mexico of clay animal figurines attached to axles with wheels. These were assumed to be toys, and were touted to be an example of a significant invention unappreciated by the barbaric Mexican Indians. Needham and Lu refer readers to Eurasian "bird-chariots" and other figurines on wheels interpreted, by Asian and European archaeologists, as tomb offerings and "cult figures," conclusions quite consonant with the Mexican examples (Needham and Lu 1985, 41). Paul (Pang-Hua) Shao, a Chinese-speaking artist who teaches design in Iowa State University School of Architecture, made field studies of monuments in Asia and Mesoamerica. He addressed the virtual absence of the true arch, or dome, in the Americas (in fact, three true arches are known from the Maya Late Classic, and Gordon Ekholm showed our conference group two low domed vaults at Tajín in Veracruz). Shao states, first, that Southeast Asian temple centers were constructed with corbelled rather than true arches until the fifteenth century A.D., and second, that the corbelled arch preferred by the Maya is not only less difficult to build but is far more earthquake-resistant than the true arch. In both Southeast Asia and Mesoamerica (and Cahokia, probably), the populace would gather for ceremonies on the grand plazas, the roofed temples being sancta rather than assembly halls (Shao 1978, 202–03; his 1976 book is an excellent survey of trans-Pacific parallels, effectively illustrated with his own photographs and drawings).

Out of our discussions with dozens of researchers, in museums and at the great Mesoamerican cities of Teotihuacán, Monte Albán, Tajín, and Palenque came an unexpected expansion of the question of trans-Pacific contacts. Customarily, contact was dichotomized into pre- and post-Columbian, time before 1492 designated "prehistoric" and after 1492, "European." It was particularly as Joseph Needham quizzed Isabel Kelly, in the collections storage in the Museo Nacional in Mexico City, that we realized that some similarities may be due to introductions by ordinary seamen fleeing the intolerable conditions on the Manila galleons during the sixteenth and seventeenth centuries. Deserters could be executed, so Asian men escaping at Acapulco, and Mexicans in Manila or Indonesia, would have hidden in villages outside Spanish control. Were these Asians, of the early historic period but avoiding inscription, responsible for the East Asian type of liquor distilling vessels in West Mexico? for the Asian-type fighting cocks that the Spanish found so widely distributed in Latin America? (Needham and Lu 1985, 56–57, Fig. 20 [Kelly's find]; Carter 1971). On the one hand, Manila galleon deserters can have introduced only a minority of the similarities adduced; the majority of postulated contact evidence is securely dated well before 1492. On the other hand, so much of the transmission of ideas and technology between China and the West chronicled in *Science and Civilisation in China* was carried surreptitiously that the possible Manila galleon deserters fall into the actual processes Simpson tells us are integral to historical science. *Science and Civilisation in China* is a model of historical science. American archaeologists' lack of interest in the work, and lack of respect for Joseph Needham's evaluation of pre-Columbian trans-Pacific contacts, betray a lack of understanding of science and of history.

The Issue of Transoceanic Contacts

In *Man Across the Sea*, I briefly described the past century's documented small boat crossings of the Atlantic. From a New England doryman celebrating the United States Centennial by rowing eastward to England (twice), to rafts, dugout canoes, folding canvas lifeboats, and an amphibian jeep, there was ample proof that the great oceans can be traversed by small boats (Kehoe 1971, 275–76). Table I updates the *Man Across the Sea* review.

Table I.

TRANS-OCEANIC CROSSINGS

Updating the contenders
for the title of Smallest Boat Crossing:

Trans-Atlantic Crossings:

1968 - Hugo Vihlen sailed *The April Fool,* 5'11-⁷/₈", Casablanca to Fort Lauderdale, Florida, in 85 days (Boehm, ed. 1983, 352).

1980 - Gerard d'Aboville, a Breton, rowed from Cape Cod to Ouessant, France, 3320 miles, in an 18-foot boat in 72 days, the first documented solo crossing from mainland to mainland.

1982 - Bill Dunlop took 78 days to sail a 9-foot boat from Maine to Falmouth, England.

1983 - Wayne Dickinson took 142 days to sail from Florida to northwestern Ireland in an 8'11" sailboat.

1985 - Two Frenchmen took 39 days to cross the Atlantic on a surfboard with a 20-*inch*-high hold for sleeping (one at a time).

1986 - Alain Pichavant and Stephane Peyron took 24¹/₂ days on a 31-foot sailboard from Senegal to Guadeloupe, whence they were continuing to New York. Peyron then sailed, in 1987, on a 25-foot sailboard from New York to La Rochelle, France, in 46 days.

1988 - Rüdiger Nehberg pedaled from Senegal to Sao Luis, northern Brazil, in a small Fiberglass pedal-rowing boat, taking 74 days.

1991 - British sailor Tom McNally sailed the Atlantic from Portugal to San Juan, Puerto Rico in a 5'4¹/₂" boat, provoking Mr. Vihlen to defend his title.

1993 - Hugo Vihlen in *Father's Day* - 5'4", 106 days, St. John's NFLD to southern England (the record for smallest boat crossing the Atlantic).

Trans-Pacific Crossings:

1972 - John Fairfax and Sylvia Cook rowed 8000 miles in a 35-foot boat from San Francisco, drifting down the coast to Mexico before crossing to Hayman Island on the central Australian coast. Fairfax had rowed from the Canary Islands to Florida in 180 days in 1969.

1978 - Webb Chiles left San Diego to circumnavigate the world in an 18-foot open boat; two years later, he sailed into Cairns Harbor, 1250 miles north of Sydney, Australia, having stopped over on islands.

1980 - On November 30, six Japanese researchers arrived in Chile, six and a half months after leaving Shimoda, Japan in a 43-foot catamaran, the Yasei-Go. They took the Kuroshio Current east to the Northern Pacific Current, taking that to San Francisco, then sailing down the coast to Chile (*Milwaukee Journal* 12/1/80).

1981 - Gerry Spiess made a 7800-mile Pacific crossing to Sydney in five months in a ten-foot sailboat; he had previously crossed the Atlantic in the boat.

1982-3 - Peter Bird rowed from San Francisco almost to Australia.

1984 - Arnaud de Rosnay disappeared at sea from a sailboard going from China to Taiwan. Earlier, his longest of seven open-water crossings was a thousand kilometers from the Marquesas to Ahé in the Tuamotus.

1987 - Ed Gillet paddled a kayak from Monterey Bay to Maui, Hawaii, in 63 days.

1991 - Gerard d'Aboville rowed a 26-foot boat from Japan to Ilwaco, Wash., in 134 days.

Thor Heyerdahl made these points, upheld by the sailors in the table: first, small boats are safer than big ones (because they are short, small boats are less stressed by long ocean swells, thus less likely to break apart); second, the open ocean is safer than coasting (where reefs, rocks, and unexpected currents pose dangers) (Heyerdahl [1978] 1980, 31–52). The curve of the globe, currents, and winds create oceanic traveling time, a better measure of difficulty than linear miles. Before the mid nineteenth century, travelers anticipated lengthy and often circuitous journeys with way-stops of weeks or months. When Tim Severin tested the feasibility of the legendary journey of St. Brendan, he overwintered in Iceland, partly to avoid unnecessary risk from August storms, partly because the medieval history of St. Brendan indicated island-hopping (Severin 1978, 172–73). Severin's large hide-covered curragh left Ireland in May 1976, and arrived in Newfoundland June 1977. Earlier, Paul Johnstone and Sverre Marstrander (1972) had demonstrated the seaworthiness of a replica of a Norwegian Bronze Age hide boat (Johnstone 1972).

Few American archaeologists are familiar with the principles of boats. Edwin Doran, a colleague of George Carter in cultural geography, analyzed these principles exhibited in watercraft around the world (Doran 1973). He found "Boatmen are conservative people," no doubt because their lives depend on cautious use of the tried-and-true. Doran recognizes three basic types of watercraft. One is the *nao* (Iberian "great ship," from an Indo-European root giving also Greek *naus*) or European keeled ship, plank-built, pointed at both ends. Another is the Chinese *junk*, bluff-ended and flat-bottomed, plank-built with bulkheads joined by transverse timbers rather than added to a frame. The third is the *vaka* or Oceanic canoe, usually built up with planks and balanced by the addition of one or two outriggers. All three great ship traditions employed sails, an energy engine complicating the stability of boats even as it delivers remarkable propulsive power. Bark- or hide-covered lashed-frame boats such as birchbark canoes, curraghs, coracles, and bullboats are historically found where wood is scarce, in Africa and the Andes as well as Northern North America, and in communities economically peripheral to mercantile centers, e.g., Ireland, Wales, Portugal. Plank sailing rafts are known from Mesoamerica and South America and southern Asia. Regarding the possibility of transoceanic contacts with America before 1492, only one fact need be stated: every type of boat—nao, junk, vaka, curragh, sailing raft—has been proven capable, in experienced hands, of traversing an ocean.[2]

The presumed utter isolation of the Americas before the heroic Columbus defied his seamen and sailed over the edge of the known world is, in a word, implausible. Polynesians on every habitable island throughout the Pacific are indubitable evidence of their ancestors' seafaring. On the Atlantic side, the Canaries, Madeira, and the Azores similarly, if not quite so dramatically, demonstrate non-European capacities for intentional long ocean voyages. Medieval Greenland Norse use of timber and other resources found across Davis Strait in America is accepted even by most American archaeologists on the basis of the Ingstads' researches and excavations in northern Newfoundland (Ingstad 1969; McGhee and Tuck 1977; McGhee 1983; 1984), although the standard interpretation is that the Norse made only brief forays south from the short-lived L'Anse aux Meadows colony (B. Wallace 1991, 193). Knowledge there is land to the west has been abundantly provided to Britons for millennia by the enormous quantity of drift timber washing up on their northwestern shores: a late Neolithic building at Stanydale in Shetland used 700 meters of dressed Labrador spruce (Calder 1950), accepted as American-originated drift by Clarke (1976, 244).

Assessment of pre-Columbian contacts is much muddied by a Manichean tendency of mainstream archaeologists to class all claims of pre-Columbian non-American Indian evidence in the Americas into the realm of "fantastic" or "cult" archaeology.[3] There are indeed hundreds of hoaxes, frauds, and silly or pigheaded identifications of artifacts and, especially, supposed inscriptions (S. Williams 1991; McGlone et al. 1993). The crux of the disagreements is the incommensurability of mainstream

Americanists' notion that salt water was an impassable barrier before the Discovery of the New World in 1492, and the avocational epigraphers' initial premise that inscriptions are likely to have been incised by ancient visitors to America. Very few of these researchers have been academically trained in epigraphy (the Semitic scholar Cyrus Gordon and the Mayanist David H. Kelley are exceptions), although several were trained in cryptography. The scientific procedure would be to follow the principle of parsimony by *demonstrating* that the petroglyphs or structures cannot possibly be the result of geological forces nor bear any resemblance to artifacts of local American Indians or post-Columbian settlers. More often than not, the non-professional researchers (who after all are sufficiently enthused and committed to work on their own time and money) do not first systematically assess the probabilities of natural, indigenous or colonial sources, but readily read Egyptian, Libyan, and Celto-Iberian, among others' symbols on rocks.

Here we have a situation very different from the work of Joseph Needham and his associates. Where Needham's scholarship is a model of thorough survey of literature, archives and artifacts plus explicit, rigorous testing of interpretations culminating in inference to the best hypothesis, the avocational epigraphers' late leader, Barry Fell, rushed into translations of often questionable petroglyphs and embraced romantic conjectures of world-circling voyages and intrepid quests over thousands of miles. Where Needham was courteous and genuinely interested in listening to others' opinions, Fell was argumentative and saw himself as a lone crusader against entrenched dogma. He was not so much mistaken in this as unwilling to concede the wide middle ground of ambiguous and inadequately researched evidence. Fell's rash statements became ammunition against him from "the archaeologists." At least a dozen of the avocational researchers more or less in his circle see his faults and in recent years have made efforts to evaluate more carefully sites and readings and to seek and discuss criticism (e.g., McGlone et al. 1993, xv). They are (understandably) reluctant to surrender their foundational position, that over three or four millennia, travelers from Europe, Western Asia, and Africa explored deeply into North America, inscribing their presence and religious faith. Efforts to date petroglyphs by physical-science techniques have not yet succeeded beyond challenge, leaving the epigraphers' identifications insecurely dated as well as open to alternate hypotheses of indigenous American Indian origin or, in some cases, possibly Mormon or other historic colonizers.

The few academically reputable researchers seriously concerned with the probability of pre-Columbian transoceanic contacts are—sometimes literally—between a rock and a hard place. The epigraphers' proclivity to recognize astronomical and religious symbols and texts hardly matches the preponderance of private trivia in actual graffiti, as seen in clearly modern graffiti interspersed with the alleged ancient inscriptions, and even in graffiti preserved on excavated Roman walls. Brief snatches of pagan creeds proposed by some of the Fell group contrast with the relatively long and mundane runic inscriptions on the Kensington Stone, from Minnesota (at the western end of the fur trade route through the St. Lawrence and Great Lakes), and Spirit Pond in Maine, both inscriptions recently analyzed by Richard Nielsen with consultation with medieval Norse specialists in Scandinavia (Nielsen 1988–1989; 1993). Nielsen explains what earlier, American professors of Scandinavian texts considered to be "errors" in the inscriptions, indicating fraud, to be dialect variation, specifically that of the Bohuslän region in western Sweden, a likely departure coast for boats sailing west across the Atlantic.

Intriguingly, it is also in the Bohuslän region that petroglyphs believed to date from the Bronze Age exhibit the "Proto-Tifinagh" symbols first recognized by Barry Fell in America on the Peterborough, Ontario, Rock (in the valley of a major tributary of the St. Lawrence). The Peterborough Rock is a massive light-colored granite dome outcropping on the north slope of the Trent Valley. This strikingly strange huge bare rock is covered with many hundreds of petroglyphs. David Kelley can accept Fell's identification of some of these petroglyphs as Proto-Tifinagh, and by implication accepts that identification of the Swedish petroglyphs, but Kelley emphasizes the difference between recognizing alphabet signs and translating short texts in ancient, poorly known languages (D. Kelley 1990). Tifinagh is hard to swallow for American archaeologists, since the Tifinagh alphabet was historically limited to northern Africa, surviving only with the Tuareg around Timbuktu; if it was once used in Scandinavia, it could have passed to or from northern Africa along the trade routes that in the Middle Ages linked the Norse with Sicily and northern Africa (in the eleventh century Sicily had Norman rulers). A parsimonious hypothesis would be that the Proto-Tifinagh words on the Peterborough Rock (that is, taking Kelley's opinion that this is the correct identification of some petroglyphs) do represent Norse traveling up the St. Lawrence and its tributary but may be somewhat later than the mid-first millennium B.C.; on the other hand, the first appearance of ceramics in the Northeast in the first millennium B.C., in technology and general style resembling Late Neolithic ceramics of northwestern Europe but not ceramics to the south in America, hints at North Atlantic Bronze Age contacts (Kehoe 1962; 1971; Porter 1981). It is interesting to note that, aside from the Proto-Tifinagh signs, at the time of historic colonization in the seventeenth century the Trent Valley was the boundary between Algonkian-speaking nations to the north and Iroquoians to the south; the Rock would have been an obvious potent site for Algonkian spiritual adepts to inscribe protective or aggressive symbols facing against Iroquois incursions.

Why the Taboo?

When James A. Ford worked on the ceramics from excavations he conducted in Preclassic sites in coastal Veracruz, he became increasingly impressed with similarities between his data and ceramics from the Southeastern United States he knew so well, from Peru where he had worked with Gordon Willey and Duncan Strong, and from the lands between. He recalled Spinden's formulation of a Nuclear American "mother culture." Half a century after Spinden's hypothesis, there seemed at last sufficient well-provenienced data to test it. Ford found his intensive review of hundreds of archaeological publications and thousands of sherds validated the hypothesis of correlated development of ceramics-producing, agricultural civilizations around the Caribbean and extending deep into northern South America. Sea travel was the sensible explanation for this widespread sharing of ceramic technology and styles. The tabooed topic!

> Archeologists have shown little interest in examining the philosophic bases of their studies. While utilizing the thesis that trait resemblances (in adjacent geographic regions) are evidence for contact, when faced with an unexplainable origin of a trait they have fallen back on independent invention theory. (Ford 1969, 194)

And what makes the origin of a trait "unexplainable" except by independent invention? Distance: linear distance shown on standard maps. Ford succinctly summed up the issue in the subtitle of his monograph, "Diffusion, or the Psychic Unity of Mankind." Nineteenth-century monogenists such as Daniel Wilson could assume instincts in primitive humans as powerful as what appeared to be instincts in other animals. Anthropology and ethology (the study of animal behavior) by the 1960s indicated far more learned behavior than instinct in the higher mammals, and surely in humans; "psychic unity" so strong as to stimulate similar sophisticated ceramic technology and styles was highly improbable. Sadly, James Ford completed his monograph on his deathbed, and could not argue beyond the manuscript he left.

Another scholar complemented Ford's approach. Margaret Hodgen was a historian collating documented innovations in Eurasia to test the question of frequency of independent invention versus innovation through contacts, and the most likely form of contacts. She concluded:

> Were it not for the tenacity with which students of cultural change now and always have adhered to the paradigm of the biological analogy, interpreted as progress, development, or social evolution (with its accompanying charac-

terizations of universality, inevitability, gradualness, and continuity), it would be unnecessary to dwell upon these rather obvious elements in the dated or historical process of change . . . [which must] fit the plain historical facts. (Hodgen 1974, 82)

Her plain historical facts pinpointed as "diffusion" agents, individuals who moved to a foreign commercial city "located . . . on a network of ancient, much-traveled roads, rivers, or sea lanes" and initiated a new enterprise based on knowledge or skill learned in their former residence (Hodgen 1974, 72). We do not know whether this situation is more likely in the mercantile capitalist political economy of her well-documented European cases, or may be more generalized. (She compares the "diffusion" of the printing press in Europe with the diffusion of Christianity—an example for which the word "diffusion" is more apt—but the Roman empire of early Christianity had strong elements of mercantile capitalism.) Hodgen found that her documented cases of cultural change "*fail completely to uphold the assumption of the universality of specific cultural changes, as implied in many theories of cultural evolution*" (64; her italics).

The issue of universal change in culture has a correlate in paleoanthropology, the study of hominid evolution. In this field, scholars recognized universal stages named as species: the australopithecine grade, the *Homo habilis* grade, *Homo erectus* grade, Neandertal, anatomically modern humans. A few researchers, notably Franz Weidenreich and, today, Milford Wolpoff, have insisted on the long duration of regional population characteristics, a picture incompatible especially with the claim that anatomically modern humans mutated once, in Africa less than two hundred thousand years ago, and replaced more primitive *sapiens* throughout the world. (How the many hundreds of thousands of other humans disappeared without trace so relatively recently is not addressed.) Wolpoff and Caspari's definition of multiregional evolution can serve for culture, too:

> humans have been a single widespread polytypic species, with multiple, constantly evolving, interlinked populations. . . . Because of these internal divisions and the processes [of selection] that maintain them, this species has been able to encompass and maintain adaptive variations across its range without requiring the isolation of gene pools. . . . Human populations developed a network of interconnections, so behavioral and genetic information was interchanged by mate exchanges and population movements. (Wolpoff and Caspari 1997, 32)

The fundamental contest, as Hodgen said, is between actualistic inference versus assumption of a universal trajectory of societal development, an essentialist position. The quest for replications of postulated evolutionary trends no longer seems a major concern, apparently because Whitean cultural evolutionism is so generally taught that younger archaeologists accept it as textbook fact. (Replicability is briefly discussed by Kelley and Hanen [1988, 116–17]; Watson, LeBlanc, and Redman do not discuss it explicitly but describe "a test case separate from" another excavator's project confirming a hypothesis [1984, 50–51].) The contrast between actualistic inferences and cultural-evolutionary "covering laws" (Watson, LeBlanc, and Redman 1984, 41) boils down to the issue of control: unilinear cultural evolution transcends human control yet an understanding of its trajectory enables people to predict development. Accepting the standard model of Progress from small and simple to large and complex, with concomitant evolution of industrial technology, Americans could impose Manifest Destiny first on Indians, Cubans, and Filipinos, then on all the Third World countries "developed" into economic dependency through American enterprises. The model of cultural evolution conveniently blots out the ugly Americans resisted by indigenous communities endeavoring to maintain relatively autonomous, sustainable economies. Actualistic inference, on the other hand, runs into disturbing observations of colonial oppression and exploitation. Archaeologists are individuals who chose *not* to become social workers, who prefer not to be embroiled in human misery. Unilinear cultural evolution is a safe haven, as Henry Adams realized.

On the face of it, discussing transoceanic voyages seems innocuously romantic. Move the topic to documented cases and it becomes history. To comprehend it as historical science requires two concessions, first that science demands actualism rather than conjectural history, and second that Destiny (in the guise of a single evolutionary trajectory) be rejected. Actualism moves us back to Daniel Wilson's observation that the populating of the eastern Pacific islands and those of the mid-Atlantic render contacts with America probable. Continuing with actualistic deductions, landings on already-populated continents would have limited effect, absent the post-Columbian combination of imperial programs of conquest abetted by a suite of diseases. Now the messianic flavor disappears, Europeans no longer the superior race salvaging the benighted savages. The whole palace of Progress becomes a mirage, its rationally constructed corridors and halls of audience dissolving into a multiplicity of tracks and niches.

Intersocietal contacts are the manifest of history. Ralph Linton put the actualistic case remarkably cogently:

> There can be no question about the average American's Americanism or his desire to preserve this precious heritage at all costs. . . . [In the morning] he places upon his head a molded piece of felt, invented by the nomads of Eastern Asia, and, if it looks like rain, puts on outer shoes of rubber, discovered by the ancient Mexicans, and takes an umbrella, invented in India. . . .

He reads the news of the day, imprinted in characters invented by the ancient Semites by a process invented in Germany upon a material invented in China. As he scans the latest editorial pointing out the dire results to our institutions of accepting foreign ideas, he will not fail to thank a Hebrew God in an Indo-European language that he is one hundred per cent (decimal system invented by the Greeks) American (from Americus Vespucci, Italian geographer). (Linton [1968] 1937, 384–85)

CHAPTER 12

Land of Prehistory

America's epic exploration of her unknown wilderness included scientific men pushing across the Columbian frontier into the Land of Prehistory to retrieve the traces of the vanishing savages. Jefferson had prescribed:

> that persons who go thither ... make very exact descriptions of what they see of that kind [antiquities], without forming any theories. The moment a person forms a theory, his imagination sees in every object only the tracts which favor that theory. (quoted in Kennedy 1994, 136)

It was too late. The Enlightenment myth assured all literate Europeans and their offspring that "positivism, inductivism, pure rationality, scientific proof, and all that" (Agassi 1981, 386) ennobled them, that they could stand above the unenlightened, observe directly, record, and reduce the teeming squirming cosmos to First Principles. Among these principles was the superiority of Western man, before whom the barbarians retreated, abandoning their rude appurtenances.

> Colonial ventures are ruptures ... archeology has been a vehicle for explaining away the obvious, for transforming a decisive break with the past into an inconsequential moment, and it can do this because its esoteric practices uncover a past invisible to the naïve observer. (Kuklick 1991, 165)

American archaeology shouldered the white man's burden, documenting a paleontological past of imperishable artifacts that ended like the Age of Dinosaurs with unheard whimpers. So long as Manifest Destiny was uncontroverted, the literal objectification of America's past seemed a natural proceeding; it only extended an Old World prehistory that celebrated the power of industrial technology through a chronicle of artifacts absolutely alienated from their makers, the mute history of the proletariat whose role is to continue manufacturing, silently. By the 1980s, sea changes in American political economy called the whole enterprise into question. The muted classes, now begrudgingly admitted to the academy as their members watched jobs transferred to the Third World, were to have their histories (Novick 1988, 469–72).

NAGPRA

Postcolonial sentiments swelled in America from the 1960s, even though the First Nations remained "domestic dependent nations," in Justice John Marshall's strange phrase from 1831. John Collier's 1930s New Deal policies during his tenure as commissioner of the Bureau of Indian Affairs had reversed the longstanding mission to destroy the First Nations, leaving their members to assimilate or disappear in remote poverty. The 1975 Indian Self-Determination and Education Assistance Act and the 1978 American Indian Freedom of Religion Act recognized what are essentially Constitutional rights for American citizens, rights that can be construed also as existing under the sovereign powers of Indian nations entered into treaty with the United States. While colonial policies consistently privileged Christians over non-Christians, the legal language of treaties acknowledged autonomy of the negotiating nations. The United States was not about to grant independence to its encapsulated colonies but it did accept that the blatant paternalism of the past was insulting, misguided, destructive, and wasting taxpayers' money. Neither the Self-Determination nor the Freedom of Religion Acts delivered immediate rectification of injustices, but they repeated policy implications of the Collier reversal and encouraged many Indian nations to greater efforts to exercise some sovereignty powers on their reservations.

The Freedom of Religion Act proved hollow in two major cases. In 1988, in *Lyng, Secretary of Agriculture, et al. v. Northwest Indian Cemetery Protection Assn., et al.*, the U. S. Forest Service was permitted to cut logging roads through a mountain area held holy by northern California Tolowa, Yurok, and Karok. In 1990, in *Employment Division, Department of Human Resources of Oregon, et al., v. Smith et al.*, the Supreme Court upheld the decision that ingestion of peyote in Native American Church worship could be used to dismiss an employee on grounds that he was a drug-user. The latter case was particularly discouraging because years of fighting to establish that peyote does not come under the definition of prohibited drugs (it is not a narcotic), a battle that included the legal incorporation of the Native American Church in 1918, had seemed successful years earlier. (Congress in 1994 reversed *Smith* by prohibiting extension of controlled substance laws to peyote used by American Indians in religious ceremonies.) Both *Lyng* and *Smith* were substantial and serious threats to free exercise of religion, and dramatic demonstration that the United States is not compelled to honor the intent of vaguely worded acts of Congress.

Senator Melcher of Montana, one of the few states in which Indian votes may swing an election, introduced a bill to counteract such disrespect by requiring museums and other owners of Indian corpse remains, grave offerings, and holy objects to return then to kin or the communities that could prove the objects were their patrimony. Hearings on the bill early in 1987 clarified the obvious point that repatriation required some documentation linking human remains or objects to living individuals or communities. Museums and research facilities usually have legal contractual obligations to curate their collections, not "deaccession" them. By the time the Melcher bill passed Congress, in 1990, as the Native American Graves Protection and Repatriation Act (NAGPRA), oceans of sentiment had ebbed and flowed over it, leaving the appearance that cold cruel White archaeologists and anthropologists habitually seized grandparents' bones and sacrosanct relics from helpless Indian people. Accounts of turn-of-the-century graverobbing for scientific collections were reprised. Protestations from curators that the bulk of collections were obtained lawfully were challenged by Indian activists insisting that everything Indian should be returned to Indians, any Indians if no direct ties are known.

NAGPRA was cataclysmic for museums and revolutionary for a large number of American archaeologists. Every institution that in one way or another had federal government ties and curated American Indian materials—in effect, nearly every U.S. museum and university—had three years to complete and submit an inventory of all its American Indian holdings. Some grants were made available for this work, but much of the expense of the painstaking, time-consuming job of not only pulling the information from records but checking each entry against actual items in storage, had to be borne by the institutions, and just at the point that most were only beginning the transfer of card-entry records to computer databases. The three-year deadline was extended upon application for many institutions, principally because they proved good-faith efforts hampered by inadequate funds. Institutions are required to provide summaries and inventories to the Indian tribes identified as originators or sources of items, upon which the tribes can negotiate with the institution for repatriation or continued curation. Regulations published in 1995 covered remains and objects discovered after NAGPRA went into effect in 1990. Every archaeologist and collections researcher working with North American archaeology now has First Nations representatives looking over their shoulder.

Issues spewed forth from the feel-good bill that failed initially to define many terms and procedures. What about federally unrecognized tribes, a category including many historically important nations east of the Appalachians who never entered into treaty with the United States? What happens when a nation split through forced removal, as happened to the Cherokee, Creek, and other eastern and midwestern nations officially removed to Indian Territory west of the Mississippi, leaving some recalcitrant families hiding out in the homelands? How do institutions determine who legally represents a tribe? And how do they deal with persons disavowed by an official Tribal Council but claiming to represent a minority, or elders, or disenfranchised descendants of tribespeople at the time of object acquisition? What about remains and objects thousands of years old? or on land disputed between two or more Indian nations? Most bizarre, what about Kennewick Man, a skeleton eroded from the Columbia River valley, dated nine thousand three hundred years old, and judged Caucasoid[1] by every biological anthropologist who examined it? Can the Euroamerican Neo-Pagans' claim to the skeleton be dismissed?

On the face of it, NAGPRA is a sign of the resurgence of America's First Nations, a population rise from 228,000 Indians in the 1890 federal census, 523,600 in 1960, to 1,959,234 in the 1990 census. Some of the population explosion in the last third of the twentieth century is due to Americans identifying Indian ancestry that they would not mention when discrimination was rife. Along with the hundreds of thousands who are biologically of Indian descent and the thousands who are socially integrated into Indian communities, thousands more announce Cherokee princesses among their forebears or proclaim spiritual kinship with these renowned primordial gurus. Thus there is a large constituency convinced that lo! the poor Indian deserves restitution of at least some of the enormous patrimony expropriated by raptor Congresses. Restore their lands? Wait a minute, that's *my* house, my fishing cabin, my National Park campground! How about restoring their ancestors' bones that no one sees, shelved in museums? Forbid logging on holy mountains? How about honoring their noble ancient pure religions with return of their primitive god statues and pipes?

Socialized in a Judaeo-Christian cosmology premising oppositional dualism, Americans assumed archaeologists who had taken Indian patrimony out of the ground must be callous arrogant scientists refusing to recognize the humanity of those they robbed. The public has no idea that the Society for American Archaeology counts a Mohican, a Muskokee, and other members of First Nations among its regular members, and elected an enrolled Osage as president just when thousands were outing their Indian ancestry, although few happened to know the tweedy Harvard graduate had that status. The agitation that gave us NAGPRA also coincided with the great shift among American archaeologists from WASP men, a number of them from wealthy or very genteel families, to a far broader spectrum including women, Jews and Catholics, working-class, and a few (very few) African Americans. Against the actual breadth of membership in SAA and the empathy many felt with others from disadvantaged communities, ranged self-appointed spokespeople for the Indians, urban residents who may or may not have some First Nation ancestry but who had little experience living within reservation communities. A few of these spokespeople seemed to derive their income from contributions and hospitality to support their campaigns. The self-appointed spokespeople were Pan-Indian rather than rooted in a particular nation's culture, and as Vine Deloria, Jr. (a Standing Rock Lakota) remarked, took John Neihardt's "Epic of the West" *Black Elk Speaks* as their bible. A good deal of their faith is Western, most particularly the notion that human bodies should be buried in the ground.

Archaeologists protested their good will, their willingness to listen and deal with First Nations, their disinclination to dig burials (take too much time to excavate properly and yield relatively little cultural information, as a rule). Anthropologists tried to point out that Plains Indians held it wrong to inter bodies in the ground, that many of the objects in museums were made to be sold or commissioned duplicates. No matter: The spokespeople who were given expense-paid trips to conferences, even to Europe, and the general public who flocked to the simplistic romanticized films *Dances With Wolves* and *Pocahontas* insisted on doing right by Indians, giving them their ancestors' bones to bury with quasi-Lakota pipe ritual. At SAA annual meetings, several hundred archaeologists jammed into ballrooms to hear panels of spokespeople, some legitimate representatives of their nations, others the impassioned champions of "The Indian." The Society itself convened a committee to prepare recommendations on ethics for American archaeologists, one section focusing on "public accountability" encompassing American Indian groups as well as a general public and local communities (Lynott and Wylie, 1995, 33–37). Commenting on the proposed guiding principles, Janet Levy remarked that an unstated assumption in discussions "seems to be that the oppressed deserve our greatest ethical concern." Fine ethos; but Levy knows situations where factions dispute within a community, and asks, "who is, or was, oppressed 'enough' to take priority. Or, in the case of American archaeology, who is Indian enough?" (Levy 1995, 91).

NAGPRA galvanized American archaeologists into accepting a post-colonial position. Melcher's bill was a symptom of the sea-change in American society during the second half of the twentieth century, the G.I. Bill lifting large numbers of working-class men, and then women, into the educated class, the Civil Rights Act greatly reducing WASP power to restrict opportunities to favored segments of the population, the growing distrust of Big Science moving federal funding from the National Science Foundation to the National Endowment for the Humanities (NEH), heightened concern with environment repercussions challenging conventional goals of productivity and management. More subtly, watching thousands of jobs taken from American workers to Third World nations, and seeing foreign corporations buy American companies and real estate, mainstream Americans began to wonder whether the United States is indeed the Redeemer Nation; perhaps we have more in common with the oppressed than our parents had thought. American archaeologists are carried like the mass on the country's politico-economic currents, and with so much larger a proportion of American archaeologists now drawn from formerly discouraged classes, the distance from hoi polloi once commonplace among archaeologists had to lessen. NAGPRA enforced accountability on a profession that, as was said of the ethnographer Malinowski, was already coming down from the veranda of the colonial officer.

Compliance with NAGPRA's deadlines for completion of thorough inventories and of research on human remains, compliance with stricter requirements for permission to excavate and for reporting discoveries, and the reliance of CRM archaeologists upon agency and private contracts, made American archaeologists more businesslike in conducting their work. NAGPRA itself reflects the diffusion of business expectations into what had been autonomous research. Although even in the good old days of primarily academic sponsorship, much work was in fact CRM in that projects were directed toward surveying and salvaging threatened sites, stringent deadlines for final reports were not the norm—preserving salvaged artifacts and bones for leisurely or eventual analyses was the goal, rather than dissemination of inventories and evaluations to authorities. It was this gentlemanly attitude, reports undertaken as noblesse oblige, that activists decried. Ancestors' bones in boxes upon shelves disrespected business efficiency, not merely Indians' kin.

"Accountability" pushed archaeologists into a postmodern realization that the discipline's known pasts may not necessarily override others' versions of the past. NEH funding opportunities legitimated discussion of contestation, where earlier reliance on NSF precluded acknowledgment of non-scientific exegeses. Larry Zimmerman, an archaeologist who worked for years at the University of South Dakota in Lakota heartland, criticized the SAA Ethics Committee's bald equation of "the best ... archaeological practice" with "most rigorously scientific" (Lynott and Wylie 1995, 25; Zimmerman 1995, 64). The conveners of the Ethics workshop, Mark Lynott and Alison Wylie, opened with an unproblematic statement typical of the positivist era, that such "rigorously scientific" practice would be "undertaken strictly for purposes of enriching our collective understanding of the past" (64) Exactly this hegemonic assumption underlay the establishment of professional control a century ago, in American history as much as in archaeology. Peter Novick links professionalization, with its insistence on professional autonomy, "the establishment of norms of objectivity," and a national scope to "transcend provincialism and particularism" (Novick 1988, 511). Credentialed salaried professionals designate the domain and it mirrors their disciplinary boundaries and scale. That First Nations might object to "our collective past" does not seem to have occurred to the SAA conveners.

Zimmerman bluntly put it:

> The problem is control. I sense that the ethics statement authors and probably most archaeologists would be reluctant to relinquish control. . . . Consultation and involvement of nonarchaeologists puts at least some of the control of research itself into hands other than ours. Are we really willing to do this? If you say yes, you have agreed to an approach that will fundamentally change archaeology. (Zimmerman 1995, 66)

He singles out the Hopi Cultural Preservation Office, described previously in the volume by its director, Leigh Jenkins, as an example of the new approach. The Hopi employ four archaeologists and an ethnohistorian, none of them Indian, to carry out directives from the tribe developed in consultation with a Cultural Resources Advisor Task Team of eighteen recognized clan elders and priests. The contracted professionals document a Hopi past frequently colliding with the national American past. Their findings are utilized in negotiations with non-Hopi to support land and water right claims, the clans' histories recounted orally, Hopi modes of agriculture and technology, and the repatriation of holy objects. The professionals use rigorous scientific and historiographic practices but are open to align these with oral history and Hopi interpretations of data, not deforming but enriching the prehistory and conventional history (Zimmerman 1995, 35).

An irony of NAGPRA is that the rhetoric attending it obscures both the diversity of Indian understandings of human existence and spiritual practice, and the real contest in America, between sovereign nations and United States control. "Respect for ancestors" is a red herring distracting the public from the postcolonial world of respect for the internationally recognized rights of nations to govern their lands and residents. CERT (Council of Energy Resource Tribes) demands for realistic royalties from mineral exploitation on reservations, Seneca insistence on its ownership of the town of Salamanca, Wanapam right to fish the Columbia from its traditional station, Chippewa hunting and spearfishing on ceded lands, Six Nations' nationals' exemption from off-reservation employment taxation, and of course the power to offer competitive commercial gambling are issues of vested sovereignty remaining after treaties. None of these will be forwarded by cases such as the elderly Wisconsin judge awarding four-thousand-year-old Old Copper skeletons to an unaffiliated urban Indian to bury with contemporary Pan-Indian rites. Unfortunately, such "justice" satisfies a public that thinks the Oglala exorbitant in demanding return of the Black Hills. Nor can NAGPRA return such patrimony.

The effect of NAGPRA is to give standing to First Nations in the Land of Prehistory. "Our collective past" is, in a sense, balkanized. Dozens of nations extend back from the nineteenth century through the contact frontier. Frank Hamilton Cushing was laughed at for his Zuni participant-observer ethnoarchaeology in the 1880s, conveying to cooler heads the wisdom of maintaining a proper distance between natives and archaeologist. With the Indian Self-Determination Act and a radical increase in college-educated American Indians, the Zuni, like the Hopi, now direct archaeologists in research. These nations whose settlements demonstrably are footed in prehistory have criteria of validity that include but are not limited to SAA's rigorous science. This is not a matter of postprocessual theory; this is everyday reality, praxis under politico-economic constraints.

The big university research departments will continue lauding charismatic egos proclaiming New Archaeologies, and continue favoring laboratory-oriented archaeology paying overhead charges. CRM archaeologists will continue filing multitudes of reports on surveys for fishing cabin pier pilings, bridge abutment repairs, highway widenings, parking lots. Tribal officials will continue examining collections, trying to connect the objects they see with orally transmitted knowledge and classic ethnographies. The fundamental change at the end of the twentieth century is the diminution of the frontier mentality. There remains plenty of excitement in exploring here and there in the past, but no more the Lone Ranger with his inarticulate Tonto. Tonto is now another Sabio. The Ranger is no longer permitted to mask his ordinary humanity. First Nations, the descendants of the enslaved, millworkers, sharecroppers, loggers, prostitutes, have their pasts uncovered by archaeologists. From the Department of the Interior to local boards, employers enjoin archaeologists to present their findings to schoolchildren and the adult public, to invite visitors to excavations and labs, and to write at the popular level. The profession of archaeology burgeoned after the 1950s, it became more open and democratic, the real source of most funding—taxpayers—was reckoned worthy of receiving archaeological information, and the inhabitants of the Land of Prehistory begat lineages into the present. The white man's burden is stowed. The Great White Way is muddied by many feet tramping.

Bastions of Law and Order

The Land of Prehistory so neatly platted by the establishment's intrepid surveyors seems, to their torch-carriers, as much as ever in need of law and order to knock sense into the mob of inchoate data. The glamor of "rigor-

ous science" still seduces some archaeologists. Universal laws may be elusive and chaos theory disconcerting, but it seems to a number of American
archaeologists that some universal principles ought to be discovered.
Biology has its backbone of evolution, so surely humans, being organisms,
should be subsumed under the mechanisms of evolution? Unilinear evolution, á là Johnson and Earle's retrograde textbook? Or the evolutionary
archaeology propounded by Robert Dunnell? Or do all of these constructions on analogy with biology miss a critical difference, human intention or
agency? In this section, I juxtapose a current claim for an evolutionary
archaeology against issues central to contemporary evolutionary biology,
and for scientific method against its unraveling under the work in artificial
intelligence. This section on persistent commitments to "objective science" is, essentially, juxtaposed to the preceding section on NAGPRA and
its postcolonial humanism.

Sites and assemblages can be placed in series. Under unilinear cultural
evolution, archaeological data are spin-doctored to illustrate Enlightenment
universal history, Whig history literally with a vengeance, obliterating the
alternate histories of conquered and "remote" nations. What Robert
Dunnell and his followers term "modern scientific evolutionary archaeology" has little in common with histories of mankind. Instead, they propose
that artifacts are as much part of human phenotypes as are somatic features, and therefore "subject to [natural] selection" for fitness (M. O'Brien
1996, xiv). Dunnell was inspired in the late 1970s by Stephen Jay Gould's
essays in the magazine *Natural History*.[2] He reproved unilinear cultural
evolutionists for scanting the essential role of natural selection. Eschewing
"Progress" and series of cultural stages, Dunnell assumes the archaeological record testifies to unceasing selection of behavior and artifacts for
greater fitness. This selection process, he premises, is no more under
human conscious agency than the evolution of social insects is under their
queens' conscious control (Dunnell 1996, 48–49, 90–91). Dunnell's version
of human/cultural evolution is selectionist; he disavows calling it adapta-
tionist yet insists that "the notion of inclusive fitness" is key to understanding the archaeological record (65). This brand of cultural evolution has the
virtue, not to be scoffed at, of leveling the playing field for human societies,
recognizing that evolutionary biology requires acknowledging that all societies that are contemporary are equally evolved. Its repudiation of human
agency adds a flavor of metaphysics in that the premise is primitive,
undemonstrated and without obvious means of empirical testing against the
competing hypothesis that conscious choice created the archaeological
record. Like the sociobiology it so much resembles, Dunnell's "modern scientific evolutionary archaeology" is radically reductionist.

Placing humans and their behavior—"cultures"—within evolutionary
biology does not require reduction to a lowest common denominator

among organisms. The foundation of evolutionary biology is variation, of which selection may affect the frequencies. Robert Chambers grasped the fundamental significance of variation when he posited his Law of Variety-Production. Histories of populations are histories of the appearance, persistence or loss of variations. Selection, as Darwin so clearly understood, is a mechanism acting upon variations; a mechanism is an efficient cause but hardly an explanation. We want to learn *what* variations occurred, *when* and *where* they occurred, to *whom* they occurred, and *why* they occurred; journalists' questions that structured the culture histories American archaeologists once worked upon routinely. Culture histories *are* evolutionary histories. They are histories of the occurrence, persistence, or loss of variations in populations. *Why* may have involved natural selection for greater fitness; it may have involved conscious human choice for one rather than another mode of living; it may have above all been happenstance contingency. To illustrate the problem with "fitness": the invention and perfection of toggle harpoons in Arctic coastal habitats certainly increased the inclusive fitness of communities there, whereas creation of celibate Shaker communities in late-nineteenth-century America is not particularly amenable to an explanation based on natural selection for inclusive fitness, although a tortured reasoning might be propounded. Explanations of humans' histories must factor in human cognitive and communicative capacities within the data set. Studying species-specific features such as these in a wide frame are the point of evolutionary biology.

The philosopher Elisabeth Lloyd characterizes natural selection theory as "a very abstract, high-level theory from which other evolutionary models are produced through specification of various aspects of the high-level theory" (Lloyd 1988, 14). She explicates the use of models wherein, for example, "the principle of natural selection is seen as part of a specification of an idealized breeding group," in contrast to the logical positivist approach of deducing axioms (17). A model is described through its state or configuration of variables, its parameters, and relations between models. Families of models constitute a theory, and theory can be confirmed by "(1) fit between models and data; (2) independent support for various aspects of the model; and (3) variety of evidence" (25). The empirical specificity of models are the strength of this approach to evolutionary biology, giving it power over a range of cases, even where human agency seems significant, and freeing analysis from the presupposition that adaptedness (or "inclusive fitness") is a universal prime mover. Lloyd emphasizes in her conclusion that "assumptions made in constructing any model play a major role in theory; I claim they should likewise play a major role in evaluation of evidence" (164).

Computer scientist Brian Cantwell Smith states this powerfully:

in that allegedly innocent pretheoretical "set-up" stage, one is liable, even if unwittingly, to project so many presuppositions, biases, blindnesses, and advance clues about the "answer," and in general to so thoroughly prefigure the target situation, without either apparent or genuine justification, that one cannot, or at least should not, take any of the subsequent "analysis" seriously. (Smith 1996, 16)

More specifically, Smith describes the trap he labels

inscription error: a tendency for a theorist or observer, first, to write or project or impose or inscribe a set of ontological assumptions onto a computational system [a program, a process to which it gives rise, a domain (33)] . . . and then, second, to read those assumptions or their consequences back off the system, *as if that constituted an independent empirical discovery or theoretical result.* (Smith 1996, 50; his italics)

The role of guiding assumptions has been examined empirically by the Laudans and Donovan (1988), who find these, rather than some grandiose schema one might term "paradigm," to be the daily bread of working scientists. Guiding assumptions tend to be indoctrinated in ordinary socialization and in formal instruction; in "cookbook science" they are routinely accepted, in more sophisticated, innovative, or reflexive scientific practice some may be adduced but others may be so embedded in customary thinking that they remain hidden. For example, what working scientist would state the assumption that there is matter in the universe? Who but a Scientific Creationist would discuss whether a stratigraphic column of fossils represents sedimentation or God's direct emplacement? The assumption, from Enlightenment histories, that humanity progressed from savagery through barbarism to agriculture and commerce guided Thomsen, Wilson, Lubbock, and Pitt-Rivers. It created a model to be sought in stratigraphic excavations and to be exhibited in museums. It is the narrative of history taught in schools. It takes the kind of jolt that Franz Boas experienced in his year of living dangerously with Baffinland Inuit to knock the assumption from its status as a given.

Dunnell's "modern scientific evolutionary archaeology" illustrates another sort of guiding assumption, one accepted a priori from another scientific discipline rather than a priori from ideology. Darwinian evolution does ground interpretation on the principles of heritable variation and selection. This does not force an evolutionary scientist to reductionist applications of the principles. Ernst Mayr warns that evolutionary biologists frequently failed to give enough attention to "(1) multiple simultaneous causations, and (2) pluralistic solutions" to "evolutionary challenge. . . . The lesson one learns from this is that sweeping claims are rarely correct in evolutionary biology" (Mayr 1991, 147–49). Contemplating this, Mayr considers the abundance of apparently neutral (non-adaptive) alleles, and concludes that these random, non-selected mutations seem to represent "non-Darwinian changes during evolution"* (152–53).

Evolutionary biologists are increasingly engaged, on the one hand, with non-linear models, or as some put it, the science of complexity, and on the other hand, with the rhetoric that molds and colors their work. Both these concerns are highly relevant to archaeology, the former opening up the world once straitjacketed by unilinear evolution models, the latter sensitizing us to the subtle manipulation of semantics, syntax, and mythos. Perhaps surprisingly, these two concerns interdigitate. Listening to stories, from nursery tales and the Bible to novels, films, sports news, commercials, we assume events in temporal sequence form a plot: someone gains or loses their goal. Speaking Indo-European, we are habituated to everything being, like Caesar's Gaul, divided into threes—beginning, middle, and end, subject, verb, object. The comfortable, "natural" way of our world is in fact a dominant model. Non-linear models, complexity, contingency, seem to fall under the rubric of chaos—Primordial Chaos, father of Night. William Blake, so ill-placed in time and class, could write of *fearful* symmetry but most of us find symmetry lovely and lulling. Letting go of plot (such as "survival of the fittest"), resisting tripartality, seem to dissolve our world into chaos.

Look again, and the monstrous threat is tamed. There are still parameters. Pigs don't fly, and we can describe the morphology that grounds them and the DNA increments that brought them to being *Sus* while *Aves* accumulated other increments. Evolutionary biology encompasses archaeology, since humans are organisms subject to the parameters of mammalian life, and it offers models of change and of stability that may be analogous to instances in the archaeological record. It cannot suffice for archaeology because DNA is conserved via cell division through generations and millions of years, while artifacts have no such robust continuity. The archaeological record parallels human evolution but it is not organic evolution.

Agency, Contingency, Complexity

Human agents are the formal causes of artifacts, that is, of the archaeological record. The intriguing question for archaeologists, once the what, where, when have been determined (as well as we can), is why a who at that place and time created *such* an artifact. Ralph Linton's analytical set of form, function, use, and meaning indicates the multifarous condition of our answers. Margaret Archer, in *Culture and Agency*, recognizes the sit-

---

*Not "non-Darwinian evolution"!

uational logic in which humans operate (Archer 1996, 145): living in a particular social group, to which has been transmitted a particular conglomeration of concepts and stories, within which experience is noted and discussed, a person is agent and simultaneously culture-carrier. The imperishable artifacts that constitute the archaeological record are neither simply functional nor, because they are material, purely ideational. The archaeologist's task is to delineate the constraints and potential of the raw material and technology of the artifact, then figure out the logic brought to bear upon it by its maker. There is a great leap between the material and the logic, not only in strength of inference but also in that the logic is situated in relationships between humans and between humans and environment—environment in the broad cosmological sense of Bourdieu's habitus. The question of human agency is thus embedded in reconstructions of culture.

Praxis is the nub of the archaeologist's confrontation with data: praxis in the past when a human acted in the context of their situation, and praxis in the present, in the actions of the archaeologist within a contemporary situation. Contemplating each situation, we can feel contingencies run amuck. What virtuoso flintknapper, driven by aesthetic sensitivity and yearning for approbation, happening to be born in the Northern Plains when Fluted Tradition knapping was still standard and Knife River chert was widely traded, flaked an Eden blade and set a model of beauty and skill acclaimed, imitated, and ensconced in the Early Holocene cultures of the region? Utilitarian function cannot explain the prevalence of this remarkable type of artifact. Limited in time and space, the arbitrariness of such an artifact makes it a good "index fossil" or "horizon marker" for a cultural value carried in some sort of wide social context.

Taking contingency into account means accepting a world without God, Progress, or any prime mover. It means forswearing the ambition of formulating universal laws. The notion of "power" deflates, seeps away, in a world where predictability is strongly compromised by chance. Contingency historicizes research problems, and as Levins and Lewontin remind us, it does so in two ways, raising the history of the research subject to prominence, and illuminating the historical context of the problem per se, its framing and method, and criteria for validity (Levins and Lewontin 1985, 286). From this point of view, the long century of denaturing history in order to transcend contingency, from Spencer through Hempel, becomes not the Age of Science but a Mythopoetic Age. The real scientist is the one who refrains from generalizing, *vide* Boas.

On a different tack—although still on the same vessel ploughing the dark sea—"complexity" is the target. Contra Spencer and his partisans, complexity is not the evolutionary goal state. Furthermore, "complexity" is an elusive concept. Some ecologists argue that hierarchy theory is a fruitful approach to "complexity": these analysts decompose a system, such as an ecosystem, into components on the basis of differences in process rates among the components (O'Neill et al. 1986, 76). "Higher" levels of the system exhibit slower rates than "lower" levels—or to phrase it less metaphorically, the analyst views the faster rates subsumed under the slower rates. (Von Bertalanffy remarked once that structures are slow processes of long duration.) These analysts try to elucidate constraints—structural, functional, spatial—on components of an ecosystem, and assume the ecosystem and its components appear to tend toward an equilibrium because various vectors meet constraints; what appears as an equilibrium at the human viewer's scale and rate is a multiplicity of movements and adjustments. Perturbations in the ecosytem or within its components may be contained within oscillations or may disrupt the oscillations, resulting in observable change. Morphogenesis, too, can be described in this way (Goodwin 1994, 106, 116). From the standpoint of morphogenesis, the generative field in which an organism grows is as vital as its genes. An organism is, in this sense, not so different from an ecosystem.

It is indeed this very point that some biologists have been wrestling with, sounding more like philosophers than the muddy T-shirted collectors of algae their research assistants see. O'Neill and his coauthors warn that analysis may be stymied if the researcher assumes significant components will always be tangible and visually bounded. Tangible boundaries, they say, are special cases of discontinuities in rate processes (O'Neill et al. 1986, 88-89). Brian Cantwell Smith puts it this way:

> the subject itself shades inexorably into unregistered contact with what is *around* it, with what it is *made of,* with the overwhelming particularity of its ineffable local surround. To *be* , therefore—to be a subject, an object, to be anything or any way at all—is a little bit like being a drop of ink on a blotter. Even if there is a center, a core—a resolute and defensible facticity about there *being* an ink blot, here and now—it nevertheless always turns out, on sufficiently close inspection, that the boundaries . . . are not . . . discrete, formal. (Smith 1996, 370; his italics)

The lesson here is that we are not dealing with a pack of cards labeled Agency, Contingency, Selection, Complexity, Environment, Function, shuffling them to make a winning hand. The archaeological record is the detritus of active fields in which individual persons perturbed their little social/environmental niches and groups of persons collectively perturbed and were dialectically perturbed by their habitats. Any boundaries, even ones such as town walls consciously constructed by inhering groups, are heuristic. One of the bizarre results of the scientism rampant in American archaeology is a book in which Suzanne and Paul Fish and Stephen Kowalewski are forced to defend the scientific validity of extensive surveys of entire geographical regions (Fish and Kowalewski 1990). Their examples show not only that exponentially more knowledge is gained from larger-scale data bases, but also how arbitrary are the conventional boundaries given for sites and archaeological cultures. At that scale, active parameters, or constraints, are more likely to be recognized as discontinuities discovered in the data. Discontinuities visible in one set of data, for example dwelling clusters or a painting style for ceramics, will probably not coincide well with discontinuities in other sets, a circumstance compatible with the image of generative fields.

The Chacmool 1993 conference "Debating Complexity" displayed a range of archaeologists' notions of "complexity." Suzanne Spencer-Wood presented a sophisticated illustration of multiscalar analysis of a set of data, framed in nonlinear theory. Her presentation of glassware from a nineteenth-century Vermont general store dramatically graphs the loss of information when forty-year groupings are collapsed into seventy-year groups: At the larger scale, the shift from local to national manufactures cannot be seen (Spencer-Wood 1996, 59–60). A similar example is given by David Wilcox, reexamining common Southwestern archaeological assumptions in the light of both the history of archaeological interpretations in the region and of its wealth of data (Wilcox 1996). In the same conference, Joseph Tainter used the colloquial meaning of "complexity" rather than the recent mathematical usage to urge against the conventional dichotomy between "simple" and "complex" societies, pleading for a view of social groups dynamically shifting between greater and lesser (structural) complexity—a subtle move from the colloquial toward the mathematical theory (Tainter 1996, 14). These and other papers in the conference volume demonstrate Randall McGuire's point that an inchoate "science of complexity" lies in many culture-historical archaeological reports (McGuire 1996, 28). Biologists Allen and Roberts put it clearly:

> complexity is tractable but demands parallel description at many explicitly specified levels. In the face of complexity it is essential to distinguish model and observables from the material system, and to recognize that the model must invoke a scale and a point of view. (Allen and Roberts 1991, x)

What Do We See in the Archaeological Record?

Archaeologists visualize entities that in biological terminology are chimeras: "individuals," for example societies, constituted from different zygotes (Rosen 1995, 343–44). The raw material of archaeology comprises what may remain of organisms, each from its zygote, plus what remains of inorganic matter affected by the humans living in the sampled locality.

Syntagmatically related in place and via stratigraphy, the recognizable elements can be said to be collated into archaeologists' chimeras; the "societies" described by archaeologists are certainly not identical with the actual living communities producing the detritus studied. The chimerical nature of archaeologists' "societies" may invalidate any facile application of principles or processes characteristic of individual organisms. Ethnographic analogy is also compromised by chimeras' freedom to incorporate disparate elements. The principle of actualism constrains us to rely upon ethnographic observations to originate and to test inferences on the significance of archaeological data, yet the chimeras we seek to picture may have been ephemeral. Equivocation becomes archaeologists on the plane of interpretation.

Balancing the equivocation befitting representations of chimeras, archaeologists must rigorously explicate their data, the disparate parts of the chimera. This is well understood on a gut level by practicing archaeologists, demonstrated by the packed little rooms where slides of data in situ are exhibited at Society for American Archaeology meetings. Michael O'Brien (1994; 1995) presents a cogent review of the frustration besetting an archaeologist attempting to construct a regional artifact history ("culture" history hardly applies to what are really exercises in ceramic sorting). The portion of the Central Mississippi Valley in which he works received a sophisticated archaeological survey by Phillips, Ford, and Griffin (1951), who sorted and seriated thousands of sherds from three hundred eighty-five sites. O'Brien quotes liberally from Phillips, Ford, and Griffin to establish that they intended their ceramic types to be provisional, envisioning ongoing resorting and refinement as normal practice. Instead, O'Brien avers, subsequent fieldworkers used Phillips, Ford, and Griffin's openly heuristic sorting as static types, resulting in ill-supported phrase designations. One confusing practice was to place undecorated sherds into one or the other of two types, according to whether shell temper was finely ground or coarse. This equated a functional trait—coarse shell temper makes the pot tougher (Feathers 1989)—with stylistic qualities of design and slip marking the other ceramic types, and gave body sherds a pair of types separate from vessels' decorated portions. Reports describe one or the other of the temper-size types as predominate of all types in sites, as if the inhabitants preferred pots without rims, *unless* the site is represented by a surface collection biased by the collector picking up the more visible decorated sherds. O'Brien continued his radical critique with a put-down of the assumption that the Late Prehistoric Central Mississippi Valley societies were "chiefdoms" fitting Service's usage of the term (O'Brien 1995, 28–30). A political history was made for these convenient "chiefdoms" out of ceramic samples, and one puzzling inference has been that a broad, fertile, populous region became a "vacant quarter" in the fifteenth century.

O'Brien deconstructs the problem with the suggestion that farther south, there were ceramic changes after 1450 out of which archaeologists made a distinctive temporal phase, while little change occurred in ceramics in the "vacant" region, inducing archaeologists to assign all ceramics to the "earlier" phase and declare the quarter vacant after 1450 (31). A complicated and conflicted house of cards had been built by reifying the pioneer heuristic sortings—positivism gone awry, to paraphrase O'Brien's 1995 title.

Examples abound of doctrinaire archaeology, one of the most obvious being a much-remarked burial in Europe cited in introductory textbooks. The "Princess of Vix" is a tumulus with wooden tomb in Burgundy, France, dated to the Iron Age, 500–480 B.C. (through Greek manufactures in the tomb) (Arnold 1991). In the tomb was an elaborately decorated wagon on which lay the body of a woman in her early thirties. An imposing imported set of wine drinking vessels, composed of an extraordinarily large bronze *krater* from Magna Graecia, four other bronze vessels, a silver bowl, and two painted Greek stemmed drinking cups occupied one quarter of the tomb. The woman in the wagon wore an impressive gold neck torque made in Iberia, amber, and bronze fibulae, waist ring, and anklets. No weapons were in the tomb. One German archaeologist identified the person in the tomb as a gracile, transvestite male priest, reasoning that so rich an assemblage of offerings would never have been allotted to a woman, however high her rank (Arnold 1991, 370). Except for this man, archaeologists have accepted the biological sexing of the person in the wagon as female, and assumed the array of wealth around her signifes a lady of both high rank *and* power. But are these qualities inevitably entailed by the syntagm of the tomb? She may have been a queen, but great wealth alone does not tell us whether this was a Boadicea or a passive ornament to the royal house. Was she high-born, or a woman who gained her status by political acumen? Was she, perhaps, a sacrifice? a serving woman to attend the feast of the gods who were to enjoy the great *krater* of wine? Surely a serving woman for the gods should be richly adorned. The "Princess of Vix" may seem in no way comparable to the Neeley's Ferry Plain sherds in Missouri that O'Brien finds such poor support for archaeological interpretations there, but these are two cases of archaeological data that, on their face, have been generally adduced as straightforward, solid material for conventional interpretations. The two cases demonstrate the inherent ambiguity of the archaeological record.

Philosopher Howard Kainz, discussing the proclivity of scientific research to raise questions with a metaphysical edge, sees that paradoxes often clarify issues (Kainz 1996). The ambiguity in most archaeological data has a similar virtue: when taken seriously, it unshackles our usually unreflective minds, pushing us to look closely at empirical phenomena, to dissociate data conventionally lumped by standard labels, to contextualize ethnographic models in their broader political as well as ecological histories, and to distinguish strong associations from merely conventional constructions. Few archaeologists are as sensitive to the fragility of our interpretations as R. Grace Morgan, who in her dissertation consistently writes of "inferred" winter campsites, "inferred" spring campsites, of data "implying" a particular use pattern, and of her assumptions structuring her work (Morgan 1991). Morgan's meticulous caution illuminates her reasoning—her chains of signification—as well as her primary data, enhancing the credibility of her conclusions. It takes courage to insist on the weaknesses inhering in most archaeological studies, while yet committed to utilizing these data toward reconstructing and analyzing past ways of life. If politics is the art of the possible, archaeology should be the art of the probable.

Ah! and how do we assess probability in a post-positivist world? Evolutionary biologists pursue that question retrodictively, employing both mathematical and experimental methods to disentangle factors in morphogenesis, which may be in some ways analogous to the histories of human societies. Kauffman seeks to identify, in organisms, genes plus the generated "families of forms" seen to arise, and the circumstances affecting the production of the actual forms studied. His "families of forms" are equivalent to ethnographic cases, particularly in that the principle of actualism limits extrapolation of unattested chimeras. He goes on to consider

> how hard it may be for selection to "pull" the set of variables to any basin of attraction [in a "fitness landscape"] ... or to hold an adapting population with the initial state.... Further, we can see whether trapping on local optima does in fact occur. (Kauffman 1993, 638)

This perspective focuses on the dynamics of variation rather than on essentialist types. Probability may be said to ride on vectors; their salience outlines parameters within which probability is enhanced.

Human societies have the interesting capacity to somewhat reverse a developmental pathway, for example, contemporary Cree in Québec and northern Alberta who have engineered governmental agreements to sustain subsistence hunting/fishing rather than continue introduced wage labor (Kehoe 1992, 516, 585). Testing the apparent relative weight of recognized factors can be amplified by examining cases of reversal. The ethnographic cases illustrate the interplay of community values, ecological conditions, human decisions, and creativity: Canadian boreal forest subsistence hunting/fishing is viable today because federal and provincial governments not only restrain capitalist intrusions but also buffer the exigencies of bush life with transfer payments and medical services (Feit 1989). Archaeological evidence of links, such as fine cherts, shell ornaments, and foreign ceramics, testify to parallel strategies of trade and probable travel to renowned healers to buffer hardship in prehistoric times.

In a provocative dissection of the semantics of the concept "cause," Mark Turner argues, with David Hume in his 1741 *Inquiry*, that what are commonly identified as cause and effect are temporal sequences, and going beyond Hume, Turner identifies the powerful metaphor "progeneration" underlying the common-sense notion of cause. This trope aligns observed temporal sequences with the fundamental experience of organic reproduction, the prior-existing organism gestating, giving birth to a newly existing creature (Turner 1987, 153–55). Turner's point that "cause" as progeneration privileges the prior-existing "state" rather than any particular element, comports very well with relational biology's impatience with mechanistic models (Rosen 1991). He declares:

> There is no notion in *causation as progeneration* that precisely the list of all the necessary conditions could ever be sorted out. The model implicit in kinship metaphor is not reductive. It illuminates salient conditions and marks them as having had the power to produce ... the whole of the situation from which an effect springs ... conditions interact to produce the effect ... *salient* causes cannot be isolated from environments. Some causes are more salient than others, but they are not isolable or complete. (Turner 1989, 155)

With such an understanding, the ambiguity of archaeological data no longer threatens the scientific character of our researches; we have moved from Newtonian mechanics to the organic world.

Where We Stand

Every natural-language word carries its bundle of associations, like a Maya chac. But formal logic, the computer scientists have found, is no panacea, because it, too, presupposes such "natural" categories as object, predicate, discreteness. Archaeology is no worse off than the physical sciences and mathematics in treading the boggy land of presuppositions.

Reviewing American archaeology through two centuries, several paradigms have been visible. First, there was the Jeffersonian project of opening a continent to Western eyes. This charge to record meticulously what is encountered could not be sustained against Manifest Destiny ideology, for Midwest earthen and Southwest stone architecture

belied the legitimating image of the bestial savage destined to be supplanted. A tacit assumption that America's First Nations never reached a
stage of civilization comparable to that of the invading conquerors has been
the framework for American archaeology, within the Modern European
paradigm of a four-stage universal history of mankind. An alternative
paradigm elevates equilibrium to cosmological status, sharing with functionalism in sociology, anthropology, and ecology the metaphor that viable
communities are organic bodies made up of separate interdependent
organs. American archaeology obscures the differences between these
two paradigms, slotting the functionalist descriptions into stages in the
unilinear evolution model. Finally, and not so clearly recognized as a paradigm, is "straight science," often disparaged as routine data-gathering.
"Ordinary science" was the paradigm of "culture history" archaeology,
picking up and laying out sherds and stones and bones to fill in the matrix of vertical time columns and horizontal regions. Ordinary science
under the New Archaeology became studies of cutmarks on bones, edge-
wear on stone, flotation analyses, GIS systems, CRM, "public education"—all the straightforward "this was in the ground and here it is
cleaned and sorted."

Every one of these paradigms objectifies its research domain. For its
first century, American archaeology followed the Common-Sense Realism
version of Baconian science. Archaeologists were inclined to be hands-
on men, contemptuous of effete bookmen, so it is not surprising that
many resisted the New Archaeology's formal philosophy of hypothetico-
deductive method, trumpeted at the start of the discipline's second century. (A bit uncanny, precisely a century between Wilson's *Prehistoric Man*
and Binford's "Archaeology as Anthropology" in *American Antiquity*. The
first pulled anthropology into the service of archaeology, the second
claimed for archaeology a dominant role in anthropology [Binford [1962]
1972, 31].) Whether straightforward field scientists or exponents of grand
theory, American archaeologists played into the ideology of modernity,
accepting its third-person analytico-referential mode of discourse as the
only proper exposition of our subject (Reiss 1982). The reification of
abstracts such as "society," "culture," "sociotechnic mode," so pervasive
in the discourse of modernism led archaeologists to work toward models
that were mirages reflected from their own syntax.

Our perspective is, curiously, quite literally a product of the discipline
inaugurated in the Renaissance foundation of modernism. Art historian
Michael Ann Holly specifies the date, 1435, when Leon-Battista Alberti
explicated the technique of perspective drawing, the ordering of what is to
be seen into a coherent, centered composition presenting an edifying
history (*istoria*). In the 1840s, that decade of bourgeois ascendancy,
Jacob Burckhardt studied Alberti's treatise and transcribed the painter's

technique into a mode of historical writing; looking thus at an ordered, centered past, Burckhardt felt he could, in his own words:

> get away from them all, from the radicals, the communists, the industrial-
> ists, the intellectuals, the pretentious, the reasoners, the abstract, the
> absolute, the philosophers, the sophists, the State fanatics, the idealists, the
> "ists" and "isms" of every kind (Holly 1996, 46–47, quoting Burckhardt's
> letter of February 28, 1846).

Until NAGPRA, American archaeologists could find such escape in their researches, too. Like Burckhardt, they could envision themselves in an outside vantage point from which they could place what they saw into a meaningful picture. Daniel Wilson told an *istoria* of the Law of Variety-Production evolving civilizations on every continent, and meritorious youths in many a humble cottage and wigwam. Sir John Lubbock and Lewis Henry Morgan, one born to wealth and the other having achieved it through investments in iron, narrated another story, the stark contrast between their class and the wretches they dominated. Holly notes, "The historical subject once ordered (even if subjectively) assumes all the characteristics of an exercise in objectivity. If it works, it does not appear possible for matters to be other than they are" (Holly 1996, 48).

For several centuries, it worked for the West. With literacy limited to a dominant class relatively unified through pan-European aristocratic and bourgeois cultures, an education based on a set of authoritative texts, and linked economies, the history formulated by the Enlightenment philosophes appeared obviously incontrovertible. NAGPRA's fallout threatening to delegitimate American archaeologists' reading of the American past indicates how insecure this accustomed dominance has become. It cannot be coincidence that ideological dominance trembles along with America's political-economic domination: Multinational corporations' global labor pool and consumer market undermine the insular superiority of the West. Disney's buckskin Pocahontas shares the multiplex cinema with Hong Kong's audacious Jackie Chan; while the Disney company retells the story of a country that hath yet her maidenhead, a swashbuckling Asian boasting financial clout dramatizes to ordinary Americans a new cast to Manifest Destiny.

The other Indians, over in India, have begun charting a world behind as well as beyond the picture constructed by that land's British raj. The Indian subcontinent, like North America, was and is home to diverse nations, diverse in ecology, population, societal structures, worldviews, languages and histories. The Archaeological Survey of India, like the Bureau of American Ethnology, was an institution of the central government established under colonial aegis, 1861 in the case of India. Indian archaeologist Dilip Chakrabarti remarks that little notice was taken of pre-historic data: "Even the discovery of the Indus civilization . . . did not lead to a change, except that history textbooks started printing photographs of the brick-built drains of Mohenjodaro" (Chakrabarti 1990, 26). The colo-nial raj could not gainsay the subcontinent nations' achievements in reli-gious and palatial architecture, artifacts, and literature but it could aver that these represented a timeless tradition-bound "archaic civilization". India, Pakistan, Kashmir, and Nepal contest interpretations of the pasts of their territories not only in law courts and academies but with armed troops. Scholars, in contrast, have been seeking common ground by recov-ering subaltern discourses and recognizing how frequently efforts to create order have ridden roughshod over the fluid and adroit competencies of daily life (e.g., Breckenridge and van der Veer 1993).

Perhaps North American archaeologists can substantiate a modus operandi emphasizing the syntagm, the actual detritus of daily life. This is not to overlook the heavy challenges of determining the degree of cohesion of assemblages, through meticulous attention to stratigraphy and tapho-nomic processes. Archaeology is scientific insofar as its observations are replicable, that is, its data available for inspection. An emphasis on syntag-mata lets an archaeologist present her or his technical work with minimal baggage, then whatever interpretation seems congruent with the data and fulfilling the legal and contractual obligations of the archaeological project. Recording data, including photographs of artifacts, on a computer disk or CD-ROM that could be sleeved with the report would enable interested readers to examine the data in greater detail without unduly burdening the publication. Potentially controversial data such as human bones that appear to have been butchered could be described in technical terms, an interpretation such as "cannibalism" given if the archaeologist is willing to defend such an emotionally loaded inference, or the data subsumed under "possible evidence of warfare" if civilty is valued over blunt opinion.

Today, chances are that any American archaeologist, even one who is a member of a First Nation and excavating under that nation's heritage management plan, will be confronted by someone unwilling to see any dis-turbance of remains from the past, or alternately, someone who objects to the appropriation of their own forebears' segment of the past. Archaeology today lies under federal, state, and local laws and regulations, and is likely to be instigated to mitigate anticipated destruction—there are no more General Pitt-Rivers exercising right of domain on their own estates to dig out barrows. Given the likelihood that excavation salvages jeopardized sites, a person who believes it wrong to uncover the buried past can be pre-sumed opposed to any displacement of existing landscape, rather a difficult position to maintain unless one is willing to live in a tent eating only wild foods and clothed in handwoven wild fiber. Less radical, the contesting of the privilege to uncover and discourse upon particular remains has been broached as an issue of intellectual property rights (Combe 1997, 93).

A more pragmatic approach is to think through the circumstance that most archaeology today is heritage management. Philip Duke emphasizes a very basic guiding assumption in Western culture, that work is carried out to achieve a designated goal. ("Work" is thus contrasted with "recreation.") The goal of archaeological work has traditionally been a culture history, whether of a particular "people," or area, or of the human species. Interpretation of an excavated syntagm is felt necessary for closure: There was a beginning, a middle, there ought to be an end. A CRM archaeologist may be obligated to provide an interpretive summary in a report. Duke proposes that archaeologists consider the descriptive report the opening of a dialog, one voice the archaeologist's own, other voices entering from their standpoints (P. Duke, personal communication 12/27/97). Interpretations of "lifeways" or "history" invariably reflect culturally loaded paradigms. The scientific report will be the presentation of data described with care to eschew merely conventional labels.

"The past" is nowhere. It cannot be discovered. What exists now and has been continuously existing since its manufacture is evidence of just that, continuous existence for whatever length of time. To identify a tangibly existing phenomenon as evidence of existence in the past requires contextualization (inscribed, geological, or in terms of radioactive decay processes)—a syntagmatic exercise. The scientific data, simply described with age and associations, may seem inadequate return for the time and funds expended for these data. Baldfaced inventories of material, metrics, and technological attributes do add up to a compilation of traces of actions carried out at a "where" and "when." If vernacular names—"knife," "bowl," "arrowpoint," "ornament"—are affixed to the objects, the leap is made from syntagm to paradigm and thereby into multivocality.

The millennium, 2001, is the sesquicentennial of Daniel Wilson's introduction of the word "prehistory" into the English language. American archaeology is ready to be a mature science, one that accepts the primacy of its empirical data—for these can outlast theories—and the political and human ramifications of its actions, as it reflectively constructs and compares interpretations. Tolerance for ambiguity is as essential as the Marshalltown trowel. More often than acknowledged, inference to the best hypothesis is a ranking of probabilities, not certitude. Relieved of the hubris that demands universal laws, archaeologists can incorporate the data of prehistory into the multiple histories of America. The Land of Prehistory is not beyond a frontier, but our own backyards.

Endnotes

Chapter 1: The Construction of the Science of Archaeology

1. A detailed synopsis of Scott's life, with references to his son-in-law's biography, is in Stephen (1897). Sutherland (1995) is the most recent life. Robertson (1994, 196–205) gives the most recent survey of critical studies of *The Antiquary*.

2. Science ran in the family. The nineteenth-century physicist James Clerk-Maxwell was a direct descendent of Sir John of Penicuik. Penicuik was the site of the first cotton mill in Scotland, erected 1778, thus in the avant-garde of industrialization.

3. William's goal was realized. Half a year after *Chambers's Edinburgh Journal* first came out, Robert was told in a letter from an acquaintance in London, "My wife, who has just returned from Scotland, says that your *Journal* is very popular among her native hills of Galloway. The shepherds, who are scattered there at the rate of one to every four miles square, read it constantly, and they circulate it in this way, the first shepherd who gets it reads it, and at an understood hour places it under a stone on a certain hill-top; then shepherd the second in his own time finds it, reads it, and carries it to another hill, where it is found like Ossian's chief under its own gray stone by shepherd the third, and so it passes on its way, scattering information over the land" (quoted in W. Chambers 1883, 245).

4. Joseph Prestwich (1812–1896) was an English wine merchant until he was sixty. Then, in 1874, after assuming the presidency of the Geological Society, he became professor of geology at Oxford, and in 1896 was knighted. His 1851 publication on aquifers in the London region was a standard authority. Prestwich parallels Robert Chambers in conducting significant geological fieldwork while "in trade."

5. For example, "*Variety-production*—that law by which nations of superior have sprung from nations of inferior endowments— may be considered as the highest that affects the natural history of our species. It produces great leaps in improvement, but these may be at long intervals. . . . It is also seen that, in the domesticated tribes of animals, and in cultivated shrubs, new varieties are constantly arising" (*Chambers's Edinburgh Journal* no. 538, May 21, 1842, 137, "Thoughts on Nations and Civilisation," unsigned but surely by Robert Chambers).

6. The best biography of Daniel Wilson is the unpublished 1980 master's thesis of Bennett McCardle. I am grateful to McCardle for allowing me to use this work. Marinell Ash was writing a biography of Wilson when she died, and her literary executors are working on the manuscript. I thank Margaret Mackay for sharing this material with me in 1989. Other biographical sources are Hannah 1930 and Langton 1929.

Chapter 2: Science Boldly Predicts

1. In this paper, Lovejoy gives Chambers full credit for presenting a strong argument for evolution compatible with sound science. Ernst Mayr, in his magisterial *Growth of Biological Thought* (1982, 381–85), also credits Chambers with an "eminently reasonable" theory, although he lamely follows the crowd by judging Chambers "unimportant" in spite of having "converted to evolutionary thinking ... A. R. Wallace, ... Herbert Spencer, ... Schopenhauer ... and Ralph Waldo Emerson."

2. The winning tender from the contractors Fox & Henderson proposed erecting the brick structure for a penny per cubic foot, and the Crystal Palace for a halfpenny per cubic foot. There were 33 million cubic feet in the Palace (twenty-five percent more gallery space than in the brick rival), and Fox & Henderson submitted a total bid of £150,000 that would be reduced to £79,800 if the contract would allow them to recover the materials after the building was dismantled, supposed to happen after six months. It remained for eighty-five years until destroyed by fire (Hobhouse 1937, 39).

Chapter 3: Consolidating Prehistory

1. "Combe was as much delighted by her powers as a musician as he was amazed and interested by her acquirements as a linguist (including Greek, Latin, Hebrew, German, French, and Italian) and her profound knowledge of the different schools of philosophy, combined with a thoroughly feminine and refined nature" (C. Gibbon 1878, II:315). None of this was enough to persuade Herbert Spencer—the Eeyore of Victorian science, James Moore (1985, 79) calls him—to marry Miss Evans.

2. George Gaylord Simpson (1970) clarifies the principles, actualism and gradualism, misleadingly linked by Lyell. Peter Bowler prefers to term Darwin's principle "scientific naturalism" and insists on the difference between this "policy" adopted by Darwin and the "materialism" more generally trumpeted by the proponents of evolution (Bowler 1985, 643, 680 n. 1).

3. Spencer wrote several versions of a definition of evolution. This is from the 1891 edition of his *First Principles*.

4. "Allo-" other, "phyl[um]" race, "other race" than the historic Celtic. Turanian referred to more or less every language not Indo-European, and by extension to Asian, American and Oceanic peoples.

Chapter 4: America's History

1. Weinberg (1935, 86) quotes Benjamin Franklin at this point, "So convenient a thing it is to be a reasonable creature, since it enables one to find or to make a reason for everything one has a mind to do." The Governor of Georgia, insisting on removal of the Cherokees, explained to the Georgia Assembly that the treaties honored Indian title only so long as the Indians hunted. "Fixed habits of agriculture ... violated the treaties" (quoted in Weinberg 1935, 87).

2. Rudolph Virchow realized, a century ago, that archaeology mirrored the proletariat (Sklenár 1983, 105).

3. Tiwanaku is a thousand years older than the Inca Empire (Tawantisuyu), which like that of the Aztecs was forged in the fourteenth century A.D. Cities with massive truncated-pyramid platforms and substantial architecture are a millennium older than Tiwanaku in the Andes and Pacific coastal valleys of South America. In Mesoamerica, the Toltecs were preceded by the empire of Teotihuacán, contemporary with Tiwanaku, and before that the Olmecs appearing in the late second millennium B.C.; Maya civilizations begin in the mid-first millennium B.C. and continue to Spanish conquests. Earthen mounds date back to 3000 B.C. in the Lower Mississippi Valley, with towns (Poverty Point) at least to the late second millennium B.C. For the archaeology of South America, see Bruhns' *Ancient South America*.

4. Some European writers disputed the similarity. Thomas Jefferson and Benjamin Franklin endeavored to prove (by their own persons, and other data) that American residence did not lead to degeneracy for descendants of Europeans: at a 1787 dinner party in Paris, reported a guest, "there was not one American present who could not have tost out of the Windows any one or perhaps two of the rest of the Company" (Cohen 1995, 86–88).

The dispute continued into Wilson's time, with Robert Knox averring, "Already, the United States man differs in appearance from the European. The ladies early lose their teeth; in both sexes the adipose cellular cushion interposed between the skin and the aponeuroses and muscles disappears, or at lest loses its adipose portion; the muscles become stringy, and show themselves; the tendons appear on the surface; symptoms of premature decay manifest themselves" (quoted in Wilson 1876, II:328).

Chapter 5: Positivists of the New Frontier

1. His *Positivist Catechism* states that "The general law of the human movement, whatever the point of view chosen, consists in the fact that man becomes more and more religious" (quoted in Bridges [1915] 1974, 208).

2. Another of Comte's observances is the Festival of St. Francis honoring people like "the mendicant [Edie Ochiltree] in Scott's *Antiquary* ... lives unfit for any special industrial office, debarred from the scientific eminence ... yet capable, in their poverty and dependence, of exercising beneficent influence on those around them" (Bridges [1915] 1974, 369).

Chapter 6: Petrified Puddle Ducks

1. After Kluckhohn's sudden death in 1960, two students from his last course, James Deetz (*Invitation to Archaeology*, 1967) and Kwang-chih Chang (*Rethinking Archaeology*, 1967), each published programmatic books about archaeology drawing heavily on lecture notes from the course, indicated by my own notes from that class.

2. Taylor is far ahead of most of his contemporaries in insisting that no one "reconstructs" the past. What historians and archaeologists do is "*projected contemporary thought about past actuality, integrated and synthesized into contexts in terms of cultural man and sequential time*" (Taylor 1948, 34–35).

3. The masculine pronoun is called for—"the man on the job" is the referent (Taylor 1948, 157). Taylor did not question the patriarchal model of a white man directing anonymous laborers including female laboratory workers. In standard postwar archaeological usage, "P. I." stands for Principal Investigator and implies Patriarch of Investigations (Gero 1983).

4. When I was a student aide in the American Museum of Natural History during the mid-Fifties, I heard Jim Ford remark, "Writing an archaeological report is verbalizing intuition."

Chapter 7: *The* New Archaeology

1. Henry Morris: "It is precisely because Biblical revelation is absolutely authoritative and perspicuous that the scientific *facts*, rightly interpreted, will give the same testimony as that of Scripture. There is not the slightest possibility that the facts of science can contradict the Bible" (1974, 15; his italics).

2. "[I]n harnessing the energy of atomic nuclei, energy in even more concentrated form is released and diffused. Thus *within* the system that is culture, we find a movement and a direction opposite to that specified for the cosmos by the second law. But in relation to the rest of the cosmos, culture is but a means of furthering the trend described by this law" (White 1959, 40 n; his italics).

3. Kuznick (1987, 107–08, 116, 122, 130, 139) chronicles Western scientists' initial

enthusiasm for the Soviet regime and their disillusionment as Stalin began repressing scientists' freedom in 1936. V. G. Childe visited the U.S.S.R. in 1935, returning highly critical of Soviet Marxism and concerned with the moral aspects of the regime (Trigger 1989, 255, 260).

4. I.e., differences in education, purchasing power, and consumer habits were far less than they had been before the Great Depression, and the trends were for working-class families to adopt business-class patterns of single-family home ownership, automobile ownership, mass-produced fashion clothing, purchased food, and entertainment.

Chapter 8: The Philosophy of the New Archaeology

1. Bayard also produced two hilarious parodies of New Archaeology, issued in mimeograph from "Phu Wiang University," a site in Thailand where the laborers addressed the graduate-student field supervisors as "Professor." See *Antiquity* 45:3, 85–87, 1971, for Glyn Daniel's appreciation.

2. At the suggestion of my colleague Robert Hall, who was invited but could not attend, I attended the conference and presented a paper, "Syntagm and Paradigm in Archaeology, or, What Can Moose Mountain Mean?" Edwin Ardener was pleased with the paper and offered constructive suggestions for revision for publication, but the organizers said they could not accommodate it in the book planned for the proceedings. Nor did editors of *American Antiquity* consider it suited to their readers. Finally it was published as a methodological note in my paper in *The Archaeology of Gender*, p. 430 (1991).

Chapter 9: Cahokia: Hidden in Plain Sight

This chapter was largely completed before historian Roger Kennedy's 1994 *Hidden Cities.* Kennedy similarly emphasizes the power of Manifest Destiny ideology.

1. Polanyi introduced the logical scheme reciprocity⇒redistribution⇒markets, but Philip Curtin states that the historical evidence he surveyed does not support Polanyi's evolutionary sequence; that redistributive economies require government bureaucracies and therefore appear much later than markets, which are in fact early in recorded histories (Curtin 1984, 87–88).

2. The British kingdoms, none of which were at all comparable to the probable extent of the Cahokian state, exported "slaves, cattle, hides, gold, silver, iron, corn, [and] hunting dogs, and imported ivory necklaces, bracelets, amber, glassware, amphorae filled with wine, olive oil, pickled olives" (Claessen and van de Velde 1991, 15). These goods were transported in sea-going boats no better than the Mayan vessel Columbus sighted in the Caribbean (the Romans described large hide-covered curraghs carrying cargo).

Chapter 10: Burrowing Through the Chiefdom

1. "Every historical change creates its mythology but indirectly related to historical fact, ... a constant by-product ... of sociological status, which demands precedent; of moral rule, which requires sanction" (Bronislaw Malinowski [1926] 1954, 146).

2. Bruce Trigger takes Willey and Sabloff to task for blaming this flattening on lack of stratified sites, unfamiliarity with stratigraphic or seriational methods, and the Indians' failure to advance beyond the Stone Age (!) (Trigger 1989, 121). In the third edition of their book, published four years after Trigger's criticism, Willey and Sabloff repeat this blaming of the victim, adding that "American archaeologists of the time [up to 1914] did not think they could adduce evidence for such dramatic macrochange [Neolithic, Civilization] on the New World scene" (Willey and Sabloff 1993, 91). This of course ignores Daniel Wilson's work.

3. This term, although popular, is inappropriate for any known society of *Homo sapiens*

sapiens, and probably for any society of *Homo.* See Kehoe 1993.

4. In Johnson and Earle's index (1987, 350) we do not find "Capital," but "Capital improvements and investments in technology," and no entry at all for "Class," although seventeen for "Clan" plus six cross references to named clans. No one can accuse these authors of Marxism.

5. Johnson and Earle's (1987, 329–48) cited sources on Northwest Coast: Codere 1950; Drucker 1955; Vayda 1961; Boas pub. 1966 (Codere, ed.); Drucker & Heizer 1967; H. Barnett 1968; Suttles 1968; Rosman & Rubel 1971; Gunther 1972; J. Adams 1973; K. Oberg 1973; Donald & Mitchell 1975; H. Stewart 1977; People of Ksan 1980; M. Morrell 1985/Gitksan. The last three sources are on the technology of fisheries.

6. There is (1992 AAA Guide) a Philip Newman on the faculty at UCLA who lists Melanesia as his area and a Paul Newman at Indiana who is a linguist and Africanist.

7. I should include myself in this group: I have conducted excavations in the Northwestern Plains and also ethnography with Blackfoot, Plains Cree, and Saskatchewan Dakota.

Chapter 11: The Taboo Topic

1. "Diffusion" is not usually the most appropriate term for the spread of ideas or artifacts via intersocietal contact; "diffusion" means the permeation of a substance, as dye through water, and is used in geography for studies of, for example, the spread of telephones or electric service throughout a region as in the work of the Swedish geographer Hägerstrand (1967) or the sociologist Rogers (1962) (see also Brown 1981). The term is unfortunately used indiscriminately to cover also intersocietal contacts when the innovation may receive only limited incorporation, for example the acceptance of the 1890 Ghost Dance or peyote ceremonies by some but not all Plains Indians.

2. Western intellectuals' distrust of unfamiliar seagoing vessels is attributed by marine historian Archibald Lewis to Roman preference for investment in roads over ships, their low valuation resulting in Romans inappropriately using Mediterranean ships on the oceans. Unsuited to riding long ocean swells, Mediterranean ships were prone to founder, seemingly justifying Romans' fear of the sea (Lewis 1958, 4–6, Lewis and Runyan 1985; archaeologist Mortimer Wheeler concurred, 1954, 31).

3. David B. Quinn (1974:22–23), commenting on Samuel Eliot Morison:

> The rejection of any pre-Columbian movement across the Atlantic apart from the Norse voyages leaves the ocean peculiarly empty for many centuries, but it is a justifiable reaction in an outstanding historian whose great merit is that he sees sharply in black-and-white terms and is therefore uniquely qualified to expound what is already known. He is perhaps too impatient to study the nuances of pre-Columbian enterprise.

Chapter 12: Land of Prehistory

1. "Caucasoid" here refers to Eurasian populations lacking characteristics generally remarked to distinguish "Mongoloids." The Ainu of Hokkaido exemplify such populations in northeastern Asia. There is no implication that Kennewick Man was of European ancestry. For a review of the questionable validity of racial classes of populations, see Keita and Kittles 1997.

2. Gould has in recent years emphasized contingency and apparent presence of non-adaptive, non-deleterious features, for which Dunnell declares Gould's "recent work … simply bad biology" (Dunnell 1996, x).

References

Adams, Henry
[1907] 1918 *The Education of Henry Adams.* New York: Random House. 1931 Modern Library edition.
Adams, John W.
1981 Recent Ethnology of the Northwest Coast. *Annual Review of Anthropology* 10:361–92.
Adams, William Y. and Ernest W. Adams
1991 *Archaeological Typology and Practical Reality.* Cambridge: Cambridge University Press.
Agassi, Joseph
1981 *Science and Society.* Dordrecht: D. Reidel.
Allen, T. F. H. and David W. Roberts
1991 Foreword to *Life Itself,* by Robert Rosen. New York: Columbia University Press.
Anderson, David G.
1994 *The Savannah River Chiefdoms.* Tuscaloosa: University of Alabama Press.
Archer, Margaret S.
1996 *Culture and Agency.* Revised ed. Cambridge: Cambridge University Press.
Ardener, Edwin
1971 The New Anthropology and Its Critics. *Man* 6:449–67.
Arensberg, Conrad M.
1968 The Urban in Crosscultural Perspective. Pp. 3–15 in *Urban Anthropology: Research Perspectives and Strategies* (Southern Anthropological Society Proceedings, no. 2), edited by Elizabeth M. Eddy. Athens: University of Georgia Press.
Arnold, Bettina
1991 The Deposed Princess of Vix: The Need for an Engendered European Prehistory. Pp. 366–74 in *The Archaeology of Gender,* edited by Dale Walde and Noreen D. Willows. Calgary: University of Calgary Archaeological Association.

Arnold, Jeanne E. and Anabel Ford
1980 A Statistical Examination of Settlement Patterns at Tikal, Guatemala. *American Antiquity* 45(4):713–26.

Ash, Marinell
1981 A Fine, Genial, Hearty Band: David Laing, Daniel Wilson and Scottish Archaeology. Pp. 86–113 in *The Scottish Antiquarian Tradition,* edited by A. S. Bell. Edinburgh: John Donald.
1986 New Frontiers: George and Daniel Wilson. Pp. 40–51 in *The Enterprising Scot,* edited by Jenni Calder. Edinburgh: Royal Museum of Scotland.
n.d. *Life of Daniel Wilson.* Ms. in possession of literary executor Margaret Mackay, School of Scottish Studies, Edinburgh University.

Barber, Bernard
1952 *Science and the Social Order.* Glencoe, Il.: Free Press.

Barker, Alex W., and Timothy R. Pauketat
1992 Conclusions and Aporia. Pp. 195–97 in *Lords of the Southeast,* edited by Alex W. Barker and Timothy R. Pauketat. Washington, D.C.: American Anthropological Association, Archeological Paper, no. 3.

Barnes, Barry, and Steven Shapin, eds.
1979 *Natural Order.* Beverly Hills: Sage.

Barrett, Richard A.
1989 The Paradoxical Anthropology of Leslie White. *American Anthropologist* 91(4):986–99.

Barton, Ruth
1990. An Influential Set of Chaps: the X-Club and Royal Society Politics 1864–85. *British Journal of the History of Science* 23:53–81.

Basalla, George, William Coleman, and Robert H. Kargon, eds.
1970 *Victorian Science ... from the Presidential Addresses of the British Association for the Advancement of Science.* Garden City, NY: Anchor (Doubleday).

Bayard, Donn T.
1969 Science, Theory, and Reality in the "New Archaeology." *American Antiquity* 34(4):376–84.

Bell, James A.
1994 *Reconstructing Prehistory: Scientific Method in Archaeology.* Philadelphia: Temple University Press.

Beniger, James R.
1986 *The Control Revolution.* Cambridge: Harvard University Press.

Bennett, Daphne
1977 *King Without a Crown.* London: Heinemann.

Berger, Peter L., and Thomas Luckmann
1966 *The Social Construction of Reality.* Garden City, NY: Doubleday.

Bieder, Robert E.
1986 *Science Encounters the Indian, 1820–1880.* Norman: University of Oklahoma Press.

Binford, Lewis R.
1962 Archaeology as Anthropology. *American Antiquity* 28(2):217–25.
1972 *An Archaeological Perspective.* New York: Seminar Press.

Bird, James
1993 *The Changing Worlds of Geography.* 2nd ed. Oxford: Clarendon Press.

Blalock, Hubert M., Jr.
 1960 *Social Statistics.* New York: McGraw-Hill.
Boehm, David A., Stephen Topping, and Cyd Smith, eds.
 1983 *Guinness Book of World Records.* New York: Sterling.
Bourdieu, Pierre
 1977 *Outline of a Theory of Practice.* Cambridge: Cambridge University Press.
Bowler, Peter J.
 1985 Scientific Attitudes to Darwinism in Britain and America. Pp. 641–81 in *The Darwinian Heritage,* edited by David Kohn. Princeton: Princeton University Press.
Bracken, Harry M.
 1984 *Mind and Language.* Dordrecht: Foris.
Braun, David P.
 1987 Coevolution of Sedentism, Pottery Technology, and Horticulture in the Central Midwest, 200 B.C.–A.D. 600. Pp. 153–81 in *Emergent Horticultural Economies of the Eastern Woodlands,* edited by William F. Keegan. Carbondale: Southern Illinois University Center for Archaeological Investigations, Occasional Paper no. 7.
Bridges, John Henry
 [1915] 1974. *Illustrations of Posivitism.* Edited by H. Gordon Jones. New York: Burt Franklin Reprints. Original, London: Watts.
Browman, David L., and Douglas R. Givens
 1996 Stratigraphic Excavation: The First "New Archaeology." *American Anthropologist* 98(1):80–95.
Brown, James A.
 1996 *The Spiro Ceremonial Center.* Ann Arbor: University of Michigan, Memoirs of the Museum of Anthropology, no. 29.
Brown, James A., Richard A. Kerber, and Howard D. Winters
 1990 Trade and the Evolution of Exchange Relations at the Beginning of the Mississippian Period. Pp. 251–80 in *The Mississippian Emergence,* edited by Bruce D. Smith. Washington, D.C.: Smithsonian Institution Press.
Brown, Lawrence A.
 1981 *Innovation Diffusion.* London: Methuen.
Bruce, Robert V.
 1987 *The Launching of Modern American Science, 1846–1876.* Ithaca, NY: Cornell University Press.
Bruhns, Karen Olsen
 1994 *Ancient South America.* Cambridge: Cambridge University Press.
Brumley, John
 1988 *Medicine Wheels on the Northern Plains: A Summary and Appraisal.* Edmonton: Archaeological Survey of Alberta, Manuscript Series, no. 12.
Bush, Gregory W.
 1991 *Lord of Attention: Gerald Stanley Lee and the Crowd Metaphor in Industrializing America.* Amherst: University of Massachusetts Press.
Butler, Anthony R.
 1982 The Historian and the Experimentalist. Pp. 107–14 in *Explorations in the History of Science and Technology in China,* edited by Li Guohao, Zhang Mengwen, and Cao Tianqin. Shanghai: Chinese Classics Publishing House.

Bynum, W. F.
1984 Charles Lyell's *Antiquity of Man* and Its Critics. *Journal of the History of Biology* 17(2):153–87.

Calder, C. S. T.
1950 Report on the Excavation of a Neolithic Temple at Stanydale in the Parish of Standsting, Shetland. *Proceedings of the Society of Antiquaries of Scotland* 84:185–205.

Caplow, Theodore
1991 *American Social Trends.* San Diego, Ca.: Harcourt Brace Jovanovich.

Carlson, John B.
1981 A Geomantic Model for the Interpretation of Mesoamerican Sites: An Essay in Cross-Cultural Comparison. Pp. 143–215 in *Mesoamerican Sites and World-views,* edited by Elizabeth P. Benson. Washington, D.C.: Dumbarton Oaks Research Library and Collections.

Carneiro, Robert L.
1981 Leslie A. White. Pp. 210–51 in *Totems and Teachers,* edited by Sydel Silverman. New York: Columbia University Press.
1996 Cultural Evolution. Pp. 271–277 in *Encyclopedia of Cultural Anthropology,* vol. 1, edited by David Levinson and Melvin Ember. New York: Henry Holt.

Carter, George F.
1971 Pre-Columbian Chickens in America. Pp. 178–218 in *Man Across the Sea,* edited by Carroll L. Riley et al. Austin: University of Texas Press.

Carter, Sarah
1990 *Lost Harvests.* Montreal: McGill-Queen's University Press.

Chamberlin, J. Edward, and Sander L. Gilman, eds.
1985 *Degeneration.* New York: Columbia University Press.

Chambers, Robert
1844. *Vestiges of the Natural History of Creation.* London: John Churchill. Facsimile reprint, 1994, with introduction by James A. Secord. Chicago: University of Chicago Press. (I used the original edition in Edinburgh University Library.)
1845 *Explanations.* London: John Churchill. Facsimile reprint, 1994, Chicago: University of Chicago Press.
1848 Letter of recommendation. Bound in *Testimonials in favour of Mr. D. W.* [Daniel Wilson], archived in Edinburgh University Library. Edinburgh.

Chambers, William
1883 *Memoir of William and Robert Chambers.* 12th ed. Edinburgh: W. & R. Chambers.

Claessen, Henri J. M., and Pieter van de Velde
1991 Introduction to *Early State Economics,* edited by Henri J. M. Claessen and Pieter van de Velde. New Brunswick, NJ: Transaction.

Clark, J. F. M.
1997 'The Ants Were Duly Visited': Making Sense of John Lubbock, Scientific Naturalism and the Senses of Social Insects. *British Journal for the History of Science* 30(105), Pt. 2:151–76.

Clarke, David L.
[1968] 1971 *Analytical Archaeology.* London: Methuen.

240 References

Clarke, David V.
1976 Excavations at Skara Brae: A Summary Account. Pp. 233–50 in *Settlement and Economy in the Third and Second Millennia B.C.,* edited by Colin Burgess and Roger Miket. Oxford: British Archaeological Reports, 33.

Cohen, I. Bernard
1995 *Science and the Founding Fathers.* New York: W. W. Norton.

Cohen, Raymond
1987 *The Theatre of Power.* London: Longman.

Cole, Douglas
1983 "The Value of a Person Lies in his *Herzensbildung:*" Franz Boas' Baffin Island Letter-Diary, 1883–1884. Pp. 13–52 in *Observers Observed,* edited by George W. Stocking, Jr. Madison: University of Wisconsin Press.

Collingwood, R. G.
1946 *The Idea of History.* New York: Oxford University Press. Galaxy edition, 1956.

Combe, George
[1847] 1872. *On the Relation Between Science and Religion.* 5th ed. Edinburgh: Maclachlan and Stewart; London: Simpkin, Marshall.
1851. *The Constitution of Man Considered in Relation to External Objects.* 6th ed. Edinburgh: Machlachlan and Stewart; London: Longman and Simpkin, Marshall; Glasgow: Griffin; Dublin: James M'Glashan.
1860. *Conslilalion of Man.... ,*9th ed. Edinburgh: Maclachlan and Stewart; London: Longman and Simpkin, Marshall.

Conrad, Geoffrey W., and Arthur A. Demarest
1984 *Religion and Empire.* Cambridge: Cambridge University Press.

Coombe, Rosemary J.
1997 The Properties of Culture and the Possession of Identity: Postcolonial Struggle and the Legal Imagination. Pp.74–96 in *Borrowed Power: Essays on Cultural Appropriation,* edited by Bruce Ziff and Pratima V. Rao. New Brunswick NJ: Rutgers University Press.

Cooter, Roger
1984. *The Cultural Meaning of Popular Science.* Cambridge: Cambridge University Press.

Cox, Robert, and James Coxe
1860 Advertisement to This Edition. Pp. iii–iv in *The Constitution of Man* by George Combe. 9th ed. Edinburgh: Maclachlan and Stewart.

Crafts, N. F. R.
1989 The New Economic History and the Industrial Revolution. Pp. 25–43 in *The First Industrial Revolutions,* edited by Peter Mathias and John A. Davis. Oxford: Blackwell.

Cremin, Lawrence A.
[1961] 1964 *The Transformation of the School.* New York: Vintage (Random House).

Curtin, Philip D.
1984 *Cross-Cultural Trade in World History.* Cambridge: Cambridge University Press.

Dalan, Rinita A.
1989 Electromagnetic Reconnaissance of the Central Palisade at the Cahokia Mounds State Historic Site. *Wisconsin Archaeologist* 70(3):309–32.

Daniel, Glyn
1967 *The Origins and Growth of Archaeology.* Harmondsworth, UK: Penguin.
1976 *A Hundred and Fifty Years of Archaeology.* Cambridge: Harvard University Press. Revised edition of *A Hundred Years of Archaeology,* 1950.
1981 *A Short History of Archaeology.* London: Thames and Hudson.

Davie, George Elder
[1961] 1964. *The Democratic Intellect.* 2nd ed. Edinburgh: Edinburgh University Press.

DeBoer, Warren R.
1996 *Traces Behind the Esmeraldas Shore.* Tuscaloosa: University of Alabama Press.

DePratter, Chester B.
1991 *Late Prehistoric and Early Historic Chiefdoms in the Southeast United States.* New York: Garland.

Desmond, Adrian, and James Moore
1991 *Darwin: The Life of a Tormented Evolutionist.* New York: Warner.

Diamond, Stanley
1964 What History *Is.* Pp. 29–46 in *Process and Pattern in Culture: Essays in Honor of Julian H. Steward,* edited by Robert A. Manners. Chicago: Aldine.

Dickason, Olive Patricia
1992 *Canada's First Nations.* Toronto: McClelland and Stewart; Norman: University of Oklahoma Press.

Diehl, Richard A.
1983 *Tula: The Toltec Capital of Ancient Mexico.* London: Thames and Hudson.

Donald, Leland
1983 Was Nuu-chah-nulth-aht (Nootka) Society Based on Slave Labor? Pp. 108–119 in *The Development of Political Organization in Native North America,* edited by Elisabeth Tooker. Washington, D.C.: American Ethnological Society.

Donovan, Arthur, Rachel Laudan, and Larry Laudan, eds.
1988 *Scrutinizing Science.* Dordrecht: Kluwer.

Drake, Samuel G.
[1836] 1837 *Biography and History of the Indians of North America.* 7th ed. Boston: Antiquarian Institute.

Dray, William H.
1957 *Laws and Explanation in History.* Oxford: Oxford University Press.

Drooker, Penelope Ballard
1989 *Textile Impressions on Mississippian Pottery at the Wickliffe Mounds Site (15Ba4), Ballard County, Kentucky.* Master's thesis, Harvard University Extension School. Ann Arbor: University Microfilms.
1992 *Mississippian Village Textiles at Wickliffe.* Tuscaloosa: University of Alabama Press.

Dunnell, Robert C.
1996 Foreword (pp. vii–xii), Evolutionary Theory and Archaeology (pp. 30–67), Aspects of the Application of Evolutionary Theory in Archaeology (pp. 86–97) in *Evolutionary Archaeology,* edited by Michael J. O'Brien. Salt Lake City: University of Utah Press.

Dyck, Noel, and James B. Waldram, eds.
1993 *Anthropology, Public Policy and Native Peoples in Canada.* Montreal: McGill-Queen's University Press.

Earle, Timothy K.
1987 Chiefdoms in Archaeological and Ethnohistorical Perspective. *Annual Review of Anthropology* 16:279–308.
———, ed.
1991 *Chiefdoms: Power, Economy, and Ideology.* Cambridge: Cambridge University Press.
Easlea, Brian
1983 *Fathering the Unthinkable: Masculinity, Scientists and the Nuclear Arms Race.* London: Pluto Press.
Emerson, Thomas E., and Douglas K. Jackson
1984 *The BBB Motor Site.* American Bottom Archaeology, FAI-170 Site Reports, vol. 6. Urbana: University of Illinois Press.
England, J. Merton
1982 *A Patron for Pure Science: The National Science Foundation's Formative Years, 1945–57.* Washington D.C.: National Science Foundation.
Esarey, Duane, and Timothy R. Pauketat
1992 *The Lohmann Site: An Early Mississippian Center in the American Bottom.* American Bottom Archaeology, FAI-270 Site Reports, vol. 25. Urbana: University of Illinois Press.
Ewen, Stuart
1976 *Captains of Consciousness.* New York: McGraw-Hill.
Fay, C. R.
1951 *Palace of Industry, 1851.* Cambridge: Cambridge University Press.
Feathers, James K.
1989 Effects of Temper on Strength of Ceramics: Response to Bronitsky and Hamer. *American Antiquity* 54(3):579–88.
Feigl, Herbert
1969 The Origin and Spirit of Logical Positivism. Pp. 3–24 in *The Legacy of Logical Positivism,* edited by Peter Achinstein and Stephen F. Barker. Baltimore: Johns Hopkins University Press.
Feit, Harvey A.
1989 James Bay Cree Self-Governance and Land Management. Pp. 68–98 in *We Are Here,* edited by Edwin N. Wilmsen. Berkeley and Los Angeles: University of California Press.
Feuchtwang, Stephan
1973 The Discipline and Its Sponsors. Pp. 71–100 in *Anthropology and the Colonial Encounter,* edited by Talal Asad. London: Ithaca Press.
Feuer, Lewis S.
1975 *Ideology and the Ideologists.* New York: Harper and Row.
Fingerhut, Eugene R.
1995 *Explorers of Pre-Columbian America?* Claremont, Cal.: Regina Books.
Fish, Suzanne K., and Stephen A. Kowalewski, eds.
1990 *The Archaeology of Regions: A Case for Full-Coverage Survey.* Washington D.C.: Smithsonian Institution Press.
Flannery, Kent V.
1973 Archaeology with a Capital "S." Pp. 47–53 in *Research and Theory in Current Archaeology,* edited by Charles L. Redman. New York: John Wiley.
1976 *The Early Mesoamerican Village.* New York: Academic Press.

1982 The Golden Marshalltown: a Parable for the Archaeology of the 1980s. *American Anthropologist* 84(2):265–78.

Ford, James A.
1969 *A Comparison of Formative Cultures in the Americas.* Smithsonian Contributions to Anthropology 11. Washington D.C.: Smithsonian Institution Press.

Fortier, Andrew C., Thomas O. Maher, and Joyce A. Williams
1991 *The Sponemann Site: The Formative Emergent Mississippian Sponemann Phase Occupations.* American Bottom Archaeology, FAI-170 Site Reports, vol. 23. Urbana: University of Illinois Press.

Fortier, Andrew C., Thomas O. Maher, Joyce A. Williams, Michael C. Meinkoth, Kathryn E. Parker, and Lucretia S. Kelly.
1989 *The Holding Site: A Hopewell Community in the American Bottom.* American Bottom Archaeology, FAI-270 Site Reports, vol. 19. Urbana: University of Illinois Press.

Foucault, Michel
1973 *The Order of Things.* New York: Vintage (Random House). Translation of *Le Mots et les Choses,* 1966, Paris: Gallimard. Translator's name not given.

Fowler, Melvin L.
1969 Middle Mississippian Agricultural Fields. *American Antiquity* 34(4):365–75.
1974a *Cahokia: Ancient Capital of the Midwest.* Reading MA: Addison-Wesley Module in Anthropology No. 48.
1974b Prehistoric Urban Evolution in North America. Discussion paper, The Center for Latin America. Milwaukee: University of Wisconsin-Milwaukee.
1989 *The Cahokia Atlas.* Studies in Illinois Archaeology no. 6. Springfield: Illinois Historic Preservation Agency.
1991 Mound 72 and Early Mississippian at Cahokia. Pp. 1–28 in *New Perspectives on Cahokia: Views from the Periphery,* edited by James B. Stoltman. Madison, Wisc.: Prehistory Press.

Fox, Jennifer
1993 The Women Who Opened Doors: Interviewing Southwestern Anthropologists. Pp. 294–310 in *Hidden Scholars,* edited by Nancy J. Parezo. Albuquerque: University of New Mexico Press.
See also entries on Dorothy Keur and Clara Lee Tanner in *Women Anthropologists: A Biographical Dictionary,* edited by Ute Gacs, Aisha Khan, Jerrie McIntyre, and Ruth Weinberg, 1988. New York: Greenwood Press.

Freidson, Eliot
1984 Are Professions Necessary? Pp. 3–27 in *The Authority of Experts,* edited by Thomas L. Haskell. Bloomington: Indiana University Press.

Fujimura, Joan H.
1992 Crafting Science: Standardized Packages, Boundary Objects, and "Translation." Pp. 168–211 in *Science as Practice and Culture,* edited by Andrew Pickering. Chicago: University of Chicago Press.

Fuller, Steve
1992 Social Epistemology and the Research Agenda of Science Studies. Pp. 390–428 in *Science as Practice and Culture,* edited by Andrew Pickering. Chicago: University of Chicago Press.

Gallagher, James P., and Constance M. Arzigian
1994 A New Perspective on Late Prehistoric Agricultural Intensification in the Upper Mississippi River Valley. Pp. 171–88 in *Agricultural Origins and Development in the Midcontinent,* edited by William Green. Iowa City: University of Iowa, Office of the State Archaeologist, Report 19.

Gallagher, James P. and Robert F. Sasso
1987 Investigations into Oneota Ridged Field Agriculture on the Northern Margin of the Prairie Peninsula. *Plains Anthropologist* 32(116):141–51.

Galloway, Patricia, ed.
1989 *The Southeastern Ceremonial Complex: Artifacts and Analysis.* Lincoln: University of Nebraska Press.

Gardin, Jean-Claude
1992 Semiotic Trends in Archaeology. Pp. 87–104 in *Representations in Archaeology,* edited by Jean-Claude Gardin and Christopher S. Peebles. Bloomington: Indiana University Press.

Gates, Henry Louis, Jr.
1995 *New Yorker* 23 Oct. 1995. Pp. 56–65.

Gibbon, Charles
1878 *The Life of George Combe.* London: Macmillan. (In two volumes; Volume I contains Combe's "Autobiography" of 1858, otherwise unpublished.)

Gibbon, Guy
1974 A Model of Mississippian Development and Its Implications for the Red Wing Area. Pp. 129–137 in *Aspects of Upper Great Lakes Anthropology,* edited by Elden Johnson. St. Paul: Minnesota Historical Society.
1989 *Explanation in Archaeology.* Oxford: Blackwell.

Gillespie, Susan D.
1991 Ballgames and Boundaries. Pp. 317–45 in *The Mesoamerican Ballgame,* edited by Vernon L. Scarborough and David R. Wilcox. Tucson: University of Arizona Press.

Givens, Douglas R.
1992 *Alfred Vincent Kidder and the Development of Americanist Archaeology.* Albuquerque: University of New Mexico Press.

Goldenweiser, Alexander
[1937] 1946. *Anthropology: An Introduction to Primitive Culture.* New York: F. S. Crofts.

Gooding, David, Trevor J. Pinch, and Simon Schaffer, eds.
1989 *The Uses of Experiment.* Cambridge: Cambridge University Press.

Goodman, Jordan and Katrina Honeyman
1988 *Gainful Pursuits: The Making of Industrial Europe 1600–1914.* London: Edward Arnold.

Goodwin, Brian
1994 *How the Leopard Changed Its Spots: The Evolution of Complexity.* New York: Charles Scribner's Sons.

Goody, Jack
1982 *Cooking, Cuisine and Class.* Cambridge: Cambridge University Press.

Griffin, James B.
1967 Eastern North American Archaeology: A Summary. *Science* 156(3772):175–91.

1985 Changing Concepts of the Prehistoric Mississippian Cultures of the Eastern United States. Pp. 40–63 in *Alabama and the Borderlands,* edited by R. Reid Badger and Lawrence A. Clayton. University, Ala: University of Alabama Press.

1989 Foreword to *The Holding Site,* by Fortier, Maher, Williams, Meinkoth, Parker, and Kelly. American Bottom Archaeology, FAI-270 Site Reports, vol. 19. Urbana: University of Illinois Press.

Hägerstrand, Torsten

1967 *Innovation Diffusion as a Spatial Process.* Chicago: University of Chicago Press.

Hall, Robert L.

1975 Chronology and Phases at Cahokia. Pp. 15–31 in *Perspectives in Cahokia Archaeology.* Illinois Archaeological Survey Bulletin 10.

1984 A Plains Indian Perspective on Mexican Cosmovision. Revised version of paper presented at symposium, "Arqueastronomía y Etnoastronomía en Mesoamerica," Mexico City.

1991 Cahokia Identity and Interaction Models of Cahokia Mississippian. Pp. 3–34 in *Cahokia and the Hinterlands,* edited by Thomas E. Emerson and R. Barry Lewis. Urbana: University of Illinois Press.

Hannah, Hugh

1930. Sir Daniel Wilson: The Man and His Work. *The Book of the Old Edinburgh Club* 17:1–16.

Hanson, Norbert Russell

1971 *Observation and Explanation: A Guide to Philosophy of Science.* New York: Harper and Row.

Hare, Lloyd C. M.

1932 *Thomas Mayhew, Patriarch to the Indians (1593–1682).* New York: D. Appleton.

Harris, Marvin

1968 *The Rise of Anthropological Theory.* New York: Thomas Y. Crowell.

1994 Cultural Materialism is Alive and Well and Won't Go Away Until Something Better Comes Along. Pp. 62–75 in *Assessing Cultural Anthropology,* edited by Robert Borofsky. New York: McGraw-Hill.

Hassig, Ross

1985 *Trade, Tribute, and Transportation.* Norman: University of Oklahoma Press.

1992 *War and Society in Ancient Mesoamerica.* Berkeley and Los Angeles: University of California Press.

Haviland, W. A., D. E. Puleston, R. E. Fry, and E. L. Greene

1968 *The Tikal Sustaining Area: Preliminary Report on the 1967 Season.* Burlington: University of Vermont.

Hawkins, Richmond Laurin

1938 *Positivism in the United States (1853–1861).* Cambridge: Harvard University Press.

Heine-Geldern, Robert

1966 The Problem of Transpacific Influences in Mesoamerica. Pp. 277–95 in *Handbook of Middle American Indians,* vol. 4, edited by Gordon F. Ekholm and Gordon R. Willey. Austin: University of Texas Press.

Heine-Geldern, Robert, and Gordon F. Ekholm

1951 Significant Parallels in the Symbolic Arts of Southern Asia and Middle America. Pp. 299–309 in *The Civilizations of Ancient America, Selected Papers of the XXIXth International Congress of Americanists,* edited by Sol Tax. New York: Cooper Square Publishers.

Hempel, Carl
1969 Logical Positivism and the Social Sciences. Pp. 163–94 in *The Legacy of Logical Positivism,* edited by Peter Achinstein and Stephen F. Barker. Baltimore: Johns Hopkins University Press.

Hesse, Mary
1980 *Revolutions and Reconstructions in the Philosophy of Science.* Bloomington: Indiana University Press.

Heyerdahl, Thor
[1978] 1980 *Early Man and the Ocean.* New York: Vintage (Random House).

Hinsley, Curtis M., Jr.
1981 *Savages and Scientists.* Washington, D.C.: Smithsonian Institution Press.
1989 Zunis and Brahmins. Pp. 169–207 in *Romantic Motives,* edited by George W. Stocking, Jr. History of Anthropology vol. 6. Madison: University of Wisconsin Press.

Hirth, Kenneth
1991 Roads, Thoroughfares, and Avenues of Power at Xochicalco, Mexico. Pp. 211–21 in *Ancient Road Networks and Settlement Hierarchies in the New World,* edited by Charles D. Trombold. Cambridge: Cambridge University Press.

Hjelmslev, Louis
[1943] 1961 *Prolegomena to a Theory of Language* (Translated by Francis J. Whitfield from *Omkring sprogteoriens grundlaeggelse*). Madison: University of Wisconsin Press.

Hobhouse, Christopher
1937 *1851 and the Crystal Palace.* London: John Murray.

Hobsbawm, Eric
1962 *The Age of Revolution 1789–1848.* Mentor edition. New York: New American Library.
1979 *The Age of Capital 1848–1875.* Meridian edition. New York: New American Library.

Hodder, Ian, Michael Shanks, Alexandra Alexandri, Victor Buchli, John Carman, Jonathan Last, and Gavin Lucas, eds.
1995 *Interpreting Archaeology.* London: Routledge.

Hodgen, Margaret T.
1974 *Anthropology, History, and Cultural Change.* Tucson: University of Arizona Press.

Hodges, Richard
1982 *Dark Age Economics.* London: Duckworth.

Holly, Michael Ann
1996 *Past Looking: Historical Imagination and the Rhetoric of the Image.* Ithaca, NY: Cornell University Press.

Hudson, Kenneth
1981 *A Social History of Archaeology.* London: Macmillan.

Hughte, Phil
1996 *A Zuni Artist Looks at Frank Hamilton Cushing.* Zuni: Zuni A:shiwi Publishing/Albuquerque: University of New Mexico Press.

Hull, David L.
1984 Historical Entities and Historical Narrative. Pp. 17–41 in *Minds, Machines and Evolution,* edited by Christopher Hookway. Cambridge: Cambridge University Press.

Hunter, Michael
1975 *John Aubrey and the Realm of Learning.* London: Duckworth.

Ingstad, Helge
1969 *Westward to Vinland.* London: Jonathan Cape. Translated by Erik J. Friis from *Vesterveg til Vinland,* 1965, Gyldendal Norsk Forlag.

Jackson, Douglas K., and Ned H. Hanenberger
1990 *Selected Early Mississippian Household Sites in the American Bottom.* American Bottom Archaeology, FAI-270 Site Reports, vol. 22. Urbana: University of Illinois Press.

Jackson, Douglas K., Andrew C. Fortier, and Joyce A. Williams
1992 *The Sponemann Site 2: The Mississippian and Oneota Occupations.* American Bottom Archaeology, FAI-270 Site Reports, vol. 24. Urbana: University of Illinois Press.

Jameson, John H., Jr.
1991 Public Interpretation Initiative. *Federal Archeology Report* 4(4):1, 4–6.

Jenkins, Ned J., David H. Dye, and John A. Walthall
1986 Early Ceramic Development in the Gulf Coastal Plain. Pp. 546–63 in *Early Woodland Archaeology,* edited by Kenneth B. Farnsworth and Thomas E. Emerson. Kampsville Seminars in Archaeology No. 2. Kampsville Ill.: Center for American Archaeology Press.

Jennings, Jesse D.
1956 The American Southwest: A Problem in Cultural Isolation. Pp. 61–127 in *Seminars in Archaeology: 1955,* edited by Robert Wauchope et al. Salt Lake City: Society for American Archaeology, Memoir no. 11.
1985 River Basin Surveys: Origins, Operations, and Results, 1945–1969. *American Antiquity* 50(2):281–96.

Johnson, Allen W., and Timothy Earle
1987 *The Evolution of Human Societies.* Stanford, Cal.: Stanford University Press.

Johnstone, Paul
1972 Bronze Age Sea Trial. *Antiquity* 46 (184):269–74.

Kainz, Howard P.
1996 Traditional Metaphysics and the Boundaries of Science. *Metaphysical Review* 3(2):1–6.

Kauffman, Stuart A.
1993 *The Origins of Order.* New York: Oxford University Press.

Kehoe, Alice Beck
1962 A Hypothesis on the Origin of Northeastern American Pottery. *Southwestern Journal of Anthropology* 18:20–29.
1971 Small Boats Upon the North Atlantic. Pp. 275–92 in *Man Across the Sea,* edited by C. Riley et al. Austin: University of Texas Press.
1981 Revisionist Anthropology: Aboriginal North America. *Current Anthropology* 22(5):503–17.
1983 The Shackles of Tradition. Pp. 53–73 in *The Hidden Half,* edited by

Patricia Albers and Beatrice Medicine. Washington, D.C.: University Press of America.

1985 The Ideological Paradigm in Traditional American Ethnology. Pp. 41–49 in *Social Contexts of American Ethnology, 1840–1984,* edited by June Helm. Washington, D.C.: American Ethnological Society.

1989 "In Fourteen Hundred and Ninety-two, Columbus Sailed . . . ": The Primacy of the National Myth in American Schools. Pp. 201–16 in *The Excluded Past,* edited by Peter Stone and Robert MacKenzie. London: Unwin Hyman.

1991 The Weaver's Wraith. Pp. 430–35 in *The Archaeology of Gender,* edited by Dale Walde and Noreen D. Willows. Calgary: University of Calgary Archaeological Association.

1992 *North American Indians: A Comprehensive Account.* 2nd ed. Englewood Cliffs NJ: Prentice-Hall.

1993 How the Ancient Peigans Lived. Pp. 87–105 in *Research in Economic Anthropology,* edited by Barry Isaac, vol. 14. Greenwich Conn.: JAI Press.

1995a Processual and Postprocessual Archaeology: A Brief Critical Review. Pp. 19–27 in *Beyond Subsistence: Plains Archaeology and the Postprocessual Critique,* edited by Philip Duke and Michael Wilson. Tuscaloosa: University of Alabama Press.

1995b Scientific Creationism: World View not Science. Pp. 11–20 in *Cult Archaeology and Creationism,* edited by Francis B. Harrold and Raymond A. Eve. 2nd ed. Iowa City: University of Iowa Press. (See also, by Kehoe, "Modern Anti-evolutionism: The 'Scientific Creationists,'" in *What Darwin Began: Issues in Evolution,* edited by Laurie R. Godfrey, Boston: Allyn & Bacon, 1985, pp. 165–85; and "The Word of God," in *Scientists Confront Creationism,* edited by Laurie R. Godfrey, Boston: W. W. Norton, 1983, pp. 1–12.)

1998 Introduction to *Assembling the Past,* edited by Alice B. Kehoe and Mary Beth Emmerichs. Albuquerque: University of New Mexico Press.

Kehoe, Alice Beck and Thomas F. Kehoe

1979 *Solstice-Aligned Boulder Configurations in Saskatchewan.* Mercury Series, Canadian Ethnology Service Paper no. 48. Ottawa: National Museum of Man.

Kelley, David H.

1987 Imperial Tula. *Quarterly Review of Archaeology* 8(1):14–16.

1990 Proto-Tifinagh and Proto-Ogham in the Americas. *Review of Archaeology* 11:1–10.

Kelley, J. Charles

1955 Juan Sabeata and Diffusion in Aboriginal Texas. *American Anthropologist* 57(5):981–95.

Kelley, Jane H., and Marsha P. Hanen

1988 *Archaeology and the Methodology of Science.* Albuquerque: University of New Mexico Press.

Kelly, John E.

1990 The Emergence of Mississippian Culture in the American Bottom Region. Pp. 113–52 in *The Mississippian Emergence,* edited by Bruce D. Smith. Washington, D.C.: Smithsonian Institution Press.

Kelly, John E., Steven J. Ozuk, and Joyce A. Williams

1990 *The Range Site 2: The Emergent Mississippian Dohack and Range Phase*

Occupations. American Bottom Archaeology, FAI-270 Site Reports, vol. 20. Urbana: University of Illinois Press.

Kennedy, Roger G.
1994 *Hidden Cities: The Discovery and Loss of Ancient North American Civilization.* New York: Free Press.

Keur, Dorothy Louise
1941 *Big Bead Mesa.* Menasha, Wisc.: Society for American Archaeology, Memoir no. 1.

Kidder, Alfred V.
1936 Speculations on New World Prehistory. Pp. 143–51 in *Essays in Anthropology Presented to A. L. Kroeber,* edited by Robert H. Lowie. Berkeley and Los Angeles: University of California Press.
1951 Some Key Problems of New World Prehistory. Pp. 215–23 in *Homenaje al Doctor Alfonso Caso,* edited by Juan Comas et al. Mexico D.F.: Nuevo Mundo.

Kitcher, Philip
1989 Explanatory Unification and the Causal Structure of the World. Pp. 410–505 in *Scientific Explanation,* edited by Philip Kitcher and Wesley C. Salmon. Minnesota Studies in the Philosophy of Science, vol. 13. Minneapolis: University of Minnesota Press.

Knorr-Cetina, Karen D.
1981 *The Manufacture of Knowledge.* Oxford: Pergamon.

Knudson, Ruthann
1985 Contemporary Cultural Resource Management. Pp. 395–413 in *American Archaeology Past and Future,* edited by David J. Meltzer, Don D. Fowler, and Jeremy A.Sabloff. Washington D.C.: Smithsonian Institution Press.

Kohl, Philip L.
1987 State Formation: Useful Concept or Idée Fixe? Pp. 27–34 in *Power Relations and State Formation,* edited by T. C. Patterson and C. W. Gailey. Washington, D.C.: Archeology Section, American Anthropological Association.

Kolodny, Annette
1984 *The Land Before Her.* Chapel Hill: University of North Carolina Press.

Kopytoff, Igor
1987 The Internal African Frontier: The Making of African Political Culture. Pp. 3–84 in *The African Frontier: The Reproduction of Traditional African Societies,* edited by Igor Kopytoff. Bloomington: Indiana University Press.

Kostof, Spiro
1989 Junctions of Town and Country. Pp. 107–133 in *Dwellings, Settlements, and Tradition,* edited by Jean-Paul Bourdier and Nezar Alsayyad. Lanham, MD: University Press of America.

Kristiansen, Kristian
1981 A Social History of Danish Archaeology (1805–1975). Pp. 20–44 in *Towards a History of Archaeology,* edited by G. Daniel. London: Thames and Hudson.
1985 A Short History of Danish Archaeology. Pp. 12–34 in *Archaeological Formation Processes,* edited by Kristian Kristiansen. Lyngby: Nationalmuseet.
1993 "The Strength of the Past and Its Great Might;" An Essay on the Use of the Past. *Journal of European Archaeology* 1:3–32.

Kroeber, Alfred L.
  1928 Native Culture of the Southwest. *University of California Publications in American Archaeology and Ethnology* 23(9):375–98.
  1952 *The Nature of Culture.* Chicago: University of Chicago Press.
Kuhn, Thomas S.
  1962 *The Structure of Scientific Revolutions.* Chicago: University of Chicago Press.
Kuklick, Henrika
  1991 Contested Monuments. Pp. 135–69 in *Colonial Situations,* edited by George W. Stocking, Jr. Madison: University of Wisconsin Press.
Kuper, Adam
  1988 *The Invention of Primitive Society.* London: Routledge.
Kurjack, Edward B.
  1979 Introduction to *Map of the Ruins of Dzibilchaltún,* by G. E. Stuart, J. C. Scheffler, E. B. Kurjack, and J. W. Cottier. Middle American Research Institute, Publication 47. New Orleans: Tulane University.
Kuznick, Peter J.
  1987 *Beyond the Laboratory.* Chicago: University of Chicago Press.
Ladd, Edmund J.
  1995 Frank Hamilton Cushing at Zuni: One Hundred Years Later. Paper presented at American Anthropological Association annual meeting, November, Washington D.C.
Lakoff, George
  1987 *Women, Fire, and Dangerous Things.* Chicago: University of Chicago Press.
Lakoff, George, and Mark Johnson
  1980 *Metaphors We Live By.* Chicago: University of Chicago Press.
Langton, H. H.
  1929. *Sir Daniel Wilson: A Memoir.* Edinburgh: Thomas Nelson.
Lathrap, Donald W., and James W. Porter
  1985 Mississippian Farmers and the Dominance of Cahokia. Pp 70–78 in *Illinois Archaeology,* edited by James W. Porter and D. Rohn. Urbana: Illinois Archaeological Survey Bulletin 1. (Note that this publication, although printed, was never distributed.)
Latour, Bruno J., and Steve Woolgar
  1979 *Laboratory Life: The Social Construction of Scientific Facts.* Beverly Hills: Sage.
Laudan, Rachel
  Introduction to *The Demarcation Between Science and Pseudo-Science,* edited by Rachel Laudan. Blacksburg: Virginia Tech Center for the Study of Science in Society.
Lemay, J. A. Leo
  1991 *The* American Dream *of Captain John Smith.* Charlottesville: University Press of Virginia.
Lesser, Alexander
  1981 Franz Boas. Pp.1–31 in *Totems and Teachers,* edited by Sydel Silverman. New York: Columbia University Press.
Levine, J. M.
  1987 *Humanism and History.* Ithaca, NY: Cornell University Press.
  1991 *The Battle of the Books: History and Literature in the Augustan Age.* Ithaca, NY: Cornell University Press.

Levine, Philippa
1986 *The Amateur and the Professional.* Cambridge: Cambridge University Press.

Levins, Richard, and Richard Lewontin
1985 *The Dialectical Biologist.* Cambridge: Harvard University Press.

Lévi-Strauss, Claude
1982 *The Way of the Masks.* Translated by Sylvia Modelski. Seattle: University of Washington Press.

Levy, Janet E.
1995 Ethics Code of the American Anthropological Association and Its Relevance for SAA. Pp. 86–93 in *Ethics in American Archaeology: Challenges for the 1990s,* edited by Mark J. Lynott and Alison Wylie. Washington D.C.: Society for American Archaeology.

Lewis, Archibald R.
1958 *The Northern Seas.* Princeton: Princeton University Press.

Lewis, Archibald R., and Timothy J. Runyan
1985 *European Naval and Maritime History, 300–1500.* Bloomington: Indiana University Press.

Lincoln, Charles E.
1985 Cahokia and the American Bottom: Evolutionary Sequence or Social Hierarchy? Seminar paper for Anthropology 208, Harvard University.

Linton, Ralph
[1937] 1968 One Hundred Percent American. Pp. 384–385 in *Every Man His Way,* edited by Alan Dundes. Englewood Cliffs, NJ: Prentice-Hall. Original, *The American Mercury* 40:427–29.

Lloyd, Elisabeth A.
1988 *The Structure and Confirmation of Evolutionary Theory.* New York: Greenwood Press.

Loeb, Lori Anne
1994 *Consuming Angels.* Oxford: Oxford University Press.

Lomask, Milton
1976 *A Minor Miracle: An Informal History of the National Science Foundation.* Washington D.C.: National Science Foundation.

López Austin, Alfredo
1988 *The Human Body and Ideology: Concepts of the Ancient Nahuas.* Translated by Thelma Ortiz de Montellano and Bernard Ortiz de Montellano. Salt Lake City: University of Utah Press.

Lovejoy, Arthur O.
1959 The Argument for Organic Evolution Before the *Origin of Species,* 1830–1858. Pp. 356–414 in *Forerunners of Darwin: 1745–1859,* edited by Bentley Glass, Owsei Temkin, and William L. Straus, Jr. Baltimore: Johns Hopkins University Press.

Lowie, Robert H.
1937 *The History of Ethnological Theory.* New York: Rinehart.

Lu Gwei-Djen
1982 The First Half-Life of Joseph Needham. Pp. 1–38 in *Explorations in the History of Science and Technology in China,* edited by Li Guohao, Zhang Mengwen, and Cao Tianqin. Shanghai: Chinese Classics Publishing House.

Lubbock, John (Lord Avebury)
1863. North American Archæology. Pp. 318–36 in *Annual Report of the Board of Regents of the Smithsonian Institution ... for the Year 1862.* Washington, D.C.: Government Printing Office. Reprinted from *Natural History Review,* January 1863.
1865 *Pre-historic Times.* 6th ed., 1912. London: Williams & Norgate.
1870 *The Origin of Civilisation and the Primitive Condition of Man.* London: Longmans, Green.

Lucas, Jack A.
1978 The Significance of Diffusion in German and Austrian Historical Ethnology. Pp. 30–44 in *Diffusion and Migration: Their Roles in Cultural Development,* edited by P. G. Duke, J. Ebert, G. Langemann, and A. P. Buchner. Calgary: Archaeological Association, Department of Archaeology, University of Calgary.

Lynott, Mark J., and Alison Wylie, eds.
1995 *Ethics in American Archaeology: Challenges for the 1990s.* Washington D.C.: Society for American Archaeology.

MacDonald, George F.
1984 The Epic of Nekt. Pp. 65–81 in *The Tsimshian: Images of the Past, Views for the Present,* edited by Margaret Seguin. Vancouver: University of British Columbia Press.

MacKenzie, Donald
1981 *Statistics in Britain, 1865–1930: The Social Construction of Scientific Knowledge.* Edinburgh: Edinburgh University Press.

MacKenzie, Robert, and Peter Stone
1990 Introduction: The Concept of the Excluded Past. Pp. 1–14 in *The Excluded Past,* edited by Robert MacKenzie and Peter Stone. London: Unwin Hyman.

MacNeish, Richard S.
1978 *The Science of Archaeology?* North Scituate, Mass.: Duxbury.

MacPherson, C. B.
1962 *The Political Theory of Possessive Individualism: Hobbes to Locke.* Oxford: Clarendon Press.

Macpherson, Hector C.
1900 *Spencer and Spencerism.* New York: Doubleday, Page.

Malinowski, Bronislaw
[1926] 1954 Myth in Primitive Psychology. Pp. 93–148 in *Magic, Science and Religion.* Garden City, NY: Doubleday.

Marcus, Joyce
1983 On the Nature of the Mesoamerican City. Pp. 195–242 in *Prehistoric Settlement Patterns,* edited by Evon Z. Vogt and Richard M. Leventhal. Cambridge, Mass.: Peabody Museum of Archaeology and Ethnology.

Martin, Paul S.
[1950] 1972 Pp. 556–69 in *Sites of the Reserve Phase, Pine Lawn Valley, Western New Mexico,* Fieldiana: Anthropology vol. 38, no. 3. Reprinted in *Contemporary Archaeology,* edited by Mark P. Leone. Carbondale: Southern Illinois University Press. Pp. 52–61.
[1971]1972 The Revolution in Archaeology. Pp. 5–13 in *Contemporary Archaeology,* edited by Mark P. Leone. Carbondale: Southern Illinois University Press. Original, *American Antiquity* 36(1):1–8.

Martin, Paul S., George I. Quimby, and Donald Collier
1947 *Indians Before Columbus.* Chicago: University of Chicago Press.
Mayr, Ernst
1982 *The Growth of Biological Thought.* Cambridge: Belknap Press of Harvard.
1991 *One Long Argument.* Cambridge: Harvard University Press.
McCardle, Bennett
1980 The Life and Anthropological Works of Daniel Wilson (1816–1892). Master's thesis, Department of Anthropology, University of Toronto.
McDonald, James A.
1994 Social Change and the Creation of Underdevelopment: a Northwest Coast Case. *American Ethnologist* 21(1):152–75.
McElrath, Dale L., and Fred A. Finney
1987 *The George Reeves Site.* Urbana: University of Illinois Press.
McGhee, Robert
1983 Eastern Arctic Prehistory: the Reality of a Myth? *Musk-Ox* 33:21–25.
1984 Contact Between Native North Americans and the Medieval Norse: A Review of Evidence. *American Antiquity* 49(1):4–26.
McGhee, Robert and James Tuck
1977 Did the Medieval Irish Visit Newfoundland? *Canadian Geographical Journal* 94(3):66–73.
McGimsey, Charles R., III
1985 "This, Too, Will Pass": Moss-Bennett in Perspective. *American Antiquity* 50(2):326–31.
McGlone, William R., Phillip M. Leonard, James L. Guthrie,
Rollin W. Gillespie, and James P. Whittall, Jr. 1993 *Ancient American Inscriptions: Plow Marks or History?* Sutton MA: Early Sites Research Society.
McGuire, Randall H.
1992 *A Marxist Archaeology.* San Diego, Cal.: Academic Press.
1996 Why Complexity is Too Simple. Pp. 23–29 in *Debating Complexity,* Proceedings of the 26th Annual Conference of the Archaeological Association of the University of Calgary, edited by Daniel A. Meyer, Peter C. Dawson, and Donald T. Hanna. Calgary: Archaeological Association of the University of Calgary.
McIntosh, Robert P.
1982 The Background and Some Current Problems of Theoretical Ecology. Pp. 1–61 in *Conceptual Issues in Ecology,* edited by Esa Saarinen. Dordrecht: D. Reidel.
McKnight, Stephen A.
1992 Science, the *Prisca Theologia,* and Modern Epochal Consciousness. Pp. 88–117 in *Science, Pseudo-Science, and Utopianism in Early Modern Thought,* edited by Stephen A. McKnight. Columbia: University of Missouri Press.
McNeill, William H.
1976 *Plagues and Peoples.* Garden City, NY: Doubleday.
Meek, Ronald L.
1976 *Social Science and the Ignoble Savage.* Cambridge: Cambridge University Press.
Meggers, Betty J.
1956 Functional and Evolutionary Implications of Community Patterning. Pp.131–57 in *Seminars in Archaeology: 1955,* edited by Robert Wauchope et al. Salt Lake City: Society for American Archaeology, Memoir no. 11.

Mehrer, Mark W.
1995 *Cahokia's Countryside: Household Archaeology, Settlement Patterns, and Social Power.* DeKalb: Northern Illinois University Press.

Mertz, David B., and David E. McCauley
1982 The Domain of Laboratory Ecology. Pp. 229–44 in *Conceptual Issues in Ecology,* edited by Esa Saarinen. Dordrecht: D. Reidel.

Miller, Jay, and Carol M. Eastman, eds.
1984 *The Tsimshian and Their Neighbors of the North Pacific Coast.* Seattle: University of Washington Press.

Milner, George R.
1986 Mississippian Period Population Density in a Segment of the Central Mississippi River Valley. *American Antiquity* 51(2):227–38.

Mitchell, Donald
1984 Predatory Warfare, Social Status, and the North Pacific Slave Trade. *Ethnology* 23(1):39–48.

Molina Montes, Augusto
1982 Archaeological Buildings: Restoration or Misrepresentation. Pp. 125–141 in *Falsifications and Misreconstructions of Pre-Columbian Art,* edited by Elizabeth H. Boone. Washington, D.C.: Dumbarton Oaks.

Moore, James R. (as Jim Moore)
1985 Herbert Spencer's Henchmen: The Evolution of Protestant Liberals in Late Nineteenth-Century America. Pp. 76–100 in *Darwinism and Divinity: Essays on Evolution and Religious Belief,* edited by John R. Durant. Oxford: Basil Blackwell.
1986 Crisis Without Revolution: The Ideological Watershed in Victorian England. *Revue de Synthèse* 4(1–2):53–78.
1988 Freethought, Secularism, Agnosticism: the Case of Charles Darwin. Pp. 274–319 in *Religion in Victorian Britain,* vol. 1, *Traditions,* edited by Gerald Parsons. Manchester: Manchester University Press.

Morgan, Lewis Henry
[1877] 1985 *Ancient Society.* Tucson: University of Arizona Press.

Morgan, R. Grace
1991 *Beaver Ecology/Beaver Mythology.* Ph.D. thesis, Department of Anthropology, Edmonton: University of Alberta.

Morrell, Jack, and Arnold Thackray
1981. *Gentlemen of Science.* Oxford: Clarendon Press.

Morris, Henry M.
1974 *Scientific Creationism.* San Diego, Cal.: Creation-Life Publishers.

Moss, Madonna L., and Jon M. Erlandson
1992 Forts, Refuge Rocks, and Defensive Sites: The Antiquity of Warfare Along the North Pacific Coast of North America. *Arctic Anthropology* 29(2):73–90.

Muller, Jon
1983 The Southeast. Pp. 373–419 in *Ancient North America,* edited by Jesse D. Jennings. San Francisco: W. H. Freeman.

Murdoch, Alexander, and Richard B. Sher
1988 Literary and Learned Culture. Pp. 127–42 in *People and Society in Scotland, 1760–1830,* edited by T. M. Devine and Rosalind Mitchison. Edinburgh: John Donald.

Needham, Joseph
  1986 *Science and Civilisation in China,* (Military Techology; The Gunpowder Epic). vol. 5, pt. 7. Cambridge: Cambridge University Press.
Needham, Joseph, and Lu Gwei-Djen
  1985 *Trans-Pacific Echoes and Resonances; Listening Once Again.* Singapore: World Scientific.
Nelson, Margaret C., Sarah M. Nelson, and Alison Wylie, eds.
  1994 *Equity Issues for Women in Archaeology.* Archaeological Paper no. 5, American Anthropological Association. Washington D.C.: American Anthropological Association.
Nenadic, Stana
  1988 The Rise of the Urban Middle Class. Pp. 109–26 in *People and Society in Scotland,* Edited by T. M Devine and Rosalind Mitchison. vol. 1, 1760–1830. Edinburgh: John Donald.
Neuman, Robert W.
  1984 *An Introduction to Louisiana Archaeology.* Baton Rouge: Louisiana State University Press.
Nielsen, Richard
  1988–1989 The Kensington Runestone: Linguistic Evidence for its Authenticity. *Epigraphic Society Occasional Publications* 17:124–78, 18:110–32.
  1993 The Spirit Pond Runestones of Maine: A Proposed Dating and Tentative Translation. *Epigraphic Society Occasional Publications* 21:92–113.
Noble, Andrew
  1982. Versions of the Scottish Pastoral: the Literati and the Tradition, 1780–1830. Pp. 263–310 in *Order in Space and Society,* edited by T. A. Markus. Edinburgh: Mainstream.
Noble, David F.
  1977 *America By Design.* New York: Knopf.
  1992 *A World Without Women: The Christian Clerical Culture of Western Science.* New York: Knopf.
Noll, Mark A.
  1994 *The Scandal of the Evangelical Mind.* Grand Rapids MI: Eerdmans.
Novick, Peter
  1988 *That Noble Dream: The "Ojectivity Question" and the American Historical Profession.* Cambridge: Cambridge University Press.
Numbers, Ronald L.
  1992 *The Creationists.* New York: Knopf.
Nutini, Hugo G.
  1995 *The Wages of Conquest.* Ann Arbor: University of Michigan Press.
Oberg, Kalervo
  1955 Types of Social Structure among the Lowland Tribes of South and Central America. *American Anthropologist* 57(2):472–87.
O'Brien, Michael J.
  1994 *Cat Monsters and Head Pots: The Archaeology of Missouri's Pemiscot Bayou.* Columbia: University of Missouri Press.
  1995 Archaeological Research in the Central Mississippi Valley: Culture History Gone Awry. *Review of Archaeology* 16(1):23–36.
  1996 Preface and Acknowledgments. Pp. xiii–xv in *Evolutionary Archaeology,* edited by Michael J. O'Brien. Salt Lake City: University of Utah Press.

O'Brien, Patricia J.
1989 Cahokia: the Political Capital of the 'Ramey' State? *North American Archaeologist* 10(4):275–92.
1991 Early State Economics: Cahokia, Capital of the Ramey State. Pp. 143–75 in *Early State Economics,* edited by Henri J. M. Claessen and Pieter van de Velde. New Brunswick, NJ: Transaction.
1994 Prehistoric Politics: Petroglyphs and the Political Boundaries of Cahokia. *Gateway Heritage* 15(1):30–47.
O'Neill, R. V., D. L. DeAngelis, J. B. Waide, and T. F. H. Allen
1986 *A Hierarchical Concept of Ecosystems.* Princeton: Princeton University Press.
Pape, W. Kevin
1995 Emerging Crises in CRM Archaeology. *SAA Bulletin* 13(2):24–26.
Parezo, Nancy J.
1993 Anthropology: The Welcoming Science. Pp. 3–37 in *Hidden Scholars,* edited by Nancy J. Parezo. Albuquerque: University of New Mexico Press.
Paterson, John L.
1984 *David Harvey's Geography.* London: Croom Helm.
Patterson, Thomas C.
1995 *Toward a Social History of Archaeology in the United States.* Fort Worth, Tex.: Harcourt Brace.
Patterson, Thomas C., and Christine W. Gailey, eds.
1987 *Power Relations and State Formation.* Washington D.C.: American Anthropological Association, Archaeology Section.
Pauketat, Timothy R.
1994 *The Ascent of Chiefs.* Tuscaloosa: University of Alabama Press.
Peace, William J.
1993 Leslie White and Evolutionary Theory. *Dialectical Anthropology* 18:123–51.
Phillips, Philip
1940 Middle American Influences on the Archaeology of the Southeastern United States. Pp. 349–67 in *The Maya and Their Neighbors,* edited by Clarence L. Hay et al. New York: Appleton-Century-Crofts.
1966 The Role of Transpacific Contacts in the Development of New World Pre-Columbian Civilizations. Pp. 296–315 in *Handbook of Middle American Indians,* vol. 4, edited by Gordon F. Ekholm and Gordon R. Willey. Austin: University of Texas Press.
Phillips, Philip, and James A. Brown
1978 *Pre-Columbian Shell Engravings from the Craig Mound at Spiro, Oklahoma,* vols. 1–3. Cambridge, Mass.: Peabody Museum of Archaeology and Ethnology.
Pickering, Andrew, ed.
1992 *Science as Practice and Culture.* Chicago: University of Chicago Press.
Pinsky, Valerie
1992 Archaeology, Politics, and Boundary-Formation: The Boas Censure (1919) and the Development of American Archaeology During the Inter-war Years. Pp. 161–89 in *Rediscovering Our Past: Essays on the History of American Archaeology,* edited by Jonathan E. Reyman. Aldershot, UK: Avebury.
Pollard, Sidney
[1968] 1971 *The Idea of Progress.* Harmondsworth: Penguin.

Porter, James Warren
1969 The Mitchell Site and Prehistoric Exchange Systems at Cahokia: AD 1000±300. Pp. 137–64 in *Explorations into Cahokia Archaeology,* edited by Melvin L. Fowler. Springfield: Illinois Archaeological Survey Bulletin 7.
1981 Marion Thick and Ertebølle Pottery: A Comparative Petrographic Study. Paper presented to Midwest Archaeological Conference, October, Madison.
Powell, John Wesley
1881. Report of the Director. Pp. xi–xxxiii in *First Annual Report, Bureau of Ethnology, 1879–80.* Washington, D.C.: Government Printing Office.
1896. Report of the Director. Pp. xxi–lvii in *Thirteenth Annual Report, Bureau of Ethnology, 1891–92.* Washington, D.C.: Government Printing Office.
Prentice, Guy
1986 An Analysis of the Symbolism Expressed by the Birger Figurine. *American Antiquity* 51(2):239–66.
Prucha, Francis Paul
1986 *The Great Father.* Abridged ed. Lincoln: University of Nebraska Press.
Quinn, David B.
1974 *England and the Discovery of America, 1481–1620.* London: Allen and Unwin.
Radin, Paul
1953. *The World of Primitive Man.* London: Abelard-Schuman.
Rapoport, Amos
1993 On the Nature of Capitals and their Physical Expression. Pp. 31–67 in *Capital Cities/Les Capitales,* edited by John Taylor, Jean G. Lengellé, and Caroline Andrew. Ottawa: Carleton University Press.
Reiss, Timothy J.
1982 *The Discourse of Modernism.* Ithaca, NY: Cornell University Press.
Richards, Robert J.
1987 *Darwin and the Emergence of Evolutionary Theories of Mind and Behavior.* Chicago: University of Chicago Press.
1992 *The Meaning of Evolution.* Chicago: University of Chicago Press.
Riley, Thomas J.
1987 Ridged-Field Agriculture and the Mississippian Economic Pattern. Pp. 295–304 in *Emergent Horticultural Economies of the Eastern Woodlands,* edited by William F. Keegan. Carbondale: Southern Illinois University Center for Archaeological Investigations, Occasional Paper no. 7.
Riley, Thomas J., Richard Edging, and Jack Rossen
1990 Cultigens in Prehistoric Eastern North America. *Current Anthropology* 31(5):525–41.
Riley, Thomas J., Gregory R. Walz, Charles J. Bareis, Andrew C. Fortier, and Kathryn E. Parker
1994 Accelerator Mass Spectrometry (AMS) Dates Confirm Early *Zea nays* in the Mississippi River Valley. *American Antiquity* 59(3):490–98.
Robertson, Fiona
1994 *Legitimate Histories: Scott, Gothic, and the Authorities of Fiction.* Oxford: Clarendon.
Rogers, Everett M.
1962 *Diffusion of Innovations.* New York: Free Press.
Rolingson, Martha Ann
1990 The Toltec Mounds Site: A Ceremonial Center in the Arkansas River

Lowland. Pp. 27–49 in *The Mississippian Emergence,* edited by Bruce D. Smith. Washington, D.C.: Smithsonian Institution Press.

Rose, Jerome C.
[1973] n.d. Mound 72 Cahokia Burial Report. Unpublished manuscript in possession of the author.

Rosen, Robert
1991 *Life Itself.* New York: Columbia University Press.
1995 Cooperation and Chimera. Pp. 343–58 in *Cooperation and Conflict in General Evolutionary Processes,* edited by John L.Casti and Anders Karlqvist. New York: John Wiley & Sons.

Rosenberg, Charles E.
1976 *No Other Gods.* Baltimore: Johns Hopkins University Press.

Ross, Dorothy
1991 *The Origins of American Social Science.* Cambridge: Cambridge University Press.

Rumney, Jay
[1937] 1966 *Herbert Spencer's Sociology.* New York: Atherton.

Rumpf, Arthur H.
1974 The Development and Assessment of a New Social Studies Program for Seventh Grade Pupils in the Milwaukee Public Schools. Ed.D. dissertation, Graduate School, Marquette University, Milwaukee Wisconsin.

Russett, Cynthia Eagle
1976 *Darwin in America.* San Francisco: W. H. Freeman.

Rydell, Robert W.
1984 *All the World's a Fair.* Chicago: University of Chicago Press.
1993 *World of Fairs.* Chicago: University of Chicago Press.

Sahlins, Marshall D.
1960 Evolution: Specific and General. Pp. 12–44 in *Evolution and Culture,* edited by Marshall D. Sahlins and Elman R. Service. Ann Arbor: University of Michigan Press.

Salmon, Merrilee H.
1989 Explanation in the Social Sciences. Pp. 384–409 in *Scientific Explanation,* edited by Philip Kitcher and Wesley C. Salmon. Minnesota Studies in the Philosophy of Science, vol. 13. Minneapolis: University of Minnesota Press.

Salmon, Wesley C.
1989 Four Decades of Scientific Explanation. Pp. 3–219 in *Scientific Explanation,* edited by Philip Kitcher and Wesley C. Salmon. Minnesota Studies in the Philosophy of Science, vol. 13. Minneapolis: University of Minnesota Press.

Saunders, Joe W., and Thurman Allen
1994 Hedgepeth Mounds, an Archaic Mound Complex in North-Central Louisiana. *American Antiquity* 59(3):471–89.

Saunders, Laurance James
1950 *Scottish Democracy, 1815–1840.* Edinburgh: Oliver and Boyd.

Scarborough, Vernon L., and David R. Wilcox, eds.
1991 *The Mesoamerican Ballgame.* Tucson: University of Arizona Press.

Scarry, John F.
1990 Mississippian Emergence in the Fort Walton Area. Pp. 227–50 in *The Mississippian Emergence,* edited by Bruce D. Smith. Washington D.C.: Smithsonian Institution Press.

Schaeffer, Francis A.
1976 *How Shall We Then Live?* Old Tappan, NJ: Fleming H. Revell.
Schávelzon, Daniel
1983 La Primera Excavación Arqueológica de America: Teotihuacán en 1675. *Anales de Antroplogía* XX(I). Mexico, D.F.: Universidad Nacional Autónoma de México.
1990a *La Conservación del Patrimonio Cultural en América Latina.* Buenos Aires: Universidad de Buenos Aires, Instituto de Arte Americano e Investigaciones Estéticas "Mario J. Buschiazzo."
1990b *Las Ciudades Mayas.* Buenos Aires: Editorial Rescate.
Scott, P. H.
1983 The Politics of Sir Walter Scott. Pp. 208–17 in *Scott and His Influence,* edited J. H. Alexander and David Hewitt. Aberdeen: Association for Scottish Literary Studies.
Scott, Sir Walter
[1815] 1871 *The Antiquary.* Edinburgh: Adam and Charles Black.
[1815] 1900 *The Antiquary.* Philadelphia: T. B. Peterson & Brothers.
Scriven, Michael
1969 Logical Positivism and the Behavioral Sciences. Pp. 195–209 in *The Legacy of Logical Positivism,* edited by Peter Achinstein and Stephen F. Barker. Baltimore: Johns Hopkins University Press.
Secord, James A.
1985 Darwin and the Breeders: A Social History. Pp. 519–42 in *The Darwinian Heritage,* edited by David Kohn. Princeton: Princeton University Press.
1994 Introduction. Pp. ix–xiv in *Vestiges of the Natural History of Creation and Other Evolutionary Writings by Robert Chambers,* edited by James A. Secord. Chicago: University of Chicago Press.
Seguin, Margaret
1985 *Interpretive Contexts for Traditional and Current Tsimshian Feasts.* Ottawa: National Museum of Man, Mercury Series, Canadian Ethnology Service Paper no. 98.
Seguin, Margaret, ed.
1984 *The Tsimshian: Images of the Past, Views for the Present.* Vancouver: University of British Columbia Press.
Service, Elman R.
1962 *Primitive Social Organization: An Evolutionary Perspective.* New York: Random House.
1971 Our Contemporary Ancestors: Extant Stages and Extinct Ages. Reprinted in *Cultural Evolutionism,* a collection of Service's essays. Pp. 151–57. New York: Holt, Rinehart and Winston. First published 1967 in *War: The Anthropology of Armed Conflict and Aggression,* edited by Morton Fried, Marvin Harris, and Robert Murphy, New York: Doubleday, pp. 160–67.
1981 The Mind of Lewis H. Morgan. *Current Anthropology* 22(1):25–43.
1988 Review of *The Evolution of Human Societies. American Anthropologist* 90(4):992–93.
Severin, Tim
1978 *The Brendan Voyage.* New York: Avon.
Shamsul A. B.
1995 Inventing Certainties. Pp. 112–33 in *The Pursuit of Certainties,* edited by Wendy James. London: Routledge.

Shanks, Michael, and Ian Hodder
1995 Processual, Postprocessual and Interpretive Archaeologies. Pp. 3–29 in *Interpreting Archaeology,* edited by Ian Hodder, Michael Shanks, Alexandra Alexandri, Victor Buchli, John Carman, Jonathan Last, and Gavin Lucas. London: Routledge.

Shao, Paul
1976 *Asiatic Influences in Pre-Columbian American Art.* Ames: Iowa State University Press.
1978 Chinese Influence in Pre-Classic Mesoamerican Art. Pp. 202–25 in *Diffusion and Migration: Their Roles in Cultural Development,* edited by P. G. Duke, J. Ebert, G. Langemann, and A. P. Buchner. Calgary: Archaeological Association, Department of Archaeology, University of Calgary.

Shapin, Steven
1979 Homo Phrenologicus: Anthropological Perspectives on an Historical Problem. Pp. 41–71 in *Natural Order,* edited by Barry Barnes and Steven Shapin. Beverly Hills: Sage.
1981. Science. Pp. 318–22 in *A Companion to Scottish Culture,* edited by David Daiches. London: Edward Arnold.

Shapin, Steven, and Simon Schaffer
1985 *Leviathan and the Air-Pump.* Princeton: Princeton University Press.

Sheehan, Bernard W.
1980 *Savagism and Civility.* Cambridge: Cambridge University Press.

Simberloff, Daniel
1982 A Succession of Paradigms in Ecology: Essentialism to Materialism and Probabilism. Pp. 63–99 in *Conceptual Issues in Ecology,* edited by Esa Saarinen. Dordrecht: D. Reidel.

Simpson, George Gaylord
1963 Biology and the Nature of Science. *Science* 139:81–88.
1970 Uniformitarianism. Pp. 43–96 in *Essays in Evolution and Genetics,* edited by Max K. Hecht and William C. Steere. New York: Appleton-Century-Crofts.

Simpson, James Young
1861. *Archaeology: Its Past and Its Future Work.* Annual address, Society of Antiquaries of Scotland. Edinburgh: Edmonston and Douglas.

Sintonen, Matti
1989 Explanation: In Search of the Rationale. Pp. 253–82 in *Scientific Explanation,* edited by Philip Kitcher and Wesley C. Salmon. Minnesota Studies in the Philosophy of Science, vol. 13. Minneapolis: University of Minnesota Press.

Sklenár, Karel
1983 *Archaeology in Central Europe: the First 500 Years.* New York: St. Martin's Press.

Slotkin, James Sydney, ed.
1965 *Readings in Early Anthropology.* Viking Fund Publications in Anthropology, no. 40. New York: Wenner-Gren Foundation for Anthropological Research.

Slotkin, Richard
1985 *The Fatal Environment.* New York: Atheneum.

Smith, Brian Cantwell
1996 *On the Origin of Objects.* Cambridge, Mass.: MIT Press.

Smith, Bruce D.
1978 Variation in Mississippian Settlement Patterns. Pp. 479–503 in *Missis-*

sippian Settlement Patterns, edited by Bruce D. Smith. New York: Academic Press.

1990 Introduction to *The Mississippian Emergence,* edited by Bruce D. Smith. Washington, D.C.: Smithsonian Institution Press.

1992 Mississippian Elites and Solar Alignments: A Reflection of Managerial Necessity, or Levers of Social Inequality? Pp. 11–30 in *Lords of the Southeast,* edited by Alex W. Barker and Timothy R. Pauketat. Washington D.C.: American Anthropological Association, Archeological Paper no. 3.

Smith, M. Estellie
1985 An Aspectual Analysis of Polity Formations. Pp. 97–125 in *Development and Decline: The Evolution of Sociopolitical Organization,* edited by Henri J. M. Claessen, Pieter van de Velde, and M. Estellie Smith. South Hadley, Mass.: Bergin and Garvey.

Smith, Marvin T., and David J. Hally
1992 Chiefly Behavior: Evidence from Sixteenth Century Spanish Accounts. Pp. 99–109 in *Lords of the Southeast,* edited by Alex W. Barker and Timothy R. Pauketat. Washington, D.C.: American Anthropological Association, Archeological Papers no. 3.

Smits, David D.
1982 The "Squaw Drudge": a Prime Index of Savagism. *Ethnohistory* 29:281–306.

Southall, Aidan
1991 The Segmentary State: From the Imaginary to the Material Means of Production. Pp. 75–96 in *Early State Economics,* edited by Henri J. M. Claessen and Pieter van de Velde. New Brunswick, NJ: Transaction Books.

Spaulding, Albert C.
1985 Fifty Years of Theory. *American Antiquity* 50(2):301–08.

Spencer-Wood, Suzanne M.
1996 Cultural Complexity, Non-Linear Systems Theory, and Multi-Scalar Analysis. Pp. 54–63 in *Debating Complexity,* Proceedings of the 26th Annual Conference of the Archaeological Association of the University of Calgary, edited by Daniel A. Meyer, Peter C. Dawson, and Donald T. Hanna. Calgary: Archaeological Association of the University of Calgary.

Spinden, Herbert J.
[1928] 1943 *Ancient Civilizations of Mexcio and Central America.* 3rd rev. ed. New York: American Museum of Natural History, Handbook Series no. 3.

Squier, E. G., and E. H. Davis
1848 *Ancient Monuments of the Mississippi Valley.* Washington, D.C.: Smithsonian Institution.

Staudenmaier, John M.
1985 *Technology's Storytellers.* Cambridge, Mass.: MIT Press.

Stephanson, Anders
1995 *Manifest Destiny.* New York: Hill and Wang.

Stephen, Leslie
1897. Scott. Pp. 80–105 in *Dictionary of National Biography.* London: Smith, Elder.

Steponaitis, Vincas P.
1986 Prehistoric Archaeology in the Southeastern United States, 1970–1985. *Annual Review of Anthropology* 15:363–404.

Stevens, Phillips, Jr.
 1996 Religion. Pp. 1088–100 in *Encyclopedia of Cultural Anthropology,* vol. 3, edited by David Levinson and Melvin Ember. New York: Henry Holt.
Stevenson, R. B. K.
 1981 The Museum, its Beginnings and its Development. Pp. 142–211 in *The Scottish Antiquarian Tradition,* pt. II edited by A. S. Bell. Edinburgh: John Donald.
Stocking, George W., Jr.
 1968 *Race, Culture, and Evolution.* New York: Free Press.
 1987 *Victorian Anthropology.* New York: The Free Press.
Strong, William Duncan
 1951 Cultural Resemblances in Nuclear America: Parallelism or Diffusion? Pp. 271–279. In *The Civilizations of Ancient America: Selected Papers of the XXIXth International Congress of Americanists,* edited by Sol Tax. Reprinted New York: Cooper Square Publishers, 1967.
Sturtevant, William C.
 1983 Tribe and State in the Sixteenth and Twentieth Centuries. Pp. 3–16 in *The Development of Political Organization in Native North America,* edited by Elisabeth Tooker. Washington D.C.: American Ethnological Society.
Sutherland, John
 1995 *The Life of Walter Scott: A Critical Biography.* Oxford: Blackwell.
Swagerty, William R.
 1989 Cahokia in Global Perspective. Presented at Organization of American Historians annual meeting, April, St. Louis.
Tainter, Joseph A.
 1996 Valuing Complexity. Pp. 10–15 in *Debating Complexity,* Proceedings of the 26th Annual Conference of the Archaeological Association of the University of Calgary, edited by Daniel A. Meyer, Peter C. Dawson, and Donald T. Hanna. Calgary: Archaeological Association of the University of Calgary.
Temple, Robert
 1990 All in His Head. *Nature* 348:591.
Thompson, M. W.
 1977 *General Pitt-Rivers.* Bradford-on-Avon: Moonraker Press.
Thompson, Raymond H.
 1956 An Archaeological Approach to the Study of Cultural Stability. Pp. 33–57 in *Seminars in Archaeology: 1955,* edited by Robert Wauchope et al. Salt Lake City: Society for American Archaeology, Memoir no. 11.
Tolstoy, Paul
 1963 Cultural Parallels between Southeast Asia and Meso-America in the Manufacture of Bark Cloth. *Transactions of the New York Academy of Sciences* Series 2, 25:646–62.
Toom, Dennis L.
 1992 Radiocarbon Dating of the Western Initial Middle Missouri Variant: Some New Dates and a Critical Review of Old Dates. *Plains Anthropologist* 37(139):115–28.
Toulmin, Stephen E.
 1969 From Logical Analysis to Conceptual History. Pp. 25–53 in *The Legacy of Logical Positivism,* edited by Peter Achinstein and Stephen F. Barker. Baltimore: Johns Hopkins University Press.

Toulmin, Stephen E., and June Goodfield
  1965 *The Discovery of Time.* New York: Harper and Row. (Harper Torchbook edition, 1966).
Townsend, Joan B.
  1985 The Autonomous Village and the Development of Chiefdoms. Pp. 141–55 in *Development and Decline: The Evolution of Sociopolitical Organization,* edited by Henri J. M. Claessen, Pieter van de Velde, and M. Estellie Smith. South Hadley, Mass.: Bergin and Garvey.
Trigger, Bruce G.
  1966. Sir Daniel Wilson: Canada's first anthropologist. *Anthropologica* n.s. 8(1):3–28.
  1980 Archaeology and the Image of the American Indian. *American Antiquity* 45(4):662–76.
  1989. *A History of Archaeological Thought.* Cambridge: Cambridge University Press.
  1992 Daniel Wilson and the Scottish Enlightenment. *Proceedings of the Society of Antiquaries of Scotland* 122:55–75.
Trombold, Charles D.
  1991 Causeways in the Context of Strategic Planning in the La Quemada Region, Zacatecas, Mexico. Pp. 145–68 in *Ancient Road Networks and Settlement Hierarchies in the New World,* edited by Charles D. Trombold. Cambridge: Cambridge University Press.
Turner, Mark
  1987 *Death is the Mother of Beauty.* Chicago: University of Chicago Press.
Tylden-Wright, David
  1991 *John Aubrey: A Life.* London: HarperCollins.
Tyndall, John
  [1874] 1970 Address [to the B.A.A.S., Belfast meeting]. Pp. 441–478 in *Victorian Science,* edited by George Basalla, William Coleman, and Robert H. Kargon. Garden City, NY: Doubleday.
Vincent, Joan
  1990 *Anthropology and Politics.* Tucson: University of Arizona Press.
Vondung, Klaus
  1992 Millenarianism, Hermeticism, and the Search for a Universal Science. Pp. 118–40 in *Science, Pseudo-Science, and Utopianism in Early Modern Thought,* edited by Stephen A. McKnight. Columbia: University of Missouri Press.
Voorhies, Barbara
  1989 *Ancient Trade and Tribute.* Salt Lake City: University of Utah Press.
Walker, Hugh
  1909 *The Age of Tennyson (1830–1870).* London: George Bell and Sons.
Wallace, Alfred Russel
  1899 *The Wonderful Century.* New York: Dodd, Mead.
Wallace, Birgitta Linderoth
  1991 L'Anse aux Meadows, Gateway to Vinland. Pp. 166–97 in *The Norse of the North Atlantic,* edited by Gerald F. Bigelow. Acta Archaeologica 61, 1990. Copenhaven: Munksgaard.
Watson, Patty Jo
  1995 Archaeology, Anthropology, and the Culture Concept. *American Anthropologist* 97(4):683–94.

Watson, Patty Jo, Steven A. LeBlanc, and Charles L. Redman
1971 *Explanation in Archaeology: An Explictly Scientific Approach.* New York: Columbia University Press. Revised edition, 1984, under the title *Archeological Explanation: The Scientific Method in Archaeology.*

Watt, Francis
1887 Chambers, Robert. Pp. 23–25 in *Dictionary of National Biography,* edited by Leslie Stephen. London: Smith, Elder.

Wauchope, Robert
1956 Preface to *Seminars in Archaeology: 1955,* edited by Robert Wauchope et al. Salt Lake City: Society for American Archaeology, Memoir no. 11.

Waugh, Linda R.
1976 *Roman Jakobson's Science of Language.* Lisse, Netherlands: Peter de Ridder.

Weinberg, Albert K.
1935 *Manifest Destiny.* Baltimore: Johns Hopkins University Press.

Welch, Paul D.
1990 Mississippian Emergence in West-Central Alabama. Pp. 197–225 in *The Mississippian Emergence,* edited by Bruce D. Smith. Washington, D.C.: Smithsonian Institution Press.
1991 *Moundville's Economy.* Tuscaloosa: University of Alabama Press.

Wheeler, R. E. Mortimer
1954 *Rome Beyond the Imperial Frontiers.* Baltimore: Penguin.

White, Hayden
1973 *Metahistory.* Baltimore: Johns Hopkins University Press.
1987 *The Content of the Form.* Baltimore: Johns Hopkins University Press.

White, Leslie A.
[1943] 1996 Energy and the Evolution of Culture. Reprinted in *Anthropological Theory,* edited by R. Jon McGee and Richard L. Warms. Pp. 239–258. Mountain View, Cal.: Mayfield. Original, *American Anthropologist* 45(3):335–56.
1949 *The Science of Culture.* New York: Grove.
1959 *The Evolution of Culture.* New York: McGraw-Hill.
1966 *The Social Organization of Ethnological Theory.* Houston: Rice University Studies 52(4), Monographs in Cultural Anthropology.

Wilcox, David R.
1996 The Diversity of Regional and Macroregional Systems in the American Southwest. Pp. 375–90 in *Debating Complexity,* Proceedings of the 26th Annual Conference of the Archaeological Association of the University of Calgary, edited by Daniel A. Meyer, Peter C. Dawson, and Donald T. Hanna. Calgary: Archaeological Association of the University of Calgary.

Willey, Gordon R.
1955 The Prehistoric Civilizations of Nuclear America. *American Anthropologist* 57(3):571–93.
1988 *Portraits in American Archaeology.* Albuquerque: University of New Mexico Press.

Willey, Gordon R. and Jeremy A. Sabloff
[1974] 1993 *A History of American Archaeology.* 3rd ed. San Francisco: W. H. Freeman.

Williams, Mark, and Gary Shapiro, eds.
1990 *Lamar Archaeology: Mississippian Chiefdoms in the Deep South.* Tuscaloosa: University of Alabama Press.

Williams, Robert A., Jr.

1990 *The American Indian in Western Legal Thought.* New York: Oxford University Press.

Williams, Stephen

1978 Foreword to *Pre-Columbian Shell Engravings from the Craig Mound at Spiro, Oklahoma,* by Philip Phillips and James A. Brown. Cambridge, Mass.: Peabody Museum of Archaeology and Ethnology.

1991 *Fantastic Archaeology.* Philadelphia: University of Pennsylvania Press.

Wilson, Daniel

1842 Archaeology. In *Chambers's Information for the People,* revised edition vol. 2, no. 93. Edinburgh: W. & R. Chambers.

1848 *Memorials of Edinburgh in the Olden Time.* 2 vols. Edinburgh: Hugh Paton.

1851 *The Archaeology and Prehistoric Annals of Scotland.* Edinburgh: Shetland and Knox; London: Simpkin, Marshall and J. H. Parker.

1853 Letter to Albert Way, 29 April. Ms. in National Library of Scotland.

1855 Letter to David Laing, 8 September. Ms. La.IV.17 in Edinburgh University Library.

1860 Letter to John Stuart Blackie, 19 March. Ms. in National Library of Scotland.

1862 *Prehistoric Man.* Cambridge and London: Macmillan.

1863 Letter to John Stuart Blackie, 2 April. Ms. in National Library of Scotland.

1865 Letter to Charles Lyell, 13 December. Ms. Lyell 1 in Edinburgh University Library.

1873 *Caliban: The Missing Link.* London: Macmillan.

1878. *Reminiscences of Old Edinburgh.* Edinburgh: David Douglas.

1900 [1878]. Archæology. Pp. 333–43. *Encyclopædia Britannica,* 9th ed., vol. 2, edited by D. O. Kellogg, American edition; original 9th ed 1878, edited by S. Baynes and W. Robertson Smith. New York: Werner.

Wiltshire, David

1978 *The Social and Political Thought of Herbert Spencer.* Oxford: Oxford University Press.

Windes, Thomas C.

1991 The Prehistoric Road Network at Pueblo Alto, Chaco Canyon, New Mexico. Pp. 111–31 in *Ancient Road Networks and Settlement Hierarchies in the New World,* edited by Charles D. Trombold. Cambridge: Cambridge University Press.

Wissler, Clark

1917 *The American Indian.* New York: American Museum of Natural History.

Withrington, Donald J.

1988 Schooling, Literacy and Society. Pp. 163–87 in *People and Society in Scotland,* vol. 1, 1760–1830, edited by T. M Devine and Rosalind Mitchison. Edinburgh: John Donald.

Wolf, Eric R.

1982 *Europe and the People Without History.* Berkeley and Los Angeles: University of California Press.

Wolpoff, Milford, and Rachel Caspari

1997 *Race and Human Evolution.* New York: Simon and Schuster.

Wood, Neal

1984 *John Locke and Agrarian Capitalism.* Berkeley and Los Angeles: University of California Press.

Woodbury, Richard B.
1993 *Sixty Years of Southwestern Archaeology: A History of the Pecos Conference.* Albuquerque: University of New Mexico Press.

Woods, William I., and George R. Holley
1989 Current Research at the Cahokia Site (1984–1989). Pp. 227–32. Appendix 5 in *The Cahokia Atlas,* by Melvin L. Fowler. Studies in Illinois Archaeology no. 6. Springfield: Illinois Historic Preservation Agency.

Woolgar, Steve
1988 *Science: The Very Idea.* Chicester, UK: Ellis Horwood.

Wylie, M. Alison
1982 Positivism and the New Archaeology. Ph.D. dissertation, SUNY-Binghamton. Ann Arbor: University Microfilms.
1985 The Reaction Against Analogy. Pp. 63–111 in *Advances in Archaeological Method and Theory,* vol. 8, edited by Michael B. Schiffer, New York: Academic Press.

Wynne, Brian
1979 Physics and Psychics: Science, Symbolic Aciton, and Social Control in Late Victorian England. Pp. 167–76 in *Natural Order,* edited by Barry Barnes and Steven Shapin. Beverly Hills: Sage.

Yellen, John E.
1991 Archaeology Proposal Submissions at NSF. *SAA Bulletin* 9(5):10–12.

Yellen, John E., and Mary W. Greene
1985 Archaeology and the National Science Foundation. *American Antiquity* 50(2):332–41.

Yeo, Richard
1993 *Defining Science.* Cambridge: Cambridge University Press.

Yoffee, Norman
1993 Too Many Chiefs? (or, Safe Texts for the '90s). Pp. 60–78 in *Archaeological Theory: Who Sets the Agenda?,* edited by Norman Yoffee and Andrew Sherratt. Cambridge: Cambridge University Press.

Ziman, John
1978 *Reliable Knowledge.* Cambridge: Cambridge University Press.

Zimmer, Julie, Richard Wilk, and Anne Pyburn
1995 A Survey of Attitudes and Values in Archaeological Practice. *SAA Bulletin* 13(5):10–12.

Zimmerman, Larry
1995 Regaining Our Nerve: Ethics, Values, and the Transformation of Archaeology. Pp. 64–67 in *Ethics in American Archaeology: Challenges for the 1990s,* edited by Mark J. Lynott and Alison Wylie. Washington D.C.: Society for American Archaeology.

Zumwalt, Rosemary Lévy
1992 *Wealth and Rebellion.* Urbana: University of Illinois Press.

Index

Understanding, 9, 55; *Two Treatises on Government,* 68
Lohmann: phase, 153–4, 158, 160; site, 154, 157, 160
London School of Economics, 137
London's Great Exhibition of 1851. *See* Great Exhibition
Longacre, William, 116
Lopéz Austin, Alfredo, 170
lord(s), 183
Louis XIV, 167
Louisiana Purchase, 169
Lovejoy, Arthur, 30, 232 Ch. 2 n 1
Lovelock Cave, Nevada, 104
Lowie, Robert, 186
Lu Gwei-Djen, 195–7
Lubbock, Sir John, xiii, 20, 21, 30, 38, 47, 50, 54, 57–62, 65–6, 81, 185, 187, 191, 194, 218, 228; *Pre-historic Times,* 20, 21–2, 50, 57–9, 69–70
Lujan, Manuel, 148
Lyell, Charles, 12, 13, 16, 20, 33, 40, 48, 57, 60, 92, 141, 232 Ch. 3 n 2; *Principles of Geology,* 30, 44; *The Geological Evidences of the Antiquity of Man, 57,* 81
Lyng, Secretary of Agriculture, et al v. Norhtwest Indian Cemetery Protection Assn., et al, 209–10
Lynott, Mark and Wylie, Alison, 213

MacArthur, Robert 127–8
MacDonald, George, 186
Mackay, Margaret, 231 Ch. 1 n 6
MacKenzie, Donald: *Statistics in Britain, 1865–1930: The Social Construction of Scientific Knowledge,* 146
MacNeish, Richard, 94, 114
maize cultivation, 156, 159, 168, 191
Malinowski, Bronislaw, 213, 234 Ch. 10 n 1
Manifest Destiny, xi, xiv, 65, 67, 79, 83, 88, 130, 150, 164, 179, 194, 206, 208, 226–8, 231
Maori, 191
markets, 38, 45, 166, 228; mass, 69, 82
Marksville culture, 95, 155
Marshall, Chief Justice John, 68–9, 209
Martin, Paul S., 93–4, 96, 116–17, 136
Martin, Paul S., Quimby, George S. and

Collier, Donald: *Indians Before Columbus,* 93, 95–6, 97, 116–17, 127
Martineau, Harriet, 12, 42
Marx, Karl, 36, 122–3
Marxism, 107, 120, 130, 234 Ch. 7 n 3
Mason, Otis, 91
materialism, 41, 48–9, 61, 107, 129–30, 132, 232 Ch. 3 n 2
Maxwell, James Clerk, 85
Maya: Late Classic, 198; Lowlands, 154
Mayan: art and architecture, 74, 76, 110; Indians, 112, 177, 179, 197–8, 232 Ch. 4 n 3
Mayanists, 194
Mayhew, Henry, 59
Mayr, Ernest, 48, 113, 141, 218–19, 232 Ch. 2 n 1
McCardle, Bennett, 231 Ch. 1 n6
McGee, W.J., 88
McGimsey, Charles R. III, 147
McGuire, Randall, 222
McIlvaine, Josiah, 175, 177
McIntosh, Robert, 128
McKern System, 100, 102–3, 105, 109, 111, 131. *See also* Midwestern Taxonomic System (MTS)
McKern, Will, 94, 101–3, 106, 111
McKnight, Stephen, 29
McNally, Tom, 199
Melcher, Senator John, 210, 212
Memorial Day, 88, 151
meritocracy, 22, 27
Mesoamerica, 110, 111, 162–3, 169–71, 179–80, 184, 192–3, 195, 197–8, 201, 232 Ch. 4 n 3; Classic, 156; Early postclassic, 153
Mesopotamia, 182, 191
metaphor, 129, 145
method: archaeological, 35, 132, 141; Baconian, 47, 124; comparative, 38; hypothetico-deductive, 127; scientific, 112, 120, 124, 133, 177, 194, 197, 216
Métis, 56, 78
meum, 67–8
Mexica empire, 65
Mexico, 65, 74–5, 95, 164, 167, 169–71, 173–4, 191, 193, 195, 197
Michigan Ceramic Repository, 127
middens, 112